Assessment Alternatives
for
Diverse Classrooms

Assessment Alternatives

for

Diverse Classrooms

Beverly P. Farr and Elise Trumbull
Far West Laboratory

Christopher-Gordon Publishers, Inc.
Norwood, MA

Christopher-Gordon Publishers, Inc.
480 Washington Street
Norwood, MA 02062

Printed in the United States of America

10 9 8 7 6 5 4 3 2 1   00 99 98 97 96

ISBN: 0-926842-50-51-X

Dedication

We dedicate this book to our daughters,
Kristin Farr and Caitlin Murphy
with the hope that their generation
will continue to strive for and benefit from
an increasingly equitable American education system.

Credits

Every effort has been made to contact copyright holders for permission to reproduce borrowed material where necessary. We apologize for any oversights and would be happy to rectify them in future printings.

Chapter 1

Figure 1.1: "The Rug Task" taken from an assessment developed by fifth-grade teachers in the Chinle Unified School District, AZ. Completed by a fifth-grader. Used with permission.

Chapter 3

Figure 3.4: *K-12 Language School Programs,*, taken from "Educating English Language Learners: A Review of the Research on School Programs and Classroom Practices," by Jorge A. Cuevas. Copyright © 1995 by Far West Laboratory, San Francisco. Used with permission.

Chapter 4

Figure 4.2: "Two Continua for Ranking Demands of Classroom Activities" reprinted by permission of the Evaluation, Dissemination and Assessment Center, School of Education, CSULA, Los Angeles, CA 90032.

Figure 4.4: "Sample Extended Interdisciplinary Performance Task" prepared by fifth grade teachers, T'saile Elementary School, Chinle Unified School District, AZ, in collaboration with Nanette Koelsch, Far West Laboratory. Used with permission.

Figure 4.5: Reprinted by permission from *A Sampler of Mathematics Assessment* © 1991 by the California Department of Education, Sacramento, CA.

Table 4.3: Reprinted by permission from *A Sampler of English Language Arts Assessment* (Elementary) © 1994 by the California Department of Education, Sacramento, CA.

Table 4.4: Adapted from Interpersonal and Academic Language Skills Checklist in J. Michael O'Malley, "Language Proficiency Testing with Limited English-Proficient Students," in James E. Alatis (Ed.), 1989, *Language Teaching, Testing, and Technology: Lessons from the Past with a View Toward the Future,* pp. 235-244. Washington, DC: Georgetown University Press.

Chapter 5

Figure 5.2: Material from "Equity and excellence through authentic science assessment" by Shirley Malcom in Shirley Malcom and G. Kulm, Eds., *Science Assessment in the Service of Reform*, copyright © 1991 by the American Association for the Advancement of Science. Used with permission.

Figure 5.5: "Generic Reading Task," developed by Nanette Koelsch, Far West Laboratory. Used with permission.

Figure 5.6: "The Mural Project," developed by sixth grade teachers, Many Farms Elementary School, Chinle Unified School District, AZ, in collaboration with Nanette Koelsch, Far West Laboratory. Used with permission.

Insert #3: Amy Shively Jackson in collaboration with the Hawaii Department of Education, Title I.

Chapter 6

Figure 6.1: Adapted with permission from a concept developed by Kenneth P. Wolf.

Figure 6.2: Original material developed by Nanette Koelsch and Elise Trumbull Estrin.

Figure 6.3: Amy Shively Jackson in collaboration with the Hawaii Department of Education, Title I.

Table 6.5: Adapted with permission from the Primary Language Record Handbook for Teachers (1988) by Myra Barrs, Sue Ellis, Hilary Hester, and Anne Thomas. Published by the Centre for Language in Primary Education, Webber Row, London, SE1 8QW, UK.

Tables 6.6 and 6.11: Juneau School District Language Arts Portfolio, 1994. Used with permission.

Tables 6.8, 6.9, and 6.10: *California Learning Record: Handbook for Teachers, K-6 and 6-12*, Preview Editions, © 1993-1994 California Department of Education.

Table 6.12: Table from "Portfolio assessment: Experiences at the Kamehameha Elementary Education Program," in *Authentic Reading Assessment: Practice and Possibilities*, Sheila Valencia, Elfrieda H. Hiebert, and Peter P. Afflebach (Eds.), © 1994 by the International Reading Association. Reprinted with permission of Kathryn Au and the International Reading Association.

Tables 6.13 and 6.14: 5th grade teachers, T'saile Elementary School, Chinle (AZ) Unified School District, in collaboration with Nanette Koelsch, Far West Laboratory.

Appendix A: "The TESOL Standards" come from *The TESOL Standards: Ensuring Access to Quality Educational Experiences for Language Minority Students* compiled by TELSOL's Task Force on the Education of Language Minority Students (K-12) in the US, 1995, Alexandria, VA: Teachers of English to Speakers of Other Languages, Inc. Reprinted by permission.

Appendix C:

"Mimi Task" developed by fifth grade teachers, Chinle Elementary School, Chinle Unified School District, AZ, in collaboration with Nanette Koelsch, Far West Laboratory.

"Science Task Assessment" developed by Dennis Rose, fifth grade teacher, Carson City School District, NV, in collaboration with Nanette Koelsch, Far West Laboratory.

"Applied Linear Measurement" developed by third grade teachers, Carson City School District, NV, in collaboration with Nanette Koelsch, Far West Laboratory.

"More Stories Julian Tells" developed by third grade teachers, Carson City School District, NV, in collaboration with Nanette Koelsch, Far West Laboratory.

"Mathematical Reasoning: Jewelry Making and Selling" developed by sixth grade teachers, Chinle Elementary School, Chinle Unified School District, AZ, in collaboration with Nanette Koelsch, Far West Laboratory.

"Measurement Task: Building a Model" developed by fifth grade teachers, Chinle Elementary School, Chinle Unified School District, AZ, in collaboration with Nanette Koelsch, Far West Laboratory.

"Heritage Task" developed by Verna Clinton, fifth grade teacher, T'saile Elementary School, Chinle Unified School District, AZ, in collaboration with Nanette Koelsch, Far West Laboratory.

"Mathematics Measurement Assessment: Designing a Dream House for Grandmother" developed by fifth grade teachers, Chinle Elementary School, Chinle Unified School District, AZ, in collaboration with Nanette Koelsch, Far West Laboratory.

"Performance Task Review Form" adapted from work conducted by Hawaii State Department of Education and Amy Shively Jackson, Far West Laboratory.

Contents

For the past several years, we have been involved at local, state, re gional, and national levels with school reform, in general, and as sessment reform, in particular. We have worked with teachers in small, rural districts as well as in medium-sized and large urban districts to support successful implementation of state-mandated assessments; with consortia of districts to explore portfolio development; and with groups developing and scoring performance tasks. We have also worked with state and district evaluators in developing new comprehensive assessment systems to meet state and federal guidelines. In the process, along with teachers, administrators and parents, we have come up against serious questions of how to ensure equity, how to make not only assessment-but curriculum and instruction-more responsive to a wide range of students. Because of the enormous influence assessment has on the lives of students–and, in particular, the disproportionately negative consequences that poor assessment can have for "non-mainstream" students–we have found ourselves focusing on how the current alternative assessment movement can be expected to affect "diverse" classrooms and what can be done to ensure that it has a positive impact. It has seemed to us that reforms are proceeding apace, with only retrospective consideration given to their impact on students for whom English is not a first language or others from "non-mainstream" communities. Certainly, this has been the case overall with so-called "restructuring" efforts.

Our background for this work stems from our own experience as teachers, as assessment specialists, as researchers, and as technical assistance providers. We bring both personal and professional knowledge to the treatment of language issues–something we believe deserves space in any book on assessment because of the central role language plays in virtually all assessment.

Our intention in constructing this book has been both to provide frameworks for thinking about assessment and related issues and to bring these frameworks alive through real-world examples, from our own experience and that of others. In addition, we have sought to include other perspectives through end-of-chapter commentaries by colleagues with expertise on the various chapter topics. We intend the book to serve as a resource to teachers, administrators, professional developers, teacher educators, and policymakers. While there are numerous excellent books on equitable education in a diverse society, on multicultural instruction, on second language learning and bilinguality, and on assessment, we have yet to find one that attempts to address all of these issues and their interrelationships. We hope that this book will serve as a step toward fulfilling that need and stimulate others to tackle the challenge in new and better ways.

In the book, we focus on diversity related to language and culture and by implication, ethnicity, race, and social class, because all of these factors are in reality intertwined. Migrant and compensatory education students, many of whom are members of non-dominant groups, are included in our thinking, though not singled out. We have focused on these sources of diversity for three reasons: 1) They are the most important in terms of numbers of students affected; 2) They continue to be poorly understood, and 3) The issues associated with them, if "language" and "culture" are used in the broadest sense, are germane to other groups. However, we recognize that potential inequities of alternative assessments based on sex differences and special education status, for example, need to be addressed as well. We have not done so here; however, many principles and practices presented will apply to all students. We want to make it clear that our decision to focus on certain aspects of diversity should not be taken to mean that we think other aspects are unimportant.

We have selected for exploration several topics that we believe educators must become conversant with in order to understand and participate most effectively in meaningful assessment reform efforts. We have asked respected colleagues with expertise in the topical areas to offer commentary at the end of Chapters 1 through 6. Our intention was to incorporate perspectives beyond our own in this way. Readers who want to focus on the "how to" of assessment development may find it most useful to turn directly to Chapter 5 or 6. We believe the other, more theoretical or descriptive chapters will also be useful in helping educators to think more deeply about assessment.

In Chapter 1, *The Challenge of Assessment Equity in a Diverse Society*, we examine the current reforms in assessment from the standpoint of their potential utility for students who have not been well-served by assessment practices in the past. We also identify some of the most salient aspects of diversity in American classrooms and define terms as they will be used in the book. The chapter discusses how attitudes toward diversity influence classroom practices and outcomes for students and reviews briefly some alternative approaches to educating a multicultural, multilingual population. The role of language in assessment and the social and ethical aspects of assessment are considered. The chapter concludes with a discussion of new views of the relationship among curriculum, instruction, learning, and assessment and how those views may positively affect teaching in diverse classrooms.

Chapter 2, *History, Trends and Critical Questions,* reviews salient historical practices and policies related to testing in the United States that form a backdrop for current assessment reform. We have also described national, state, and local assessment reform efforts-some of which have already shifted direction. We believe that there is much to be learned from these examples, and that their alterations reflect the evolving nature of the development of new assessments. Implications for the issue of equity with larger-scale assessment movements are explored, along with specific strategies and policies suggested by various groups to achieve equity in assessment. Critical questions that frame the discussion are also raised in this chapter.

In Chapter 3, *Curricular Considerations,* we discuss implications of a constructivist view of learners for instruction, with particular focus on its relationship to equity and culturally-responsive pedagogy for diverse students. Multicultural and bilingual education are discussed in greater depth, emphasizing the congruence of recommended practices in these two fields with the theory of constructivism. Effective teaching strategies and examples of their use are presented. We also question standard notions of "disadvantagement" in relation to school success.

In Chapter 4, *Language in Instruction and Assessment,* we provide a framework for understanding the concept of language proficiency and how it is assessed, as well as the relationship of language to learning. We explore some issues in second language learning, including cross-cultural differences in ways languages are used. We examine the language demands of performance assessments and make suggestions for evaluating these demands, giving recommendations for ways to support English language learners or students from non-dominant cultures. This in-depth treatment of language issues is offered because of the centrality of language to learning and because teacher preparation programs do not routinely expose teachers to language topics.

Chapter 5, *Developing Equitable Assessment Systems,* is focused on district and school processes for developing comprehensive assessment systems. It is important to recognize that the policymaking and design efforts taking place at the national level can provide impetus and support for local and state development efforts. Such tracking procedures should be undertaken with the goal of achieving alignment and complementarity among systems. A philosophical framework and specific strategies for development, administration, interpretation and use are provided. The chapter is intended to help educators at all levels think about how to fit the pieces together.

In Chapter 6, *Portfolio Assessment: Potential for Equity,* we discuss what we believe to be a beneficial assessment tool for a diverse student population. Because of their content and process flexibility and the opportunity they provide for contextualizing student work, portfolios are an appealing assessment approach. We explore some of the many ways of using portfolios and describe some specific examples drawn from communities around the country.

The final Chapter, *Getting Real: Reports from the Field*, is a compendium of narratives written by teachers, administrators, researchers, and others engaged in developing and carrying out new assessment procedures. Although nearly everyone we have talked with about assessment innovations insists that the work of his or her colleagues is "incomplete" or "under development," the ones whose stories are included were willing to share their ongoing learnings, so that others may get a sense of the complexity and promise of such innovations. We are especially grateful to these contributors for opening their work for the benefit of other pioneers.

We are also grateful to all of our colleagues at Far West Laboratory (now WestEd), who have contributed to our understanding and recognition of the complexity of the issues. Among those with whom we have had ongoing dialogue and worked collaboratively are Paula Alexander, Stan Chow, Jorge Cuevas, Gary Estes, Sylvie Hale, Jo Ann Izu, Amy Jackson, Nanette Koelsch, Ann Muench, Sharon Nelson-Barber, Rose Owens-West, Celia Reyes, Jerome Shaw, Kathleen Tyner, and Kathy Whealdon. We extend great thanks as well to all of those who have directly contributed to the book—our final chapter contributors and end-of-chapter commentary authors: Amalia Mesa-Bains, Julia Lara, Virginia Gonzalez, Sharon Nelson-Barber, Linda Winfield, and Kathryn Au. We also feel extremely fortunate to have two such highly-regarded educators as Geneva Gay and Edmund Gordon provide the foreword and afterword for the book. We believe that their participation is not so much a tribute to this book as it is a recognition of the urgency of dealing with the issues we raise, issues that they, themselves, have addressed in powerful ways through their own work and writings. Finally, there are other colleagues and mentors who have given us uncredited support—past and present. Among these are John Oller, Paula Menyuk, Henriette Langdon, Kenji Hakuta, Cecilia Navarrete, Richard Figueroa, Annie Calkins, Sheila Short, and Roger Farr.

B. F. and E. T.
March 1996

Foreword

This volume is a needed and welcome addition to the scholarship in multicultural education. It extends the dialogue on education for and about cultural diversity to a domain that has only been implied in other discussions. The need for assessment techniques that are culturally relevant in determining the academic achievement of diverse students is acknowledged or implied in most multicultural writings, but it has not been fully developed or explicated. And, the long-standing debate over cultural bias in teaching and testing is well known. Upon first hearing the topic of this book—assessing the achievement of culturally, racially, socially, and linguistically diverse students—one might expect for old arguments to be resurrected. But that is not the case.

The authors of this volume bring some new perspectives and illuminating insights to the issue of assessing culturally diverse students. They provide a rich body of information about the nature, dimensions, and functions of assessment, alternative approaches to assessment, and how to operationalize assessment equity and fairness within the *context of cultural diversity.* Their explanations of and suggestions for developing culturally sensitive assessment techniques complement other notions about making the educational process more relevant for diverse students, such as multicultural curriculum, instructional materials, pedagogy, counseling, and supervision. Their contributions, thus, enrich and extend the dialogue on multicultural education.

Far and Trumbull use a tone and approach to discuss the assessment of diverse learners that is consistent with the way other multiculturalists deal conceptually with critical issues in the field. Increasingly, there is a tendency for advocates to explicate the conceptual linkages between multicultural education and related educational issues, ideologies, and innovations. For example, Gay (1994) explains the similarities between principles of multicultural and general education; Banks (1990; 1991/92), Bennett (1995), and Nieto (1992) demonstrate the strong affinity between the goals and visions of multicultural education and democratic principles of freedom, equality, justice, and human dignity; Sleeter (1991) shows how multicultural education is related to personal and social empowerment; and Suzuki (1984) explains how it is good quality pedagogy for a culturally pluralistic society.

The authors of this text continue this theoretical tradition by situating their discussions about appropriate ways to assess the achievement of diverse students in the conceptual parameters of constructivism, cultural diversity, and authentic assessment. By so doing, they model the idea that multiculturalism is not an end in itself, but an instrumental tool for achieving other educational ends. It is most effective when it is infused throughout or embedded in all dimensions of the educational process. This conceptual integration is successfully accomplished, to the extent that it is virtually impossible for the reader to divorce assessment from the context of cultural diversity.

The ideas offered about what culturally sensitive assessment is and why it is imperative for achieving educational equity for diverse students are both imaginative and transformative. The authors challenge the readers to transcend existing assessment paradigms to devise measures that are more valid and viable for ethnically, racially, socially, and linguistically diverse students. The major premise underlying this challenge is that assessment procedures should be contextualized in cultural diversity and aligned with multicultural curricula taught in schools. This is necessary because the cultural socialization of students affects how they learn to construct knowledge and assign meaning to experiences, achieve self-identity, and acquire skills in self-presentation (Pai 1990). Consequently, assessment that is authentic can never be totally objective, unbiased, generalized, or culturally neutral; nor are these desirable aspirations to pursue. Instead, it must be culturally-, socially-, and task-specific. Therefore, a more plausible strategy for educators to undertake is to ensure that the assessment measures used with culturally diverse students reflect and incorporate their cultural orientations, preferences, and styles of demonstrating mastery.

Like other multiculturalists, the authors of this volume ground their arguments in the belief that a strong interactive relationship exists between culture and educational relevancy, validity, and effectiveness. As Young Pai (1990, p. 3) explains, "there is no escaping from the fact that education is a sociocultural process . . . the relative worth of special goals and educative means is rooted in the social, cultural, political, and economic contexts in which people learn and educational institutions function." This is true for the macroculture as well as the many microcultures that comprise the United States, and individuals within the various groups. Consequently, a plethora of notions about what should be learned and how best to demonstrate task mastery exists in most classrooms. The extent to which teaching and learning encompass a variety of cultural perspectives, experiences, and presentation styles, the chances of fully engaging all students increase considerably. Conversely, the use of values, norms, and structures from only one cultural system to determine school programs, policies, and procedures constitutes a form of cultural hegemony. Students who are not members of this culture are unfairly handicapped and denied unrestricted participation in the schooling process. Their educational opportunities and outcomes reflect this disadvantage as evident in lower levels of academic and social achievements.

The kind of curricular, pedagogical, and assessment measures educators use can facilitate or obstruct students' achievement, depending upon how congruent they are with the cultural frames of reference and performance styles of different ethnic and cultural groups. Because ethnically, socially, and culturally diverse students demonstrate what they consider is worth knowing, what they know, and what they are able to do in different ways, a variety of assessment techniques and procedures must be employed in pluralistic classrooms. It is imperative for these to be *culturally relevant* if high academic achievement is to be made more accessible to and equitable for diverse students. This point is made convincingly throughout the different topics examined in this text.

Several other major multicultural principles and themes are woven throughout the discussions in this book. To begin with, *multicultural educations is viewed as a process* instead of a program. It is more of an ideological orientation, a methodological guide, and set of quality control criteria for making all educational actions culturally pluralistic, rather than a discrete program of instruction which teaches content about cultural and ethnic groups. As such, multiculturalism should permeate all aspects of the educational enterprise, both within and across dimensions. It should be evident in policy, curriculum, instruction, school climate, administration, counseling and guidance, and assessment. And, all of the dimensions of these domains should be revised to reflect cultural diversity. In the arena of assessment this includes the types of measures used, the substantive content of each measure, how the measures are administered, and which ones are determined to be more appropriate for use with which ethnic, social, and cultural groups.

Implicit in this conception of multicultural education is the need for *a diversity and plurality* of culturally appropriate means to achieve common learning outcomes, to become the new normative standards for all parts of the educational process. The acceptance of this principle requires changes in the fundamental belief systems that are the foundations of U. S. education. For so long these have been driven by standards of cultural monism and homogeneity. Given the pluralism that characterizes today's schools and society, this is a dysfunctional orientation. Instead, the more diversity there is in the formal structures and dynamics of the educational process, the greater is the likelihood that more students will be empowered through higher academic competence and accomplishment. This principle is embodied throughout the narrative text of *Assessment*

Alternatives for Diverse Classrooms. The authors consistently invite and encourage readers to explore *multiple measures, perspectives,* and *explanations* in pursuit of greater assurance that cultural relevance, validity, equity, and fairness will characterize the assessment of culturally diverse students' achievement.

Three other multicultural principles conveyed throughout this text are *cultural contextuality, congruency,* and *responsiveness.* These themes build upon the fact that students and teachers are cultural beings, and how they demonstrate what they know is strongly influenced by their cultural socialization. Some cultural groups give priority to verbal and visual ways of learning and demonstrating skill mastery; others convey competence through tactical, kinetic, and performance means. Some are rational and mechanical, while others are more aesthetic, affective, and dramatic. These variations require the use of *multiple measures that reflect multicultural sensitivity* to assess the performance of ethnically, socially, linguistically, and culturally diverse students. Just as instructional techniques need to be varied and diversified in order to match the learning styles of students from different cultural groups, assessment techniques must be similarly varied to match the communication, presentation, and performance styles of diverse students.

This kind of pluralism is necessary for all students to have *comparable quality opportunities* to demonstrate what they know without being unduly constrained by the procedural mechanisms of the assessment systems. Otherwise, cultural incompatibilities in the formats of assessment measures can interfere with students' ability to demonstrate the substance of their knowledge. For instance, demanding that limited English speakers demonstrate their understanding of what "equal representation" means by writing an explanatory essay in standard English can be a form of culturally unfair assessment. The same is true when students who perform better orally are always expected to demonstrate the mastery of academic tasks in writing. They may understand the concepts and tasks quite well, but appear not to because the *format* in which they are expected to perform is problematic for them. Researchers of cultural diversity and school achievement have shown this to be true.

Some graphic cases in point are the Kamehameha Early Elementary Project (KEEP) for Native Hawaiian children and the findings of research on the speech behavior of Native American students in classrooms. When eductors expected these children to perform according to middle class, European American styles, the results were very poor. However, when the presentation and performance formats where changed to more closely approximate the styles students were accustomed to in their home cultural communities, school achievement improved radically, and without making any changes in the substantive content of the instruction or assessment. These results substantiate the positions taken in this volume that is as important to make the *styles* of assessment as culturally relevant as the content of what is assessed. Therefore, culturally diverse students should be provided with a variety of options for *how* they will demonstrate what they know. This is what *culturally responsive, culturally relevant,* and *culturally contextualized assessment* means.

Virtually all multiculturalists agree that if efforts to incorporate cultural diversity into the educational process are to be maximally successful, they should be *holistic* and *comprehensive.* This means that the reform initiatives should impact all levels and parts of the education process for all students in all school settings. It also means that multiculturalism should be understood to have content, process, climate, context, and structural dimensions. It encompasses more than cognitive information; Personal and social skills, as well as values, ethics, and morality must be included as well. This principle of thoroughness and comprehensiveness comes through powerfully and persuasively in this volume. The authors apply it to the domain of assessment by explaining that the process includes the content of what is "tested," as well as the styles and administration procedures of assessment. Also, there are different types of assessments that should be conducted, including curriculum, language, literacy, subject matter competencies, standardized testing, and a variety of informal evaluations. Embedded in each of these "dimensions of an assessment system" are many opportunities for making them culturally responsive. Some are substantive, procedural, structural, interpretative, and utility. It is not enough to merely change a few items on a test, or to add a specific measure for cultural diversity to claim that one is doing culturally responsive assessment. This is analogous to assuming that the curriculum is sufficiently multiculturalized when a lesson or unit or ethnic achievements or special celebrations for Black History month are added to the list of students learnings. Classroom curriculum, instruction, and assessment require much more extensive changes for them to be culturally responsive. Cultural pluralism must be evident throughout their content and process, their substance and syntax, the "what" and the "how," of their respective domains.

For assessment, this may include multiculturalizing the content of standardized tests, using different kinds of culturally-specific behavioral performances, pluralizing portfolios, and culturally contextualizing such informal measures as story retelling, observations, logs (written, audio, and video), and think alouds. The point of all these is to use assessment techniques that are more compatible with the cultural performance styles of diverse students, and are amenable for use in different settings for different purposes. Here the ideas of multiple intelligences and situational competencies are meaningful. Students perform differently based on time, place, purpose, and audience. Culturally responsive assessment is attuned to these differences and include a variety of measures to capture the *socially situated* skills embedded in them.

The question of *placement* is a critical issue in discussions about how to improve the effectiveness of education for diverse learners. Some educators feel that the most appropriate way to bring cultural diversity into the instructional arena is through additions, supplements, extensions, and enrichments. However, all of these have a common flaw. They are marginal and peripheral to the instructional mainstream. As long as these approaches are used, cultural diversity will be seen as "exceptional," "extra-ordinary," even "exotic" (whether positively or negatively), and therefore, relegated to "special occasions" only. As such, it can be easily distorted and dismissed since it does not penetrate the fundamental cores and routine functioning of the educational process. For this reason, multicultural advocates believe that a better approach to dealing with cultural diversity is *infusion*. That is, *it should permeate the most essential components of all aspects of the educational enterprise.*

In *Assessment Alternatives for Diverse Classrooms*, this principle comes across loudly and clearly from how the authors organize the topics examined, and how they address the substantive content of the discussions. The book begins with a discussion of some major concepts and principles of multicultural education. These create the conceptual context and contours for the analysis of all subsequent topics. And, cultural diversity is a central theme and point of reference within the examination of each separate topic. Consequently, the text models as it advocates for the principle of multicultural education infusion.

The issue of *accountability* plays a major, and often contentious, role in discussions about multicultural education. Questions arise about "Whose responsibility is it?" from the perspective of personnel, programs, and even components within programs. Even some educators who appear to be proponents of cultural diversity and embrace the idea of it being part of the content of instruction shy away from multiculturalizing assessment procedures. They often see these dimensions of the educational process as the last bastion of quality control, and to culturally diversify it is analogous to "lowering academic standards." Individuals who take this position do not understand and value cultural diversity as thoroughly as they claim. More authentic advocates suggest that multicultural education is everybody's business, and cultural diversity must have a prominent place in all parts of the educational process.

The authors of this volume help to operationalize this idea by showing how cultural diversity can and should be incorporated into assessment procedures. In addition to the substantive quality of their specific discussions, the general symbolic significance of their position is even more profound. Within U. S. education we have cultivated a belief and practice that what is included in assessment and evaluation is what really counts. Thus, students know that the real important information appears on tests. Teachers and principals know that those things included in their performance appraisals are of critical importance. The values attached to these cause individuals to focus their energies toward mastering them. Conversely, the things we say are importance during instruction, but not at the point of assessment receive second-order significance. Teachers, students, and administrators know this and act accordingly. They do not attach as much importance to issues and information that are not "tested."

Whether intentional or not the authors of this volume begin to "deconstruct" these notions as they relate to cultural diversity and assessment. They say in many different, deliberate, and powerful ways that the assessments of diverse learner must, of necessity, be culturally pluralistic and responsive. This is imperative if assessment results are to be accurate, valid, and reliable. By evoking these fundamental quality control variables of assessment, Farr and Trumbull demonstrate how cultural diversity and the assessment of diverse learners are inextricably interrelated. One cannot be effectively achieved without attending to the other. This line of argument nests multiculturalism into the heart of the bottom line of educational accountability—that is, "what's really important is one the test."

Farr and Trumbull tell us, without equivocation, that cultural diversity is "on their test" for assessing diverse students. They argue persuasively that it must be on everyone else's as well, whether their "test" is curriculum, instruction, policy, classroom climate, materials, or guidance, if educators are to make any real progress in improving the quality of the educational opportunities and outcomes of ethnically, racially, socially, and linguistically diverse students. Their contributions to this struggle extend the hope and enrich the possibilities for success. The field of multicultural education welcomes their voices, insights, and suggested reforms.

Geneva Gay
Professor of Education
University of Washington, Seattle

References

Banks, J. A. (1990). Citizenship education for a pluralistic democratic society. *The Social Studies 81* (5), 210-214.

Banks, J. A. (1991/92). Multicultural education: For freedom's sake. *Educational Leadership 49*, 32-36.

Bennett, C. I. (1995). *Comprehensive multicultural education: Theory and practice, third edition.* Boston: Allyn and Bacon.

Gay, G. (1994). *At the essence of learning: Multicultural education.* West Lafayette, IN: Kappa Delta Pi.

Nieto, S. (1992). *Affirming diversity: The sociopolitical context of multicultural education.* New York: Longman.

Pai, Y. (1990). *Cultural foundations of education.* New York: Macmillian (Merrill Imprint).

Sleeter, C. E. (Ed.). (1991). *Empowerment through multicultural education.* Albany: State University of New York Press.

Suzuki, B. H. (1984). Curriculum transformation for multicultural education. *Education and Urban society, 16* 294-322.

Chapter 1

The Challenge of Assessment Equity in a Diverse Society

Hopes and Fears Surrounding Assessment Reform

> . . . ultimately, the success of any reform effort in our schools must be measured by the degree to which it is able to effect meaningful change in the educational lives of poor students and students of color, whose problems in, and with, our schools have been a major catalyst for seeking reform in the first place.
>
> Nelson-Barber and Harrison, 1994

We believe the current education reform efforts—of which assessment reform is a significant part—offer both hope and concern for traditionally underserved students. Unfortunately, vast numbers of students, continue to be underserved by the American educational system: second-language learners, students from non-dominant ethnic and racial groups, immigrants, children of poverty, and—sometimes—special education students, females, and those who reside in rural areas. Some students are, of course, members of several of these groups. Assessment reform holds out the hope of practices that are at once more useful because they reveal more about what students have learned and more fair because they take into consideration students' contexts of learning. The potential for new practices to fall short of utility and equity lies at least in part in the common practice of moving ahead to get reforms in place for "the majority" and then trying to adapt them to "special populations," usually after most of the financial and human resources have been allocated or exhausted.

The reforms risk serious failure if they cannot truly address the needs of all students—in ways that respond to what Lauren Resnick calls their "right to achieve at levels that allow [them] to participate productively in society" (Resnick, 1994, p.2). We argue that a priority of all reforms should be the needs of underserved students *before* those of any others, because without such concerted attention, their needs are likely to go unmet once again. Existing inequities will be perpetuated if not multiplied. Such an outcome cannot be in the best interests of our society from either a moral or practical standpoint.

The belief that "good instruction is good instruction," and, by extension, "good assessment is good assessment" is a seductive and tenacious one. In the most general terms, education that is responsive to students' needs, that reflects high expectations for students, that offers multiple routes to learning to the same standards, and that promotes increasing responsibility of students for their own learning is good for everybody. However, good instruction and assessment should look different in different environments, depending on the students served. Many of the specific techniques that are associated with instructional reform (such as thematic instruction, cooperative learning, and project-based learning) have proven to be effective with different kinds of students. But, again, *they cannot be carried out in a uniform way across all populations, without consideration for students' own experiences, ways of learning and communicating, and the goals and values of the communities from which students come.* Similarly, assessments designed at the state or national level for "all fourth-graders" should be tailored to suit various contexts. For example, a mathematics assessment that requires students to design a tile floor may present unnecessary obstacles for American Indian children living on a reservation who have perhaps never seen a tile floor. Teachers on the Navajo reservation in Arizona have modified such an assessment to connect with experiences of their students by asking students to design a rug pattern of certain dimensions rather than a tile pattern. The revised assessment, they believe, addresses the same mathematical skills and knowledge as the original task. Table 1.1 shows the original assessment, Figure 1 shows how teachers modified the task (complete with a segment of student performance). The assessment has also been modified to suit the needs of fifth-graders.

FIGURE 1.1
"The Rug Task"

A tourist to the canyon came through on a jeep tour and stopped to watch Grandmother weave. She was so impressed with Grandmother's weaving that she asked Grandmother to weave her a rug using her favorite pattern. Use the pattern below to design a rug. Use only this pattern in as many ways as you want.

Sample pattern grid:

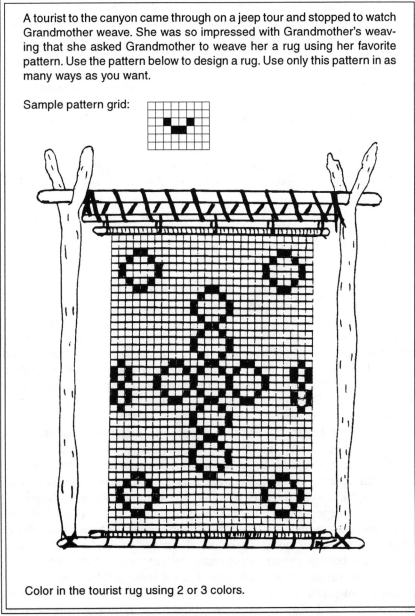

Color in the tourist rug using 2 or 3 colors.

Taken from an assessment developed by fifth-grade teachers in the Chinle Unified (Arizona) School District; completed by a fifth-grader.

Though standards-linked assessments are not intended to compare districts or schools or to rank student performances, scores on these new assessments are being used in just such a manner, with at times devastating consequences for some districts and their students. The public, on the whole, has not been adequately educated about what constitutes appropriate use of these assessments; and so new systems risk being co-opted, invalidated, or simply rejected by the public virtually from the outset. Problems of this nature have arisen in California, Arizona, and elsewhere. Not only state-developed assessment, but also classroom-level assessment can lead to negative outcomes in terms of student loss of motivation, lack of trust, and disengagement with the assessment process. If students sense wrongful or unfair comparisons, they will not have faith in the assessment system used with them. A poignant example of this phenomenon was described by the principal of a large urban high school at a meeting on fairness in testing convened at Far West Laboratory in early 1994. When annual statewide tests are administered, 40 to 50 percent of students from the grade being tested will be absent. Students stay home on testing days, he explained, because they believe the tests do not assess what they know, and they expect only negative consequences.

Educational Reform and the Place of Assessment

One reason for investing hope in the potential of current reform efforts to increase equity is that there is now an extensive theoretical and research base that helps us understand students' cognitive development as well as the nature and impact of linguistic and cultural factors in the classroom. There is also a growing body of literature on multicultural and pluralistic education that investigates what constitutes democratic, anti-racist schooling. Perhaps even more important, educators are subscribing increasingly to the belief that student success is heavily dependent on the curriculum and instruction and not just on inherent, individual psychological differences. This belief is necessary for real reform, because until the assumptions and practices that perpetuate inequities are recognized, only trivial progress can be made. It is not only macro-level social inequities or micro-level instructional practices that contribute to unequal student achievement but mediating beliefs about who can and should achieve that result in the empowerment of same students and alienation of others.

Our alarm arises in part from an increasing sense that traditional power relations that serve to maintain the *status quo* have not been disturbed enough to allow for meaningful participation in reform efforts of those professionals who have the deepest understanding of the needs of underserved students, i.e., those educators who are themselves members of non-dominant groups. Assessment, in particular, has had catastrophic consequences for students from such groups in the past, by virtue of incorrectly labeling them as deficient (without evaluating their opportunities to learn) and thus preventing them from having access to educational opportunities they deserve. For this reason, it seems to us that assessment performs a pivotal role in ensuring equitable opportunities for students. Although our focus in this book is on assessment reform and its relation to students from non-dominant ethnic and linguistic communities, the general issues pertain to all underserved students and their communities.

Defining Diversity

To understand the implications of assessment reform for a diverse society, we need to have a very clear notion of what we mean by "diversity." "Diversity," "pluralism," "culture," "multicultural[ism]," "ethnicity," "race," "minority"—all are terms that are used by different people to mean different things; and all will be used at various points in this book. Some of these terms overlap in meaning (culture/ethnicity/race, for example). All are subject to misunderstanding or misuse, and all evoke philosophical and emotional associations linked to complex social issues. If we, as educators, parents and community members, genuinely seek fair assessment practices for all students, we need to examine first our ways of thinking about these terms and concepts. Their meanings will perhaps become clearer in context; however, we believe it is important to establish some common ground of understanding with our readers at the very beginning of the book.

"Diversity," as applied to human beings, can refer to a vast array of physical, psychological and social differences. "From the subjective point of view, diversity is 'otherness' or those human qualities that are different from our own and outside the groups to which we belong, yet present in other individuals and groups" (Loden and Rosener, 1991). But let's look a little deeper:

diversity: difference, unlikeness, variety . . .

from the Latin noun *diversitas*, meaning "difference," associated with the verb *divertere*, meaning "to turn different ways", that is, "to differ."

When applied to student populations, "diversity" may be intended to refer to differences in language, culture, race, ethnicity, social class, sex, age, religion, learning style, abilities, or sexual orientation (Zeichner, 1993; Loden and Rosener, 1991). In this book, we focus on linguistic and cultural diversity and—by implication—race, ethnicity and social class. Some educators find fault with the words "diverse/diversity," believing that they connote "division," which is from the Latin *dividere*, meaning "to separate." However, the term "diversity" need not imply division—as its derivation shows. Perhaps the one caution vis-à-vis the term is that "diversity" should not be thought of as representing only those students who come from particular ethnic, racial or linguistic groups but as representing all students. "Otherness" is not situated in certain students; where one sees difference is relative to where one stands.

Race and Ethnicity

"Race" and "ethnicity" are sometimes used almost interchangeably, with the former having a stronger force as a biological category. Biologists and geneticists reject "race" as a *biological* category, however, pointing out that there are no discrete, genetically identifiable groups that have specific physical characteristics not manifested in other groups. It would be more accurate to think in terms of a continuum of characteristics rather than discrete categories such as "negro" or "caucasian." There is great variability within a single family, not to mention a designated population. There are no absolute differences between populations from different geographic areas, only differences in relative frequencies of given characteristics. For example, as Lewontin, Rose, and Kamin (1984) observe, "The Kikuyu of East Africa differ from the Japanese in gene frequencies, but they also differ from their neighbors, the Masai, and although the extent of the differences might be less in one case than in the other, it is only a matter of degree. This means that the *social and historical* definitions of race that put the two East African tribes in the same 'race' but put the Japanese in a different 'race' were biologically arbitrary" (p.120). The question, then, is how much difference is required to declare two populations to be separate races; and where does one set boundaries *between* the extremes, for people who have characteristics of more than one "race" as it has been defined?

Nevertheless, race functions *socially* as a distinct category; people respond to each other on the basis of perceived race, and much of social conflict is race-based. Therefore, the notion of race cannot be dismissed as a factor in understanding the impact of diversity in the classroom. In this book, although we speak largely of "culture" rather than race or ethnicity, it should be remembered that ethnic and racial group membership are powerful determinants of status and social relationships in the classroom. We use "culture" in its broadest sense, recognizing that at times it is actually race or ethnicity that may explain behaviors or social phenomena better.

"Ethnic group" is not easily defined, but it is often used to refer to a microcultural group that has common ancestry, culture, tradition, language, religion and history. Ethnic group membership entails both the sensing and expressing of "collective, intergenerational cultural continuity" (Fishman, 1988,p.10). When we think of "ethnic group," we may think of "peoplehood" (Banks, 1988, p.81). In fact, "ethno," derives from the Greek *ethnos*, meaning "people, culture, or race." The reader will begin to see the difficulties in sorting out these terms. A person's "ethnicity" is dependent upon his/her psychological identification with an ethnic group, rather than on some objective analysis of the degree to which he/she speaks a language or dialect or shares traditions or religion with the group.

Reflecting on the importance of culture, race, and ethnicity, James Banks (1988) has said:

> The cultural and ethnic differences among racial groups must be reflected in educational programs designed to reduce intergroup tension and to foster interracial understanding. Overemphasis on cultural differences and cultural pluralism, however, may divert attention from racial differences and hostility. We err seriously when we try to understand ethnic conflict in the schools by focusing exclusively on cultural differences between dominant ethnic groups and ethnic minorities . . . If we develop educational programs and policies designed to make students more accepting of cultural differences but fail to deal seriously with problems caused by racial differences, we will not solve our basic intergroup problems . . ." (p.87).

Racism is, of course, not a necessary outgrowth of ethnic identity or of differences among ethnic groups coexisting in a society, but is "one of the excesses into which ethnicity can develop" (Fishman, 1988, p. 19). Racism goes beyond ethnic identity and pride to assertions of superiority and dominance of one group over another. Racism can be characterized as fostering a system of privilege and penalty (Nieto, 1992) in which some groups routinely benefit at the expense of others, because of the ways resources are allocated. Institutional racism results when official policies and practices of schools and other institutions have inequitable results for certain ethnic or racial groups. For example, tracking has had a disproportionately negative effect on students from non-dominant groups.

Minority

The term, "minority", can be both misleading and socially loaded, and we have tried to avoid using it in this book. In the first instance, groups that have been traditionally considered ethnic or racial minorities actually constitute the majority of a given region or school district. Furthermore, with current trends in population growth and changes, Whites will no longer be a clear majority for many more decades; "people of color," taken together, will constitute equal numbers. With regard to the second concern, American Indian and African- American colleagues have told us that the term "minority" carries a pejorative tone and implies diminished value or importance. In seeking to use language that does not perpetuate or create distance, erroneous beliefs, antagonism, or deprecation, we avoid the term "minority," in favor of "non-dominant group." However, because language betrays often inaccessible assumptions, we recognize an ongoing need to examine all of the terminology we use and what it implies. Perhaps we need new language created by a broader spectrum of members of the entire society.

Culture

There are many definitions of "culture." Current sociological definitions include the following elements: systems of knowledge and values of groups, ways of being/knowing/behaving, acquired and transmitted by symbols, that distinguish a group. Some of the components of a culture are values, behaviors, languages and dialects, nonverbal communications, arts and artifacts, and world view. Culture may be considered "The sum total of ways of living built up by a group of human beings and transmitted from one generation to another." (*Webster's Encyclopedic Unabridged Dictionary of The English Language, 1985*). The emphasis in most current conceptualizations of culture is on "The intangible, symbolic, and ideational aspects of group life" (Banks, 1988, p. 72). Americans belong—at least to some degree—to a national *macroculture*, despite membership in smaller *microcultures*. The macroculture, though often characterized as "Anglo" or "WASP," is actually much more complex. It has been influenced by many cultures. From the outset of colonization and conquest, for example, invading Europeans interacted with and adopted ways of living of American Indians who lived on the continent. Nevertheless, the dominant educational approach appears to have its roots largely in European-American history and values. The degree to which individuals identify with a group is variable, as is the degree to which groups or their members are aware of the distinct features of their own culture.

Microcultures

Individuals are actually members of several smaller cultural groups simultaneously, such as social class, sex, race, religion, or even learning style or lifestyle. These identities interact, so that to focus on any single one is to oversimplify a multidimensional dynamic. There are many aspects of diversity in each person, representing a complex set of values, roles, experiences and perceptions from which he/she draws meaning (Loden & Rosener, 1991). Of course, there is diversity within groups as well as across groups; and knowledge of a cultural group's values or world view, for example, cannot predict those of a specific student. Moreover, cultural values and behaviors change over time, particularly as groups influence each other.

Something that is often forgotten is that a single individual may be multiethnic or multiracial. Oddly, in a society of immigrant and Native groups who have quite naturally intermarried, there is considerable pressure on individuals to choose a single ethnic or racial identity. Bureaucratic requirements for racial identification, intended to be used to monitor for discrimination and access to services, both foster and reflect an oversimplified notion of personal identity (Glass and Wallace, 1995).

Language Group

Language is the principal symbol system through which human beings communicate and represent their knowledge, and it is the primary means for transmitting culture across generations. Language is so clearly at the heart of personal and group identity that it has been said that "Any scorn for the language of others is scorn for those who use it, and as such is a form of social discrimination" (Haugen, 1974, cited in Daniels, 1985, p. 33). As the premier symbol system of a culture, language is eminently associated with world view, both reflecting and shaping it. In fact, it is difficult to disentangle language and culture. Each language is attuned to the needs of its speakers, and even though value judgments about the primitiveness, beauty, or expressiveness of one language compared to another abound, each language is a "fully-formed, logical, rule-governed variant of human speech" (Daniels, 1985, p. 33).

People learn to describe and interpret their environment and experience through their own language(s), and the ways in which different cultural groups organize information through language are quite variable. For example, languages differ in their counting systems and associated terminology. In Japanese there are suffixes attached to ordinals (first, second...) that designate characteristics of the item being counted: *sanbon* = third in a series of long, slender objects such as pencils. *San* means three, and *bon* is the descriptive suffix. At even deeper levels, languages reflect important social values of a culture. The Japanese system of verbs for giving and receiving is much more complex and refined than that in English. Different verbs are used, depending on the social status of giver and receiver. A younger person giving something to an older person uses the verb "sashiageru," but when giving something to an age peer uses "ageru," and to his pet cat (further down the social ladder) "yaru" There are parallel verbs meaning "to receive." Such a system reflects the hierarchical nature of social interchange, and its absence in other languages must be startling indeed to Japanese speakers.

Our native language is the speech of our parents, siblings, friends, and community. It is the code we use to communicate the most powerful and intimate experiences of our lives. It is a central part of our personality, an expression and a mirror of what we are and wish to be. Our language is as personal and as integral to each of us as our bodies and our brains, and in our own unique ways, we all treasure it. And all of us, when we are honest, have to admit that criticism of the way we talk is hard not to take personally. This reaction is nothing to be ashamed of: it is simply a reflection of the natural and profound importance of language to every human being (Daniels, 1985, p. 32).

Social Class or Status

Another important element of diversity in the classroom is social class or socioeconomic status. Considerable educational research argues that membership in the microculture of *class* is the greatest determinant of school success. Of course, social class, race, ethnicity, language and culture are not independent of each other. There is a disproportionately high representation of non-dominant cultural and linguistic groups in the lower socio-economic strata. Despite the egalitarian goals of universal public education to reduce class inequities, students from higher socioeconomic brackets continue to have access to better schools—including better facilities, materials, and instruction. As a result of unequal opportunities to learn, students from lower socioeconomic strata perform less well as a group on assessments (Leinhardt, 1983; Winfield, 1987). However, these differences are often not taken fully into account in interpreting assessment outcomes. The unfair consequences of norm-referenced testing on students from socially non-dominant groups are well-known (Shepard, 1991, among others).

Effects of Unequal Status

Cultural and linguistic groups have different social status and function differently in the macroculture, partly because of their different histories within it. These status differences are mirrored in the classroom when teachers and students hold lower expectations for some students; and such differences contribute to inequitable outcomes for students. Lowered expectations can affect what students are taught, how their performances on classroom assignments and assessments are interpreted, and the sorts of subsequent instruction and placement offered to students (often producing an ongoing cycle of diminished opportunities) (Shepard, 1991).

Groups such as American Indians and African-Americans have been characterized as "caste-like, involuntary minorities" in contrast to immi-grants, "voluntary minorities," who chose to come to the country and ex-pected to join the mainstream (Ogbu, 1992). Critics of such categorization would argue that it is too neat and tidy. After all, what is meant by "vol-untary?" Are we to say that refugees from a war zone "volunteered" to leave, or that all descendants of slaves are "involuntary" Americans? Yet, by their own accounts, African-Americans and American Indians may find themselves in opposition to identification with the dominant group—feel-ing deeply compromised to emulate the values and behaviors of those groups who have had a hand in relegating them to a low status.

The behavioral attributes associated with "Whiteness"—those most often valued by the school—may not coincide with the cultural values of African-American students. According to Perry (1993), these "White" at-tributes are likely to be "the ability to be reserved, to subordinate emo-tions and affections to reason, to constrain physical activity, and to present a disciplined exterior" (p. 13). Moreover, for African-American students, school may not simply be a place to acquire skills but "an appropriate place . . . to struggle for a redefinition of their social and political position in the larger society" (Perry, 1993, p. 15). This relationship to school is in keeping with the African-American community's longstanding intellec-tual tradition of linking "schooling to citizenship, leadership and racial uplift" (Perry, 1993, p. 21). For teachers to grasp the significance of their students' ways of participating in schooling, they need to be able to un-derstand how ideology, culture, historical values about schooling, and jux-tapositions of possibly conflicting culturally-based behavioral expectations converge to promote success or failure for individual students. Even in schools where most or all students are from a non-dominant group, teach-ers and administrators tend to be from the dominant group; thus the norms of the school reflect those of the mainstream.

Attitudes toward Diversity

. . . we have all been programmed to respond to the human difference between us with fear and loathing and to handle that difference in one of three ways: ignore it, and if that is not possible, copy it if we think it is dominant, or destroy it if we think it is subordinate. But we have no pat-terns for relating across our human differences as equals. As a result, those differences have been misnamed and misused in the service of separation and confusion (Audre Lorde, cited in West, 1993, p. 63).

Diversity is touted by some as a threat to the unity of the larger soci-ety and by others as something to celebrate. Those holding the former position see recognition and maintenance of diversity as rending the fabric of the society, creating divisions, introducing conflict in beliefs and values—even destroying the nation's sacred academic canon, that is, the essential body of knowledge—especially works of literature—that ought to be studied (for example, Bloom, 1987; Hirsch, 1987, Schlesinger, 1990). They wish to push for a common culture. Those in the latter camp value the opportunities to learn new ways of being, doing and thinking and seek greater understanding of self through interactions with those from other cultures. They may also believe that in a democracy expression of multiple perspectives and empowerment of all groups are desirable goals (e.g., Banks, 1988, 1993; Gay, 1988; Villegas, 1991). These two stances toward diversity have been characterized as *assimilationist* and *pluralistic*, and we will see shortly how they are translated into approaches to multicultural education in the classroom.

People tend to be comfortable with others like themselves, and teachers can be expected to have greater discomfort with students they see as being unlike themselves. Unfortunately, "otherness" can come to be seen as a deficiency; equality can be interpreted by teachers as bringing students to "sameness" (Loden & Rosener, 1991). When teachers claim to be blind to diversity, as in "When I look at my students, I don't see them as Black or White," it suggests an unconscious expectation for students to assimilate, to become like members of the dominant culture (of which the teacher is usually a member). Teachers, too, may see diversity as a threat to unity in the classroom and fall into an "assimilationist" modus operandi. As Nieto (1992) has observed, it is not students' differences per se that marginalize them; rather, it is the *value* placed on those differences by the dominant society that makes differences matter.

Negative attitudes toward teachers from non-dominant cultures can subvert their ability to teach, or to get hired in the first place—even by representatives of their own cultural or ethnic group. Many examples of this phenomenon could be given, but the following one illustrates it well. Lipka (1993) has documented difficulties that certified Yup'ik teachers in Alaska have in getting hired by their own communities. They are often passed over for non-Yup'ik teachers, offered jobs as classroom aides (even though they are fully certified teachers), or hired, only to be displaced when an "appropriate" White mainstream teacher comes along. Both community members and non-Yup'ik administrators seem to fail to see the Yup'ik teachers as capable of being professional educators. By definition, a teacher is a White person, or one who acts like one. Such attitudes block the most natural way of introducing continuity between students' home communities and schools. The loss to schools is great when teachers from culturally diverse backgrounds are prevented from teaching. Such teachers, many of whom will have encountered similar social obstacles to those their students are facing, can bring particular insights to the task of educating culturally non-dominant students. Their life experience can be the source of bridges between cultures for students—something that is all the more important because traditional teacher education does not prepare teachers to know how to build such bridges (Olsen & Mullen, 1991). The decline in representation of teachers from non-dominant groups is something deserving of deep concern (see "Demographic Trends" below.)

Even if a teaching faculty is not from the dominant group, it may well reflect the values of the mainstream. For example, in the Solomon Islands, it is typical for Native teachers to duplicate the didactic style of British colonial education by lecturing and drilling students. One would expect those teachers to use their first-hand knowledge of the ways Solomon Island children learn in their communities to bridge cultural gaps; but, almost by definition, those who succeeded in British-style schools have acquired a British style of learning and carry on the traditions of their British-style teachers (Watson-Gegeo, 1992). Other studies have shown that when non-dominant culture teachers do get hired and use strategies that are culturally congruent for students of like background, their teaching may be devalued by other teachers and administrators (Delpit, 1986; Ladson-Billings, 1989; Nelson-Barber, 1989). They themselves may not be fully conscious of their strategies (since they engage in them naturally) and may not be able to explain or defend them, despite intuitive knowledge of their appropriateness.

Demographic Trends

Classrooms are diverse, and they are going to become more diverse, if current trends continue. From 1990-2010, the U.S. population is expected to grow by 42 million. Hispanics are expected to account for 47 percent of the growth, African-Americans 22 percent, Asians and other people of color 18 percent, and Whites only 13 percent (Loden & Rosener, 1991). By the early twenty-first century, it is anticipated that one-third of Americans will be people of color (American Council on Education and Education Commission of the States, 1988); and nearly half of the school-age population (46 percent) will be of color (Pallas, Natriello, and McDill, 1989). This trend away from an overwhelmingly White majority has been underway for some time and is attributable to both an influx of immigrants from Asia and Latin America during the 1980s and higher birth rates among people of color. Of course, many factors influence population dynamics—among them are immigration policies and economic well-being (poorer people have more children).

Table 1.1 shows changes in several population groups from 1980 to 1990. The growth in culturally and linguistically non-dominant groups is greater than that of Whites, as can be seen. Although they still constitute a relatively small percentage of the total U.S. population, their rates of increase are noteworthy (see Table 1.2). Particularly striking are the statistics on American Indians, Eskimos, and Aleuts (Aleuts are elsewhere referred to as "Alaska Natives"), Asian and Pacific Islanders, and Hispanics. With regard to American Indians (who constitute most of the change in the first set of categories), their numbers may have increased so dramatically in part because of cultural and ethnic awareness movements among many American Indian communities; people who felt marginalized in the past have in many cases come together to reconstitute communities and traditions.

TABLE 1.1

Changes in Population Groups as a Percentage of Total Population from 1980 to 1990

	1980 Census % of total population	1990 Census % of total population
White	83.1	80.3
Black	11.7	12.1
American Indian, Eskimo, Aleut	0.6	0.8
Asian or Pacific Islander	1.5	9.0
Hispanic	6.4	9.0

TABLE 1.2

Within-Group Percentage Changes in Population Groups from 1980 to 1990

Population Group	% Change
White	6.0
Black	13.2
American Indian, Eskimo, Aleut	37.9
Asian or Pacific Islander	107.8
Hispanic	53.0

Note: Change in total U.S. population was 9.8%
Source: U.S. Bureau of the Census, 1992.

At the same time as students of color are increasing, teachers of color are decreasing—from 12.5 percent of the teaching force in 1980 to a projected five percent in 2000 (American Council on Education and Education Commission of the States, 1988). This is not surprising in light of attitudes held by some toward non-dominant culture teachers. Another factor in this declining figure must surely be the decrease in funding for programs that attracted and supported such teacher candidates in the past.

Although diversity is greatest (because of historical patterns and ongoing immigration) in states such as California, Texas, New York, and Florida, no state is truly homogeneous culturally and ethnically. Vermont folklorist Mac Parker (1993), for example, has documented how Vermont's current culture has been influenced by American Indians, Scots, French-Canadians, Poles, Russians, Swedes, Laotians, Vietnamese, African-Americans, and people from other cultures and nationalities. The influences of all of these groups are felt today in Vermont, and culturally distinct practices continue among them, including use of languages other than English, traditions in cooking and arts, and membership in different religions.

Differences in Ways of Knowing and Learning

𝒫 Cultural and linguistic diversity bring with them diversity in cognitive and communicative styles and strategies, problem-solving approaches, systems of knowledge and methods and styles of assessment. What counts as intelligent behavior is variable from culture to culture; what counts as knowledge and evidence for knowing something, as well as appropriate ways of displaying knowledge are also culturally variable. For example, the European-American style of argument is to make an allegation and then support it with pieces of evidence. Apparently, Chinese tend to do just the *opposite*: they *first* offer a series of pieces of evidence that support a concluding statement (Tsang 1989) to *follow*.

The occasions chosen for displaying knowledge and who chooses these occasions also vary from culture to culture. For example, it is common in many American Indian communities for children to observe an adult or older sibling in a "target" activity for some time (perhaps on several different occasions) and then to practice the same activity in private. Once a child determines that he or she has mastered the activity, he or she will choose to perform it publicly or in view of the adult or older sibling (Deyhle, 1987; Philips, 1983). This scenario is quite distinct from the common trial-and-error approach favored in many American households and schools. In the latter approach, adults may demand that a child try to use or demonstrate a skill before the child has any competence in doing so—sometimes in front of an audience as large as an entire classroom.

It is easy to see from these few examples how diversity in the classroom requires multicultural understanding on the part of teachers. How a student formulates an argument or expresses it can influence a student's performance on classroom assessment tasks and, in turn, teachers' evaluations of students. Without awareness of the ways in which cultural differences can affect student classroom participation and performance, teachers will not understand fully why students behave and perform as they do. Moreover, "the challenge that teachers face is how to make effective instructional use of the personal and cultural knowledge of students, while at the same time helping them to reach beyond their own cultural boundaries" (Banks, 1993. p. 8).

Teachers' attitudes toward diversity and the actions they motivate can have potent effects in the classroom. Students benefit from seeing multiple ways to solve a problem and to interpret events and phenomena. By not acknowledging or understanding differences, teachers deny students the opportunity to be themselves and to learn from each other's approaches. This shortcuts the necessary processes people must go through to get to common ground—by exploring their individual perspectives and by experiencing the tensions of difference. Even standing on common ground, people stand in different spots on that ground; each one "sees and hears from a different position" (Greene, 1993, citing Arendt, 1958, p. 57).

The rush to sameness can result in failure to draw upon students' particular strengths and ways of knowing, disenfranchisement of students as active learners in the classroom, and in a lack of motivation to participate at all. Learning entails risk; risk depends on trust; and if students cannot trust that they are appreciated for who they are, they will be unlikely to take risks.

Multicultural Education

Multicultural education is one response to diversity and is, itself, a multiform phenomenon. At one extreme are methods that treat multicultural education as something a teacher does with students from particular ethnic or racial groups in order to teach them the culture of the dominant group (an assimilationist approach). This is the philosophical position of one school of educators and policymakers who hold that there is a core of cultural knowledge that all students ought to possess, and that is largely European-American (Hirsch, 1987). "The implication is that only certain Americans can define what it means to be American—and the rest must simply 'fit in'" (West, 1993, p. 3). Implicit in this approach is a deficit view of non-dominant cultures that assigns little or no value to maintaining or drawing from a student's home culture or sharing elements of that culture with dominant culture students. Other multicultural programs have the goal of building on home cultures to promote "positive group identity" (Sleeter and Grant, 1987) or self-concept and may include units in ethnic studies that show the contributions of a particular group.

Broadly construed, a third approach to multicultural education embodies goals of empowering students from all groups, promoting a school culture that reflects perspectives of all students and allows groups to maintain their identities ("pluralistic," "radical," and "social reconstructionist" approaches). The common thread between the latter two approaches is the assumption that it is desirable to incorporate aspects of content and ways of learning/knowing of more than one culture in the classroom and that doing so is harmonious with the goals of a democratic society.

Cultural pluralism is associated with systemic strategies toward equity, such as diversifying the staff and changing curriculum to include multicultural content as well as various points of view. It also implies to many educators the goal of working with students to prepare them to be citizens working for social equality—engaging in democratic decision-making and applying social action skills. Pluralism emphasizes that while there is a common American culture, each cultural group continues to have its own unique characteristics (Ayalon, 1993). "Pluralism" or "educating for cultural pluralism" entails not only recognizing different cultural/ethnic/racial perspectives in the classroom but actively promoting the liberation of all groups and teaching in ways that do not alienate students from different groups from their home cultures (Banks, 1988).

As Banks (1991, 1993) notes, there is ongoing vigorous public debate over what constitutes the "cultural canon," that is, the official list or catalogue of knowledge/texts/ways of knowing that form the basis of "cultural literacy" (Hirsch, 1987) for all members of the macroculture. Many argue that the canon needs to change to reflect the racial, ethnic, and cultural diversity that exists. Banks suggests that if there is to be a common core of knowledge, it should be determined by all voices in the macroculture. He proposes "multicultural literacy" (in contrast to Hirsch's "cultural literacy"), which represents "knowledge and understanding that reflect the broad spectrum of interests, experiences, hopes, struggles, and voices of society" (Banks, 1991, p. 142). In harmony with this orientation is Fishman's (1989) assertion that *unum* and *pluribus* go together in America (*E pluribus unum* = from many, one). The unum grows out of pluribus but does not replace it.

Language as Part of Multicultural Education

An element that often gets lost in the multicultural agenda is *language*, although one of the greatest casualties of an assimilationist approach is often a student's first language. Education for students who are not proficient speakers of English has most often been conceived of as *compensa-*

tory, reflecting a devaluing of students' first languages. Such a stance is unfortunate for many reasons. It shows lack of appreciation for the meaning of a first language to both the student's personal identity and to his/her continuing home relationships that may depend on that language, as well as a failure to understand the cognitive benefits of multilingualism. Some have pointed out the irony of ignoring a student's first language and then later encouraging or requiring second-language learning in middle or high school. The terms "folk bilingual" (for students who are bilingual by accident of birth) and "elite bilingual" (for those who learn a second language by choice or privilege) capture the social values associated with this policy. A further irony of the compensatory approach—based on the assumption that the only important language in primary school is English—is that students who have had the opportunity to maintain their first language while learning English have been shown to have important linguistic and cognitive skills that monolingual students do not have or acquire only later on in development (Bialystok and Ryan, 1985; Hakuta, Ferdman, and Diaz, 1987).

A strong multicultural program would promote maintenance and development of students' first languages and offer language education as enrichment for English speakers. One does not have to give up a first language to learn English, but that is most often what happens. Nearly all immigrants lose their mother tongue by the second or third generation of living in America (Fishman, 1989). It is ironic that numbers of third-generation Hispanic-Americans who have lost their first language now find themselves studying Spanish in school in order to communicate with and work within their own communities. Advocates of multilingualism do not reject the importance of all students' becoming highly proficient in English. They believe that learning English should not preclude maintaining a first language and learning additional ones.

The loss of a language can have negative social, cognitive, and emotional consequences. For this reason it is crucial that we look below the surface of the "English only" movement to see it clearly as one of the most unfortunate representations of an assimilationist (if not racist) agenda. There is no educational or economic justification for the movement; rather it draws its energy from sometimes unconscious fears of "the other," in this case the person who speaks a language other than English. One can see why a majority culture might wish to stamp out others' languages. Language is at once the most powerful vehicle of culture, is inscrutable to non-speakers (hence making the majority culture member feel excluded or less in control), and is probably the personal capacity most closely tied to one's identity and humanness.

The Role of Language in Assessment

Because of its centrality in assessments, including alternative forms, language will continue to be at the core of discussions about fairness and accuracy of student assessment. Appreciation of the role of language in cognition and in personal and group identity—and, thus, in students' variable ways of participating in classroom activities—is necessary if teachers are to make best sense and use of "new" forms of assessment. It is virtually impossible to eliminate reading ability as a variable in any kind of written assessment. In fact, it is difficult to design assessments (or instructional events) that do not rely heavily on language; and so language proficiency becomes a key to success with them. This fact is of special concern when the students taking the assessments are English language learners, or when they are students whose customary ways of using language do not match those of the school and demanded by the assessments.

Language proficiency is often a prerequisite for entry into programs—whether as a proxy for intelligence, as the prime skill required for succeeding on an achievement test, or as an indicator of readiness for advanced academic work. Young children are declared eligible for programs on the basis of instruments such as the *Peabody Picture Vocabulary Test*. It has been permissible to use a vocabulary subtest alone to identify students for compensatory education. English language learners are sorted and slotted into programs on the basis of such instruments as the *Language Assessment Scales*. The verbal portion of the *SAT* is considered the best indicator of a student's potential for success in college, and high scores are essential for admission to many schools.

Despite the importance of language in learning and assessment, teachers are not universally exposed to frameworks for understanding language development or relationships between language and cognition. Moreover, assessment of language proficiency and methods of isolating the language demands of an assessment against the demands for content domain knowledge have not been adequate. (See Chapter 5.)

Democracy and Diversity

As Gunnar Myrdal observed decades ago in *An American Dilemma: The Negro Problem and Modern Democracy* (1944), the United States is faced with a moral conundrum in that its stated ideals promote equality, while many of its social practices undermine it. Perhaps the increasingly diverse nature of our population will focus us—particularly educators—once again on attempting to realize our democratic ideals. Cornel West (1993) suggests that we need a new social framework that acknowledges the basic humanness and Americanness of each of us. He, too, invokes the motto,

"E pluribus unum," in saying that the destinies of Blacks and Whites are inextricably linked. "If we go down, we go down together" (West, 1993, p. 4). Paradoxically, respect for and maintenance of differences can pave the way for addressing the common good. If multicultural schooling is to be effective, it needs to foster all students' participation in constituting a shared cultural reality. As West (1993) has said, the challenge facing America in the next century is to somehow fashion a common public culture that is responsive to the long-silenced cultures of color. Several other writers speak of deepening and broadening our sense of community by a more inclusive, multicultural approach to education and life. Educational philosopher Maxine Greene (1993) speaks eloquently about the challenge:

> There have always been newcomers in this country; there have always been strangers. There have always been young persons in our classrooms we did not, could not see or hear. In recent years, however, invisibility has been refused on many sides. Old silences have been shattered; long-repressed voices are making themselves heard. Yes, we are in search of what John Dewey called "the Great Community," but, at once, we are challenged as never before to confront plurality and multiplicity (p. 13).

Myths about Diversity

Difference as Deficit

The myth that difference equals deficit is an entrenched one with a long and inglorious history. It has its roots in racism, classism, and ethno- and linguacentricism. This myth has alternately been based in erroneous beliefs about nature/biology (genetic causes of human differences) and nurture/culture. Both biological determinism and cultural determinism offer oversimplified explanations of people's differences—attributing them strictly to either biological or cultural causes. Both extremes fail to account for the complexities and interactions of biology, culture, and inter-personal and inter-cultural experience. According to the former, people are as they are because of their genes. There is an inevitability, a destiny to unfold that is genetically determined. Biological determinism is associated with ranking people on (fixed) properties they are believed to possess, reflecting a static view of human abilities. Norms are established, and deviations from these norms are by definition *abnormal*. One can readily see how such a philosophy could be used to explain differences in social status and many other variables including school performance—and to rationalize improving not opportunities but the gene pool, that is, encouraging the poor to use birth control!

Many questionable, if not cruel, social policies have been based on a belief in biological determinism. For example, in the early part of the twentieth century, U.S. immigration laws were written to limit the number of eastern and southern European immigrants, because it was believed that they were genetically predisposed to intellectual dullness; the German racial and eugenic laws of the 1930s were based on similar beliefs (Lewontin et al., 1984). During the same era in England, where there was a class-based society, children were sorted into educational tracks on the basis of biased and sometimes actually fabricated test scores. The history of intelligence testing is clouded with biological determinist belief, despite efforts by some, such as Alfred Binet, himself, to disparage the notion that IQ is an unchangeable trait rather than a flexible index of performance in a restricted set of domains (Lewontin et al., 1984).

Although an extreme biological determinist position is not likely to be taken by an educated person today, remnants of this philosophy influence current understandings of why people are different. Many people now believe that it is a simple "50-50 nature-nurture" proposition: half of a person's intelligence, for example, is accounted for by genes, half by environment. But this is a vast oversimplification. In fact, even when a trait has some genetic basis, one does not know as far as an individual is concerned what the genetic contribution is. Genetics (or the index of heritability of a trait) explains only probabilities of occurrences of traits in populations, not individuals. Moreover, even traits that have some genetic basis are amenable to change in interaction with the environment— height in relation to nutrition, for example, not to mention complex, socially constructed "traits," such as intelligence (see Anastasi, 1990).

"Actually, heritability indexes give the proportional contribution of hereditary factors to the total variance of a specified trait in a given population at a given time, that is, under existing conditions. One limitation of such an index is that any change in either hereditary or environmental conditions in that population will alter the heritability index" (Anastasi, 1990, p. 21).

Cultural determinism, the belief that one is permanently defined by one's culture or limited by it (as in the myth of "cultural deprivation") is equally pernicious. It, too, denies the capacity of people to learn throughout their lifetimes and implies that cultures are static entities, unresponsive to the needs of people. Humans in their ethno- and linguacentrism believe that one language is superior to another; that there is one best way to eat at table (or not), to give and receive a gift, to express anger or state an opinion. It is difficult to espouse cultural values, to believe in certain standards yet appreciate difference. How much easier it is to say, "This is the one best way and all others are misguided." It is easy to see the relationship of this kind of thinking to the concept of test norms, the notion that variation from norms of behavior (often White, middle-class norms) is equivalent to *abnormality*. This issue is an essential one in the current debate over the value of performance-based, standards-linked assessment versus norm-referenced assessment. If sorting and ranking students in relation to [dominant culture] norms is no longer the purpose of testing, it should be possible to accommodate students' differences in cognitive style, language, and experience while holding steady some broad content and performance standards. At least, that is the challenge.

In the past, deficit views have led to inferior programs for English language learners rather than an "ability centered" approach that posits different but valuable abilities of students from different cultures and experiences (Miramontes and Commins, 1991). Misguided assessment processes can reinforce these beliefs that difference is equivalent to deficit, resulting in special education placements from which children virtually never emerge to rejoin their peers in the regular education program.

Bilingualism as Handicap

In a particular version of the "difference as deficit" myth, many teachers view speaking another language as an educational handicap. "Spanish holds students back." Why does our society not see bilingualism as an asset in a diverse society (Garcia and Pearson, 1991)? We would argue for a philosophical position that actively focuses on identifying student strengths or abilities (Miramontes and Commins, 1991) and counts among them knowledge of languages other than English.

As mentioned above, the notion of *compensatory* programs for deficits has been the basis of many programs for English language learners. Language differences may be observed in style, usage, dialect, accent, vocabulary—associated with not only different languages per se but registers or classes within a language. Judgments about children's intelligence based on pronunciation and grammar are often unconscious, yet have palpably unfair consequences. As with imputations of the inferiority of some languages, beliefs that non-preferred dialects are inferior on a logical or linguistic basis are specious. It has been shown that whether socially approved or devalued, dialects are systematic variations of a language, with rules of their own which are learned by their speakers. Dialectal differences in grammatical usage are not "errors," but the result of the application of different rules. Although social prejudice against unfavored dialects is not likely to disappear, it should be recognized for what it is. In the meantime, teachers need to be wary of their own tendencies to equate mastery of the standard or "received" dialect of English with superior intellect or learning.

Sociopolitical and Ethical Issues in Assessment

Educational practices have long-term, if not permanent, effects on students; and we—as educators and as a society—cannot afford to focus on the technology of assessment without equal attention to sociopolitical influences on the development, use and consequences of assessments. Some of the most common assessment policies have resulted in highly negative schooling experiences for students. One high school student interviewed in conjunction with an institute on school transformation said the problem with schooling was that "This place hurts my spirit" (Poplin & Weeres, 1992). Schools that hurt children's spirits would not be overtly sanctioned by any reputable educator, and yet many current educational practices (tracking, test misuse, labeling difference as deficit, for example) that are known to be highly damaging to children's spirits and to their prospects for learning continue to enjoy widespread use. With regard to the impact of assessment on students, feelings of self-worth and perceptions of self-efficacy are often negatively affected by achievement tests and test scores (Paris, Lawton, Turner, and Roth, 1991)—out of proportion to what the tests are actually capable of revealing about individual students. Surveys of middle and high school students have suggested that over time testing tends to increase students' disillusionment about tests, decrease their motivation to expend effort on tests, and increase their use of inappropriate strategies (Paris et al., 1991). It is not surprising that lower-achieving students exhibit these effects in greater numbers. Reflecting on their own and others' research data, Paris et al. (1991) conclude, "It appears that the results of standardized achievement tests become increasingly less valid for low achievers, exactly the group who are most at risk for educational problems and who most need diagnostic testing. Their scores may be contaminated by inappropriate motivation and learning strategies in ways that further debilitate their performance and affirm a self-fulfilling prophecy of low scores" (p. 16). How valid can student performances be in such circumstances? Worse yet, what good is a testing system that has such unfortunate impact on students?

As Edmund Gordon has said, the "problem of equity is a problem of the larger society outside school. As long as society continues to reward winners and to screen out people 'not like us,' inequities will remain regardless of what happens to assessments" (cited in Rothman, 1994, p. 2). For us, the challenge to change such a societal stance looms larger than any of the others associated with educational reform. One question that arises is whether our society can be induced to address the challenge on moral grounds alone. Lorraine McDonnell (1994), for example, has argued that the redistribution of resources that would be required in order to produce "substantive equity" or equal results would be difficult to achieve solely through appeals to altruism. Rather, she believes, it will be accomplished through appeals to voters' self-interest in developing a better economy and society. Lorrie Shepard (1991) echoes the doubt that moral suasion will be sufficient to ensure equity but sees assessment reform as a true opportunity to engage in a process of developing a system that addresses opportunities to learn as integral to the whole reform effort.

New Thinking about Instruction and Assessment

Assessment reform is best understood in the wider context of changes in views of teaching and learning.

Relationship of Assessment to Curriculum and Learning

One essential shift in perspective has to do with the relationships among curriculum, instruction, and assessment. Teaching, learning, and assessment are now seen as inextricably linked: good performance assessments mirror good instruction, and both engage children in critical thinking from the beginning (of the grades, of the year, of the instructional unit, of the activity . . .). From this point of view, it is not valid to sort children into those who can engage in high-level thinking or project-based learning and those who need to focus on basic skills and simple tasks. "Authentic assessment supports [such] good teaching by not requiring teachers to redirect attention away from important concepts, in-depth projects, and the like" (Shepard, 1991).

Curricular reform, the redesign of instructional practices, and an increase in professional development support for teachers need to be synergistically applied if the larger goals of educational reform are to be accomplished. The existing measurement culture has been generally associated with an accretion model of learning: a gradual and hierarchical acquisition of skills—new ones building upon already acquired ones in a predictable order. In such a model, a clear scope and sequence can be specified, with low-level algorithms as prerequisites to larger concepts, powerful strategies, or independent thinking. Benjamin Bloom's taxonomy depicts learning as progressing in linear fashion from basic forms of recognition and imitation to higher cognitive activities such as analysis and synthesis. Many of today's teachers rely on this model as a guide for instructional practice (probably in ways that Bloom did not intend). Moreover, the bulk of instructional and assessment materials proceed as if this description held, despite abundant evidence that even sophisticated thought "follows a 'zigzag' course between craft and vision" (Polya, 1954; Wolf et al., 1991, citing Lakotas, 1976). In addition, even very young children's thought processes include the same kinds of mental processes entailed in higher-order thinking (Resnick & Resnick, 1989).

A constructivist view of learners who build their own meaning and their own schemata (frameworks for understanding situations or problems), stresses the dynamic rather than the static—active knowing and thinking rather than the passive acquisition of bodies of knowledge. Rather than gradually adding to a store of knowledge, learners experience "qualitative and uneven shifts in understanding" (Wolf et al. 1991, p. 50). Moreover, they develop as thinkers not in isolation but in interaction with other learners. Influences of a more socially-oriented psychology (such as espoused by Russian psychologist Lev Vygotsky) and the fields of sociolinguistics and anthropology have come to bear more strongly on educators' thinking in recent years. Learning and knowledge are seen to exist in social context, relative to the culture of the individual. As Resnick (1991) has noted, theories of situated cognition (e.g., Brown, Collins & Duguid, 1989; Lave, 1988) "challenge the dominant view in cognitive science that assumes a cognitive core can be found that is independent of context and intention. Instead, they argue, every cognitive act must be viewed as a specific response to a specific set of circumstances. Only by understanding the circumstances and the participants' construal of the situation can a valid interpretation of the cognitive activity be made" (p.4). People's beliefs and values about what to learn and how to go about learning it originate in their home experiences, as do norms of language use. Cognition is not a solitary act committed by an individual, dependent only on his or her inherent learning potential; it is a social act—sometimes in the sense of immediate collaboration with others, sometimes in the sense of being situated within multiple layers of social history and current social context.

The currently operative word relating curriculum and assessment is "alignment." In traditional educational practice, it was common for educators to emphasize the need to "match" testing objectives to teaching objectives. Many actually went about the rather technical and clerical task of doing side-by-side comparisons of a scope and sequence chart in a basal reader teacher's guide (for example) with the testing objectives given in a test manual. Test selection was often based on the apparent closeness of the match. Such a process is not equivalent to what is now addressed as "alignment"—the matching of assessments with content standards and classroom instruction. The focus is on broader, more complex units, both in terms of standards versus minute skills and integrated assessment tasks versus multiple-choice or short-answer questions. As performance-based tasks are being developed that are open-ended and challenging, that invite multiple approaches to solutions and often require the use of multiple resources, educators are coming to see that classroom instruction must incorporate such activity as well. At the same time, it is clear that a range of performance tasks must have reference to a set of content standards that reflect a consensus about what knowledge and skills a student must acquire in a particular domain. Such alignment is essential to the development of a coherent system that provides adequate opportunities to learn, broadens the concept of what it means to learn, and assesses learning in fair and useful ways.

From a Testing Culture to an Assessment Culture

Some say we are moving away from a "testing culture" toward an "assessment culture," one of "defining and documenting what it is to use a mind well" (Wolf et al., 1991, p. 32), with an emphasis on *informing* rather than *measuring*. The contrasts between these two cultures do not reside merely in the forms of assessment used. "They derive from radical differences in underlying conceptions of mind and of the evaluation process itself" (Wolf et al., 1991, p. 33), as well as differences in assumptions about the nature and distribution of intelligence in people. The "assessment culture" approach is a more natural counterpart of social constructivist conceptions of cognition and learning, than a "testing culture" approach that assumes context to be neutral. It is based more in clinical judgment (Wolf et al., 1991, p. 59), negotiating meaning, critically examining evidence to confirm or reject a judgment of competence or excellence, taking circumstances into account. Even the process of assessment is seen as a social one, with meaning jointly constructed by teacher and student(s), rather than a one-way act of judgment. Others, such as Taylor (1994), have distinguished a "measurement" from a "standards" approach to assessment. The "measurement" approach has been associated with the practice of ranking people along various dimensions and a belief in the predictability and immutability of intelligence or learning capacity. Tests reflecting this belief system have been designed explicitly to magnify differences among students. The "assessment" approach (associated with standards) is based on the belief that learning potential is more a function of experience than destiny. The practice of sorting and ranking students in relation to each other gives way to assessment against agreed-upon standards, using agreed-upon criteria.

Portfolios, performance tasks, exhibitions, and the like will not be powerful or useful assessment process tools unless those who use them have a fundamental understanding of and belief in the views of learning and knowing to which they are conceptually linked. Without an awareness of the past theories of learning and practices and policies that are based on them, we will not understand the current movement well. As it is, the old and new paradigms co-exist, with notions of controlling the conditions of assessment to ensure reliability bumping up against demands for tailoring assessment and its administration to student contexts and needs. As the education community continues to consider what role assessment reform needs to play in educational reform, it needs to avoid such over-reliance on assessment reform to leverage educational reform that its weaknesses become exaggerated (Shepard, 1991).

Teacher Involvement and Professional Development

The kinds of educational innovations proposed currently, whether characterized as "restructuring," "school improvement," or "systemic reform," require fundamental changes in the roles of teachers, administrators, parents, community, and students. However, the greatest demands fall upon teachers: new conceptualizations of assessment hinge on teachers' taking responsibility for creating (or modifying), administering, scoring, and interpreting assessments. If teachers are to assume such responsibilities, they will need major support in the form of professional development. In Arizona, for example, where a new statewide assessment system was mounted in 1991, large cadres of teachers have attended workshops on how to score performance assessments. Provision of so much professional development has been a difficult and costly undertaking for the State Department of Education, but teachers themselves say that without opportunities to talk and argue at length over how to apply rubric-based criteria to actual student performances, they would never have understood the assessment reform of which they are such a central part. Now, back in their own districts, teaching faculties throughout Arizona are struggling to find the time and financial support to engage in the kind of professional practice essential to implementing what is really a full-fledged reform of the ways they teach and assess. Commenting on the reform, one rural Arizona teacher said, "[This] is so different. It's far more than a [new] test. It's the whole process of instruction, and it really is altering the whole system. The trend has been moving toward that anyway—whole language, integration of subjects . . . You can see it all coming together" (Estrin, 1996, p. 19).

Districts are using all the existing resources they can muster, seeking grant support, and relying on the good will and leadership of their teachers to meet professional development needs. Studies such as *Prisoners of Time*, the report of the National Commission on Time and Learning (1994), and pilot projects around the country have begun to provide much-needed examples and suggestions for creative solutions to these needs. Organizational conditions that support "professional practice" schools, where professional development is built into the social fabric of schooling, are being identified and means for achieving them described (see, for example, Lieberman and Miller, 1990; Rosenholtz, 1989).

Concluding Comment

It is in this broad context of changes in thinking about how students learn, about who can and should achieve, about what it means to teach and assess, about the roles of teachers and students, and about how culture-based knowledge and ways of knowing can be capitalized on in the classroom that we will explore the potential of current assessment reforms in the following chapters.

Commentary

Amalia Mesa-Bains

I am gratified that the authors of this book have taken the time to lay a foundation about concepts of "diversity" for their readers, as they introduce the topic of assessment. Sorting out some of the categories of diversity such as "race," "ethnicity," and "culture" is very important, because these aspects of personal and group identity affect students' educational opportunities and have particular implications for equity in assessment. One of the problems we have had in the field of education—particularly when it comes to the notion of "diversity"—is the persistent use of euphemistic terms that are never defined. The specificities that pertain to "race" versus "class" or "ethnicity" are rarely defined. Rather, they are treated as though they are equivalent in terms of social effect or meaning. We need mechanisms for examining our beliefs about diversity, the roots of our perceptions. Where do these ideas come from—ideas such as the "noble savage," the Spanish debates in Meso-America about whether Indians have a soul, and the concept of slaves as human chattel? They are the roots of the negative perceptions about diversity held today. These roots of perception put people on a pathway. For example, the group of families that did not send their children to school on the day of testing (mentioned in the chapter) anticipated only the negative potential of testing. For assessment reform to have any hope of equity, schools and society at large must cultivate deeper understanding of diversity—both what it is and what it means—in the United States.

One of the most serious errors of a naive multiculturalism is that everything is presented as being on a level playing field: group differences in sociopolitical histories that place those groups in very different relations to present-day United States society are often ignored. For example, Irish American and Chicano history may be treated similarly, but the histories are in no way the same; and a teacher needs to understand that in order to help students address those histories in a meaningful way. Ireland was never annexed by the United States, and Irish-Americans are not living on the continent on which their great-great grandparents were born. Multicultural education is often applied in a simplistic way that glosses over important differences among group histories. John Ogbu (whose work is mentioned in the chapter) has gotten at this issue to some extent: he at least gives some parameters for understanding how it is that people got to be in this place called the United States and the roles they are cast in, based on how they were originally brought into this nation's patrimony. He really begins to open this issue up, but we need to go further if we are going to conceive of multicultural education that is meaningful and moves us all toward greater mutual understanding and equality.

With Ogbu, I believe that to understand the roles of particular groups in current American society, some reference to history and the social contexts various groups found themselves in historically is necessary. But I want to highlight the concept of *class and economics* as a powerful element of diversity in terms of effects on people's lives. To some degree this category collapses or cuts across perceived race and culture. The colonial histories that we are all beset with are, even in the contemporary age, trajectories that we have been set on in terms of labor roles. People were brought to this country for particular jobs (the Chinese to build railroads, Mexicans to work in the fields, for example); their countries of origin were in many cases colonized to gain access to certain resources. The places our great grandparents were born in are not irrelevant: they have to do with current expectations, access, and equity. Labor and economic histories are linked to what is effectively a caste system in the United States. And, whether we like it or not, very few people rise out of the caste into which they were born.

As an example, one can see a continuous trend for Mexican workers from the 1500s forward, but especially in the 1800s after the U.S. annexation of over half of Mexico. Following that event, the remaining Mexicans were tracked almost uniformly into a laboring caste from which they have not, on the whole, emerged even up to the present time. Considering that those people will at some point be a majority, at least in California, the issue of the labor role needs to be given great thought. What will the labor force of a future generation be like, and will Mexican-Americans be accepted in a greater variety of roles, as will be needed? This concern pertains very much to the migrant and bilingual education programs in place today. They are largely compensatory in both cases: in the first, focused less on strong academic preparation for equal entry into advanced studies than on basic skills; in the second, focused more on acquiring English than on maintaining and developing a first language while developing English—reflecting a deficit view of native languages. In neither instance do we see expectations equal to those held for "majority" students.

Bilingualism and bilingual education need to be understood in historical context as well. In the case of Spanish-English bilingualism, at least for Mexican Americans, there is a whole history of associating the speaking of Spanish with educational or intellectual deficit. The Spanish language is inherently tied to the notion of disenfranchisement through the history of the colonial occupation. When the colonies that now constitute large portions of our southwestern states were annexed from Mexico, the process that the United States government used was one that effectively disenfranchised Spanish speakers. In order to maintain ownership of any of their property, Mexicans had to negotiate through an English-only legal and taxation system, so that overnight monolingual Spanish-speaking people lost all of their holdings, including the silver and gold mines. The Spanish land grants were lost. The use of English—and, more explicitly, the removal or oppression of the Spanish language—was the vehicle of oppression by which those resources could be acquired; that process was a prime vehicle by which the United States was able to take the Mexican empire. Consequently, the use of Spanish became a transgression, a taboo.

It is not possible to just turn around and reinstate the Spanish language with a positive sentiment, because of this history. There are historical parallels to Native languages and to various African languages. When Africans were brought in as slaves, they were separated from those who could speak the same language. That practice was a means of controlling the slaves: people are disempowered when they cannot communicate. We cannot expect to simply enfranchise those languages at a later point without consideration for the history. And, in the same way that the United States government reduced the perceived power of a large population of newly-annexed Spanish speakers through the legal system, modern-day Mexican Americans in California are being held in check by increasingly oppressive legislation. The current xenophobic trend is based on fear of this linguistic and cultural group that is an increasingly large proportion of the population.

Efforts to intimidate or hold in check a "minority" group are not unrelated to perceptions of ability, expectations for learning, ideas about who will achieve, and systems of instruction and measurement. There is one dimension that cuts across the present and the past, the dimension of knowledge, of learning. In the colonial enterprise, in order to rationalize the appropriation of resources and oppression of people, there had to be a notion constructed that those who were oppressing had superior knowledge and culture. This was a governing idea in any colonial enterprise. If we consider how such a notion might play out or unfold over the years and look—a couple of centuries later—at what is being measured and what systems of knowledge are being assessed and valued, along with assumptions about who is capable of knowing and learning, we should not be surprised at what we find. We are trying to develop new instruments without having developed a new attitude about knowledge, about whose knowledge is valid, and about what the historical truth is. We are operating with an old idea—the myth of colonial superiority—and trying to adapt instruments, processes, and practices that will somehow mediate that false knowledge, but it is very difficult. I believe that assessment that is equitable and relevant has to be tied to new systems of knowledge and teaching. In the same way that we must take away the euphemistic layers from "diversity," we need to say what we really mean when we talk about "knowledge."

Something else that I would like to emphasize that was brought up rather briefly in the chapter is the concept of "complex identity." To understand human identity and human behavior, we need to realize that, in a single individual, gender, class, ethnicity, race, nationality, citizenship and other elements all come together in various composites to form a complex identity. We now see the interplay of gender and race, for example, and have a deeper understanding of what Black women face than there was during the Black nationalist movement. These issues of complex identity make complex assessment all the more important. We cannot just be looking at ethnic groups and how they perform. Within any given student, we need to be able to look at many facets. One cannot say "All Blacks perform this way . . ."

All people live in multiple realities—at work, at home, in their friendships and social lives, in their hobbies. People are not as simple-minded as portrayed, for example, by pessimists like Schlesinger (1990, 1991), who do not seem to trust students to learn how to negotiate multiple worlds. People may not believe that a young person could have a strong sense of group reference and still be a member of another larger group. A bilingual, bicultural person learns to do that all his life. Group reference gives a foundation, a sense of who you are; but you learn to switch languages and behaviors. And as you grow older, you also switch dress to be appropriate for different situations. It is odd to assume that human beings are so simple that they cannot do that—that they are incapable of such a complex and multi-referenced reality. We are willing to accept *cyberspace*, and we expect kids to handle all sorts of processes and realities through computers; but we are somehow not willing to accept complex *social space!*

The fulfillment of my vision of a multicultural classroom depends on a great deal more professional preparation for teachers. As I have discussed, I believe a deep understanding of the historical roots of current social realities must be understood by teachers. In my observations, it has been rare to find even discussions about regional histories in classrooms.

Far from believing that to engage in them would be fractionalizing, as some do, I believe they are essential and constructive to the democratic process in the classroom. Those discussions cannot take place, because the most fundamental aspects of history (such as the annexation of Mexico) are not well taught in teacher preparation programs. I think for Mexican-descended people, the annexation is probably the most important aspect of United States history. It is comparable to slavery as a historical trauma for African-Americans. It has affected everything that has happened to us since then, but it is totally disregarded in the content of history courses.

What is ignored in a curriculum is as powerful in its effects as what is taught. What does it mean to immigrants from Latin America to notice, for example, that the names of counties, towns, and streets in California are Spanish (a language they are discouraged from speaking) more often than English and yet to be taught nothing about why that is the case? The process by which these things are ignored is the same process by which certain histories are not taught.

I think that, in fact, the kinds of social processes that go on in classrooms are the key to being able to have a multicultural classroom, whether the content material is multicultural or not. Practices may include or exclude certain students and their perspectives. Students can role-play by taking different historical or current roles; they can learn to mediate conflict or substantiate their ideas through debate and exchange. These are process skills entailing interpersonal communication that can flourish when teachers provide structures that allow young people to explore and even "live in" these multiple perspectives. Activities like role-playing can help students learn how to switch codes and languages. But such experiences are often missing in the classroom. We, as teachers, are often too afraid to engage in any activity that is not paper-and-pencil or book-oriented, because we will lose control. But I have seen these kinds of activities work very well in classrooms. When a student has to role-play someone quite different from herself, it forces understanding in terms other than what she is used to. It makes her feel more competent. It is easy to talk with people who understand your codes, your way of talking and thinking, but it is challenging to communicate with others who come from a different language, culture, or history. Teachers need to help children accrue these skills. I think some of the most effective curricula in terms of helping people to live in a diverse society are not multicultural curricula per se. They are focused on media literacy, cross-cultural communication, practices in the ability to analyze social contexts that students and teachers are going to have to operate in. Another effective approach to helping students take on different perspectives is through literary characters, through literature. A book is a more neutral space (than personal experience) through which people can engage the concerns and conflicts they have.

One final issue I want to emphasize with regard to assessment is something that is dealt with throughout this book: assessment is not just about what you know. It is also about what you are willing to say you know. Some groups do not privilege individual displays of achievement. Such displays may be considered bad manners. Or, if one's acknowledgement of what one knows will embarrass someone else, that may be taboo. Children may come from cultures in which it is unacceptable to show that someone else is wrong, so that in public questioning they will not produce a right answer following a wrong answer, whether they are able to or not. Teachers must learn the cultural conventions of their students so that they can anticipate the best ways to assess them, or at the very least understand the limitations of existing practices and use assessment results judiciously and fairly.

—— ❧ ——

Dr. Amalia Mesa-Bains is a psychologist, educator, artist, and cultural critic who lives in the San Francisco Bay Area. She is an author of scholarly articles and a nationally-known lecturer on both Latino art and multicultural issues. Dr. Mesa-Bains was for several years a professional development specialist in the Department of Integration in the San Francisco Unified School District, a unit charged with carrying out a consent decree to integrate the schools. In that capacity, she was deeply involved in bringing multicultural perspectives to educational programs. Dr. Mesa-Bains was recognized for her art and her contributions to education by the MacArthur Foundation in 1992 with a Distinguished MacArthur Fellowship.

References

American Council on Education and Education Commission of the States. (1988). *One-third of a nation: A report of the Commission on Minority Participation in Education and American Life.* Washington, D.C.: American Council on Education.

Anastasi, Anne. What is test misuse? Perspectives of a measurement expert. (1990). In *The uses of standardized tests in American education. Proceedings of the 1989 ETS Invitational Conference.* Princeton, NJ: Educational Testing Service.

Arendt, H. (1958). *The human condition.* Chicago: University of Chicago Press.

Ayalon, Aram. (1993). Does rural white America need multicultural education? Paper presented at the annual meeting of the National Rural Education Association, Burlington, VT.

Banks, James A. (1988). *Multiethnic education: Theory and practice.* Second Edition. Boston: Allyn and Bacon, Inc.

Banks, James A. Multicultural literacy and curriculum reform. (1991). *Educational Horizons,* Vol. 69, No. 3.

Banks, James A. (1993). The canon debate, knowledge construction, and multicultural education. *Educational Researcher.* Vol. 22, No. 5, 4-14.

Bialystok, Ellen and Ryan, Ellen Bouchard. (1985). Toward a definition of metalinguistic skill. *Merrill-Palmer Quarterly,* Vol. 31, No. 3, 229-251.

Bloom, Allan. (1987). *The closing of the American mind.* New York: Simon and Schuster.

Brown, John Seely, Collins, Allan, and Duguid, Paul. (1989). Situated cognition and the culture of learning. *Educational Researcher, Vol. 18,* No. 1, 32-42.

Cassell's Latin Dictionary. (1977). New York: Macmillan.

Daniels, Harvey A. (1985). Nine ideas about language. In Clark, Virginia P., Eschholz, Paul A., and Rosa, Alfred F. (Eds.). *Language: Introductory readings.* New York: St. Martin's Press.

Delpit, Lisa. (1986). Skills and dilemmas of a progressive black educator. *Harvard Educational Review,* Vol. 58, No. 4.

Deyhle, Donna. (1987). Learning failure: Tests as gatekeepers and the culturally different child. In Trueba, Henry (Ed.), *Success or failure.* Rowley, MA: Newbury House.

Estrin, E. T. (1996). *A case study of assessment reform in Arizona, part II: Consolidating change.* San Francisco: Far West Laboratory.

Fishman, Joshua. (1989). *Language and ethnicity in minority sociolinguistic perspective.* Clevedon, England: Multilingual Matters, Ltd.

Garcia, Georgia Earnest and Pearson, P. David. (1991). The role of assessment in a diverse society. In Hiebert, Elfrieda H. (Ed.), *Literacy for a diverse society*. New York: Teachers College Press.

Garcia, Jesus and Pugh, Sharon L. (1992, November). Multicultural education in teacher preparation programs: A political or an educational concept? *Phi Delta Kappan*.

Gates, Jr., H.L. (1991). Goodbye, Columbus? Notes on the culture of criticism. *American Literacy History*, 3(4), 711-727.

Gay, Geneva. (1988). Designing relevant curricula for diverse learners. *Education and Urban Society*, Vol. 20, No. 4.

Glass, Ron and Wallace, Kendra R. (1995). Challenging race and racism: A framework for educators. In Root, Maria P. P. (Ed.) *Racially mixed people in a new millenium, A second anthology*. Thousand Oaks, CA: Sage Publications, Inc.

Gordon, Edmund (1994, Winter). Cited in Rothman, Robert. *Assessment questions: Equity answers*, Proceedings of the 1993 CRESST Conference, Los Angeles, p. 2.

Greene, Maxine. The passions of pluralism: Multiculturalism and the expanding community. (1993). *Educational Researcher*, Vol. 22, No. 1.

Hakuta, Kenji, Ferdman, Bernardo M. and Diaz, Rafael M. (1987). Bilingualism and cognitive development: three perspectives. In Rosenberg, S. (Ed.), *Advances in applied psycholinguistics*, Vol. 2.

Haugen, Einar. (1974). The curse of Babel. In Haugen, E. and Bloomfield, M., *Language as a human problem*. New York: W.W. Norton, p. 41.

Hirsch, E.D., Jr. (1987). *What every American needs to know*. New York: Vintage Books.

Kochman, Thomas. (1989). Black and white cultural styles in pluralistic perspective. In Gifford, B. (Ed.), *Test policy and test performance: Education, language, and culture*. Boston: Kluwer Academic Publishers.

Ladson-Billings, G. (1989). Like lightning in a bottle: Attempting to capture the pedagogical excellence of successful teachers of Black students. Paper presented at the College Board Colloquium Celebrating Diversity: Knowledge, Teachers, and Teaching. New York, NY.

Lave, Jean. (1988). *Cognition in practice*. Cambridge, England: Cambridge University Press.

Leinhardt, G. (1983). Overlap: Testing whether it is taught. In Madaus, G. (Ed.), *The courts, validity, and minimum competency testing*. Boston: Kluwer-Nijhoff. pp. 151-170.

Lewontin, R.C., Rose, Steven and Kamin, Leon J. (1984) . *Not in our genes*. New York: Pantheon Books.

Lieberman, Ann and Miller, Lynne. (1990). Teacher development in professional practice schools. *Teachers College Record. Vol. 92,* No. 1.

Lipka, Jerry. Schools failing minority teachers: Problems and suggestions. Paper submitted to *Educational Foundations.*

Loden, Marilyn and Rosener, Judy B. (1991). *Workforce America! Managing employee diversity as a vital resource.* Homewood, Illinois: Business One Irwin.

McDonnell, Lorraine. (1994, Winter). Cited in Rothman, Robert. *Assessment questions: Equity answers,* Proceedings of the 1993 CRESST Conference, Los Angeles, p. 3.

Miramontes, Ofelia B. and Commins, Nancy L. (1991). Redefining literacy and literacy contexts: Discovering a community of learners. In Hiebert, E. (Ed.), *Literacy for a diverse society.* New York: Teachers College Press.

Myrdal, Gunnar. (1944). *An American dilemma: The negro problem and modern democracy.* New York: Harper and Row.

National Commission on Time and Learning. (1994, April). *Prisoners of time.* Washington: U.S. Government Printing Office.

Nelson-Barber, Sharon. (1989). (Ed.), *Thinking out loud.* Proceedings for the Teacher Assessment Project Forum on Equity in Teacher Assessment. Stanford University, Stanford, CA.

Nelson-Barber, Sharon and Harrison, Margaret. (1996). Bridging the politics of identity in a multicultural classroom. Forthcoming in *Theory into Practice..*

Nelson-Barber, Sharon and Meier, Terry. (1990, spring). Multicultural context a key factor in teaching. *Academic Connections.*

Newsweek. (August 9, 1993). America: Still a melting pot?

Nieto, Sonia. (1992). *Affirming diversity: The sociopolitical context of multicultural education.* New York: Longman.

Ogbu, John U. (1992). Understanding cultural diversity and learning. *Educational Researcher,* Vol. 21, No. 8.

Olsen, Laurie and Mullen, Nina A. (1991, spring). Embracing diversity: California teachers are finding new ways to bridge cultural chasms. *Equity and Choice.*

Pallas, Aaron M., Natriello, Gary, and McDill, Edward L. (1989). The changing nature of the disadvantaged population: Current dimensions and future trends. *Educational Researcher,* Vol. 18, No. 5.

Paris, Scott G., Lawton, Theresa A., Turner, Julianne C., and Roth, Jodie L. (1991). A developmental perspective on standardized achievement testing. *Educational Researcher, Vol. 20* No. 5, 12-20.

Parker, Mac. (1993). Address to National Rural Education Association Annual Meeting, Burlington, VT., October.

Perry, Theresa. (1993). *Toward a theory of African-American school achieve-ment*. Report No. 16, Center on Families, Communities, Schools and Children's Learning.

Philips, Susan Urmston. (1983). *The invisible culture: Communication in class-room and community on the Warm Springs Indian Reservation*. New York: Longman.

Poplin, M. and Weeres, J. (1992). *Voices from inside the classroom*. Claremont, CA: Institute for Education in Transformation at The Claremont Gradu-ate School.

Resnick, Lauren. (1994, Winter). Cited in Rothman, Robert. *Assessment ques-tions: Equity answers*. Proceedings of the 1993 CRESST Conference, Los Angeles, p. 2.

Resnick, L. and Resnick, D. (1991). Assessing the thinking curriculum: New tools for educational reform. In Gifford, B. R. & O'Conner, M. C. (Eds.), *Changing assessments: Alternative views of aptitude, achievement and in-struction*. pp. 37-76. Boston: Kluwer.

Rosenholtz, Susan J. (1989). *Teachers' workplace: The social organization of schools*. New York: Longman.

Rothman, Robert. (1994, Winter). *Assessment questions: Equity answers*. Pro-ceedings of the 1993 CRESST Conference, Los Angeles.

Schlesinger, Arthur M., Jr. (1990, summer). When ethnic studies are un-American. *Social Studies Review*, Vol. 5.

Schlesinger, Arthur M., Jr. (1991). *The disuniting of America: Reflections on a multicultural society*. New York: W.W. Norton and Company.

Shepard, Lorrie. (1991). Negative policies for dealing with diversity: When does assessment and diagnosis turn into sorting and segregation? In Hiebert, Elfrieda H., *Literacy for a diverse society: Perspectives practices, and policies*. New York: Teachers College Press.

Shepard, Lorrie. (1991). Interview on assessment issues with Lorrie Shepard. *Educational Researcher*. Vol. 20, No. 3.

Taylor, Catherine. (1994). Assessment for measurement or standards: The peril and promise of large-scale assessment reform. *American Educa-tional Research Journal*. Vol. 31, No. 2, 231-262.

Tsang, Chui Lim. (1989). Informal assessment of Asian Americans: A cul-tural and linguistic mismatch? In Gifford, B. (Ed.), *Test policy and test performance: Education, language and culture*. Boston: Kluwer Academic Publishers.

Watson-Gegeo, Karen Ann. (1993). Keeping culture out of the classroom: Teacher practices andiInstructional constraints in the Solomon Islands. Paper presented at the Annual Meeting of the American Association for Educational Research, Atlanta, Georgia.

Webster's encyclopedic unabridged dictionary of the English language. (1985). New York: Portland House.

West, C. (1993). *Race matters.* Boston: Beacon Press.

Winfield, Linda F. (1987). Teachers' estimates of test content covered in class and first-grade students' reading achievement. *The Elementary School Journal.* Vol. 87, No. 4.

Wolf, Dennie, Bixby, Janet, Glenn, John III, Gardner, Howard. (1991). To use their minds well: Investigating new forms of student assessment. In Grant, Gerald (Ed.), *Review of research in education.* Washington, D.C.: American Educational Research Association, 31-74.

Zeichner, Kenneth M. (1993, February). Educating teachers for cultural diversity. National Center for Research on Teacher Learning. *NCRTL Special Report.*

Chapter 2

History, Trends,
and
Critical Questions

The European examination systems were developed as instruments to sort, select, and direct the distribution of scarce resources (jobs, education, university positions). How do we use examination systems if we want to improve learning for all in a country where education is accepted as a right, indeed, as an imperative? In reality, examinations are also used in the United States to sort, select, and distribute resources. We would have to *reinvent* assessment for it to work as a cultivating, standard-raising tool that is effective in a highly decentralized educational system, with an extremely heterogeneous population. These are challenges the European systems have never addressed.

Shirley Malcom, 1991

History of Testing in the United States

To suppose that the use (and misuse) of tests or assessments for purposes of sorting and ranking individuals belongs to the modern age—or at most originated with the Army Mental Tests of the 1920s—is a serious misapprehension of the facts. From a wealth of carefully-documented research, Stephen Gould synthesized a landmark work, *The Mismeasure of Man* (1981), in which he relates the ignoble history of attempts to measure the intelligence of *Homo sapiens*. In Gould's introduction, he alludes to a pronouncement by Socrates that citizens of the republic "should be educated and assigned by merit to three classes: rulers, auxiliaries, and craftsmen." Gould recounts that because of Socrates' inability to devise a logical argument to support such a process, he fabricated a myth. In response to his question to Glaucon, "Is there any possibility of making our citizens believe in it?", Glaucon replied: "Not in the present generation; there is no way of accomplishing this; but their sons may be made to believe in the tale, and their sons' sons, and posterity after them."[1]

As related by Gould, the "mismeasure of man"—particularly *his* [2] intelligence—stretches back two centuries to the study of craniometry, "the leading numerical science of biological determinism during the nineteenth century," through which the most extensive data compiled before Darwin was used to rank races by the size of their brains. Gould's examination of the various sets of data reveals fallacious assumptions made (most likely unintentionally) through the use of faulty procedures.

The use of craniometry in the 19th century gave way to the intelligence testing of the 20th. Gould details the work of Robert Yerkes, who sought to establish the field of psychology—then known as a "soft science"—by proving that it could be as rigorous as physics. Yerkes eventually assembled a team of experts to develop the Army Mental Tests. Three types of tests were developed: Army Alpha, given to literate recruits as a written examination; Army Beta, a pictorial test given to those who had failed Alpha; and individual examinations for failures in Beta by Army psychologists who graded each man from A to E and made suggestions about military placement. While the Army made little use of the scores (except in screening men for officer training), Yerkes, himself, believed that mental testing had "helped to win the war." His lieutenant, E. G. Boring, who later became a psychologist, analyzed a large sample of the available data and proclaimed three "facts":

1. The average mental age of white American adults stood just above the edge of moronity at a shocking and meager thirteen.

2. European immigrants can be graded by their country of origin. The average man of many nations is a moron. The darker peoples of southern Europe and the Slavs of eastern Europe are less intelligent than the fair peoples of western and northern Europe.

3. The Negro lies at the bottom of the scale with an average age of 10.41 (Gould, 1981).

Boring's analyses were rife with errors and misinterpretations. A few examples will serve as an important backdrop for thinking about new forms of assessment and the problems and risks associated with the interpretation of complex performances.

The Alpha and Beta tests had numerous parts; some of those parts appear in similar form on modern intelligence tests and are not as subject to charges of cultural bias—analogies, filling in the next number in a sequence, unscrambling sentences. Other parts of the test, however, could only be thought of as "ludicrous measures" of innate intelligence. "How could Yerkes and company attribute the low scores of recent immigrants to innate stupidity when their multiple-choice test consisted entirely of questions like:

> • Crisco is a: patent medicine, disinfectant, toothpaste, food product
> • The number of a Kaffir's legs is: 2, 4, 6, 8
> • Christy Mathewson is famous as a: writer, artist, baseball player, comedian?" (Gould, 1981, p. 200).

The conditions for administering the exams were also horrendous—in a sense adding grave insult to terrible injury. As the procedures for moving recruits through the exams began to fall apart, the administrative conditions and standards also began to deteriorate. Frustration and tension mounted, and little attention was paid to the administrative procedures that had been prescribed. The most common blunder was for recruits to be given the wrong test, or not to receive the correct follow-up examination. As Gould points out, it is one thing to look at the written form of data and analyze it for miscalculations and misjudgments; it is quite another to imagine what it was like for these young men. "What was it like to be an illiterate black or foreign recruit, anxious and befuddled at the novel experience of taking an examination, never told why, or what would be made of the results: expulsion, the front lines? In 1968, an examiner recalled his administration of Beta: 'It was touching to see the intense effort . . . put into answering the questions, often by men who never before had held a pencil in their hands'" (Gould, p. 204). While the Beta examination only included symbols, pictures, and numbers, it still required pencil work and a knowledge of numbers and how to write them.

Gould's analysis of an enormous amount of data and reports produced by Yerkes and Boring revealed further horrifying interpretations, particularly instances of ignoring correlations with environmental factors. Yerkes found correlations between average scores and infestation with hookworm, between intelligence and amount of schooling, between average scores and country of origin, and between average test scores for foreign-born recruits and years of residence in America. He attributed lower scores for blacks to a "disinclination based on low innate intelligence" and never mentioned the effects of segregation, poor school conditions, or economic conditions for blacks and other impoverished groups who were forced to work to survive. The fact that most Latins and Slavs were recent arrivals in America and spoke English either poorly or not at all, and that Teutonic immigration had occurred much earlier did not affect Yerkes's conclusion that those of Nordic ancestry had greater innate intelligence than those of Latin or Slavic heritage. "Again and again, the data pointed to strong correlations between test scores and environment. Again and again, those who wrote and administered the tests invented tortuous, *ad hoc* explanations to preserve their hereditarian prejudices" (Gould, p. 221).

The Army Mental Tests paved the way for the development and widescale use of standardized, norm-referenced tests that may have served mostly to reify intelligence (and other abstract concepts such as achievement) by turning them into entities that could, we came to believe, be measured to a precise number. This could then be used to sort and rank individuals by fixing their performance along a gradual ascending scale designed to order what is, in reality, a picture of "complex variation." Gould's work is worth reviewing, if only to remind ourselves of the serious potential for misjudging and "mismeasuring" individuals' aptitudes, abilities, learning, and behavior. As he notes, his book is "about the use of (these) numbers to rank people in a single series of worthiness, invariably to find that oppressed and disadvantaged groups—races, classes, or sexes—are innately inferior and deserve their status" (Gould, p. 25).

It is not particularly surprising that the early development and use of mental ability tests in the military was followed by a rapid increase in their use in education. The large influx of immigrant students and the advent of compulsory schooling led to an emphasis on the use of tests for instructional placement. Unfortunately, the myths of racial group differences that were initiated with the Army Mental Tests were perpetuated by the schools. "For African-Americans and Latinos, tests have been used primarily to perpetuate myths of inferiority and restrict access rather than to select educational opportunities" (Winfield & Woodard, 1994).

National Trends in Assessment—1990s

> Reinventing assessment to support equity can only be achieved through reinventing schooling; reinventing schooling can only be achieved by reinventing assessment to support equity. What must come first is the will to do both. (Shirley Malcom, 1991).

Restructuring Schools through Changes in Assessment

At various points in the history of American schools, efforts have been initiated to reform the educational system. These endeavors often reflected pressure on the schools to respond to changes in society. In the 1950s and 1960s, school desegregation demands imposed a significant responsibility for moving the society toward greater integration. During the 1980s, a wave of educational reforms washed across the nation, commonly legislated by individual states and frequently stimulated by reports about the dire state of affairs in America's schools; for example, *A Nation at Risk*. The results of these reform efforts were less than satisfactory, although some positive outcomes are often cited. In general, however, such reforms as higher graduation requirements—imposed without coordinated support for students who did not meet the standards—helped to push low-performing students out of school. Achievement gains that are sometimes cited as outcomes of such reforms may, in fact, have resulted from the reduction in the numbers of such students.

In the current era, schools again find themselves under inordinate pressure to reform, this time under the banner of "restructuring" or "systemic reform." Cherry Banks (1993) uses the term, "restructuring" to mean "the implementation of programs designed to improve the organization and performance of schools." As have other educators, Banks points out that such restructuring is, in theory, entirely possible because "we know what to do." Much of that knowledge was generated from the reform research of the late 1970s and early 1980s, the work of a number of scholars who conducted research in the area of school effectiveness. Most often cited is the work of Ronald Edmonds (1978), who found that high student performance was correlated with specific factors identified in the schools the students attended: clear school mission, strong leadership, supportive and safe school climate, clear curricula and instructional strategies, monitoring of student progress, and positive school/community relations.

Restructuring, then, as one version of reform, is nothing new to the American school system. What is somewhat new or different, perhaps, in the current wave of reform is the focus on new forms of assessment as the impetus to reform. Several factors played a significant role in bringing about this change in focus. The period from about 1975 to 1990 was graced with an abundance of cognitive research aimed at developing a better understanding of the processes of learning and teaching. This developing and changing knowledge base led quite irrevocably to the exploration of its educational implications, two of which were: (1) new curriculum frameworks would need to be articulated to reflect new knowledge about learning; and (2) if instruction were to be changed as desired to reflect the new knowledge, assessments of learning would also have to be changed. These implications are reflected in two major national movements intended to bring about the development of programs and systems to address these needs: (1) the crafting of federal and state legislation to provide support; and (2) the development of content standards and associated assessments for use in local and national contexts and for varying purposes. The development work has been undertaken by national educational organizations, state departments of education, local school districts, and school personnel.

Federal and State Legislation

In 1994, two pieces of federal legislation were passed that, if implemented as intended, would profoundly affect the development of assessment systems across the nation. These legislative efforts to support the development of content standards and performance-based assessments are: (1) reauthorization of the entire package of ESEA (Elementary and Secondary Education Act) legislation under the new title, *Improving America's Schools Act of 1994*, and (2) the *Goals 2000* legislation proposed by the Clinton administration and signed into law March 31, 1994.

The main themes of the *Improving America's Schools Act of 1994* are presented below:

Five Directions for ESEA

1. High standards for all children—with the elements of education aligned, so that everything is working together to help all students reach those standards.

2. A focus on teaching and learning.

3. Flexibility to stimulate local school-based or district initiative, coupled with responsibility for student performance.

4. Links among schools, parents, and communities.

5. Resources targeted to where needs are greatest and in amounts sufficient to make a difference.

Several of the "Titles" in the *Improving America's Schools Act* will have some bearing on the development of equitable school programs. Probably most significant is the strong emphasis in the law on the development and implementation of programs that reflect "high standards for *all* children." Although it might seem that only those students served through programs under this Act will be affected by its provisions, this is not likely to be the case. Title I, for example, is the largest federally-funded educational program and, combined with the other federal programs, represents a major and very influential presence in American schools. These programs and the regulations associated with them tend to affect almost everything else that goes on in schools. For example, the requirement that all Chapter 1 students be tested using a pre-post administration of a standardized, norm-referenced instrument often affected testing decisions for all students in the schools. Similarly, the requirement in the Hawkins-

Stafford Amendments of 1988 emphasizing that all students served in the program would be taught not only the basics of reading and mathematics but also "more advanced" skills, has had some effect on instructional programs.

The second piece of legislation that is likely to play a significant role in the development of new assessment systems is referred to as *"Goals 2000: The Educate America Act* (S.846)." The purpose of this legislation is to provide a framework for meeting the national education goals by:

- establishing a framework for relating federal education programs to education reform;

- endorsing the National Education Goals and establishing the National Education Goals Panel;

- establishing the mechanisms for developing a national, voluntary system of internationally competitive elementary and secondary-level standards and assessments and workforce standards;

- providing support to states and localities to stimulate the development and implementation of comprehensive state-wide school improvement strategies centered around high standards.

This law would lead to a considerable expansion of national standards-setting efforts in "core" academic subjects that is already ongoing, because it would support local and state efforts as well. It also adds the arts and foreign languages to the core subjects named in the education goals originally set under the Bush administration.

The two pieces of legislation, the *Improving America's Schools Act* and *Goals 2000: The Educate America Act*, were written with the intent of having them fit together and support one another. *Goals 2000* is intended to provide a framework for the reauthorization of ESEA by creating a vision of excellence and equity that will guide all federal education and related programs.

State-level Efforts

There are a number of state-legislated efforts to develop new curricular standards and assessments that represent examples of concerted efforts by states to reform assessment and thereby to restructure their schools. In 1987, **Arizona** launched an ambitious reform effort when the legislature, in cooperation with the State Board of Education and the Department of Education, initiated the Goals for Educational Excellence Project. A Joint Legislative Committee was created to set reform goals in the areas of K-12 achievement, graduation rate, and postsecondary success in employment or higher education. In setting achievement goals, the Committee validated and extended Arizona's curriculum frameworks—the Essential Skills. The Committee also authorized the Department to develop a high-quality, broad-based assessment system. The Department's response to this request was the *Arizona Student Assessment Program (ASAP)* [3]. The state saw the assessment as a validation of more thorough, close-to-instruction district assessment. Districts are required to assess all students on the Essential Skills, using one or a combination of options:

- Forms of the state's performance assessments
- District assessments that match the Essential Skills
- A portfolio system that accounts for acceptable student work

The new Essential Skills assessments developed by the State look quite different from typical multiple-choice standardized tests. The tests are *performance based;* they measure student performance or application of skills, not just recall or comprehension (Arizona State Department, 1992).

In response to calls from a range of constituent groups—educators, business leaders, and the public—to change the way students are evaluated in school, the **California** legislature mandated a new testing system (SB 662, 1991) for public schools known as the *California Learning Assessment System (CLAS)*. The testing system was designed to:

- provide useful information to teachers, students, and parents on a timely basis;
- increase the ways students can demonstrate what they know and can do;
- focus on the real-world knowledge and skills necessary to be a successful adult;
- integrate assessment with instruction, calling for students to think and solve problems and motivating them to read at higher levels of achievement;
- be based on tests that are fair and sensitive to students' language, culture, and disabilities.

As designed, CLAS was to have two major components: (1) annual end-of-year assessments in reading, writing, and mathematics at grades 4, 8, and 10, and in history-social science and science at grades 5, 8, and 10; and (2) portfolio type assessment for the same grades and subjects as the annual assessments. Selected student work was to be collected in portfolios throughout the year for evaluation by groups of teachers. The portfolios could also include state or locally-developed activities similar to those in the end-of-the-year assessment. It was intended that student work done in languages other than English could be included.

The California legislation emphasized that the system would be designed for all students and further specified that CLAS be fair and sensitive. To that end, the CLAS development process included the following: balanced treatment reviews; student and teacher questions integrated with the test items to determine how well the items reflected what is being taught in the classroom; recommendations for English learner assistance; and consideration of special administrative procedures for students with special needs (California Department of Education, 1993.)[4]

The **California** Assessment Collaborative (CAC) was also authorized by the California State Department of Education through Assembly Bill 40 to support and study a number of alternative student assessment projects around the state and report on its findings. The intent of CAC was to facilitate the process of school restructuring by studying and disseminating information on alternative assessment projects being implemented in school districts across the state. The CAC encouraged participation of districts that were developing and implementing alternative assessment strategies as a part of their restructuring efforts. It was also the intent of the California legislature that information gathered through this project would inform the development of CLAS.

The goals of the Collaborative were to assist a variety of alternative assessment projects statewide, examine the effects of these projects on teaching and learning, and disseminate its findings and recommendations to practitioners and policymakers. To accomplish these goals, the Collaborative identified approximately twenty projects across a variety of grade levels and subject matter areas that were developing and implementing a wide variety of alternative assessment approaches, including portfolios, performance assessments, teacher observations systems, computer-based assessment systems, and written constructed responses.

The **Kentucky** Educational Reform Act (KERA) of 1990 called for substantial changes in the educational system statewide. A major component of this reform was the establishment of an innovative assessment program—*Kentucky Instructional Results Information System (KIRIS)*. KERA called for the development of a primarily performance-based system that, combined with other aspects of school life, could create a more comprehensive picture of the health of Kentucky schools. Aspects that have to do with student participation, ranging from student attendance and retention to mental and physical barriers that prevent learning are referred to as noncognitive indicators. By combining both noncognitive and cognitive indicators, KERA called for statewide standards that could define successful students and schools.

The Council on School Performance Standards translated seven capacities stated in KERA into six goals for Kentucky schools. The first, and perhaps most important, goal was to expect a high level of achievement of all students; it is divided into six sub-goals and requires that schools develop their students' ability to use and apply key learnings from a wide array of subject areas, so that they can think critically and become self-sufficient and responsible members of society.

The final system developed by the state will reflect the efforts of many educators throughout Kentucky, combined with the findings of experts throughout the nation. The system will integrate Kentucky's vision, capabilities, and needs, as well as current research on school effectiveness indicators, state-of-the-art technology, and data collection systems in other states (Kentucky Department of Education, 1992).

In May, 1989, the State Board of Education in **Vermont** invited eight Vermont teachers to draft a plan that would use writing portfolios in an assessment of the writing programs in Vermont's schools. Although at first intended only for grades 4 and 11, the Vermont State Legislature suggested that it be designed for grades 4 and 8, with implementation of a grade 11 assessment being implemented when resources permitted. Vermont was the first state to institute a statewide portfolio-based assessment program: following a pilot year, the first year of implementation was 1991-92. During that same year, a Mathematics Portfolio Assessment Program was also initiated; a committee had been established in 1989 to explore ways in which portfolios might be used for statewide assessment in mathematics. Both the writing and mathematics portfolio assessments include three components designed to "view programs through three different lenses":

- Best pieces of student work
- Whole portfolios
- Uniform assessments

"Best pieces" are used to assess specific abilities (such as problem-solving, communication skills, and dispositions in math—drawn from NCTM standards); "portfolios" provide a picture of the instructional context and the content representativeness of programs; and "uniform tests" are administered to gauge the knowledge and understanding of concepts and procedures and to link to national comparative data. One of the findings pertinent to the discussion in this book from the pilot year implementation of mathematics portfolios was that "additional specification of portfolio content is necessary to provide an equitable basis for evaluating student performance" (Vermont State Board of Education, 1991).

Local Efforts

To a great degree, the policymaking and design efforts that take place at national levels—either through the passage of new laws that include evaluation or assessment policies or through the development of sample standards and assessments—can protect, support, and inform efforts at the local level. The national work, on the other hand, should not proceed without serious consideration of how it will match or support (rather than detract from) local efforts. This means that policymakers at the national level need to be keenly aware of how school, district, and state personnel are approaching the work, what barriers have arisen, and what productive strategies have emerged. Such knowledge will help them determine and make recommendations that are reasonable and practicable given the local reality of schools. Local innovators, likewise, need to know about national efforts that will eventually and in some way affect their work. Some guidance for developing assessment systems is found in a general understanding of the context in which assessment changes are taking place.

The Special Programs Management Section (SPMS) of the **Hawaii** State Department of Education worked with Far West Laboratory (FWL) to provide both Chapter 1 and regular classroom teachers with the opportunity to fashion a collaborative assessment system. It was designed to support teachers' assessment needs. After a year of introductory portfolio workshops and classroom exploration, teachers began work on building the assessment system. A working group discussed and generated eight performance standards for elementary literacy. These standards provided the template for what was to be measured. The next phase of the project involved teachers and administrators in the development of performance assessment tasks. This process started with a discussion about high-quality performance tasks and rubric (or scoring guidelines) development. Performance rubrics explicate performance standards in a task-specific way. The outcome of the design work was the development of eight elementary literacy standards, seventy initial tasks, and rubrics for the standards and tasks.

Teachers who were part of the working group conducted task trials in their own classrooms. In the spring of 1993, they came together to discuss task trials, select exemplary tasks, refine rubrics and begin a discussion about high-quality student work based on examples of student responses to tasks. Future work will focus on developing and implementing a portfolio model, constructing a meaningful scoring moderation process for teachers, and developing processes for reporting portfolio data to parents and the educational community.

In June, 1991, the Juneau, **Alaska** School Board endorsed a plan for the portfolio process to be used in the school district. It was a multi-year plan by which a new grade would be added to the process each year. Currently, all of the first and second grade teachers build a portfolio with each child to represent his/her work from a year spent in an integrated whole language classroom, as outlined by the City and Borough of Juneau School District's Language Arts Curriculum. In designing the portfolio process, developmentally appropriate practices, as defined by many well-known researchers and advocates for the education of young students (for example, Piaget, Clay, Barrs, Hornsby, Kamii, and Tierney), were considered.

The district philosophy states, "When we think about the art of communication, we must include reading, listening, writing, and speaking. The four processes all require initiation of thought and communication of ideas. Communication, then, is always filtered through the individual's own background and experience, and is very personal." It is the belief of the primary teachers and the Juneau District that communication/language arts is the essential key to academic success in all curriculum areas. Through the portfolio process, Juneau's first and second graders demonstrate that they can meet the state's essential language and literacy outcomes.

Development of Standards and Assessments

The second trend in assessment reform that has had considerable momentum in recent years is the development of content standards or curricular frameworks reflecting new knowledge about the process of learning. This work is being conducted by national organizations, state departments of education, and local schools and districts. The efforts described below are largely those being orchestrated by national organizations.

The National Council of Teachers of Mathematics (NCTM) led the way in developing an articulated framework for mathematics instruction in grades K-12 (*Curriculum and Evaluation Standards for School Mathematics, 1989*). One of the underlying premises of their work is that " 'to learn' means more than to memorize and repeat. Learning involves investigating, formulating, representing, reasoning, and using appropriate strategies to solve problems, and then reflecting on how mathematics is being used." In addition, the group notes the fact that "teaching mathematics to 'all students' emphasizes that anyone who is to be a productive citizen in the 21st century must be mathematically literate—including not only 'talented white males' but all underrepresented groups" (Romberg, 1993). As will be elaborated below, this notion of developing standards for *all* students is a linchpin for discussions of equity in education.

The *NCTM Standards* were a prominent part of the discussion at the education summit convened by President George Bush in 1989 when the National Governors' Association adopted six national education goals to be met by the year 2000. The *Standards* became a focal point of the strategy for school reform pushed by the Bush administration and were adopted by the National Education Goals Panel. It was clear to the governors at the education summit that the goals would be meaningless unless they defined what was meant by academic excellence. The *Standards* were seen as a good example of what was needed.

Subsequent to the education summit, both educators and politicians embraced the need for standards and moved forward with uncommon quickness. The development of national standards for what students need to learn became widely supported as the most promising first step in the improvement of the U.S. education system. Lauren Resnick (1992), a key figure in the development of standards and assessments, stated this potential quite strongly:

> Two problems face our nation as we prepare for the 21st century: creating the economic conditions that will build and maintain prosperity for all of our people; and creating a social and political environment in which our diverse populations can work together amicably and productively as Americans. Education alone can solve neither of these problems. But neither can be solved without significant changes in the way our education system now functions.
>
> A system of national standards and locally developed assessments tied to them is the key to a high performance education system that can simultaneously raise overall achievement and open new opportunities for all Americans.

The movement toward the development of curriculum standards has not only been rapid, but it has also generated activities that once seemed difficult to orchestrate. Specialists representing various perspectives within disciplines have attempted to set aside their biases in the interest of agreeing on a core of knowledge and abilities that *all* students should acquire. Curriculum standards have been or are currently being developed in eleven subject areas (see Appendix). Many states have also been engaged in the development of state standards in various content areas, in most cases building on and drawing from the national efforts. More than forty states, for example, have been revising their curriculum frameworks to reflect the mathematics standards.

In addition to the efforts on the part of national organizations to develop standards, the New Standards Project (NSP) has been working on the development of national standards and assessments designed to improve curriculum and instruction.[5] Nineteen states and six urban school districts, representing nearly half of America's school children, participate in the NSP. Teachers and specialists who are part of the NSP consortium work hand-in-hand to "design and implement a system of performance standards, authentic assessments, and professional development intended to change the way the American school system works" (Resnick, 1993). The NSP also collaborates with the efforts of national organizations that are developing sets of standards—building on them as frameworks.

In order to represent identified learning outcomes more clearly, the NSP participants are designing an assessment system that will include tasks or activities intended to elicit the desired behaviors, as well as student portfolios with samples of student work that exemplify the learning outcomes. The standards and assessments developed by the Project will eventually be available for use by states, local districts, or schools. In addition, the NSP is using a "trainer-of-trainers" approach to provide professional development in scoring and task development for teacher teams from each partner state; these teachers will become "senior leaders" to respond to the need for meaningful teacher engagement in the new assessment strategies.

Not to be overlooked in what could be considered a nationwide stampede to develop curriculum frameworks or standards is the effort on the part of the National Board for Professional Teaching Standards (NBPTS) to establish rigorous standards for what *teachers* should know and be able to do. Thirteen standards committees have been involved in the process of developing standards in various subject areas and for various age levels. The standards for the Early Adolescence Generalist certificate, the Early Adolescence English Language Arts certificate, and the Early Adolescence English Language Arts assessment package were approved by the NBPTS in March, 1993.

Attention to Equity

If one imagines this trend toward the development of new standards and assessments as a stampede, it is likewise easy to imagine how difficult it is to get those involved to dither[6] a while, to give serious thought to issues of equity, and to consider the potential implications for America's children. Certainly we would agree that the national movement toward an articulation of well-structured, research-based standards and accompanying performance assessments that may potentially drive instruction toward new heights is creditable. It has already spurred a national conversation in education that heretofore did not occur. "We never had a passionate yet reasoned discussion about what was worth teaching and what students ought to know" (Resnick, 1993). Resnick also points out that the current attempt to better define essential outcomes is different in that "we've really never had content standards that were applied to all students. I remember surveying high school teachers in a school district where I worked about what they expected all students to know when they graduated from high school. Their most frequent response was: 'It depends.' So there's been no common understanding of desired outcomes for all students."

"For all students" is a phrase that highlights the focus of this book. Some educators have already been raising serious questions about the lack of attention to the needs of students who might be learning English, who perform poorly in academic areas, or who are for other reasons at risk of failing in school. "Anytime you have a change in systems and start moving ahead and you leave kids behind, there's going to be a gap in attention and resources" (Martin Gould in Viadero, 1993). Our intention with this book is to encourage consistent attention to issues of equity throughout the process of developing alternative assessment systems. "Concerns for equity are the cornerstone of this wave of educational reform. Equity concerns must then be at the heart of assessment design if we expect assessment to play a central role in moving the reform agenda" (Malcom, 1991).

Efforts to Address Equity

Some efforts have been made to address issues of equity as new standards or assessments are developed at local, state, and national levels. These efforts are reflected in the following strategies:

- Development of frameworks, guidelines, or leadership statements
- Inclusion of equity as an assessment standard
- Use of focus and advisory groups
- Studies of instructional/assessment practices
- Institution of special administrative procedures

Frameworks, guidelines, or leadership statements

Much of this work has been pursued by groups with a specific interest in ensuring equal learning opportunities for students who may be less than fully proficient in English or who are otherwise disadvantaged within the American school system. One example is the Stanford Working Group on Federal Education Programs for Limited-English (LEP) Students. Their goal—as proposals for restructuring and reform receive serious consideration—is to encourage the investigation of "all available avenues for ensuring that LEP students fully benefit from these promising new directions." Recognizing that LEP children have been "kept on the margins of American education and education reform" for too long and that current efforts to raise educational standards for all may "worsen matters for LEP students if those students' unique needs and potential contributions are not addressed," the Stanford Working Group has developed documents related to assessment and equity. A statement developed by a leading group of educators, along with the others listed below, is presented in its entirety in the Appendix. These statements constitute an important resource for teachers, administrators, and other researchers and educators involved in the development of standards and assessments.

- **Leadership Statement of Nine Principles on Equity and Educational Testing and Assessment** (statement by concerned educators, March 12, 1993)
- **Guidelines for Equitable Assessment** (Diversity and Equity in Assessment Network, FairTest, Cambridge, MA)
- **Principles for Improvement** (New Standards Project)

Inclusion of Equity as an Assessment Standard

After developing a set of cutting-edge *content* standards, the National Council of Teachers of Mathematics developed *teaching* and then *assessment* standards. The assessment standards (Figure 2.1) present criteria for judging the adequacy of mathematics assessment practices.

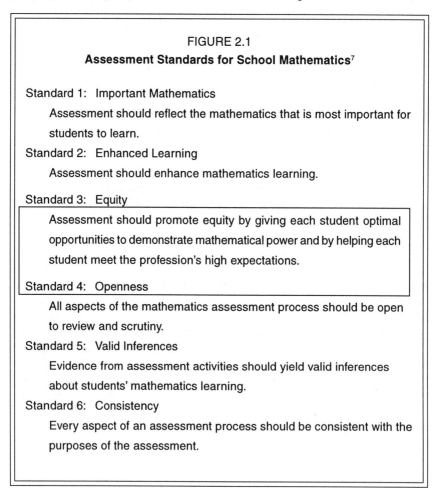

FIGURE 2.1
Assessment Standards for School Mathematics[7]

Standard 1: Important Mathematics

Assessment should reflect the mathematics that is most important for students to learn.

Standard 2: Enhanced Learning

Assessment should enhance mathematics learning.

Standard 3: Equity

Assessment should promote equity by giving each student optimal opportunities to demonstrate mathematical power and by helping each student meet the profession's high expectations.

Standard 4: Openness

All aspects of the mathematics assessment process should be open to review and scrutiny.

Standard 5: Valid Inferences

Evidence from assessment activities should yield valid inferences about students' mathematics learning.

Standard 6: Consistency

Every aspect of an assessment process should be consistent with the purposes of the assessment.

Certainly the inclusion of an equity standard is a major step in maintaining a focus on this issue as assessment approaches are developed. It will be noted, however, that while these standards provide specifications for the *design* of assessments, they present criteria that are relevant mostly to *administration*. In the case of the "Equity Standard," for example, it will be incumbent on those who administer the assessment to give each student "optimal opportunities to demonstrate mathematical power" and help each student "meet the profession's high expectations" (NCTM, October, 1993). For many of the criteria that are specified in the standards, it will not be possible to build them into the assessment items themselves. Much will depend, as has been the case with standardized multiple-choice tests as well, on how the assessments are administered and how the results are used.

Use of Focus and Advisory Groups

The use of advisory groups seems to be, by far, the most common approach to addressing equity issues as groups of educators pursue the development of standards and assessments. The New Standards Project (NSP) staff, for example, have used advisory groups at various stages of their work. In the fall of 1991, NSP ran a series of focus groups "seeking information about the opinions of Americans of different social, economic, and ethnic groups on the desirability of national education standards and assessments." Interestingly enough, they found that the low-income and minority parents offered the strongest support, indicating that they wanted their children judged by the same standards as other children. They viewed the development of standards as an opportunity to improve their children's chances for a high-quality education.

NSP also conducts focus groups with equity advocacy organizations to obtain advice about how to address equity concerns. NSP advisory groups include "scholars and practitioners with expertise in culture, gender, and language issues." One advisory group helps the NSP staff think about ways to administer tasks for students who are learning English in order to enable them to display their competence in English as well as in their native language (Resnick, 1993).

The use of advisory groups is an important step in bringing all parties with relevant expertise—cultural and linguistic, for example—"to the table", but some critics do not feel that it is enough. The strongest critics see such a solution, perhaps, as slight compensation. It is critical, however, that participation in this process be as broad-based and direct as possible so that varying perspectives are taken into account. Pauline Brooks (1993) points out that the involvement of minority group representatives is more often during the review process than during the development process; she has also indicated the need to have more linguists involved in assessment development. Direct involvement of such experts during development phases helps to ensure that varying cultural and linguistic perspectives are taken into account when items are written or when discussions focus on anticipated responses. For example, certain animals hold sacred significance to American Indians, so that passages about them may add a layer of conflict, misunderstanding, or discomfort.

Studies/reports focused on instructional/ assessment practices

Studies or reports that address the issues associated with the development of effective instructional and assessment strategies based on current thinking and research have been commissioned or conducted by a number of states and organizations. These reports have helped to elucidate some of the issues associated with the goal of providing a sound education to a diverse population of students.

The New York State Department of Education commissioned a series of essays on "Standards for Excellence" as part of a process in which the state engaged to "rethink the ways in which it organizes, manages, supports, and assesses education so as to promote greater equity and higher levels of educational excellence in all schools." The state's *Compact for Learning* provides guidance to help communities redesign their schools. In one of the commissioned papers, "Standards of Practice for Learner-Centered Schools" (July, 1992), Linda Darling-Hammond presents a framework for standards of excellence, including those that will govern equitable access to learning opportunities, professional practice, and accountable school functioning. Darling-Hammond presents a strong point that should not be lost sight of as we pursue the development of standards and assessments. It will be reinforced throughout this book. "Genuine accountability—that is, responsible practice and responsiveness to clients—occurs only when a useful set of processes exists for guiding practice and for using information to improve practice" (Darling-Hammond and Ascher, 1991). When we judge school effectiveness only in terms of aggregated measures of student achievement outcomes and do not evaluate the quality of educational practice effectively, we create powerful incentives for schools to restrict, push out, or depreciate the performance of students who perform at a lower-than-proficient level for reasons which may be directly attributable to the quality of the instruction. "A purely outcome-based accountability system would confuse the quality of education offered by schools with the needs of the students they enroll; it would work against equity and integration, and against possibilities for fair and open school choice, by discouraging good schools from opening their doors to educationally needy students." It is generally hoped that this conflict will be addressed by articulating "opportunity to learn" standards as discussed later in this chapter. Such standards cannot relate solely to inputs; they must also address the quality of the educational program provided to students. Accountability cannot be achieved solely through the development of standards and assessments and by establishing associated consequences; the "distribution of schooling opportunities" must be addressed.

A report on bilingual programs was prepared for the California Department of Education by Berman et al. in February, 1992. *Meeting the Challenge of Language Diversity: An Evaluation of Programs for Pupils with Limited Proficiency in English* was the result of a study funded by the California legislature. In the state that now boasts the largest and fastest-growing multicultural and multilingual population, the researchers found that "California public schools do not have valid and ongoing assessments of the performance of students with limited proficiency in English. Therefore, the state and the public cannot hold schools accountable for LEP students' achieving high levels of performance." Noting that authentic assessment procedures are particularly appropriate for language minority students, they recommended to the state that "authentic and alternative assessment procedures should be developed to bring LEP students into the state's accountability structure and to enable teachers to better diagnose the needs of LEP students" (Berman et al., 1992).

These two reports represent a small sample of efforts to address the concern for equitable assessment in a coherent way. Information provided through such reports will help to clarify the issues and to keep a light trained on those students most in need of our understanding.

Institution of special administrative procedures

States that have already gone through a development phase for new assessments and are piloting or using new assessments have also already had the opportunity to wrestle with the establishment of equitable administration procedures. With the implementation of the *Arizona Student Assessment Program,* the Arizona Department of Education developed guidelines for mediating the administration of the English form of the assessments. This process of mediation is permitted for students who are limited English proficient or who are in special education programs or have disabilities. It is specified that these procedures do not mean giving answers or an out-of-level assessment. Rather, teachers are allowed to use techniques they might ordinarily use with such students. These techniques include:

- flexible scheduling to allow extended time for completion;
- flexible setting to allow separate administration or in a small group;
- translation to the student's primary language;
- simplification of the language by paraphrasing, using synonyms, or using shorter sentences;
- reading to the student;
- taking dictation;
- using visuals such as pictures in a dictionary (Wiley, June, 1993).

Additional adjustments or accommodations in administration procedures that are being considered or implemented through other exploratory efforts include such procedures as giving choice of task, peer consultation, use of native language, scaffolding approaches, and scoring. (These are discussed more extensively in Chapter 5, Developing Equitable Assessment Systems.)

Critical Questions Related to Equity

While concerns about equity are many, several stand out as ones that must be addressed as part of the dialogue related to the establishment of national standards and assessment systems. As the national trends described in this chapter continue, we agree with Malcom that the goal must be to "reinvent assessment to support equity," and this will require finding answers to these questions.

Is it really possible?
In response to the question, "Is it really possible to create standards that apply equally to *all* students?" John O'Neil (1993) proposes that the great variability among students' access to learning, variations in motivation and interest, as well as other factors, will make it difficult to design challenging standards that are appropriate for all students. While the developers of standards are variously considering anywhere from one to three *performance* levels, those proposing only one are doing so because they are worried that more than one will encourage differing expectations and tracking. Under the proposed Chapter 1 reauthorization legislation (*Improving America's Schools Act of 1994, Title I*), the first of five stated directions for the program is "High standards for all children—with the elements of education aligned, so that everything is working together to

help all students reach those standards." But while the legislation was crafted in part to respond to calls for reform such as are commonly generated by poor assessment results,[8] whether it is possible to accomplish equitable reform by setting the same standards for all is not easy to know or predict.

"Attempting to help *all* students attain higher standards is an unprecedented venture for American education. So it remains to be seen if the isolated examples of Jaime Escalante and others can become more widespread" (O'Neil, 1993). It is important to note that several research studies have lent support to the "Escalante phenomenon" in the areas of math and science. A 1983 study by the American Association for the Advancement of Science looked at programs operating outside of school settings designed to improve the pre-college education of women and minorities in math, science, and technology. The evaluators identified characteristics of exemplary programs and focused on student success in the programs, improved attitudes, and later success in school. Other studies (Clewell and Anderson, 1987; Cole and Griffin, 1987; Stage et al., 1985) supported the findings of the earlier AAAS study. "One could easily surmise that if the schools attended by minorities and females more closely approximated in standards, character, and intent the most successful of these projects, American education would be well on the way to reinvention" (Malcom, op. cit.).

Is the development of standards the place to start?

Diversity in America's classrooms is a reality and requires a response in the form of educational programs that will adequately address the needs of a wide range of students. While there is evidence that schools are actually doing substantially better than they were 60 or 70 years ago,[9] it seems clear that they are not doing what is required for the future. The American school system is more attuned to the 1920s than to the 1990s and beyond. Despite the fact that some criticisms of the American school system are exaggerated and the fact that educators are generally not held in high regard by many Americans,[10] educators are not unaware that school reform is an increasing demand, one that is viewed as essential for meeting the challenges of a global economy. Eighty-one percent of people polled in 1992 stated that "if poor and minority children are not well educated, it will have a 'major effect' on our ability to compete in world markets" (Harris, 1992). In the face of such demands and expectations, educators cannot fail to respond. But is the development of standards in the curricular areas the appropriate place to start?

Educators who have disparaged standards as the appropriate starting place for educational reform seem generally committed to correcting basic inequalities in the schools as the first priority. Some of these critics are among those who have written forcefully about the need for educational reform or have themselves been architects of school reform models that have been implemented with a considerable degree of success. James Comer, for example, believes that "what poor children need first are the social skills and community bonds that children of privilege take for granted." He argues that it will not be possible to reform schools "until we address the larger developmental factors that make it possible for students to learn." His model, developed at the Yale Child Study Center, includes an emphasis on parent and community involvement, child study teams, and a social skills curriculum. Similarly, the Coalition of Essential Schools' founder, Ted Sizer, warns that racing ahead with a plan to establish standards and tests before basic inequalities among schools—class size, outmoded facilities, inequitable school financing—are addressed is "the wrong sequence. We will end up proving once again that poor kids don't score as well as rich kids" (O'Neil, 1993). Jonathan Kozol likewise argues that the first priority must be to eliminate separate and unequal school systems. He believes this goal is attainable by paying the highest salaries to the best teachers who serve the poorest children in classrooms with a class size of no more than 20 in urban schools.

Will all children be given equal opportunities to learn?

This concern is certainly related to the preceding one, but it is worth mentioning, because those who are developing standards must remember that if they are using that process as the starting place for reform, they must maintain a parallel focus on standards that ensure access to learning. What were initially referred to as "school delivery standards" are now more commonly referred to as "opportunity to learn" standards and are intended to provide a basis for judging whether schools are providing students with sufficient opportunity to attain high standards. Absent such assurance, it is easy to understand how unfair it would be to impose standards on students who do not have access to the teaching and resources necessary to ensure the highest level of learning. As Resnick (1992) points out:

> American children today do not have an equal chance to learn in school. Dramatic differences in resources available in rich and poor school districts persist and are growing. But the most profound inequities are often hidden from view; they persist even when children from different backgrounds attend the same schools. Even in such schools, expectations are not the same for all, and the opportunities for learning are not equivalent. Almost everywhere, schools expect less of children from poor and minority families; they therefore ask less of them, and, above all, they offer them less.

Will the development of standards and new assessments, alone, ensure that these inequities will disappear?

Of course not. Concerted attention to the development of opportunity to learn standards may provide needed protection, but educators who have begun to grapple with the difficult problem of equity are finding it tough going. The challenge is to characterize the opportunities that must be provided to all students without resorting to checklists of requisite items, for example, number of books, computers, students per class, and the like. Such lists have not worked to improve education in the past. As the number of schools across the nation that are implementing powerful instructional programs and innovative assessment strategies continues to increase, it will become easier to define the opportunities to learn that must be available to all students. This could be a long journey, however, and it would seem best to embark on the path, outfitted with the wealth of information now available about how children learn—including children who may be learning English or who may be from a cultural group different from the "mainstream."

In a Ford Foundation report issued in 1990, it was charged that the "American testing system has become a 'hostile gatekeeper' that has limited opportunities for many, particularly women and minorities" (Rothman, 1990, quoted in Freeman and Freeman, 1991). Part of the solution to this state of affairs *may* reside in the consensus-building process in which many educators are now engaged to develop curriculum standards and assessments. As content standards and performance standards (levels of student competence in the content) are established, assessments tied to those standards are developed. It is critical that participation in this process be as broad-based and direct as possible so that varying perspectives are taken into account. This is a factor that it seems more groups conducting development projects should take into account. Many have established advisory or focus groups, but if there is not more involvement from start to finish by participants who represent our diverse population, then there is less chance for accommodating the needs of all.

Brooks' (1993) mention of the need to involve linguists (and we might suggest anthropologists as well) should also be given serious consideration. Performance-based assessments, like most assessments, are largely language-based, and language reflects culture (see Chapter 4). There are strong connections between a culture's ways of organizing life, its ways of using language, and its approach to problem-solving. Students' beliefs, ways of construing the world, and presuppositions about what is possible or meaningful will affect their interpretation of problems (Estrin, 1993). For example, an examination of Ute Indian students' assumptions when engaged in mathematics problem solving showed that they were quite different from those of their Anglo counterparts. Reflecting their cultural values, they were more concerned with the actual truth value of a problem statement than they were with the hypothesized truth. Asked how much it would cost for gas to drive a truck from X to Y at $1.20 a gallon, a Ute Indian student is more likely to be sidetracked by the fact that he does not have a truck. Asking students to imagine things as other than what they are and then take action on the basis of such an hypothesis is said to be contrary to Ute cultural values (Leap, 1988). Thus, a deep understanding of the linguistic elements that will affect both the design of an assessment and students' performance is a critical factor in the development of assessments that are valid and support equity.

Will performance assessments make a difference for children who are traditionally low-performing?

This is a crucial point, because many critics of standardized, norm-referenced tests who are now advocating for performance-based assessments believe that these new assessments will provide a richer, more complete picture of what children have learned. But, as noted earlier in a comment by Sizer, we may, once again, merely emphasize the performance gap between poor kids and rich kids. While many—ourselves among them—believe that the new assessments will eventually present the greatest potential for learning about the learning of our diverse student population, it is folly to presume that low-performing students—often those from linguistic and cultural minorities—will suddenly do better on such assessments, or, at least, that we will (potentially) get a truer picture of their learning. The latter is likely, but, in fact, initial studies seem to indicate that the use of such assessments may widen the gap between disadvantaged students and their more advantaged counterparts. While these studies are clearly preliminary, it is not difficult to see why this might be the case.

Lorrie Shepard (1993) has conducted several studies to evaluate differences in performance among student groups. Based on a review of her own studies and others conducted in Great Britain, she concludes that the results refute the assumption that because performance assessments are more valid, there will be fewer differences in performance. A widened gap seems, in fact, to have materialized for most minorities, with the exception of females, who appear to do better with open-ended questions. Shepard offers two possible explanations for this outcome: biased measurement and lack of opportunity to learn.

Test bias does not simply go away with the design and implementation of performance-based assessments. Potential causes of test bias include a greater reliance on language-dependent skills: more reading and writing is required for extended problems and such activities as writing explanations for mathematical solutions. In addition, performance assessments are often based on situational contexts or cultural items that may be unfamiliar to students from certain cultures. The critical thinking demands typical of such assessments, such as making judgments or expressing values, may not be compatible with some cultures' norms.

Banks (1993) cites an example from Lisa Delpit who wrote about an African-American student who was angry because a white professor used a process approach to the teaching of writing. While the approach was effective with many mainstream white students, this student felt that the professor was not making an effort to teach the class. The approach was "more culturally congruent" for the white students than for African-American students. "Instructional innovations that focus on process rather than on the direct teaching of skills can be detrimental to students who equate a lack of structure with a lack of caring." While this example relates to instruction, we believe that it illustrates quite well the issues that arise from a failure to consider "cultural congruence" when developing innovative approaches to assessment. This factor is tangentially related to another source of test bias noted by Shepard—that of students' differential experience with assessment formats. Some formats penalize certain students, especially English language learners.

"Opportunity to learn" is also noted by Shepard as a potential cause for poor performance by disadvantaged students. Evidence suggests that minority students have been subjected disproportionately to rote-level, test-oriented teaching practices (Madaus, 1992). Validity and fairness questions that need to be evaluated include: Do majority and minority students have equal access to instruction intended to improve performance? Do all students benefit equally from such instruction?

Shepard does qualify the results of her own studies by saying that while the gap appeared to widen with the introduction of performance assessments, it was noted with considerable encouragement that on subsequent administrations, there was a huge shift in the number of lower-performing students who completed the tasks, gave explanations, and seemed more willing to "talk" mathematically. Such a shift leads one to conclude that the students became more comfortable with the performance-based approach, perhaps through involvement in similar instructional activities.

Will there be high-stakes consequences from the use of performance assessments?

While Shepard (1993) counsels against the attachment of high stakes to performance assessments, others argue in favor of using them for accountability purposes because "the evidence is just incontrovertible that whatever kind of test matters in the system has a heavy influence on classroom practice" (Resnick in O'Neil, 1993). Resnick argues further that performance-based assessments should, in fact, be used for accountability purposes primarily because of a stronger potential link to instruction than is possible with most standardized tests. "A great deal can be done by changing those tests to ones worth teaching to." Other researchers also posit that unless these assessments are viewed as having value because they are tied to important educational decisions, they will not survive as a meaningful part of the system.

The debate leaves the educational community with serious questions about how the assessment reform scenario will play out. It is a particularly critical debate when one bears in mind the serious consequences that have been suffered by many minority students whose educational and vocational futures have been determined by single test scores. The initial results from pilot tests of performance-based assessments do not give reason to hope that students' futures would be safer if determined by such assessments. One fact should begin to become clear in this discussion— the issues surrounding the restructuring of schools "for equity and excellence" with a focus on the development of new assessments are inextricably linked, and the successful resolution of any one of the issues is largely dependent on the resolution of all the others. But as Edmund Gordon (1992) has written: "Unfortunately, for those of us who prefer to deal with simple problems, this one is complex beyond measure."

Larger Issues

An examination of the history and current trends of assessment development does not, by itself, present a complete picture of the complexity involved. Educators as a whole, and those who develop assessments, in particular, certainly do not and cannot work in a vacuum. They must recognize the social, political, and economic aspects of what they do and reflect that acknowledgment in the design of assessments. Edmund Gordon points out that the skills that are measured only represent the abilities of those who do the best with such. "We succeed in promulgating ourselves. If there are winners, you've got to have losers. We are finding now that we have too many losers who are trying to win in antisocial ways" (Gordon, 1993).

Gordon and Lorraine McDonnell, who has conducted studies on the education of immigrants, are two of several educators who have attended to the notion that a society that has unequal members cannot assume that equal distribution of resources (in this case educational) is adequate or appropriate. Some redistribution of resources may be necessary to remedy what has been an inequitable distribution; school delivery standards would be seen as "fair shares." The new targeting formulas proposed in the reauthorization legislation for Chapter 1 that call for a greater allocation of funds to districts in deepest poverty also represent an attempt to redistribute resources. It is clear that there are economic implications involved in reinventing a schooling system so that all children can meet the same challenging standards and become productive citizens. Others would argue that it is morally imperative that we create schools that optimize every student's learning opportunities. "Equity references fairness and social justice" (Gordon, 1993). "Our collective future depends on fair shares to all" (McDonnell, 1993).

At the same time that we consider each individual's right to his or her fair share of the educational pie, we might also consider what Lauren Resnick refers to as a student's "right to achieve." One way to define equity is the right to achieve at a level that allows an individual to participate fully in the social system, the "right to have what we need to become true participants."

The following quote from McGee Banks represents a thread we drew from the tapestry of this dialogue and harkens back to an earlier quote in this chapter (p. 42) taken from a paper by Shirley Malcom. We found it interesting that both of these scholars focused attention on the same essential ingredient.

> Creating schools in which all the nation's children receive a high-quality education will not be easy. But behind every significant achievement are dreamers and visionaries. . . . We must have a vision, but we must also have the will to act. Forging that will is perhaps our greatest challenge.

Endnotes:

1. For a complete rendition of the tale, see Gould (1981).
2. Gould apologizes for and explains the apparent sexism.
3. The ASAP is currently being restructured.
4. Funding for CLAS was vetoed by the governor of California in 1994 after the first year of implementation. California will continue to work on the development of a new statewide assessment.
5. The work of the New Standards Project is guided by a set of ten principles and a "Social Compact". This document is included in the Appendix.
6. On the Editor's Page of the November, 1991, issue of *Phi Delta Kappan*, Pauline Gough wrote a column called "A Vote for Dithering". In it she states that "we must accept the fact that intelligent change takes *time*. We have to give serious thought to an abundance of ramifications *before* we act."
7. National Council of Teachers of Mathematics, working draft, October, 1993.
8. In the recent report of the National Assessment of Chapter 1, *Reinventing Chapter 1: The Current Chapter 1 Program and New Directions*, it is stated: "Program

participation does not appear to significantly reduce the test score gap for disadvantaged students."

9. This is even true on some indicators related to the performance of such groups as African-Americans. Twenty years ago, for example, the dropout rate for African-Americans was much higher than that of whites; today they complete high school at about the same rate. In 1971, 82% of 17-year-old African-Americans read at a "basic level"; in 1992, that figure had increased to 97%.

10. A Louis Harris poll conducted in 1992 found that only 7% of the individuals surveyed thought that educators were doing an excellent job.

Commentary

Julia Lara

State Policy Directions:
Standards and Assessments and LEP Students[1]

The following observations are intended to highlight briefly a few state level policy directions in the area of standards and assessment development and LEP students. These policy directions hold some promise for enhancing equitable educational opportunities for LEP students. They are based on a review of responses to a selected number of questions posed to state education agency officials. The survey was conducted during the summer of 1994 by the staff of the Council of Chief State School Officers.

At the outset it is important to note that the standards-based reform movement is in the early stages of implementation in most states. The general sequence of implementation is to first develop content standards (academic expectations, curriculum framework) and subsequently work on the assessment programs and professional development activities. Currently, many states are working on both content standards and the development of assessment programs in specific grades/subject areas. Questions concerning the implication of the standards reform movement for "special needs" students are now being considered and debated in many states. Thus, the following observations are tentative and may not reliably foretell the outcome of state education deliberations and planning.

In examining the responses of state specialists to the issue of inclusion of all students in systemic planning, content standards, performance standards, and assessment programs, there is some grounds for optimism: Twenty-three states reported that they have involved persons knowledgeable about the education of LEP students in their systemic reform planning process.[2] Almost all (33 out of 34) of the states that have content standards noted that those standards will apply to LEP students, and 19 of 21 states that have developed performance standards indicated that these will apply to LEP students.[3] This is an important policy shift, because it signals states' willingness to recognize the need to include these students in their accountability system and thereby hold schools accountable for the education of LEP students in the content or performance standards statements. Not explicitly mentioning LEP students in the content and performance standards statements might be reasonable, as long as states do not use a "one size fits all" approach in the development of curriculum, assessments, and teacher development efforts. Unfortunately, there is a tendency among "systemwide" reformers to disregard the unique characteristics of culturally and linguistically diverse students in their attempts to institutionalize broader school reforms.[4] The result is that the benefits to be gained by the particular innovation do not accrue equitably to all students.

Currently, 37 states exempt LEP students from their statewide assessment program.[5] A review of state policy statements show that, in most states (18), these exemptions are based on the number of years (two or three) LEP students have been enrolled in language support programs. Fourteen states exempt students based on the students' level of English language proficiency. Another nine do not exempt students at the state level. The remaining five states with exemption policies combine both criteria or leave it up to the school level to determine criteria for exemption. Four states do not have an exemptions policy. Two of these states indicated that they did not have a statewide assessment program. The remaining two states noted that the decision resides with staff at the local level.[6]

Given the states' desire to be inclusive of "all" students, new assessment systems will need to be developed by more states to accommodate a greater number of LEP students. States have started to move in this general direction. A significant number have already put in place mechanisms to assess LEP students' knowledge of subject matter while students are still in the early stages of learning English. These approaches range from use of primary language assessments to use of accommodations in the test instrument, or administration of English language assessments. For example, ten states reported that they already assess academic knowledge or skill in a non-English language (mostly Spanish).[7] Most of these assessments are either norm-referenced or criterion-referenced tests. As cited in Chapter 2 of this publication, Arizona is the only state with a performance-based system that includes assessment in a non-English language (Spanish)8. More states than was the case five years ago are now implementing accommodation procedures that allow simultaneous translations, use of dictionaries, small group test environments, and help with the test directions. These are positive signs, although not sufficient if the goal is to assess LEP students' achievement of challenging academic content.

Recognizing the challenge established by a higher set of academic expectations, some states are considering the development of primary language assessments that are more performance-based. This is the case in California, Illinois, Massachusetts, Colorado, and others that are already testing in the students' primary language. This interest on the part of these states is bolstered by recent federal legislation that requires that all students be included in the accountability system (Title I of IASA), and that provides incentives for states to develop assessments in non-English languages (Goals 2000: Educate America Act).

Given the diversity of languages represented within each state and the level of primary language competence of LEP students, states will need some flexibility in the development of their assessment programs. Ultimately, states may have to design an assessment program that allows for exemptions, uses multiple measures (performance based, criterion based), and a combination of primary and English language assessments.

The observations made above were culled from responses of state officials to a series of questions concerning systemic reform. They are encouraging because they signal states' willingness to assume a stronger leadership role regarding the education of students who in some instances were not fully integrated into the fabric of the school community. However, whether state education agencies will have the support to continue work on standards-based reform seems to be an open question. Considerable work remains to be achieved in all key facets of this reform strategy, particularly in assessment development. This component requires substantial financial investment at the state and local levels. Fortunately, collaborative efforts like those of the Council of Chief State School Officers, New Students Project, and the PACE project have considered the inclusion of LEP students in their assessment development efforts and will produce products that will be useful to classroom teachers and policy makers.

— ❧ —

Dr. Julia Lara is the Director of Services to Language Minority Students and Co-Director of the IASA (Improving America's Schools Act) Implementation Project at the Council of Chief State School Officers, Washington, D.C. Her expertise is in advising CCSSO staff and others on appropriate programs for English language learners. She has had a key role in working with various national and state entities to analyze services to language minority students and make recommendations for improvement of policies that affect those students. Dr. Lara has published numerous articles and reports through the CCSSO. Among the best-known are "School Success for Limited English Proficient Students" (1990), "Reflections: Bridging Two Cultures," (1992), and "State Data Collection and Monitoring Procedures Regarding Overrepresentation of Minority Students in Special Education" (1994).

Endnotes

1. Disclaimer: The observations outlined in this commentary are those of the author, not of the Council of Chief State School Officers.

2. Question: Have persons knowledgeable about the education of LEP students or parents of LEP students been involved in the planning process? Total number of states responding to this question was 38.

3. Other states were in the process of developing their content standards.

4. See Minicucci and Olsen. (1992). *Meeting the Challenge of Language Diversity;* and J. Lara, *Middle School Reform and Second Language Learners: A Case Study of a School in Transition* (to be published by CCSSO. 1995).

5. Question: Are LEP students exempted from the state assessments required of other students? A total of 41 states responded to this question.

6. There is an overlap in these categories of states. For example, states may not exempt Spanish-speaking students from tests administered in Spanish in a given grade level, but will need to exempt non-Spanish-speaking LEP students. Also, some Spanish speakers might be exempted when enrolled in grades with no primary language assessments.

7. Arizona, District of Columbia, Delaware, Hawaii, New Jersey, New Mexico, New York, Texas, Connecticut, Utah.

8. Conclusion is based on information obtained through the CCSSO Survey.

References

August, D. et al. (1993). *Federal education programs for limited-English-proficient students: A blueprint for the second generation.* Report of the Stanford Working Group. Stanford, CA.

Banks, C. A. McGee. (1993, September). Restructuring schools for equity: What we have learned in two decades. *Phi Delta Kappan*, Vol. 75, No. 1.

Berman, P., et al. (1992, February). *Meeting the challenge of language diversity.* Berkeley, CA: BW Associates.

California Department of Education. (1993). *California Learning Assessment System (CLAS)equity guidelines.*

Clewell, T.T. & Anderson, B. (1987). *Intervention programs in math and science and computer science for minority and female students.* Princeton, NJ: Educational Testing Service.

Cole, M. & Griffin, P. (Eds.). (1987). *Contextual factors in education: Improving science and mathematics education for minorities and women.* Madison: Wisconsin Center for Education Research, University of Wisconsin-Madison.

Darling-Hammond, L. (1992). *Standards of practice for learner-centered schools.* New York: National Center for Restructuring Education, Schools, and Teaching.

Darling-Hammond, L. & Ascher, C. (1991). *Creating accountability in big city schools.* New York: ERIC Clearinghouse on Urban Education and NCREST.

Delandshere, G. & Petrosky, A. (1994). Capturing teachers' knowledge: Performance assessment. *Educational Researcher, Vol. 23,* No. 5, pp. 11-18.

Edmonds, R. & Fredericksen, J. (1978). *Search for effective schools: The identification and analysis of city schools that are instructionally effective for poor children.* Cambridge, MA: Harvard University, Center for Urban Studies.

Educational Researcher (March 1991). Interview on assessment issues with Lorrie Shepard. Vol. 20, No. 2.

Estrin, E. T. (1993). *Alternative assessment: issues in language, culture, and equity.* San Francisco: Far West Laboratory.

FairTest. (1994). *Guidelines for equitable assessment.* Cambridge, MA.

Freeman, Y. and Freeman, D. (1991, January). Portfolio assessment: an exciting view of what bilingual children can do. *Bilingual Education Outreach.*

Gordon, E. W. (1993). Presentation at 1993 Conference of the Center for the Study of Evaluation & The National Center for Research on Evaluation, Standards, and Student Testing: *Assessment questions: Equity answers.* UCLA, September, 1993.

Gordon, E. W. (1992, April). *Implications of diversity in human characteristics for authentic assessment.* Los Angeles: National Center for Research on Evaluation, Standards, and Student Testing.

Gordon, E. W. (1992). Implications of diversity in human characteristics for authentic assessment. CSE Technical Report 341. Los Angeles: National Center for Research on Evaluation, Standards, and Student Testing.

Gould, S. J. (1981). *The mismeasure of man.* New York: W.W. Norton.

Leadership statement of nine principles on equity and educational testing and assessment, March 12, 1993.

Leap, W. (1988). Assumptions and strategies guiding mathematics problem solving by Ute Indian students. In Cocking, R.R. & Mestre, R.P. (Eds.), *Linguistic and cultural influences on mathematics.* Hillsdale, NJ: Lawrence Erlbaum Associates.

Madaus, G.S. et al. (1992). The influence of testing on teaching math and science in grades 4-12: Executive summary. Boston: Center for the Study of Testing, Boston College.

Malcom, S. (1991). Equity and excellence through authentic science assessment. In Kulm, G. & Malcolm, S. (Eds.), *Science assessment in the service of reform* (pp. 313-330). Washington, D.C.: American Association for the Advancement of Science.

McDonnell, L. (1994). Cited in Rothman, Robert, *Assessment questions: Equity answers,* Proceedings of the 1993 CRESST Conference, p. 3.

National Committee on Science Education Standards and Assessment. (July 1993). *National science education standards: July '93 Progress Report*. Washington, D.C.: National Research Council.

National Council of Teachers of Mathematics (Assessment Standards Working Groups). (October 1993). *Assessment standards for school mathematics (working draft)*.

O'Neil, J. (1993, February). On the New Standards Project: A conversation with Lauren Resnick and Warren Simmons. *Educational Leadership*, 17-21.

O'Neil, J. (1993, February). Can national standards make a difference? *Educational Leadership*, 4-8.

Resnick, L. B. (1992, Spring). Why we need national standards and exams? *State Education Leader*, Denver, CO: ECS.

Resnick, L. B. and Resnick, D. P. (1992). Assessing the thinking curriculum: new tools for educational reform. In Gifford, B.R. & O'Connor, M.C. (Eds.), *Future assessments: Changing views of aptitude, achievement, and instruction*. Boston: Kluwer Academic Publishers.

Romberg, T. (1993, February). NCTM's Standards: A rallying flag for mathematics teachers. *Educational Leadership*, 36-41.

Simmons, W. & Resnick, L. (1993, February). Assessment as the catalyst of school reform. *Educational Leadership*, 11-15.

Stage, E.K., Kreinberg, N., Eccles, J., Becker, J.R. (1985). Increasing the participation and achievement of girls and women in mathematics, science, and engineering. In Klein, S. S. (Ed.), *Handbook for achieving sex equity through education*. Baltimore, MD: Johns Hopkins University Press.

Stanford Working Group. (1994). *Blueprint for the second generation*. Palo Alto, CA: Stanford University.

Viadero, D. (June 2,1993). The rhetoric and reality of high academic standards. *Education Week*.

Wiley, C. Strategies for involving all students in national and state assessments: Presentation notes and background information. Arizona Student Assessment Program. Presentation at National Conference on Large Scale Assessments, Albuquerque, NM, June 1993.

Winfield, L. & Woodard, M. (1994). Assessment, equity, and diversity in reforming America's schools. *CSE Technical Report 372*, Los Angeles: National Center for Research on Evaluation, Standards, and Student Testing.

Chapter 3

Curricular
Considerations

If our destination is excellence on a massive scale, not only must we change from the slow lane into the fast lane; we literally must change highways. Perhaps we need to abandon the highways altogether and take flight, because the highest goals that we can imagine are well within reach for those who have the will to excellence.

Asa Hilliard, September 1991

From an article titled with the question, "Do we have the *will* to educate all children?", this quote sets the theme once again for a consideration of the broader context in which issues of assessment and equity are placed. In this chapter, we will discuss curricular and instructional issues that cannot be avoided or neglected if our goal is to develop assessments of student learning that will provide well-focused lenses with which to observe the processes involved. Many educators involved or interested in the development of performance-based assessments are optimistic that these assessments will have a positive effect on classroom instruction. They assume that measurement-driven or test-driven instruction will become a goal worth achieving—a goal that stands in stark contrast to the long-decried process of "teaching to the test," the result of wide-scale, high-stakes testing so common over several decades.

While we agree that assessments designed to engage students in challenging tasks, allow them to reflect on the learning involved, and validate processes as well as products of learning *do* have the potential to change the ways teachers design curriculum and plan instruction we cannot assume that this will be a clear and direct result. More importantly, even if changes in classroom instruction begin to emerge, such changes will not ensure equity for all students. What we are saying, essentially, is that *excellence* (the envisioned goal of changing instruction in the way that many educators are supporting [1]) does not always equal *equity*. Gay (1988) does not see these attributes as incompatible but notes an interrelationship:

> In fact, equity is a precondition and a means for achieving excellence. Whereas equity is a methodological input issue, excellence is an evaluative outcome measure. Excellence finds expression in common standards and expectations of high achievement for all students, and equity translates into appropriate methodologies and materials according to specific group or individual characteristics. Excellence occurs when individual students achieve to the best of their ability, and equity is accomplished when each student is provided with learning opportunities that make high level achievement possible.

In the field of curriculum and instruction, research over the last two decades has produced knowledge that is changing the "color and texture" of America's classrooms and, ideally, will continue to change many more classrooms in expansive and extensive ways. This information is also reflected in many curriculum frameworks, content standards being developed at local, state, and national levels. Much of this knowledge and the related instructional strategies belong in a theoretical category often referred to as "constructivist." This theoretical construct has important relevance to the development of equitable assessments, since most performance-based assessments are aligned with an approach to teaching and learning based on constructivism.

A second body of research and educational dialogue that has relevance to this discussion centers on approaches to bilingual and multicultural education. This dialogue has persisted for several decades and has often been (and still is) quite contentious. It is likely to become more contentious as the demographic picture of the United States continues to change, and as issues involved in developing "high standards for all children" and equitable assessments continue to arise.

In the first part of this chapter, we will review some of the tenets of constructivism and highlight issues associated with bilingual and multicultural education. This will serve as a backdrop for the set of issues or curricular considerations that must be addressed as we approach the design and development of equitable assessments.

Constructivism in the Classroom

Much of cognitive psychology research in recent decades has led to the understanding that learning is an active process. Knowledge is not a fixed entity to be passed on to a learner[2]; rather learners *construct* their own knowledge. A *constructivist* view of the learner is one of an active builder of knowledge and knowledge structures. In this view, learners do not simply "acquire" knowledge and skills; they use their existing knowledge based on their own experience to understand and organize new information. Constructivists would argue that isolated facts or information that is not structured by the learner is not meaningful. A constructivist approach to teaching incorporates notions of different learners solving problems in different ways, using different strategies, from different vantage points. In theory, then, no two learners would construct exactly the same understanding or representation of meaning from a given classroom experience/lesson/exposure/piece of information. This point, alone, has overwhelming importance when considering the learning challenges faced by children who are English language learners or whose cultures are distinct from those of the mainstream culture. Indeed, it is significant for all children—each of whom approaches learning in an idiosyncratic way.

If it is true, as Eleanor Duckworth (1991) says, that children develop intellectually only when they test out ideas that they find significant, we must—when "teaching" literature, for example—be sure they get to explore those ideas. But it is not a matter of simply allowing students to discover on their own how their significant ideas intersect with a literary experience. Teachers can help students find "something worthy to think about"; yet our intentions for what children should learn must include the awareness that they will construe what we are teaching in their own terms— that we cannot/should not overspecify the "lessons" they should learn. Thus, the meaning of a text will vary from child to child. Constructivism does not posit that all students' constructions are equally valid because some explanations are better than others. What we want to do as teachers is facilitate improved or expanded constructions and development of the necessary intellectual tools through our offerings to students, through the kinds of conversations we help them through, through the experiences we structure for them. Higher-order thinking would not be something to gradually work up to, but something supported from the start.

By helping students to make connections to their own experiences and interests, we are potentially merging classroom cultural context with the student's home cultural context. In so doing, we are getting away from fully-packaged activities (no matter how enticing they may seem) and leaving room for interpretations and content based on the student's experiences and interests. If we weave program elements into a coherent whole, we avoid teaching students a series of apparently unrelated events.

Goodlad, Klein, and Tye (1979) refer to the "common" experiences in which children participate in the classroom as the *taught* curriculum and the learnings that they develop as the *experienced* curriculum.

The primary question for the teacher, therefore, is how to help students build a foundation of skills and information while they simultaneously use their creative, intellectual abilities to solve real problems and incidentally develop positive dispositions toward such endeavors. The powerful concept of *constructivism* can help us find solutions to this question (Grennon Brooks, 1993).

Constructivist learning contrasts markedly with what Jackson (1986) refers to as the *mimetic* tradition in education in which students are expected to master skills and facts largely through drill and practice exercises. One has only to think or speculate about the ways infants and young children go about figuring out and organizing the world they enter in order to gain some insight about constructivist learning. Children create rules and formulate hypotheses and test them out as they experiment and play with the sounds, words and word parts, and syntactic structures of their language. Weir (1962) even noted this propensity to play and experiment with the sounds of language in very young children in her work that studied "language in the crib." In the same way that children do not master a complex linguistic system merely by imitation, they do not construct theories of the world around them by having it explained to them or through drill and practice exercises. Traditional schooling is based on the premise that there is a fixed world that the learner must come to know. Duckworth (1991) counters the mimetic tradition with a vision of teaching that reflects constructivism: "I propose situations for people to think about and I watch what they do. They tell me what *they* make of it rather than my telling them *what* to make of it."

Discrepancy resolution is the student's "fundamental quest" according to Sigel and Cocking (1977). As the learner encounters objects or experiences that are discrepant with his/her operating view of reality, he or she must find a way to resolve the discrepancy, accommodate the new information, and seek validation for this learning. With this in mind, it is not difficult to comprehend the discrepancies encountered by a student whose language or culture is different from the dominant language or culture of the school. While these students face the dual challenge of mastering the information presented and at the same time accommodating a different language and culture, it is important to note that the cognitive, linguistic, and cultural learnings they have already accomplished will support new learning. For example, a child who has "constructed" the rules of his native language quickly recognizes that a second language has structures and rules that vary in ways that are largely predictable. Similarly, we have come to understand that the process of reading comprehension involves the application of *schemata* (cognitive structures) or *scripts* to text that is presented. A child will generally have a particular "script," for example, for "going to the park to play," and she applies that script when she reads a story about such an event. The script, itself, is often common to children regardless of the language they speak or world culture they have experienced. These scripts, then, help them to comprehend stories they read in a new language. The scripts—along with cognitive strategies such as predicting, inferring, generalizing, and hypothesizing—constitute elements of "positive transfer" for children as long as we, as educators, don't confound this process by emphasizing the presumed barriers of "negative transfer."

For too long, many teachers and American educators, in general, have operated on the assumption that a child's first language or experience with his native culture will constitute a major hindrance to learning English and the curriculum of American schools. One can see how this conclusion is reached more readily when the concept of education is one of transmission, and the goal is for the child to memorize and master a very long list of facts and skills. If, however, one views learning using a constructivist lens, it is much easier to understand the potential of positive transfer, indeed even the advantage of learning and being able to use more than one language and to experience more than one culture.[3]

Because constructivist teachers typically "ask one big question" or lead students into a consideration of complex concepts, they enhance the opportunity for second-language learning and for learning within the context of a culture different from that of the learner. They give the students time to think and connect them with the resources necessary to explore big ideas and to use multiple paths to seek multiple solutions. Rigid timelines conflict with research on how human beings form meaningful theories about the ways the world works (Duckworth, 1986), how students and teachers develop an appreciation of knowledge and understanding (Eisner, 1985), and how one creates the disposition to inquire about phenomena not fully understood (Katz, 1985). "Most curriculums simply pack too much information into too little time—at a significant cost to the learner" (Grennon Brooks and Brooks, 1993).

It is important to note that while all of the research on learning and instruction that has occurred over about the last two decades is not always identified as constructivist per se, there is great consistency in the information that has shaped current thinking about teaching and learning. There is always the risk that a term will become a piece of jargon and/or will become part of a jingoistic approach to education, and we hope that that can be avoided in this case. The term "constructivism" synthesizes a significant body of research across a variety of domains—reading, math, science, for example—but it will only fulfill its promise of reshaping our educational practices if we do not allow it to be reduced to an educational style or trend as ephemeral as any fashion trend. One way that constructivist theory has been translated into classroom practice is through discussion and exploration of instructional strategies that lead to "powerful learning." A vignette—drawn from commentary on the "Accelerated Schools" [4] model—is presented in Figure 3.1. It provides a good classroom example of an activity that reflects a constructivist approach to teaching and learning.

FIGURE 3.1

Powerful Learning in "Accelerated Schools"

Mission Control bustles with activity as up to 24 students and their parents and visitors huddle around computer terminals and video monitors. There are three communications stations in this room: one for the Mission Director, one for the Physical Science Director, and one for the Biological Science Director. These positions are staffed on a rotating basis by trained sixth graders, who are responsible for providing information, encouragement, and feedback to their Mars-based counterparts. Frequently, this coaching is done in Spanish or Portuguese, the native languages of many of the students. Once all the preparations are made, the shuttle crew enters the cockpit, leaving behind their teacher and classmates. Once they pass through the circular hatch, they strap themselves into four brightly colored airline seats and await further instructions from Mission Control. The pilot and co-pilot sit in the forward seats and wear headsets that put them in voice contact with the ground crew. . . . They receive the message to begin the launch sequence, and a flight simulation program appears on the computer screen. . . . The ground crew in the next room views a video of an actual shuttle launch, just as if they were watching it through Mission Control's windows. . . . After taking their first steps on "Planet Mars," a classroom adjoining the classroom housing Mission Control, the astronauts are responsible for setting up a habitat for themselves and conducting approximately ten biological and physical science experiments. The students begin working together on the experiments and realize that each one of them is uniquely qualified to operate certain instruments, or answer certain questions. They must rely on the strengths and knowledge of everyone in their group, or they cannot successfully complete their work.(Their teacher engineered the situation this way by meeting for individual pre-launch training sessions with each one of them, and giving them all different information.) Only about 40 percent of the students' activities are scripted for them, with clear instructions on what to do, and who should do what. The rest of the time, the students know only the goal of the experiment, and they must figure out how to conduct it themselves. Students also must manage all of the inevitable mission glitches; their teacher is present at Mission Control with the other students, but he intervenes only when absolutely necessary.[1]

---

[1] The Mars Flight is a project created by George O'Neel, a teacher at Burnett Academy in San Jose, California. The description of this simulation is taken from Hopfenberg, W.S., Moore, M.A., & Rodriguez, G. (1994). *Curricular change in Accelerated Schools.* CA: Stanford University.

It is important to emphasize how important a consideration of school curricula and instructional practices is to the improvement of the general condition of education. The reform proposals that have been put forth and the innovative practices that are being explored often do not require enough attention to the heart of the educational matter—the content of instruction and the strategies for delivering it. "These (reform) proposals suggest overhauling assessment practices to make them more relevant for students, establishing site-based management teams in schools, rethinking the efficacy of tracking and ability grouping, and freeing school districts from federal and state mandates . . . these proposals don't go deep enough. They don't speak openly enough about the educational system's underlying suppositions about what it means to learn, about what it means to become educated" (Grennon Brooks and Brooks, 1993).

It is clear to us that if we are to produce assessments that are characterized by fairness, we cannot abstain from a consideration of how students learn—students from situations of poverty or affluence, students who are learning a second or third language or having difficulty with their first, students whose cultural background differs from that which typifies the school or whose life experiences have been so restricted that building a prior knowledge base for learning through an enriched, rather than impoverished, curriculum is essential.

Multicultural Literacy, Bilingual Education, and the School Curriculum

The educational reforms of the 1980s paid relatively little attention to issues associated with developing a citizenry that would have the knowledge and skills as well as the attitudes to function competently in a world that was becoming increasingly diverse—ethnically, racially, and culturally—and increasingly complex.

Disproportionate failure and dropout rates among students of color have led to an ever-growing recognition that these students are clearly "at risk." While it is unlikely that the label serves them well,[5] it is important to acknowledge those factors that influence these students' encounters with public schools. It is undeniable that American schools are controlled by and reflect a dominant white culture. In the face of an awareness that "the maintenance of one's community, history, language, talents, and skills is of paramount importance to any group of people" (Hidalgo, McDowell, and Siddle, 1990), it is not difficult to understand why students of color develop coping strategies that limit their chance of school success. As Wyman (1993) notes, these students may camouflage their successful academic efforts in order to maintain acceptance by their peers, participate in a "resistance culture," or suppress their cultural heritage and become "raceless."

Cummins, who has written extensively on the topic of multicultural education, "examines the academic problems of minority students in light of a school's ability to mirror or reverse power relations within society" (Wyman, 1993). According to Cummins [and others such as Sleeter (1991), Pang (1990), and Molnar (1989)], whether students become "empowered" or "disabled" depends explicitly on the quality of their encounters with school. "These encounters are influenced by the degree to which the language and culture of non-majority students are part of the school program, the minority community's participation in the educational system is fostered, and educators are supportive of students of color in instruction and assessment" (Wyman, 1993).

Sleeter and Grant (1990) conducted a thorough analysis of multicultural education programs and developed a taxonomy of teaching approaches that helps to define the concept of multicultural education. Their taxonomy which includes five approaches is presented in Figure 3.2.

FIGURE 3.2

Taxonomy of Approaches to Multicultural Education*

- **Teaching the Culturally Different** guides students of color in their transition into the dominant culture.

- **Human Relations** fosters harmony and appreciation among students of varying cultural backgrounds.

- **Single Group Studies** exposes students to experiences, ideas, contributions, and various cultural groups through different courses.

- **Multicultural Education** changes the school program, including staffing, curriculum and instruction, to reflect the diverse cultures of populations within the school, promoting cultural pluralism and social equality.

- **Education that is Multicultural and Social Reconstructionist** educates students to take action against social structural inequality and fosters cultural pluralism.

---

*Sleeter, C., and C. Grant. (1990). An analysis of multicultural education in the United States. In *Facing Racism in Education*, edited by N.M. Hidalgo et al. (pp. 138-161). Cambridge, MA: Harvard Educational Review.

It is not a trivial task for school personnel to examine their approach to multicultural or multi-ethnic education and to explore the options for designing a program that meets the needs of their culturally diverse students.[6] These decisions cannot be made without a consideration of the overall goals of such programs and the well-ingrained social issues that have affected such decisions throughout our political and educational history. Metaphors to explain this history abound. Immigrants were often attracted to America by promises that they would be coming to the "horn of plenty" only to find that they were relegated to the "back of the bus." While the humiliation of social degradation has been experienced by many ethnic groups, the "back of the bus" was often reserved for Blacks who were descendants of African slaves brought to the United States as "involuntary immigrants," as Ogbu (1992) refers to them. The differences in the immigration and assimilation experiences of various racial and ethnic groups are significant when school programs designed to address their needs or school performance by students from these nondominant groups are examined.

Historically, educators thought there was justification for erasing ethnicity because they believed that people of color would have greater difficulty if they attempted to maintain their ethnicity. "Hence, cultural domination in the guise of acculturation and assimilation has been the *modus operandi* for American education and curriculum development" (Nobles, 1990). The motivation for eradicating ethnicity, however, was not merely out of generous consideration for the learning challenge faced by culturally divergent students. Americans have generally felt threatened by the idea of potential separatist movements. Reference to America as the "great melting pot" was a reflection of the intention to create one homogenous mix by submerging a legion of diverse ingredients.

One way to characterize ways in which these various theories play out in the curriculum and instructional practices of the classroom is to use Figure 3.3 as a reference point.

In this figure, the various approaches to multiculturalism are characterized as "invisibilizing," "marginalizing," "expanding," and "deciphering." We find the taxonomy is useful for thinking about the subtle differences that are frequently unacknowledged by those who are planning a multicultural program or who profess to have a multicultural program in place. Like many of the educators whose work we have referenced in this chapter, we advocate a curriculum that "expands" ideas about our pluralistic heritage beyond the standard characterizations of the dominant group and gives students many opportunities to consider how that heritage gives us unique vantage points and enriches both our society and everyone who is a member of it. Such a curriculum also strengthens students' ability to confront (and potentially resolve) conflicts in viewpoint or interpretation. If we cannot—as a society—develop a language and way of talking publicly about the more complex aspects of our multicultural, multiethnic,

and multiracial character, we will continue to have unresolved social issues. An "expanding" approach to multiculturalism offers hope for current and future generations of empowered/enfranchised students to participate more fully in (and contribute more to) the society at large.

FIGURE 3.3
Forms of Knowledge/Approaches to Multiculturalism*

Invisibilizing	**Marginalizing**
Reflects the assimilationist agenda; largely ignores individual and group differences, voices, perspectives.	Relegates attention regarding minority groups to special days, weeks, celebrations; reflects a trivializing of cultural differences.
Expanding	**Deciphering**
Open-ended exploration of pluralism; reflects joint construction of knowledge, understanding; equal participation by all; empowering perspective.	Reflects beginning efforts to understand differences and their meanings; explorational perspective.

*Constructed by Estrin as an interpretation of information presented by Joyce King
(April, 1994): Perceiving reality in a new way: Rethinking the Black-White duality of
our time. Annual Meeting of the American Educational Research Association, New
Orleans.

While the "cause" of pluralism has had a host of advocates over the
years who recognize the plight of linguistic and cultural minority children in our schools, the struggle to develop and maintain educational programs that will permit them to become the recipients of a quality education has been and continues to be a difficult one. In a report on teacher
education in which "Professional Development Schools" are described and
explicated, the Holmes Group[7] addresses the issue of education and social justice:

> In the kind of country that we are, and aspire to be, teaching and learn-
> ing for understanding cannot be rationed to a few. The Professional De-
> velopment School will be a place where everybody's children partici-
> pate in making knowledge and meaning—where each child is a valued
> member of a community of learning. A very great challenge to the Pro-
> fessional Development School is to create such communities in a society
> whose families live on very unequal terms (Young et al., p. 29).

Many writers and researchers have been extolling the virtues of a multicultural curriculum, but perhaps none as eloquently as James Banks. He recognizes the potential of such a program to help students "to know, to care, and to act in ways that will develop and foster a democratic and just society where all groups experience cultural democracy and empowerment. Knowledge is an essential part of multicultural literacy, but it is not the only component. Knowledge, alone, will not help students develop empathy, caring, and a commitment to humane and democratic change" (Banks, 1991).

Banks' concept of the multicultural classroom is directly related to the "constructivist" notions discussed above because he sees knowledge construction as an important aspect of multicultural education. In this case, the process of constructing knowledge relates to how teachers help students "understand, investigate, and determine how implicit cultural assumptions, frames of references, perspectives, and biases within a discipline influence how knowledge is created. This process teaches students that knowledge reflects the social, political, and economic context in which it is created" (Banks, 1991).

The process of knowledge construction may be applied across the disciplines. In science, students might study how racism was perpetuated by genetic theories of intelligence or how the anthropological work of Franz Boas and Ruth Benedict challenged racist beliefs and practices.[8] A study of the "New World" might give rise to discussions of differing perspectives on the "settlement" of the land that came to be known as the United States. Students might examine why earlier newcomers (mostly from England) are commonly referred to as "settlers" and "pioneers," while later arrivals from other countries are referred to as "immigrants." Native Americans, on the other hand, might feel inclined to refer to them all as "invaders," "conquerors," or "foreigners." They might also consider the term, "westward movement" from the point of view of the Sioux Indians for whom the "West" was not the West, but the center of the universe (Banks, 1991, p. 142).

> Only a curriculum that reflects the collective experiences and interests of a wide range of groups is truly in the national interest and consistent with the public good. Any other curriculum reflects only special interests and, thus, does not meet the needs of a nation that must survive in a pluralistic, highly independent global world (Banks, 1991, p. 140).

No one could argue that the challenge that classroom teachers face in trying to meet this goal is formidable. Not only must the teacher face the racial, social-class, linguistic, and cultural differences of her students, but she must also consider how to create a community of learners using an approach that involves teaching for understanding—not just the attainment of skills. To accomplish this task in the face of sometimes severe inequalities of race, class, and gender and also think about the need to help youngsters develop "empathy . . . and a commitment to democratic change" should be enough for all of us to acknowledge teachers with a much deeper respect than they typically enjoy from their fellow citizens. How many of those who are so quick to criticize teachers would want to enter a classroom every day with that challenge before them? But this is the challenge of teaching.

Bilingual education is framed and defined by its own set of theories and theorists, approaches, issues, and terms. Nonetheless, while the focus and goals are clearly distinct from those of multicultural education, there is considerable overlap in the target population, in the cognitive learning research base from which they draw much of their theoretical underpinnings, and in the issues related to assessment.

The rights of language minority students to have access to a high-quality education have been adjudicated in several court cases. According to the decisions of *Brown v. Board of Education* and *San Antonio Independent School District v. Rodrigues*, immigrants are entitled by law to receive an education equal to that of all other citizens (Carrera, 1989). Also well known is the case of *Lau v. Nichols* (1974), which decision required that limited-English proficient students receive some sort of special language services from their school district. The vast disparity of interpretation for "special language services," of course, has led to somewhat contentious debate about approaches to the teaching of students whose first language is not English. Embedded in this general discussion is the question of how to establish and evaluate levels of language proficiency. These issues are discussed in detail in Chapter 4, but the range of bilingual education program options as presented in Figure 3.4 is a useful framework for thinking about how the issues related to assessment would be rendered for each approach. (For example, if students are in a "submersion" program where "English-only" is the operating principle, what does that imply for assessments used to evaluate the learning progress of those students?)

The court decisions and legislative mandates related to bilingual education have been unevenly successful across the nation in terms of compliance. Compliance can only truly be achieved when it is "rooted in sympathy with the intended aims and understanding of the conceptual issues" (Cummins, 1982, p. 1). The latter is a critical issue that is not consistently acknowledged, that is, that teachers need to know enough about second-language acquisition and bilingual academic development to implement effective educational practice.

FIGURE 3.4

K-12 Language Schooling Programs
English Language Focus

CHARACTERISTICS

	Goal of Program	Methods for English Language Development	Methods for Second Language Development
LATE-EXIT **TRANSITIONAL** BILINGUAL EDUCATION	high academic achievement & language proficiency in **English**	-ESL (pull-out or within class) -gradual introduction of English for reading in latter half of elementary -gradual introduction of English for content area instruction (4-6 years)	-gradual diminishing of native language for reading -gradual diminishing of native language for content area instruction -interactions with fluent, native-speaking peers
EARLY-EXIT **TRANSITIONAL** BILINGUAL EDUCATION	high academic achievement & language proficiency in **English**	-ESL (pull-out or within class) -prompt introduction of English for reading in first half of elementary -prompt introduction of English for content area instruction (1-3 years)	-prompt diminishing of native language for reading -prompt diminishing of native language for content area instruction -interactions with fluent, native-speaking peers
STRUCTURED **IMMERSION** EDUCATION	high academic achievement & language proficiency in **English**	-ESL (pull-out or within class) -immediate introduction of English for reading from first day -immediate introduction of English for content area instruction	no attempt to promote a second or native language

K-12 Language Schooling Programs
Second/Foreign Language Focus*

CHARACTERISTICS

	Goal of Program	Methods for English Language Development	Methods for Second Language Development
ENGLISH AS A SECOND LANGUAGE (ESL) PULL-OUT	high academic achievement & language proficiency in **English**	-intensive and/or individualized instruction of English as a content area -immediate use of English for content area instruction in regular classroom	no attempt to promote a second or native language
SUBMERSION EDUCATION	high academic achievement & language	-all subjects taught in English in a mainstream classroom immediately -peer support and/ or tutoring	no attempt to promote a second or native language
FOREIGN LANGUAGE ACADEMIES **(FLA)**	high academic achievement & language proficiency in *both* **English & a foreign language**	-ESL (pull-out or within class) -interactions with fluent, English-speaking peers -content area instruction in English	-foreign language taught as a subject area -interactions with fluent, foreign language speaking peers -content area instruction in the foreign language
FOREIGN LANGUAGE ELEMENTARY SCHOOLS **(FLES)**	high academic achievement & language proficiency in *both* **English & a foreign language**	-gradual introduction of English for reading in latter half of elementary -interactions with fluent, English-speaking peers -use of English by students' families at home	-immediate use of second language for reading -second language taught as a subject area -content area instruction in the second language

MAINTENANCE BILINGUAL EDUCATION	high academic achievement & language proficiency in *both* **English & a foreign language**	-ESL (pull-out or within class) -gradual introduction of English for reading in latter half of elementary -gradual introduction of English for content area instruction	-immediate use of native language for reading -interactions with fluent, native speaking peers -content area instruction in the native language
DUAL **IMMERSION/** TWO-WAY BILINGUAL EDUCATION	high academic achievement & language proficiency in *both* **English & a foreign language**	-systematic increase of English for content area instruction -gradual introduction of English for reading in latter half of elementary -interactions with fluent, English-speaking peers	-immediate use of second/native language for reading -interactions with fluent, native-speaking peers -content area instruction in the second/native language

*Cuevas, J. (1995). Educating limited-English proficient students: A review of the research on school programs and classroom practices. San Francisco: Far West Laboratory.

Misconceptions about the development of bilinguality abound. Two of these misconceptions have direct relevance to issues of assessment. The first is the assumption that the first language of a student must be eradicated if that student is to learn English (or the second language) and become part of the dominant cultural group. While this belief is not as pervasive today, remnants of it remain in certain educational practices, for example, ones that convey a valuing of English over a student's first language. When assessments are evaluated only in terms of one's success with English, a student who is learning English is taught that her first language has no value and cannot support her academic development.

The second misconception that affects both instruction and assessment is the notion that individuals who have acquired enough of a second language to interact with their peers on a day-to-day basis (generally attainable between eighteen months and two years) have adequate proficiency to engage in any learning or assessment task without undue difficulty. This is a misconception of what it means to "know" a language and leads to misjudgments regarding student learning. "As a result, low academic

performance or test scores among language minority students are attributed to deficiencies in the student or in his or her background experiences. In this way, the process of 'blaming the victim,' which has characterized the 'education' of minority language children in North America
throughout this century, is perpetuated" (Cummins, 1982, p. 6). There is,
in fact, no need for there to be a "victim."

A familiarity with current research and thinking on the design of curriculum and instructional practice is vital as a backdrop for an explication
of the issues related to assessment. Most important is to be aware of changes
that are occurring in classrooms, trends that can be identified, and contro-
versies that still rage about how best to provide an educational experience
that not only meets the learning needs, but also challenges a diverse population of students. In the next section, we will discuss the important curricular issues that must be taken into account when designing new forms
of assessment or assessment systems that will serve the various purposes
established in the American educational system.[9]

Curricular Issues Related to Equitable Assessment

*Parents provide their children as best they can physical and cultural nourish-
ment in the home. That a home fails to provide a student the fundamental elements of success in our system of education indicts our system as a failure and
not the home. The uniqueness as well as the culture-base of each person needs to
be celebrated in the educational process. The discovery of one's self, and one's
heritage, should be education's cause and growth into one's potentials its end*
(Waters, no date indicated).

Literacy Development and Culture

In the design of curriculum and instructional practices, we must consider how we will create opportunities for children to develop language
proficiency. But language proficiency must be defined in terms beyond
language structures. We also must ensure that students develop their capacity to use language for specific purposes—to choose the suitable use of
language register, style, or tone to interact in different situations—to report or to describe, to make inquiry, to regulate behavior, or to accomplish
other purposes through language.

There are also vast differences among cultures regarding what it means
to be literate, and what it means within the same culture at different times
or for different purposes. These differences should not be ignored, but
their subtlety and the fact that we are often not conscious of them, or do

not articulate them, makes it quite difficult to convey their import for classroom instruction and the design of assessments. In a society tending toward homogeneity, it is easy to think of literacy simply in terms of specific skills and activities. Given broad cultural consensus on the definition of literacy, alternative constructions are either remote or invisible, and so literacy becomes a seemingly evident personal attribute that is either present or absent.

Thus the English language learner will find herself faced with a wide array of alternative methods, and she will become aware that different values are placed on different behaviors. Ferdman (1990) gives a good example of this when he discusses American educators who tend to see creative writing by children as a "valued activity" and incorporate it into school curricula. "This may appear strange in other countries, however, where students are encouraged to learn and copy the work of great thinkers rather than to produce original work." How often do teachers view the reluctance or resistance of a child from a non-dominant culture to participate in literacy activities as a result of a different perspective of what it means to be literate and how writing should be used?

The development of language proficiency and literacy behaviors represents the most vital part of our being as humans. It is through language that we learn about the world that surrounds us—how to interact with others and objects within that world, how to think about it, how to represent ourselves within it. When one's language is rejected or devalued in some way, it constitutes a fundamental rejection of that individual. "Literacy, I believe, touches us at our core in that part of ourselves that connects with the social world around us. It provides an important medium through which we interact with the human environment" (Ferdman, 1990). In this context, it is not difficult to understand how the process of becoming literate is also the process of becoming identified with a particular culture. Kádár-Fülop (1988) describes the development of "language loyalty"—the encouragement of positive attitudes toward the language—as an important function for literacy education.

In situations where the language learner views the "teachers" or those who are encouraging the development of a particular language as oppressors or as hostile in some way, there will, not surprisingly, be conscious or unconscious resistance to learning the target language. In such cases, the process is a destructive one. In other cases, the language learner may choose one language over another for reasons that result from a host of factors within the individual and the social context; the choice, itself, is likely to affect the learning that takes place. Linguists often refer to this exercise of choice as "code-switching," a behavior that is reflected in the conscious use of one language over another in particular situations. Two personal examples cited by Ferdman are presented in Figure 3.5.

FIGURE 3.5

As a child, I delighted in reading anything I could get my hands on. But one of my favorite types of stories as an eight and nine-year-old was *midrashim*, myths and legends based on the Bible. If Norse legends were given to me, I was just as likely to read them; but they did not have the same impact on me, and I did not see them in the same light. Because of my Jewish identity, my relationship to King David or to Abraham was a more personal and significant one than my connection with Thor. The Biblical stories, because they touched on my cultural identity, had practical and symbolic meanings that went beyond the story and extended into helping me learn more about myself and my group in a social context and gave me conceptual tools with which to interact with other group members. Similarly, when I want to read a Latin American author, I will do so in Spanish, my native tongue, rather than in English translation. My choice is based not only on a desire to read the original, but also to reaffirm my connection with Latin American symbols and texts. In spite of ostensibly similar content, I experience the images and meanings differently in the two languages (Ferdman, 1990, p. 196).

Castell and Luke (1987) also provide an excellent example of the process of learning a language within the context of a culture that is alien to one's native culture. They describe Alaska Native teenagers' feelings about acquiring Western written literacy as a metaphor for adopting a new ethnic group identity. "To become literate in school terms would be to disaffiliate symbolically from their parents and other members of the Alaska Native village, a few of whom are 'literate' in traditional knowledge and skill, such as that involved in hunting, and many of whom are marginally literate in school-like practices of literacy." Kwachka (1994) contends further that many Alaska Natives in small villages choose "non-literacy." They rely on the schooled members of the community such as lawyers, accountants, and bank personnel to carry out the few necessary literacy tasks. Kwachka uses the term, "non-literate," rather than "illiterate" because of the element of choice: as suggested above, many Natives have chosen not to learn to read and write. Use of the word, "illiterate," suggests failure to learn.

One more example from the research literature will further adorn our tapestry of understanding regarding differences in literacy development that are related to culture. Villegas (1991) uses the example to explain the miscommunication that can occur due to ethnic differences. She reports on the research of Michaels (1981), who compared the narrative styles of African-American and White first graders, focusing on narratives related during "sharing time," a classroom activity that involved students' telling about some past experience. "In primary classrooms, where sharing time is used most frequently, it can serve as a bridge between the oral language that pupils bring to class and the literate discourse of written text, which emphasizes decontextualized language" (Villegas, p. 17). Michaels found, however, that the two groups of students used different strategies to construct their narratives. While White students focused on a single topic and organized sequentially and assumed less shared knowledge on the part of the listener, African-American students frequently presented a series of implicitly associated anecdotes. It was also apparent that the teacher's criteria for good narratives corresponded closely to the "topic-centered" style of the White students. Michaels argued that the sociolinguistic disparity prevented the White teacher from interacting effectively with the African-American students during this classroom activity. One can easily deduce how much significance such disparities would have when students are directed to write narratives on an assessment and when such narratives are scored.

The distinct differences in perspective regarding what it means to be and to become literate have obvious implications for classroom instruction and assessment. It would certainly be an impossible task to develop a culturally-appropriate curriculum, instructional strategies, and assessments that take into account and accommodate in specific ways a wide range of linguistic and cultural differences. What is important to recognize, however, is that a heightened awareness of such differences and the use of multiple measures will take us a long way down the road toward equity. While the use of multiple measures should be the norm for any student in a classroom, this is especially important in cross-cultural classroom settings. Strategies might include observations of students in various contexts, examination of students' work products, or anecdotal records related to students' answers to oral questions or comments during class discussions.

What is needed, then, is what Knapp et al. (1990) refer to as a different "view of the disadvantaged learner"; students whose first language is not English or who come from non-mainstream cultures are definitely at a disadvantage when they attempt to learn not only the content but the culture of the school.[10]

> (First), stereotypical ideas about the capabilities of a child who is poor or who belongs to an ethnic minority will detract from an accurate assessment of the child's real educational problems and potential. Second, by focusing on family deficiencies, educators may miss the strengths of the cultures from which many disadvantaged students come. The adverse consequences of these conceptions include (1) low expectations for what these students can accomplish in academic work; (2) failure to examine

carefully what the schools do that exacerbates (or facilitates the solution of) these learning problems; and (3) misdiagnosis of the learning problems these students face (e.g., interpreting dialect speech patterns as decoding errors). . . . The disadvantaged child may well bring to school speech patterns, cognitive predispositions, and behavior patterns that do not match the way things are done in school. These students must learn the culture of the school while they are also attempting to master academic tasks (Knapp et al., 1990, p. 4).

While there *may* be gaps in disadvantaged students' experience, the teacher must build on their background of experience and at the same time challenge them to expand their repertoires of experiences and skills.

Other issues that arise at the juxtaposition of curriculum and assessment have to do with *content* and, specifically, the relevance of the assessments to a variety of cultures and the alignment of the assessments with the curriculum that is presented in the classroom.

Curriculum Design and Instructional Practices

Curriculum is "at the heart of assessment decisions." The problem of assessment is really a problem of curriculum and of educational goals. We must move toward direct observation of the kinds of performances that a curriculum focused on the development of thinking skills educators value rather than toward indicators and probes of lesser interest. The alignment of curriculum and assessment is certainly critical, but it is also important to acknowledge first the importance of designing a curriculum and implementing instructional practices that will result in the kind of learning that current educational research supports. Often referred to as the "thinking curriculum," it requires the "recognition that all real learning involves thinking, that thinking ability can be nurtured and cultivated in everyone, and that the entire educational program must be reconceived and revitalized so that thinking pervades students' lives beginning in kindergarten" (Resnick & Resnick, 1992). While those who are developing and using performance-based assessments need to ask how well the assessment matches the classroom instruction that precedes (or follows) it, it will not be enough to simply add more "hands-on," self-reflection, problem-solving, cooperative learning or other such activities to the content of the classroom.

Wolf et al. (1991) offer some general guidance that posits thinking as a "performance, a combination of humility and risk: It takes on noisy, ill-defined problems, alternately collecting data, observing, and hazarding guesses (Holt, 1990; Lakotas, 1976; Lampert, 1990; Polya, 1954). It involves large projects that combine invention and investigation with craft and insight and embedded accuracy." The authors go on to explain that like other performers, those engaged in thought typically sustain work over a period of time, surmounting obstacles, rehearsing, revising, and making new attempts. Thinking also involves interpretation—deciding how to make sense of information and beliefs. When one considers students who are ethnically or linguistically different from the mainstream student, it is not difficult to see how a curriculum framed in the way described would be better suited to meet their needs—allowing for multiple interpretations, multiple answers, multiple paths to success. As constructivist theorists point out, students must construct a point of reference from their own experience and relate it to new learning. The classroom subject matter or experience must be close enough to his own that he can form meaning from it.

One method for organizing the curriculum to better meet the needs of diverse learners that has proven successful is the use of a thematic approach. In a review of programs in schools where language minority students were particularly successful, Garcia (1991) noted that effective instructional approaches for these students were consistently organized around thematic units. "In the majority of classrooms studied, the students actually selected the themes in consultation with the teacher, either through direct voting or through some related negotiation process. The teacher's responsibility was to insure that the instruction revolving around the chosen themes covered the school district's content and skill-related goals and objectives for that grade level."

For those designing curriculum, a few cautions are in order. While there are undoubtedly more, these strike us as common hazards: (1) "dis-integrating" the curriculum; (2) erring on the side of coverage; (3) trivializing content. In the proceedings from a recent conference on "Assessment and Equity," Mary Lee Smith of Arizona State University reported on the progress of Arizona's Student Assessment Program (ASAP). "Whether they will take the high road—undertaking the time-consuming and expensive professional and curriculum development work necessary to teach toward ambitious standards and a thinking curriculum—or the low road—finding the tricks to inflate scores—remains to be seen." Smith discussed instances they had observed of "dis-integrating," in which "teachers who lack a thorough understanding of constructivist teaching take what was designed to be an integrated unit, break it into bits, and teach toward mastery of the bits."

Many curriculum designers are also still making the mistake of thinking that comprehensive coverage of a subject domain must be the goal. For many years, this has meant that topics are covered very superficially and, most often, too quickly for meaningful assimilation of the concepts. This makes learning particularly difficult for students who are new to

English or whose home culture is different from that of the school. What we have come to recognize is that more in-depth study must be an integral part of the "thinking curriculum." As Howard Gardner (Brandt, 1993), who has written about "multiple intelligences," has stated, "Another obvious implication, one that only a few people have begun to take seriously, is that we've got to do a lot fewer things in school. The greatest enemy of understanding is coverage. As long as you are determined to cover everything, you actually ensure that most kids are not going to understand. You've got to take enough time to get kids deeply involved in something so they can think about it in lots of different ways and apply it—not just at school but at home and on the street and so on."

Lastly, we want to caution against trivializing aspects of the curriculum by adding a few problem-solving activities, science experiments, math manipulatives, or exercises with a multicultural bent. The generally well-known Foxfire curriculum is based on a philosophy that involves sustained exposure to topics in an environment characterized by independent student research and inquiry regarding various aspects of culture. Eliot Wigginton (1992), the educator/philosopher responsible for Foxfire, points out that "the fact that time is so precious has led many educators to conclude that there simply is not enough room in the curriculum for subjects with a cultural focus. This belief has sometimes led to contrived half-remedies from well-meaning teachers: word problems with an Appalachian slant in a math class ("If three dogs tree a mother bear and two cubs . . .") or American history taught through a text revised to acknowledge a contribution or two from each of several ethnic groups." This inclination toward developing a curriculum that is "multicultural" by adding insignificant details about foods and festivals, or other surface cultural details, will not allow students to think deeply about the meaning of cultural and linguistic differences.

Recommendations for effective instructional practices designed to provide access to learning for as many students as possible and to prepare them for open-ended and performance-based assessments are remarkably consistent and focused. They essentially converge on several points:

1. Constructing knowledge based on experiences, conceptions, and opportunities for first-hand inquiry should be the goal of instruction. Students must be deeply engaged in hands-on developmental work.

When students engage in inquiry activities that require them to think deeply and for which there is no single best approach to learning, it helps them develop problem-solving and other reasoning strategies that serve them well in every opportunity for learning that occurs both in and outside of school. As they engage in such activities, they learn to pose questions, interact with other individuals and with resources, and extend their learning in ways that could not be anticipated. These situations allow them to bring their own culturally-based experiences and perspectives to the learning.

2. *Teachers must design instructional experiences that accommodate the fact that students from different linguistic and cultural backgrounds use language in different ways.*

Villegas (1991) points out that even when students and teachers speak the same language, they sometimes have different ways of using it. Researchers often point out the discontinuity that minority children experience in the use of language at home and in school. When such is the case, children's prior experience is of little use because their "established ways of using language and making sense of the world are deemed unacceptable in the classroom." Several examples from researchers who have explored this issue highlight a few of these differences that would not be immediately recognized by the classroom teacher.

Shirley Brice Heath (1983) conducted an extensive study of language use in the Carolinas. She became interested in the use of questions at home and in school, particularly in an African-American working-class community. She found the children in Trackton were immersed in language, but adults did not regard them as "legitimate conversational partners until they were old enough to be competent communicants." Trackton adults tended to use directives rather than questions; in the classroom, however, the children were expected to participate in conversations with the teacher frequently. Questions dominated classroom exchanges, and directives were used far less frequently than in the community. Rather than asking "real" or analogical questions, the teachers most often asked "test" questions, that is, questions that required students to display academic knowledge (for example, What is this color?) (Villegas, 1990). It is not surprising that students did not respond as expected.

In a study conducted by Phillips (1972, 1983) on the Warm Springs Indian Reservation in central Oregon, the researcher confirmed what teachers observed—that the children were silent in school. She found, however, that the children were most reluctant to talk during whole class or group lessons directed by the teacher, which required students to speak out individually in front of their peers. When the children were asked to work independently, they occasionally volunteered to speak to the teacher, and when students controlled interactions as in small groups, the Native American children spoke freely with their peers. These differences in patterns of participation resulted from the instructional format. Such sociolinguistic behavior differences will also result from assessment formats that do not accommodate culturally-determined differences. And since the choice of instructional format may adversely affect children's opportunity to learn, these differences will also influence how well children are able to perform on assessments.

3. Instructional strategies carefully designed to bridge the gap between the children's home and school experiences should be used.

Students whose cultural socialization has conditioned them to learning in informal, cooperative, and collaborative styles should not be placed in situations that are highly structured, individualistic, and competitive. Those who prefer a tactical or an affective approach to learning will be placed at an unfair disadvantage by being exposed constantly to curricula that emphasize visual activities and cognitive content. Their achievement on any given academic task is as much a function of their ability to master the performance style as it is an indication of their intellectual competence (Gay, 1988).

Villegas (1991) identifies a number of specific examples of strategies designed to bridge the gap. She cites one that is often mentioned in discussions of multicultural education: The Kamehameha Early Education Project (KEEP). Because observations of native Hawaiian children in their homes revealed that they were adept learners, despite the fact that they seemed unresponsive to classroom instruction, KEEP researchers introduced more culturally sensitive strategies. According to Au et al. (1985) and Gallimore (1985), a collaborative orientation derived from the structure of family life and from early socialization practices involving siblings as caretakers led to the establishment of peer learning centers in the classrooms. As used in the project, the centers encourage children to help one another with academic tasks. A second example of cultural accommodation in KEEP was the use of a "talk story," a recurrent speech event in Hawaiian culture, during reading lessons. This strategy of collective turn-taking allows students to build joint responses during storytime, either among themselves or together with the teacher. These strategies have worked very well for native Hawaiian students.

The San Diego Project is another that uses culturally responsive pedagogy (Villegas, 1991). While the everyday experiences of minority children from low-income backgrounds are often considered unsafe terrain for educators to explore, and thus are often avoided, in this project the introduction of community-related themes into instruction (even though these themes may appear controversial at times) has increased students' motivation to learn.

Finally, the success of Marva Collins with African-American students is worth noting (Villegas, 1991). Collins' approach has been well documented in scholarly journals and in the press. As reported by Hollins (1982), the climate of Marva Collins' classroom is similar to that found in the traditional African-American family setting. Both the classroom and the family foster "cooperation, flexibility, collective responsibility, autonomy, and strong adult leadership." Collins' classroom also evidences the use of interaction patterns commonly found in the African-American church. These patterns include "choral and responsive reading, audience participation, use of analogies, and the identification of a moral or personal message from the passage read." By engaging students in culturally relevant learning, Marva Collins has improved her pupils' academic performance, and she has helped the students maintain and strengthen their sense of identity and personal worth. (See Figure 3.6 for five cultural criteria that Villegas has identified for researchers to consider when developing performance assessments for beginning teachers.)

FIGURE 3.6
Cultural Criteria for Instructional Planning*

1. Teachers should have an attitude of respect for cultural differences, a belief that all students are capable of learning, and a sense of efficacy.

2. Teachers must know the cultural resources their students bring to class, and they must be aware of the culture of their own classrooms.

3. Teachers should implement an enriched curriculum for all students.

4. Teachers must build bridges between the instructional content, materials and methods, and the cultural backgrounds of the students in their classrooms.

   - Establishing links between instructional materials and student cultural experiences.

   - Varying instruction to accommodate students' cultural differences.

   - Promoting skills in interactive decision-making.

   - Creating a classroom climate that encourages students to express themselves.

   - Managing the classroom in culturally sensitive ways.

5. Teachers should be aware of cultural differences when evaluating students.

---

* Villegas, A. M. (1991, September). Culturally responsive pedagogy for the 1990s and beyond.   Educational Testing Service.

As does Villegas, Bartolomé (1994) refers to instructional strategies that bridge the gap between the student's home culture and the culture of the school as "culturally responsive instruction: teaching approaches and strategies that recognize and build on culturally different ways of learning, behaving, and using language in the classroom." Bartolomé argues convincingly that innovative instructional strategies that have become well-known and have been successful at creating "humanizing learning environments where students cease to be treated as objects and yet receive academically rigorous instruction" may produce negative results if implemented uncritically. She cites Lisa Delpit's (1986, 1988) important research as evidence of this fact. Delpit examined the process writing approach as used with African-American students and found that many students had quite negative reactions to the pedagogical style:

> I didn't feel she was teaching us anything. She wanted us to correct each other's papers and we were there to learn from her. She didn't teach anything, absolutely nothing.

> Maybe they're trying to learn what Black folks knew all the time. We understand how to improvise, how to express ourselves creatively. When I'm in a classroom, I'm not looking for that. I'm looking for structure, the more formal language (1988, p. 287).

Most current literature on effective teaching practices stresses the need to build on students' knowledge bases or on their "prior knowledge." Several researchers (Anyon, 1988; Diaz et al., 1986; Moll, 1986; Oaks, 1986) have found, however, that teachers of affluent White students are much more likely to use this common-sense approach than teachers of students from "marginalized populations." Operating on the prevalent "deficit model," it is probable that teachers of working-class, poor, or ethnic minority students see these students as lacking the "necessary cultural capital" to use as a basis for extended learning. The failure to build on students' knowledge base is a failure to recognize that learning can only occur when students are able to access prior knowledge and link it to new information. By acknowledging student's existing language and culture, we are better able to humanize the educational experience of children who often feel dehumanized and disempowered in schools.

4. Teachers should use scaffolding and other strategic teaching approaches to support student learning.

Many authors have used the phrase, "strategic teaching," over the last decade or more to describe an approach by which students are explicitly taught strategies that help them monitor their own learning. Various methods are designed to "prepare independent and metacognitively aware students" (Bartolomé, 1994): use of frames and graphic organizers, scaffolding, question generation, predicting and testing predictions, paraphrasing, and several others. While much of the initial research on strategic teaching was conducted with English monolingual mainstream students, recent studies have demonstrated that such teaching improves the reading comprehension and use of effective learning strategies of linguistic minority students (Avelar La Salle, 1991; Chamot, 1983; Hernandez, 1991; O'Malley & Chamot, 1990; Reyes; as reported in Bartolomé, 1994). Some of these studies show that the students' use of effective learning strategies in their native language improved and that they "were able to transfer or apply their knowledge of specific learning strategies and text structure to English reading texts" (Bartolomé, 1994, p. 187), this despite limited English proficiency.

"Scaffolding" refers to a process of providing a set of supports constructed for students that enable them to move through related experiences from the home toward the demands of the school and is one example of a teaching strategy that can help students gain access to learning or information. Scaffolding can be considered another way to bridge the gap between home and school, but it is also a general way to help students approach an instructional or assessment task by providing related information, asking questions, having students describe their thinking up to the point of confusion, using visual or tactile aids, making useful comparisons, and so forth.

5. The materials, approaches, and types of questions used in the classroom should be varied and allow students to respond in ways that accommodate cultural differences.

There is no question that learning to read is a desirable educational goal, but no one set of reading materials and methods is equally effective with all students. It is imperative that these materials and methods be ethnically and culturally diversified in order to make opportunities to learn to read equivalent or comparable across different groups of students. Such diversification of the content, context, and techniques used to facilitate learning will improve the academic success of a broader spectrum of students, develop knowledge and appreciation of cultural pluralism, and better equalize social, economic, and political opportunities among ethnic and cultural groups (Gay, 1988).

Teachers' heavy reliance on "display" or "test-type" questions seems to work to the disadvantage of many working-class and minority students socialized in language communities where little emphasis is placed upon asking children to display information for its own sake. Also in these communities, "stating the obvious" or "saying what everyone knows" is not encouraged because it is perceived as having no communicative purpose (Nelson-Barber and Meier, 1990).

6. The ideal situation for language learning consists of instructional activities that allow children to interact freely in the course of working on mutually involving tasks that invite discussion, questioning, responding, and so forth (Wong-Fillmore & Valadez, 1986).

In all classrooms, but especially in those where language is being learned or where the cultural environment is novel to students, it is important that there be a high level of interaction and cooperative activity. In his review of the literature on effective instructional practices used with linguistically and culturally diverse students, Garcia (1991) found that "functional communication between teacher and students and among fellow students was emphasized more than might be expected in a regular classroom. Teachers were constantly checking with students to verify the clarity of assignments and the students' roles in those assignments. Classrooms were characterized by a high, sometimes even noisy, level of communication emphasizing student collaboration on small group projects organized around 'learning centers'." An analysis of instructional events in literacy and math indicated that teachers in Latino language minority classrooms organized instruction in such a way that students were required to interact with each other utilizing collaborative learning techniques. It was during student-student interactions that most higher order cognitive and linguistic discourse was observed." As a result of her work on tracking practices, Oakes (1986) suggests that classroom changes in task structures, student interaction (especially cooperative learning), and evaluation processes are particularly promising as alternatives to tracking because they can "alter teachers' and students' conceptions of the intellectual ability of low-achieving students."

Alignment of Curricular Content and Outcome Measures

If new performance-based assessments point at more challenging learning goals for all students, they may ameliorate some of this source of inequality. However, this will be true only to the extent that teachers who serve these students are able to teach in the ways demanded by the assessments—that is, in ways that support the development of higher order thinking and performance skills and in ways that diagnose and build upon individual learners' strengths and needs (Darling-Hammond, 1994).

Matching curriculum and instructional practices to the form of performance-based assessments must have primacy in our development efforts and deliberations. Many educators are anticipating positive changes in the design of curriculum and instructional strategies to result from the use of the new assessments. But the potential effect of alignment, or "overlap" as Lauren and Daniel Resnick refer to it, cannot be overestimated, and it is essential that educators at all levels—from classroom teachers to assessment developers—develop an awareness of this connection and support the design of instructional practices that will result in greater alignment.

One way to characterize a desired outcome of educational reform is that it be more learner-centered. To gather the kind of learner-centered information that is required to approach this goal, there must be "extensive involvement in looking at children and their work from many different vantage points" (Darling-Hammond, 1994). Schools are more often characterized by instructional routines that allow minimal variation of approach and a limited range of options in solving learning problems. In order to accommodate the culturally- and linguistically-based learning styles of a diverse population of students, a concept of learning must be adopted that is reflected in much more adaptation of instruction to individual students—their talents, background experiences, and interests.

It should be obvious that the criteria we use for new forms of assessment that are designed to gather the most accurate information about students' learning should be the same criteria that we use for instructional programs designed to optimize student learning. "Whether we like it or not, what is taught and what is tested are intimately related. No serious possibility exists for creating accountability tests that will not eventually influence what is taught and how it is taught in the schools" (Resnick, 1989).

Use of Assessment Data for Instructional Decisions

> . . . changes in the forms of assessment are unlikely to enhance equity unless we change the ways in which assessments are used as well: from sorting mechanisms to diagnostic supports; from external monitors of performance to locally-generated tools for inquiring deeply into teaching and learning; and from purveyors of sanctions for those already underserved to levers for equalizing resources and enhancing learning opportunities (Darling-Hammond, 1994).

The development of new forms of assessment must embrace the possibility that the rich information about student learning that is gathered will be used to shape teaching in ways that will be more effective for students; otherwise the outcomes of education will not be changed. The goal must be for these assessments to support better teaching and transform schooling, particularly for students who are traditionally underserved.

Student strengths, interests, and talents are not commonly visible on standardized tests. Performance assessments should illuminate possible "entry points" (Kornhaber and Gardner, 1993) for instruction that will build on children's developed intelligences and extend them into new areas of learning. This approach stands in stark contrast with the more common practice of using the results of standardized tests to misinterpret the behavior of minority students in ways that lead them to underestimate the true academic potential of such students. These judgments often have profound and long-lasting effects on students' lives. "What is needed instead are culturally informed diagnoses of the various performance problems diverse students have in learning, thorough understanding of how they learn, and carefully designed programs of instruction that respond to these needs, preferences, and learning deficiencies" (Gay, 1988).

Access and Equity

The development of "opportunity-to-learn" standards has been part of the national conversation on standards and alternative assessments. Those who support the development of such standards in tandem with the development of content and performance standards do so because they are concerned that setting "high standards for all students" will merely result in raising the bar without providing those students most in need with the necessary support to clear the bar. In short, they are afraid that traditionally underserved students will not have access to a curriculum and an instructional program that will allow them to meet "high standards." This fear is not without basis. The literature describing the typical educational program for low-performing, minority, or poor children is extensive; it describes instructional practices consistent with an "impoverished curriculum." The misuse of basic skills tests have had unfortunate effects on students placed in the lowest tracks or in remedial programs— disproportionately low-income and minority students. These students are most apt to experience instruction geared only to multiple-choice tests. They work at low cognitive levels on test-oriented tasks that are profoundly disconnected from the skills they need to learn. Rarely are they given the opportunity to talk about what they know, to read real books, to write, or to construct and solve problems in mathematics, science, or other subjects (Darling-Hammond, 1994).

Other researchers have found that instruction for low-ability students generally has less academic orientation; classroom activities lack clear purpose and focus; material is introduced less clearly and covered at a slower pace; objectives are lower and also less likely to be explained to the students; and academic standards are vague and less rigorously applied. Textbooks that are used often give less information, pose fewer questions for students to think about, emphasize facts, and typically do not mention potentially controversial topics (Anyon, 1981; Oakes, 1986). In reading, the focus is often on pronunciation and decoding; the unit of instruction is most often a word or word part; meaning is represented only in the form of responses to literal recall questions. These students experience reading as a mechanical activity and most often fail to make any connection to their personal lives. These instructional practices tend to accentuate any inequality in skills and knowledge between these and more advanced students. The overrepresentation of minority children in low-level tracks has thus been a cause for considerable alarm.

Low teacher salaries and poor working conditions are enough to ensure a steady supply of unqualified teachers in poor districts, and low-income and minority students are routinely taught by the least-experienced and least-prepared teachers. Unlike programs designed for "gifted and talented" students, programs for "disdvantaged" students are often staffed with paraprofessionals or aides who may only have a high school education. In areas of the country where bilingual education is a required part of the instructional plan, the shortage of qualified bilingual teachers has resulted in a pervasive use of bilingual paraprofessionals. In many cases, they are the ones providing most of the instruction for English language learners. From a policy perspective, the single greatest source of educational inequity is a disparity in the availability and distribution of highly qualified teachers.

If we are to ensure that all students have adequate opportunities to learn, it will be necessary to enhance the capacity of all teachers. This means that teacher education policies must ensure that all teachers have a stronger understanding of how children learn and develop, how assessment can be used to evaluate what they know and how they learn, how a variety of curricular and instructional strategies can address their needs, and how changes in school and classroom organization can support their growth and achievement (Darling-Hammond, 1990, 1994).

Wolf et al. (1991) suggest that new modes of assessment may provide one means for exposing the abilities of less traditionally skilled students by giving a place to world knowledge, social processes, and a great variety of excellence. They further suggest that this may be possible if assessments are used to "unify, rather than stratify, access to knowledge and strong educational practices. For example, teachers writing Pittsburgh's Shakespeare exam are insisting that all students, not only the best and the brightest, be enrolled in a literature course that permits them to think and interpret what they read. And clearly the hope is that it draws instruction in its wake, so that the exam is not the first occasion when students are asked to read and think like actors and directors."

Measuring achievement without knowing the instructional conditions under which achievement occurs poses a serious dilemma. Studies of opportunities to learn have, however, only taken place in low-stakes environments, not in situations where schools are held accountable for providing those opportunities (Burstein, 1993). Aschbacher (1994), for example, in reviewing portfolios for a program known as *Humanitas,* found that the portfolios showed a direct relation between the kind of assignments teachers gave their students and what students learned. Students' work showed more higher-order thinking skills and interdisciplinary connections when their class assignments *required* them to make those connections and to use complex thinking. Recall the guidelines for accountability assessments offered by the Resnicks and presented in Figure 3.7: "You get what you assess; you do not get what you do not assess." At this point, we can only hope that this will eventually be the case, but as educators, we will need to do all we can to make it a reality.

FIGURE 3.7

Guidelines for Planning Equitable Assessments*

1. **You get what you assess.** Educators will teach to tests if the tests matter in their own or their students' lives.

2. **You do not get what you do not assess.** If the goals of solving complex problems or writing extended essays are educationally important, these activities need to be sampled directly in an assessment program aimed at encouraging improved instruction.

3. **Build assessments toward which you want educators to teach.** Assessments must be designed so that when teachers do the natural thing—that is, prepare their students to perform well—they will exercise the kinds of abilities and develop the kinds of skill and knowledge that are the real goals of educational reform.

*Resnick, L. & Resnick, D. (1991). Assessing the thinking curriculum: New tools for educational reform. In B.R. Gifford & M.C. O'Connor (Eds.), *Future assessments: Changing view of aptitude, achievement, and instruction.* Boston: Kluwer Academic Publishers.

One final issue related to access and equity that we think is important but is often skirted in the literature has to do with the acquisition of power and options for minority students. Lisa Delpit (1988) is one researcher who has tackled it more directly. She advocates changes in school that would reflect cultural awareness, a belief that all students can learn, and the use of students' communicative styles in teaching—as do many others. Delpit acknowledges issues of power and the fact that students must acquire the mainstream culture because it provides a means of access to power. This means acquiring the communicative codes and linguistic forms of those in power. At the same time, she emphasizes that "students should be taught to value ethnic distinctions and be helped to learn that the culture of the group in power, while instrumental in our society, is not intrinsically superior to the cultures of the less powerful minority groups." Along this same vein, Gay (1988) identifies the real focus of equity as the "equivalency of effect potential, quality status, and significance of learning opportunities. . . . More of the same for all kinds of students will not work."

Larger Issues

As we did in Chapter 2, we feel that it's important here to present some larger issues that are related to curricular design. Henderson (1992) highlights some of these issues by posing some key questions: "(But) how many people desire collaborative empowerment to solve common social problems? How many people trust in the viability of participative democracy or want to stretch their ideological horizons?"

In essence, these larger issues emerge from the politics of difference. The changes in school processes related to instruction and assessment that we are calling for in this book require changes in the fundamental belief system that forms the basis for education. We and the many educators we cite seek the establishment of an educational system that will provide conditions for teachers, students, and others to "learn the knowledge and skills necessary to live in a manner in which they have the opportunity to govern and shape society rather than being consigned to its margins" (Giroux, 1992), a system that will not, as Cummins (1986) asserts, use assessment to play the "role of legitimizing the disabling of minority students." We must recognize and acknowledge how we have "disabled" minority students by accepting over time a deficit view of these students. The notion of disadvantagement is disturbing because it situates the cause of school failure in individuals rather than in social systems—where it belongs or must be examined. Students who are members of certain demographic groups are, to be certain, at some disadvantage when they go to school, but it is not something inherent. It is a transactional disadvantage: they are disadvantaged *with regard to* the educational system. As a result, we have designed programs to "compensate" for their deficits or to "intervene" in a cycle of disadvantagement.

Secada (1992) also decries the tendency to transform the description of a social profile/problem into predictive and causal statements:

> For example, it is one thing to note that Hispanics from lower-class backgrounds do not, as a group, perform as well in mathematics as do middle-class Hispanics, or even as well as Whites who are similarly situated. It is another thing, however, to argue that being Hispanic from a lower-SES background places one at risk of such an event; that is to say, mem-

bership in a group is predictive of a certain event. It is an even stronger claim to argue that membership in a group causes such an event . . . The prediction that should be made, if there is one, is that *unless we modify the educational experiences that students from these backgrounds receive, we will fail to educate them as fully as we believe they can be educated* (p. 640).

It is important to consider, both historically and internationally, how power structures have affected the learning of students from minority groups. Many researchers have reviewed the patterns of minority group failure from an international perspective. An oft-cited example of negative influence is the academic failure of Finnish students in Sweden, where they are a low-status group, compared to their success in Australia, where they are regarded as a high-status group (Troike, 1978). Ogbu (1978) also reports that the outcast Burakumin perform poorly in Japan but just as well as other Japanese students in the United States. These examples serve to teach us that school failure does not occur in minority groups that do not perceive themselves—and are not perceived by others—as inferior. Failure for minority groups does not occur where they do not feel alienated from the dominant culture. The failure of a low-status group to succeed results from a multitude of factors that includes limited access to economic and educational resources. By contrast, students who are empowered by their school experiences develop the ability, confidence, and motivation to succeed academically. They participate competently in instruction as a result of having developed a confident cultural identity as well as appropriate school-based knowledge and interactional structures (Cummins, 1983).

A number of other persuasive writers (Paulo Freire, 1987; Bartolomé, 1994) have exhorted educators to develop "political clarity" in order to be able to adopt and modify teaching strategies that respect and challenge learners from diverse cultural groups. "A teacher's political clarity will not necessarily compensate for structural inequalities that students face outside the classroom; however, teachers can, to the best of their ability, help their students deal with injustices encountered inside and outside the classroom" (Bartolomé, 1994, p. 178). To accomplish such an important goal, teachers can create heterogeneous learning groups with the intention of modifying low-status roles of students[11], engage students in explicit discussions about their experiences, and otherwise create "democratic learning environments" where students become accustomed to being treated as competent. "I believe that the students, once accustomed to the rights and responsibilities of full citizenship in the classroom, will come to expect respectful treatment and authentic estimation in other contexts" (Bartolomé, *Ibid.*). Bartolomé's use of the phrase, "authentic estimation," brings us back to the consideration of assessment. It should not be difficult to see that if students are not given full opportunity to enhance and demonstrate their competence as learners that assessment tools will continue to be tools of oppression.

We close this discussion of larger issues with the passionate words of two authors who eloquently describe the educational and social goals we must pursue in the interest of fairness and justice:

> To restructure we must first look deeply at the goals that we set for our children and the beliefs that we have about them. Once we are on the right track there, then we must turn our attention to the delivery systems, as we have begun to do. Untracking is right. Mainstreaming is right. Decentralization is right. Cooperative learning is right. Technology access for all is right. Multiculturalism is right. But none of these approaches or strategies will mean anything if the fundamental belief system does not fit the new structures that are being created (Hilliard, 1991).

> Since the days of De Tocqueville, Americans have wondered how to deal with the conflicts between individualism and the drive to conform. They have wondered how to reconcile the impassioned voices of cultures not yet part of the whole with the requirements of conformity, how not to lose the integrity of those voices in the process, how not to allow the drive to conformity to determine what happens at the end. . . . Something life-affirming in diversity must be discovered and rediscovered, as what is held in common becomes always more many-faceted—open and inclusive, drawn to untapped possibility (Greene, 1993).

Endnotes

1. In this case, we are using "excellence" to mean "quality"; others use it to refer to outcome measures, as indicated in the quote from Gay which follows.

2. Miller and Seller (1985) refer to this "curriculum position" as the "Transmission" model. From this perspective, the goal of education is to transmit "facts, skills, and values to students," and knowledge is seen as fixed and unchanging.

3. Evidence to support this notion is found in a considerable body of research. Evidence exists, for example, that indicates that adults actually learn a language faster than children (Snow & Haefnagel-Hoehle, 1978). Since older learners have mastered most of the language mechanisms in their first language as adults, language researchers believe that adults can frequently access abilities learned in their native language, like grammar comprehension or life experience, to master a second language. Researchers have also discovered that

bilinguals tend to be especially adept at tasks that require metacognition (Diaz, 1985; Hakuta & Diaz, 1985).

4. The "Accelerated Schools" is a model of school reform developed by Henry Levin, Stanford University.

5. In fact, our society, itself, is at risk if we cannot soon muster the will and sense of urgency to confront the multiple causes of school failure.

6. We also submit that it is important to establish a multicultural program even when a school's student body is not diverse. All students in our nation need to grow into an understanding of cultural diversity and the richness and complexity it adds to our society.

7. The Holmes Group is a consortium of nearly 100 American research universities "committed to making our programs of teacher preparation more rigorous and connected—to liberal arts education, to research on learning and teaching, and to wise practice in the schools" They use the term, "Professional Development Schools," to describe the schools they envision (*Tomorrow's Schools*, p. vii).

8. Franz Boas, *Race, Language, and Culture*, New York: Macmillan, 1948; Ruth Benedict, *Patterns of Culture*, Boston: Houghton Mifflin, 1934.

9. It may be important to note that: (1) purposes range from accountability and reporting, to sorting and ranking, and to a wide range of instructional uses; (2) these are not the same in the educational system of every country.

10. See the discussion at end of this chapter (under "Larger Issues") on the use of the term, "disadvantaged."

11. Elizabeth Cohen (1986), for example, devised an approach referred to as "complex instruction" by which teachers create learning conditions where students working in groups can demonstrate their knowledge and expertise and thus enable themselves and others to see them as capable and competent.

Commentary

The Effects of Educators' Attitudes on the Assessment and Instruction of Culturally and Linguistically Diverse Students

Virginia Gonzalez
The University of Arizona

Drs. Estrin and Farr present as their major conclusion in this chapter that changes in the educational system in our assessment and instructional practices cannot take place if an attitudinal change in educators does not occur. They include in this attitudinal change needed for educators to gain awareness of their belief systems, prior knowledge about developmental and learning constructs, and cultural and linguistic differences in their students. An attitudinal change can be stimulated by exposing educators to new educational models stemming from a multicultural/bilingual paradigm through formal training in higher education institutions, and by engaging educators in "hands-on" developmental experiences related to constructivistic perspectives for learning. Then, this chapter builds a bridge between cognitive psychology and bilingual/multicultural education, a framework that is very appropriate for both educating teachers and culturally and linguistically diverse (CLD) students. Thus, the major contribution and issue raised in this chapter refers to the application of concepts stemming from (1) a constructivistic perspective within cognitive psychology, including developmental and schema theory; and (2) a pluralistic curriculum linking performance-based assessment with instruction derived from a bilingual/multicultural educational perspective. In addition, I consider that this chapter proposes an educational psychology perspective with major theoretical and applied educational implications for the field of bilingual/multicultural education.

From a constructivistic perspective, learning is considered to be an active process as children construct connections between their prior cultural and linguistic experiences within their minority family environments with new experiences encountered within the mainstream school culture. Within a constructivistic classroom, educators function as mediators and facilitators for students to develop their higher-level thinking processes such as problem-solving, conceptual critical thinking, and learning strategies. Then, instructors need to use scaffolding to help CLD students construct connections between their two cultural and linguistic worlds, encompassing their minority family and mainstream cultural environments. Moreover, the use of performance-based assessments allow educators to be active agents of change of the educational system. That is, educators can use evaluations as integrated experiences for CLD students within the curriculum, and they can respect individual differences. Presently, more and more classroom teachers are being integrated into the assessment process of CLD students by becoming members of interdisciplinary assessment teams. Teachers can open a whole new window for assessment into "real-life" performance at school. It is an absurdity to think that within a psychological typical assessment situation, an evaluator can get "a complete picture" of the CLD child after administering a battery of standardized tests during three or five hours. Teachers and parents can provide valuable and meaningful information about the performance of the child across different sociocultural contexts and periods of time that creates "a dynamic videotape" of the CLD child.

Moreover, to have a dynamic and connected view of assessment and instruction is important as the CLD child is continuously adapting when using assimilation and accommodation processes of learning. Learners are continuously interpreting and re-interpreting experiences lived within their two cultural and linguistic worlds in order to construct meaningful concepts. Whenever the CLD child encounters an experience that is similar across cultural, linguistic, and conceptual symbolic representations of the world, she will just transfer prior conceptual knowledge from either the first (L1) or second (L2) languages and cultures. For instance, when the curriculum includes content such as vocabulary learning in English in relation to meaningful contexts, the Hispanic Spanish dominant child will transfer her knowledge of linguistic gender for some words common to both languages for animate referents (for example, the use of two different words for denoting linguistic gender such as "hen" and "rooster"— *gallina* and *gallo*, the Spanish equivalents). In contrast, when cultural, linguistic, and conceptual dimensions of representations of lived experiences of a CLD child differ in both worlds, then he will need to construct a new concept that will be related only to his L1 and L2 and cultures. For instance, when the curriculum points to the concept of verb conjugations encompassing difference tenses related to temporal concepts in English, the child whose L1 and culture is Chinese will need to construct new concepts. This child will begin learning as he is immersed within the mainstream American school culture the social conventions and context of use of these new linguistic rules in relation to the concept of time. Furthermore, bilingual developmental programs that use both L1 and L2 and cultures as a tool or method for instruction will stimulate the CLD child to construct conceptual connections for transferring prior knowledge, as well as to construct new culturally and linguistically embedded concepts. Thus, the characteristics used by Drs. Estrin and Farr in this chapter for describing high-quality bilingual developmental programs lead to positive influences of bilingualism on cognition, such as metalinguistic awareness (the ability to think about language), creativity, and additive bilingualism.

From a bilingual/multicultural perspective, Drs. Estrin and Farr highlight in this chapter the importance of high educational standards for assuring excellence in the education of all CLD students, and equity for meeting the individual needs of all CLD students. Thus, equality in education does not mean to treat every minority and majority student in the same way, but to respect and meet idiosyncratic strengths and weaknesses when designing individualized educational programs. In order to be of high quality for CLD students, the curriculum needs to use appropriate teaching methods, educational materials, and especially have an underlying philosophical model that values diversity. That is the reason why teachers need to understand and believe in the theoretical and philosophical assumptions and principles based on which multicultural/bilingual educational models and derived educational programs are developed. Drs. Estrin and Farr refer to the negative effects of misconceptions held by teachers on the educational services that CLD students receive. For instance, most in-service teachers, even with years of experience, have a misunderstanding of the construct of intelligence. It is a common misunderstanding to believe that intelligence equals language development, and that therefore a limited English proficient child cannot be gifted because his verbal performance is delayed in comparison to monolingual peers. Another common misconception held by teachers is that intelligence equals the IQ score obtained from administering standardized tests to CLD students. Actually, intelligence is a socially constructed concept that encompasses cultural and linguistic ways of thinking within a particular sociohistorical environment. Moreover, intelligence standardized tests pretend to measure innate abilities connected with genetic and racial factors, but this assumption is a fallacy, given that most of these tests measure learning within a particular cultural and linguistic environment. Thus, learning influences the development of our innate learning potential and the acquired knowledge that results from the actualization of this potential.

Thus, to make a long story short, lack of knowledge of educators of theoretical and methodological issues related to major developmental constructs, such as intelligence, results in false attributions made by educators. Two examples are the misconception that "learning problems" are due to internal causes, and the belief that psychological assessment using standardized testing can identify the "genuine learning potential, or lack of it" of a CLD child. This lack of knowledge results not only in false attributions, but also in prejudices, stereotypical perceptions, mislabeling, misdiagnosing, oppression, racism, discrimination, and blaming victims for their learning problems. When, in fact, educators suffering from attitudinal problems are the ones who have a "teaching problem," due to their lack of knowledge and understanding of what it means to come from culturally and linguistically different backgrounds. Model educators are the ones who take responsibility for changing the teaching situation and their own attitudes in order to become advocates of CLD students. These model educators are themselves good learners and thinkers who can use moral reasoning for understanding the "subjectivity" involved in the process of knowledge construction. As stated by Estrin and Farr in this chapter, "Teachers need to create a community of learners that involves teaching for understanding" (p. 83).

In summary, teachers who have positive attitudes toward CLD students can understand the value of performance-based assessment for linking assessment with instruction, as they need to collect evidence for acting as advocates for their students. As stated by Estrin and Farr in this chapter, "We need to measure thinking in action" embedded in the curriculum activities because "the problem of assessment is really a problem of curriculum and of educational goals" (p. 92). Performance-based assessments encompass different kinds of instruments such as portfolios, problem-solving tasks, and observations; all of these are derived from the same constructivistic developmental perspective within cognitive psychology that measures individual differences and learning processes. Validity of developmentally-based instruments is increased by allowing them to follow the train of thought of CLD students in order to discover what problem-solving strategies and higher-level thinking abilities they express in their performance. That is, performance-based measurements show construct validity when used for assessing intelligence development in CLD students because the underlying constructivistic perspective considers the double interaction between internal (for example, maturation, sensitive developmental periods, potential for learning, etc.) and external (for example, curriculum, teaching methods, teachers' expectations and attitudes, parents' socioeconomic status and educational background, culture, language, etc.) factors. Moreover, when using performance-based measurements, the emphasis is placed on assessing potential for learning, which also increases the construct and concurrent and predictive validity of these instruments for CLD students. Concurrent and predictive validity are increased because classroom teachers can use performance-based assessments that generate qualitative and descriptive information directly for instructional programs especially designed for CLD students. Thus, performance-based assessments have ecological validity because they measure high-level thinking skills and learning potential by providing culturally meaningful contexts of learning for CLD students.

— ❧ —

Dr. Virginia Gonzalez is an Assistant Professor of Educational Psychology at the University of Arizona whose areas of specialization include cognitive and language development in language-minority young children and second language-learning in adults. She has been nationally recognized for her innovative research contributions to the improvement of the assessment of bilingual Hispanic children by the National Association for Bilingual Education in 1992 and by the American Psychological Association in 1993. She is has also been honored with a Certificate of Appreciation from the National Honor Society in Psychology for Community and Junior Colleges for her outstanding contributions and mentoring of ethnic minority students in the field of psychology. Dr. Gonzalez is a frequent presenter at national conferences, has published numerous articles and has written two books to be published in 1996.

References

Au, K., Tharp, R.G., Crowell, D.C., Jordan, C., Speidel, G.E., & Calkins, R. (1985). The role of research in the development of a successful reading program. In J. Osborn, P.T. Wilson, & R.C. Anderson (Eds.), *Reading education: Foundations for a literate America,* Lexington, MA: Heath, 272-289.

Banks, J. (Spring, 1991). Multicultural literacy and curriculum reform. *Educational Horizons,* Vol. 69, No.3.

Bartolomé, L. (1994, Summer). Beyond the methods fetish: toward a humanizing pedagogy. *Harvard Educational Review Vol. 64,* No. 2.

Brandt, R. (1993, April). On teaching for understanding: A conversation with Howard Gardner. *Educational Leadership.*

Brooks, J.G. & Brooks, M.G. (1993). *In Search of Understanding: The case for constructivist classrooms.* Alexandria, VA: Association for Supervision and Curriculum Development.

Burstein, L. (1993). Validating national curriculum indicators: A conceptual overview of the RAND/CRESST NSF project. Paper presented at the annual meeting of the American Educational Research Association, Atlanta, GA.

Castell, S., & Luke, A. (1987). Literacy instruction: technology and technique. *American Journal of Education, 95,* 413-440.

Cummins, J. (1982, February). Tests, achievement, and bilingual students. *NCBE Focus.* No. 9.

Cummins, J. (1986, February). Empowering minority students: A framework for intervention. *Harvard Educational Review, Vol. 56,* No. 1, pp. 18-36.

Darling-Hammond, L. (1994). Performance-based assessment and educational equity. *Harvard Educational Review,* Vol. 64, No. 1.

Delpit, L. (1986, November). Skills and other dilemmas of a progressive Black educator. *Harvard Educational Review.* Vol. 56, 4.

Delpit, L. (1988). The silenced dialogue: Power and pedagogy in educating other people's children. *Harvard Educational Review, Vol. 58,* No. 3, 280-298.

Delpit, L. (1990). The silenced dialogue: Power and pedagogy in educating other people's children. In *Facing racism in education,* edited by N. Hidalgo et al. (pp. 84-102). Cambridge, MA: *Harvard Educational Review.*

Diaz, R. (1986). Bilingual cognitive development: addressing three gaps in current research. *Child Development, 56,* 1376-1388.

Duckworth, E. (1986, November). Teaching as research. *Harvard Educational Review, Vol. 56,* No. 4, 481-495.

Duckworth, E. (1991, February). Twenty-four, forty-two, and I love you: Keeping it complex. *Harvard Educational Review,* Vol. 61, 1.

Eisner, E., Ed. (1985). Aesthetic modes of knowing. *Learning and teaching the ways of knowing, 84th yearbook of the National Society for the Study of Education.* Chicago: University of Chicago Press, pp. 23-36.

Ferdman, B. (1990, May). Literacy and cultural identity. *Harvard Educational Review,* Vol. 60, No. 2.

Freire, P. (1987). Letter to North-American teachers. In I. Shor (Ed.), *Freire for the classroom.* Portsmouth, NJ: Boynton/Cook.

Gallimore, R. (1985, May). The accommodation of instruction to cultural differences. Paper presented at the University of California Conference on the Underachievement of Linguistic Minorities, Lake Tahoe, California.

Garcia, E. (1990). Educating teachers for language minority students. In W.R. Houston (Ed.), *Handbook of research on teacher education,* pp. 712-729. New York: Macmillan.

Garcia, G., and Pearson, P.D. (1990). Modifying reading instruction to maximize its effectiveness for "disadvantaged" students. In *Better schooling for the children of poverty: Alternatives to the conventional wisdom,* M. Knapp and P. Shields (Eds.), Office of Planning, Budget, and Evaluation, under Contract No. LC88054001.

Gay, G. (1988, August). Designing relevant curricula for diverse learners. *Education and Urban Society, Vol. 20,* No. 4.

Giroux, H. A. (1992, Summer). Language, difference, and curriculum theory: Beyond the politics of clarity. *Theory into Practice,* Vol. 31, No. 3.

Goodlad, J., Klein, M.F., & Tye, K.A. (1979). The domains of curriculum and their study. In John Goodlad, (Ed.), *Curriculum inquiry: The story of curriculum practice.* New York: McGraw-Hill.

Gordon, E. (1992). *Implications of diversity in human characteristics for authentic assessment.* Los Angeles: CRESST.

Greene, M. (1993). The passions of pluralism. *Educational Researcher*, January-February 1993.

Heath, S.B. (1983). *Ways with words: Language, life, and work in communities and classrooms.* London: Cambridge.

Henderson, J.G. (1992, Summer). Curriculum discourse and the question of empowerment. *Theory into Practice*, Vol. 31, No. 3.

Hidalgo, N.M., McDowell, C.L. and Siddle, E.V., Eds. (1990). *Facing racism in education.* Cambridge, MA: *Harvard Educational Review.*

Hilliard, A. (1991, September). Do we have the *will* to educate all children? *Educational Leadership*, September 1991.

Hollins, E. (1982). The Marva Collins story revisited: Implications for regular classroom instruction. *Journal of Teacher Education, Vol. 33*, No. 1, 37-40.

Jackson, P.W. (1986). *The practice of teaching.* New York: Teachers College Press.

Kádár-Fülop, J. (1988). Culture, writing and curriculum. In A.C. Purves (Ed.), *Writing across languages and cultures: Issues in contrastic rhetoric,* pp. 25-50. Newbury Park, CA: Sage.

Katz, L.G. (1985). Dispositions in early childhood education. *Eric/EECE Bulletin* 18, 2. Urbana, IL: ERIC Clearinghouse on Elementary and Early Childhood Education.

Knapp, M., Turnbull, B. & Shields, P. (1990, September). New directions for educating the children of poverty. *Educational Leadership.*

Kornhaber, M., & Gardner, H. (1993). *Varieties of excellence: Identifying and assessing children's talents.* New York: Columbia University, Teachers College, National Center for Restructuring Education, Schools, and Teaching.

Kwachka, P. (1994, May). Presentation at American Indian/Alaska Native Literacy and Language Roundtable, Denver.

Lakotas, I. (1976). *Proofs and refutations: The logic of mathematical discovery.* New York: Cambridge University Press.

Lau v. Nichols. (1974). 414 U.S. 563.

Michaels, S. (1981). Sharing time: Children's narrative styles and differential access to literacy. *Language in Society*, Vol. 10, 423-442.

Moll, L. (1990). Social and instructional issues in educating "disadvantaged" students. *Better schooling for the children of poverty: Alternatives to the conventional wisdom*, M. Knapp and P. Shields (Eds.), Office of Planning, Budget, and Evaluation, under Contract No. LC88054001.

Molnar, A. (1989, October). Racism in America: A continuing dilemma. *Educational Leadership* Vol. 47, No. 2: 71-72.

Nelson-Barber, S. & Meier, T. (1990, Spring). Multicultural context a key factor in teaching. *Academic Connections*, The College Board.

Nobles, W. (1990). The infusion of African and African-American content: A question of content and intent. In *Infusion of African-American content in the school curriculum*, edited by A. Hilliard et al., pp. 5-26. Morristown, N.J.: Aaron Press.

Oakes, J. (1986, September). Keeping track, Part 1: The policy and practice of curriculum inequality. *Phi Delta Kappan.*

Oakes, J. (1986, October). Keeping track, Part 2: Curriculum inequality and school reform. *Phi Delta Kappan.*

Ogbu, J. U. (1978). *Minority education and caste: The American system in cross-cultural perspective.* New York: Academic Press.

Ogbu, J. U. (1992, November). Understanding cultural diversity and learning. *Educational Researcher,* Vol. 21, No. 8.

Pang, V.O. (1990). Ethnic prejudice: Still alive and hurtful. In *Facing racism in education,* edited by N.M. Hidalgo et al., pp. 28-32. Cambridge, MA: *Harvard Educational Review.*

Phillips, S. (1983). *The invisible culture: Communication in classroom and community on the Warm Springs Indian Reservation.* New York: Longman.

Polya, G. (1954). *Induction and analogy in mathematics.* Princeton, NJ: Princeton University Press.

Ramirez, M., & B. Cox. (1980). Parenting for multiculturalism: a Mexican-American Model. In *Parenting in a multicultural society,* edited by M. Fantini et al., pp. 151-178. New York: Longman.

Resnick, L. & Resnick, D. (1991). Assessing the thinking curriculum: New tools for educational reform. In B.R. Gifford & M.C. O'Connor (Eds.), *Future assessments: Changing view of aptitude, achievement, and instruction.* Boston: Kluwer Academic Publishers.

Rogers, V. (1989). Assessing the curriculum experienced by children. *Phi Delta Kappan, Vol. 70,* 714-717.

Rothman, R. (1994, Winter). Assessment questions: Equity answers, Proceedings of the 1993 CRESST Conference. In *Evaluation comment,* UCLA: Los Angeles.

Secada, W. (1992). Race, ethnicity, social class, language, and achievement in mathematics. In Douglas A. Grouws (Ed.), *Handbook of Research on Mathematics Teaching and Learning.* New York: Macmillan.

Shields, P. (1990). A review of research on school and community influences on effective curriculum and instruction. *Better schooling for the children of poverty: Alternatives to the conventional wisdom,* M. Knapp and P. Shields (Eds.), Office of Planning, Budget, and Evaluation, under Contract No. LC88054001.

Sigel, I.E., and Cocking, R.R. (1977). *Cognitive development from childhood to adolescence: A constructivist perspective.* N.Y.: Holt, Rinehart and Winston.

Sleeter, C. (1991). *Empowerment through multicultural education.* Albany, N.Y.: S.U.N.Y. Press.

Sleeter, C. (1993, April). This curriculum is multicultural . . . isn't it? Paper presented at the American Educational Research Association, April 27, 1993.

Sleeter, C. & Grant, C. (1988). Education that is multicultural and social reconstructionist. *Making choices for multicultural education.* Columbus, OH: Merrill Publishing.

Sleeter, C., & Grant, C. (1990). An analysis of multicultural education in the United States. In *Facing Racism in Education,* edited by N.M. Hidalgo et al. (pp. 138-161). Cambridge, MA: *Harvard Educational Review.*

Troike, R. (1978). Research evidence for the effectiveness of bilingual education. *NABE Journal, Vol. 3,* 13-24.

Villegas, A. M. (1991, September). *Culturally responsive pedagogy for the 1990s and beyond.* Educational Testing Service.

Waters, William V. (no date). Constructivist theory into practice in a secondary linguistic minority classroom: Shared teacher and student responsibility for learning. *ERIC,* CS211604.

Weir, R. (1962). *Language in the crib.* The Hague: Mouton.

Wigginton, E. (1991, December/1992, January). Culture begins at home. *Educational Leadership.*

Wolf, D., Bixby, J., Glenn, J. III, & Gardner, H. (1991). To use their minds well: Investigating new forms of student assessment. *Review of Research in Education.*

Wong-Fillmore, L. & Valadez, C. (1986). Teaching bilingual learners. *Handbook of research on teaching,* 3rd ed., Merlin Wittrock (Ed.). New York: Macmillan.

Wyman, S. L. (1993). *How to respond to your culturally diverse student population.* Alexandria, VA: Association for Supervision and Curriculum Development.

Chapter 4

Language in Instruction and Assessment

... educational failure is often, in a very general and rather deep sense, language failure. The child who does not succeed in the school system may be one who is not using language in the ways required by the school ... If the teacher's image of language is narrower and less rich than that which is already present in the minds of those he is teaching ... it will be irrelevant to him as a teacher. A minimum requirement for an educationally relevant approach to language is that it takes account of the child's own linguistic experience, defining this experience in terms of its richest potential and noting where there may be differences of orientation which would cause certain children difficulties in school ... (Halliday, 1973, pp. 18-20).

In this chapter we explore the role of language in the classroom, particularly in the context of new approaches to assessment, with a focus on implications for students who are still learning English or who belong to culturally non-dominant communities. As a prelude to specific issues of language and assessment, we will talk about the nature of language as a system of human communication and its relationship to cognition and to other representational systems. We will inquire into current notions of "language proficiency" and ways of assessing it, as well as how language proficiency affects students' school success. The chapter will also present information about the relationship between first and second language learning and proficiency along with key theoretical ideas and research findings suggestive of appropriate instructional and assessment strategies for students learning English. (See Chapter 3 for greater treatment of curriculum and instruction.)

Examples of prototypical performance assessments will be examined in light of their language demands, and suggestions for evaluating the language load of assessments and for accommodating language differences will be presented. Advice offered here for ways of regarding language and of enhancing the effectiveness of classroom instruction and assessment must be interpreted in light of particular settings, if it is to be applied usefully. We cannot prescribe for local needs, but we hope to provide some perspectives and "scaffolding" that will assist teachers and program planners to think about the role of language in learning and assessment.

Language and the New Assessments

Language is the most widely used symbol system for learning and for representing knowledge (whether orally or in writing). Even much of so-called "visual" learning is linguistic: when people say they learn better when something is written in addition to or rather than spoken, they are asking for another form of linguistic input (though they may also be asking for pictures or diagrams). Alternative assessments, though ideally *multi-intelligence*, or *performance-based*—suggesting use of modalities other than language—most often rely quite heavily on language. Language is inevitably used at the very outset in the directions, influencing how the student conceptualizes the task, and is usually a major factor in successful completion of a task or assessment item. In fact, one could easily argue that the language demands of the majority of alternative and performance-based assessments are considerably greater than those of traditional short-answer or multiple-choice norm-referenced tests.

Because language is the usual medium for understanding any problem and solving it, its influence is virtually omnipresent in the classroom or in daily endeavors. Even tasks that appear to be primarily visual (such as following a map or solving a jigsaw puzzle) are often mediated by language. People translate visual information into verbal form in order to remember it (Roth, 1978, cited in Oller, 1991, p. 54). For example, Russian psychologist Luria showed, through multiple experiments, that "the integration of verbal skills with certain motor tasks was essential to successful performance of those tasks for children at an early stage of development" (Oller, 1992, p. 66).

In any case, one cannot go directly from visual perception to problem solution even with a test such as Raven's Progressive Matrices—a test often used as a non-verbal index of intelligence. The test-taker, asked to determine which of a number of visual designs should logically follow in a progression, will need to represent to him/herself in some way the designs and their relationship to each other mentally, whether using such terms as "square," "circle," "dot," or some others (Oller, 1991, p. 54). Perception itself, whether visual, auditory, tactile, olfactory or gustatory, is not pure and direct; even the most basic sensory experiences are mediated by mental interpretation, most probably by language.

Language, Thought, and Learning

Much inquiry and argument among psychologists, linguists, and philosophers (Whorf, Vygotsky, Piaget, and Chomsky, among others) has been directed to the issue of the relationship between language and thought. Some have believed language to be dependent on thought, that is, a tool of thought/cognition. Others suggest that there is no propositional thought as we know it without language, that it is only through language that thought takes shape. A third position is that language and thought are interdependent, facilitating each other (Crystal, 1987).

Semiosis: The Basis of Human Intelligence?

semiotic: pertaining to signs

semiotics: "a general theory of signs and symbolism usually divided into three branches: pragmatics [concerns contexts influencing language use], semantics [concerns linguistic meanings], and syntactics [concerns sentence and word structures]"

(Webster's Encyclopedic Unabridged Dictionary, 1989, p. 1298)

Oller (1991) asserts that there is strong theoretical support for conceiving of intelligence itself as "a kind of *semiotic* or representational capacity" (p. iv) and cites C.S. Peirce's logical proof that all ordinary reasoning is a manifestation of representational capacity, an underlying ability to abstract from concrete sensory and motor experience and *re-present* that experience.

Oller (1991) identifies three major semiotic systems. The first is *sensory-motor*, through which we have mental images of our bodies in space, objects around us, and how objects can be expected to behave under certain circumstances. Sensory-motor representations are more or less directly, and iconically, related to the facts of experience; that is, their form is almost a "photograph" of the events they represent. The second is *kinesic;* it is gestural, as in motioning to someone to do something, or pointing out someone or something (giving so-called "deictic" or directional information). The kinesic system is somewhat more abstract than the sensory-motor. The third is *linguistic*, in which sequences of sounds are used to represent all manner of concepts. It is the most abstract system of the three.

These three systems are integrated; that is, humans can translate from one to another—suggesting that they draw on a common underlying representational capacity. We can envision what someone else is talking about or what we are reading (going from language to sensory-motor); we can convert linguistic representations to gestures—or, more likely, enhance them with gesture; we can translate our physical experiences into language. We can also express meanings through the arts in ways that seem to variously combine different aspects of semiotic function (varying both among art forms and among artists—linking more or less clearly to sensory-motor images, gesture, or language). Sculpture, painting, drawing, architecture, dance, literature, and music reflect more or less directly semiotic intent. Unfortunately, as our readers will readily understand, we cannot do justice to theories of art and the relation of artistic expression to semiotics and language here in this book. However, neither do we want to minimize the meaningfulness and importance of artistic forms of representation (or artistic forms of intelligence) to human development and experience.

Language is the only one of the three semiotic systems identified by Oller as using true *symbols*. A symbol, as opposed to a *signal* or *sign*, is fully abstracted from what it represents. That is, there is nothing in the form of the symbol that would suggest what it refers to. (There is nothing about the actual word "book" that suggests "something to read," or "a set of pages bound by a paper or cardboard cover.") Unlike iconic representations, which either directly (as in the case of sensory motor images) or partially (as in the case of gesture) maintain a connection to the physical experience, words bear no physical relationship to the objects or concepts they stand for. This feature of *arbitrariness* of the relation between form and meaning makes the linguistic system the most flexible, productive, and powerful.

"Sign" (American Sign Language, in the United States) the primary language of the deaf, has complexity and power equal to that of oral language. Even though Sign uses gesture, and some individual signs seem to mimic the objects or actions to which they refer, it is not equivalent to the kinesic system mentioned above. In fact, signed languages use hand and face movements, handshape, location of the hands, and orientation of the palm to communicate simultaneously all the same kinds of information that spoken languages communicate. Space, for example, can be used to show verb tense; eye blinks can show where a phrase ends and another begins (Tartter, 1986).

For purposes of communication with others as well as one's internal cognitive/intellectual activity, language (spoken or signed) is clearly the most important of the three systems. As Oller has said,

> Since language, especially one's primary or best-developed language,
> represents the most powerful and most general semiotic system for nearly
> all normal human beings, it follows that primary language abilities will
> play a central role in all sorts of abstract representational tasks. It is in
> this refined sense that the hypothesis that intelligence may have a kind
> of abstract semiotic (even a sort of deep linguistic) basis has, it would
> seem, its greatest plausibility and theoretical strength (Oller, 1991, p. iv).

If, as Oller has suggested, "the child's primary language is probably
the most likely basis for the development of general semiotic capacity"
(Oller, 1991, p. 21), much of cognitive development rests on proficiency in
the first language. When learning a language, however, children have the
support of other semiotic systems—gestural and sensory-motor. "We do
indeed understand representations . . . beyond our reach in one system
(namely the target language) by appealing to representations in another
semiotic system. The one provides an interpretation of the other" (Oller,
1991 p. 21). Teachers show an intuitive grasp of this *intertranslatability*
among representational systems when they encourage children to envision what is happening in a story (using one system to bolster comprehension via another), to talk their way through a jigsaw puzzle or complex
motor act, or when they enhance their own verbal expression with gesture.

Some information that links the physical world of experience to the
more abstract world of language is usually present or explicitly invoked
by teachers in instruction, particularly with students being taught via a
second language. Typically, programs for students learning English employ
many means to support the linguistic input with visual input—photographs, illustrations, drawings, diagrams, gestures, dramatizations—
something that may not be done with an assessment. Supplying additional
context can make unknown words and sentence structures become
"comprehensible input" (Krashen, 1981). For students who still need to
rely on contextual information (visual or otherwise), taking a test where
such enhancements are missing may leave them feeling stranded in a sea
of abstraction.

We do not want to equate all symbolizing with *linguistic* symbolizing;
as mentioned above, representation can take other forms and can indeed
be much more abstract and less linear-analytical and more holistic than
language (think of painting). Physicists, for example, have described how
they "see" and mentally manipulate hypothetical physical phenomena in
three-dimensional space. Painting and music have semiotic elements, but
there is no fully conventionalized mapping between form and meaning,
as in language; so for communicating explicit intentions, they are less reliable than language. With language, words have agreed-upon meanings

by convention (although meanings can change as well by convention); and word order and word endings show relationships among words in sentences. There are sociolinguistic or "pragmatic" conventions as well, "rules" for ways people speak to each other, depending on the social situation.

Gardner's Theory and Semiotic Systems

In his theory of multiple intelligences (1983), Howard Gardner proposes as one of the criteria for an *intelligence* that it have an associated symbol system. Besides language, musical, mathematico-logical, and visuo-spatial "intelligences" have identifiable symbol systems (though all three systems, especially the last two, depend also on linguistic symbols as well). For each of these symbolic or semiotic systems there is a grammar or *syntax* (rules governing the organization of the system), a *semantic* component (a set of meanings attached to the symbols), and a *pragmatic* component (a set of uses or functions to which the symbols are put) (Gardner, 1991). As mentioned earlier, symbol systems often have forms of notation: there are musical notation, mathematical notation, and conventions for mapping/drawing/diagramming (visuo-spatial representation).

Gardner's bodily kinesthetic intelligence would presumably use as a semiotic system, though not a true symbol system, the sensory-motor representational system to which Oller refers. Inter- and intrapersonal intelligences would depend a great deal on the linguistic system. By requiring that "his" intelligences have symbol systems (or perhaps, more accurately, *semiotic* systems), Gardner seems to be acknowledging that at heart human intelligence is representational capacity—or at least that representational capacity is a core component of intelligence.

Gardner gives substantial attention to the cultural variability in symbol systems. He says that the primary task of a child in the first few years is

> to master the syntax, semantics and pragmatics of those symbol systems
> that are valued in the surrounding culture . . . The particular symbol sys-
> tems favored—or spurned—within a culture form the agenda that the child
> must master in the "semiotic," "symbolic," or "representational" stage.
> And just as important a part of the child's learning at this time are the
> particular ways in which the symbol systems are used. Indeed, in observ-
> ing the child's acquisition of symbolic competence, we witness that con-
> tinual interplay between inborn proclivities and cultural options that char-
> acterizes human development forever after (Gardner, 1991 p. 57).

Thus, although all children develop symbolic competence, they do so in different ways that reflect the values and needs of their culture.

Language: A Human Capacity

The ability to design and use symbol systems is a distinguishing feature of human beings. Many species of animals signal each other with purposeful sounds—alerting others to danger, showing readiness to mate, for example—or communicate in some other ways (bees dance to show the location of flowers; some fish develop a colorful stripe to indicate fertility). But only humans have an abstract symbol system (language) that is open-ended and productive in the sense that novel utterances can be created almost endlessly on any topic. New words can be coined as needed; and through the "miracle" of syntax, the system for combining words to form sentences, relationships among words are signalled. Though some higher primates such as apes, chimpanzees, and gorillas have been taught various forms of human language (most successfully elements of signed English and American Sign Language, because of limitiations of their articulatory-vocal apparati), they have not used language in the same ways as humans do. Most of their utterances have to do with daily concrete needs and desires ("more cookie," "want doll," etc.); however, they do not tend to muse on the meaning of life or problem-solve via language. And, for some reason, non-human primates do not seem to grasp syntax; rather, they combine signs in largely random order, so that the relations among terms are not clear (Tartter, 1986). ("Gorilla eat." and "Eat gorilla." are not interchangeable.)

Although some signing primates have reportedly taught their offspring how to communicate using elements of American Sign Language or signed English, it is not clear that a true social need exists for them to use language—except in the company of humans. Perhaps it is because they do not have or need culture as we know it. Or, perhaps it is the other way around: they do not have the learning capacity of humans that would allow them to develop culture as we know it.

"Culture" has been defined as including systems of knowledge and values of a group, ways of being/knowing/behaving, *acquired and transmitted by symbols*, that distinguish a group (Chapter 2). A core element of culture is the transmission of knowledge and values from generation to generation. Culture is, by definition, transmitted behaviorally rather than genetically. The large size of the human brain, with its advanced learning capacity and ability to symbolize in ways not fully developed in other animals, has made the development of culture possible. With the advent of the capacity to learn and transmit learning effectively through symbols (including through notational systems that preserve learning), humans are not held to the inflexibility of genetically-determined behaviors. As biologist John Tyler Bonner has observed, "Passing information by behavioral rather than genetic means has made it possible in some cases to pass kinds of information that either cannot be transmitted genetically at all or are less effectively transmitted by genes" (Bonner, 1980, p. 4). Bonner suggests that first the capacity to learn grew, then the capacity to teach; and with these true culture arose. Cultural transmission of information has given humans an adaptive advantage; while genetic evolution is very slow, cultural evolution may be very rapid (Bonner, 1980). All humans have the capacity to learn the content of any culture because of equivalence in brain capacity. This principle has been expressed as "psychic equivalence" by anthropologists and psychologists who have conducted cross-cultural studies, including studies of individuals transplanted from one culture to another (Cole and Bruner, 1971).

Language, though not the only bearer of symbolic content, is the preeminent medium used to transmit culture, to communicate cultural information within and across generations.

The Language of Math

We mention this topic here, because it has often been alleged that language and mathematics are independent, or that mathematics has its own language apart from the "normal" code. However, it has been argued strongly by philosophers Bertrand Russell and C.S. Peirce that "mathematics as a kind of reasoning is parasitic and derivative inasmuch as it is entirely dependent upon language" (Oller, 1991 p. 22). There is, however, a specialized language of mathematics, what has been called a *mathematics register*, that is explicitly structured to express mathematics concepts (Halliday, 1975, cited in Spanos et al., 1988). Words that signal logical relations are frequent in mathematical problems (*if . . . then, because, for example, such that, but, either . . . or, given, therefore*). In addition, there are words that appear to be drawn from "natural" language (for example, *root, power, diagonal, square*) that have particular meanings in a mathematics context that they do not have in general conversation. Students need to learn the mathematical uses of these words. As with any kind of problem-solving, students need to be able to use language to represent the problem to themselves. Research has shown that the quality of problem representation is a key to successful problem solution (Duran, 1985). Recognition of the importance of language in mathematics is reflected in one of the standards put forth by the National Council of Teachers of Mathematics (NCTM): "Learn to communicate mathematically."

To express and expand their understanding of mathematical ideas, students need to learn the symbols and terms of mathematics. This goal is best accomplished in the context of problem solving that involves students in reading, writing, and talking in the language of mathematics. As students strive to communicate their ideas, they will learn to clarify, refine and consolidate their thinking (NCTM, 1989). This standard highlights the connections among reasoning, thinking, and communicating—

all of which are dependent on language. Performance assessments developed by states and other groups are often quite linguistically complex, both in terms of the text that sets out a problem and in terms of the language the student is required to produce to explain his/her procedures and solution path.

Language Proficiency

Because of the essential role language plays in instruction, learning, and assessment, it is important for teachers to have a framework for understanding what is meant by "language proficiency." Such a framework enables teachers to interpret student performance more accurately and thus to target instruction more effectively. Unfortunately, teachers have not routinely had the opportunity to develop in-depth knowledge about language proficiency and its development; and misperceptions about the relationships between comprehension and production, and between conversational skill and academic language skill have often led to inappropriate instruction (Cummins, 1989; Diaz, Moll, and Mehan, 1986). Teachers' ratings of students' language proficiency are also colored by their own language backgrounds and their attitudes toward bilingual and language minority programs, among other factors (De Avila, 1990).

Teachers' ability to make judgments of language proficiency would likely contribute to improved education for English learners in the areas of program placement, design of classroom instruction, interpretation of language issues in classroom performance or social adjustment, and assessing the need for additional instruction in the student's first language. Because of their unique opportunities to observe students' language use in many situations and their opportunities for communicating with family members, teachers can contribute information that greatly enhances the picture presented of language proficiency by formal tests. There are daily opportunities in instruction and assessment to draw on such a framework as well, whether to evaluate students' language proficiency per se (as part of language arts assessment) or to gain insight into its contribution to performance in other subject matter domains. These arenas of assessment (language assessment and educational assessment) intersect, and both have high potential impact on students.

Concerns about the confounding of language proficiency with educational proficiency are longstanding (see Chapter 1). Some of the questions relating to language and educational assessment that have haunted theorists, researchers, and practitioners alike are:

- What is the role of language proficiency in learning/education and in assessment?

- Can we determine what assessments are actually measuring? To what degree are they (including so-called "non-verbal" assessments) assessing language proficiency rather than or in addition to other constructs?
- Can effects of educational disadvantage (lack of opportunity to learn) be separated from effects of language through assessment?
- What is the relationship between the first and second language as it affects classroom performance?
- How do cultural, ethnic and social class differences influence language use and performance in the classroom?
- What can be done to clarify the role of language and to make assessments more fair and informative?

These are complex questions that language researchers have been addressing for decades, and there are no simple answers to them. However, there is substantive information bearing on them that we can draw on to make better decisions about instruction and assessment.

Conceptualizations of Language Proficiency

Ways of thinking about language proficiency lead to ways of assessing it, practices in student placement and instruction, and ultimately high-stakes consequences for students. It must be acknowledged that "language proficiency" is not an agreed-upon, fully operationalized construct (De Avila, 1990); however, theories and research in sociolinguistics, psycholinguistics, and bilingual education have contributed greatly to our understanding of what it means to be proficient with a language. (See Figure 4.1 for a summary of three views of language proficiency.)

FIGURE 4.1
Three Views of Language Proficiency

Language Arts View

Listening   Speaking   Reading   Writing   (Performing)
             (Signing)

Traditional Linguistic View

Phonology   Syntax (and Morphology)   Semantics   Pragmatics

Communicative Competence (Sociolinguistic) View

Grammatical Knowledge   Sociolinguistic   Discourse   Strategic
(phonology, syntax,   Competence   Competence   Competence
semantics, morphology)

Social Context

Teachers tend to think of language proficiency in terms of the components of language arts: listening, speaking, reading, and writing (and sometimes "performing"). Although these are not the elements of a classic linguistic definition, they constitute one useful typology that is not in conflict with others that will follow here. Legislation and policy documents use this broad classification scheme to refer to assessment of bilingual students or those in the process of learning English (see below). To these components, one might add "internal language," the language of thought, which does not really fall into any of the four categories above, but whose importance teachers would certainly acknowledge.

Legal Definitions of Language Proficiency

The Bilingual Education Act of 1978 describes a limited English-proficient (LEP) student as one who:

(a) meets one or more of the following conditions:

- was born outside of the United States or whose native language is not English;

- comes from an environment where a language other than English is dominant; or

- is American Indian or Alaska Native and comes from an environment where a language other than English has had a significant impact on his/her level of English language proficiency; and [who by reason thereof]

(b) has sufficient difficulty speaking, reading, writing, or understanding the English language to deny him or her the opportunity to learn successfully in English-only classrooms or to participate fully in the society. (Cited in CCSSO, 1992)

An advisory committee to the Council of Chief State School Officers crafted a definition of what it is to be fully English-proficient (FEP):

A fully English-proficient (FEP) student is able to use English to ask questions, to understand teachers and reading materials, to test ideas, and to challenge what is being asked in the classroom. Four language skills contribute to proficiency, as follows:

- Reading—the ability to comprehend and interpret text at the age- and grade-appropriate level.

- Listening—the ability to understand the language of the teacher and instruction, comprehend and extract information, and follow the instructional discourse through which teachers provide information.

- Writing—the ability to produce written text with content and format fulfilling classroom assignments at the age- and grade-appropriate level.

- Speaking—the ability to use oral language appropriately and effectively in learning activities (such as peer tutoring, collaborative learning activities, and question/answer sessions) within the classroom and in social interactions within the school. (CCSSO, 1993, p. 7)

The CCSSO document goes on to elaborate functionally on the LEP definition by saying,

A limited English-proficient student has a language background other than English, and his or her proficiency in English is such that the probability of the student's academic success in an English-only classroom is below that of an academically successful peer with an English-language background (p. 7).

Two cautions are in order: (1) It is important to avoid equating speaking of a language other than English with LEP status; some students whose primary language is not English will not be limited in English proficiency. (2) "Fully English-proficient" cannot be taken to be equivalent to "native-like proficiency." Many extremely proficient speakers of a language never reach native-like speech because of their accent or difficulties with idiomatic language.

However straightforward these provisions may appear, they have not resulted in simple solutions to identifying limited English-proficient students because of lack of adequate assessments or practical methods for surveying all students and lack of agreement as to what would constitute proficiency in English. In short, any current census of LEP students is undoubtedly flawed (Casanova and Arias, 1993). We do know that during the 1980s, a surge of immigration contributed to a sharp increase in the numbers of students who speak languages other than English. In California, where change was greatest, the LEP student population grew by 73 percent between 1980 and 1986 (Casanova and Arias, 1993). One current estimate of the number of students who could benefit from bilingual services places the number at more than five million (Casanova and Arias, 1993). However, because of inconsistent methods in the ways states and districts identify LEP students, it is almost impossible to derive a meaningful statistic. Obviously, there are major ramifications of (and political agendas for) inflating or deflating the LEP population, not the least of these being impact on federal funding levels for bilingual education (Casanova and Arias, 1993).

Ideally, to determine a student's level of proficiency, school personnel should evaluate the student in all four language areas (listening, speaking, reading, and writing). Moreover, students must be assessed along these dimensions in both their first language and in English (CCSSO, 1992, pp. 6-7). It is certainly desirable to have the student evaluated by a speech-language clinician who is proficient in the student's first language. The clinician may use a combination of interviews with family and teachers, observations in various settings, oral and written language samples, and formal and informal testing (Langdon, 1992) to assess a student's proficiency in the four areas mentioned (in both the first language and in English). However, in many cases a school or district does not have the luxury of a clinician for every language represented in the school, nor does time permit the kind of thorough evaluation that would be ideal. Particularly if the immediate need is to identify students for program placement, a timely process is imperative. In states with high LEP populations, the recommendation is that screening, identification, and placement be completed within thirty days (Lara, 1992).

Functional Definitions

In practical terms, when it comes to determining a student's level of (English) language proficiency, most school districts probably do not have an explicit, fully developed concept of language proficiency beyond the legal definition; although some may have curriculum content and performance standards for language arts that, if linked with appropriate educational assessment, could serve to reveal important information about a student's overall language proficiency. Rather, most districts have an implicit definition of language proficiency represented by the particular language proficiency tests they choose or that are chosen by speech-language clinicians to establish students' eligibility for special programs and services or readiness to exit them.

To evaluate a student's proficiency in language, traditional language tests often have focused on the systems of language: phonology (sounds of the language and their pronunciation), syntax/morphology (sentence and word structures), semantics (word meanings), and pragmatics (practical choices in use of language in social contexts).

Some tests have been designed to classify the student in terms of oral fluency and language dominance as well. For example, the LAS (Language Assessment Scales, Duncan and De Avila, 1985), a frequently-used test, includes measures of auditory discrimination, vocabulary, phoneme production, sentence comprehension and oral production in both English and Spanish to determine language dominance. Many tests actually examine a very narrow range of language skills or even a single kind of skill. "Discrete-point tests" assess single aspects of language proficiency, such as syntactic skill or auditory discrimination ability.

Communicative Competence

The most dramatic shift of perspective regarding language proficiency in the last two decades has been from a primarily formal-structural approach to one that focuses on a child's ability to communicate meaning through language. The term "communicative competence" has been proposed to refer to "the ability to use linguistic knowledge and skills appropriately in particular settings for particular communicative functions" (Greenleaf, 1992). In this conceptualization, language proficiency is not abstracted from its social context. The communicative competence interpretation of language proficiency is harmonious with the perspective of this book; however, we have chosen to use the more familiar term "language proficiency," because it is more widely used in legislative and educational policy documents. A communicative competence version of language proficiency would have the following components (see also Figure 4.1):

1. Grammatical competence—mastery of the language code, including rules of phonology and pronunciation, vocabulary and word meanings, rules of syntax (sentence formation), and morphology (root words, prefixes, suffixes, grammatical endings)

2. Pragmatic (or sociolinguistic) competence - mastery of the appropriate use of language in various social contexts (how to speak to a teacher or respected elder vs. a peer; how to make a request, show gratitude, or greet someone, for example)

3. Discourse competence—Mastery of production of texts of various types according to accepted rules of organization and cohesion (for example, telling a story, holding a telephone conversation, recounting a past event, explaining a step-by-step process, participating in a group discussion);

4. Strategic competence—Mastery of verbal and non-verbal strategies to repair or keep communication going, enhance one's ability to communicate (for example, by using gesture or looking a word up in the dictionary)

(adapted from Canale, 1981 in Cummins, 1981, p. 7).

To the fourth component—strategic competence—we might add "metalinguistic knowledge," or awareness of language itself, its forms and functions, along with knowledge of how to talk about language. As students become readers and writers, they need to be able to bring to conscious awareness their own tacit knowledge of language, including knowledge of phonology (or how sounds work in the language), syntax (or what makes for an acceptable sentence), semantics (word meanings), and written discourse (for example, what makes for a story). Students who are able to make judgments about the acceptability (grammaticality) of what they read are more likely to self-correct errors, and it is known that good readers are more sensitive to their own errors in reading than are poor or even average readers (Menyuk and Flood, 1981). With regard to the writing process, one could argue that access to usually tacit linguistic information is even more critical.

The other aspect of metalinguistic skill alluded to is facility with using the "language of language." All three views of language proficiency presume that a student will be able to correctly interpret and use terms such as "word," "sentence," "syllable," "sound," "letter," "paragraph," "story."

While some students acquire metalinguistic awareness seemingly without explicit instruction, many do not; however, such awareness can readily be taught to school-age children (Trumbull, 1984). For example, through games they can improve their understanding of what a word is, how to use the word "word," and that a word is not physically related to its referent (for example,"snake" is not a long word) (Estrin and Chaney, 1988). Of course, reading and writing contribute to metalinguistic awareness in very important ways; for example, students who know how to read for meaning are more likely to pay attention to errors that interfere with comprehension (Garcia 1992). And reading contributes to students' awareness of word boundaries, helping them to distinguish between other linguistic units such as sounds, syllables, and phrases.

Non-Verbal Communication

Of course, human communicative competence entails more than just language; it includes facial expression, gesture, and tactile information (embracing, handshaking, patting, kissing, and so on) (Crystal, 1987). It entails conventional proxemic (bodily distance) and oculesic (eye movement) information as well—information that is extremely culturally variable. And aspects of language modulation, such as volume and pace of speech, also contribute communicative information and are variable culturally as well as within a single speaker, depending on situation. "Communication" refers to sharing of information between or among people (including between reader and text). It implies a speaker and a hearer, or transmitter and receiver; and communication cannot be said to have occurred unless a message has been received, that is, understood. In direct, interpersonal communication, speakers do not need to rely entirely on the spoken message; they may use gesture, elements of the physical/interactive setting, facial expression, linguistic intonation and stress, and many other sources of information to make sense of the message. Much of this information is unconsciously transmitted and received, making cross-cultural (and even male-female) communication all the more troublesome at times.

Assessment in a Communicative Competence Orientation

A communicative competence or pragmatic approach to assessment would imply examining meaningful communication in context. This constitutes an "integrative" approach, because students use multiple language skills during one performance or communication activity (Canales, 1992). Speech-language clinicians may try to capture naturally-occurring language or elicit a sample of discourse from a student who is being assessed. However, it is difficult to maintain psychometric rigor and use informal assessment practices; so, many clinicians use formal tests that elicit language samples with standardized prompts. Other integrative measures used are observation checklists, interviews, dictation tests, and cloze tests (Canales, 1992). Instruments of these types can be used by teachers to great advantage.

Despite the difficulties of maintaining "pragmatic naturalness" (Oller, 1992, p. 55) in assessing students' language, it may be worth the trouble.

> What [is] . . . important about pragmatic tests, and what is yet to be appreciated fully by theoreticians and practitioners is that all of the goals of discrete-point items, e.g., diagnosis, focus, isolation, etc., could be better achieved in the full rich context of one or more pragmatic tests. As a result, it has been argued that the valid objectives of discrete-point theory could be completely incorporated within a pragmatic framework. (Oller, 1992, p. 56)

Non-Comparability of Assessment Outcomes

Unfortunately, tests are not comparable. They use different criteria to arrive at their diagnoses of NEP, LEP and FEP, so that different tests will identify different percentages of students tested as limited English proficient, because they are measuring different aspects of language. Worse, they may not be based on clear theory regarding the purpose for or method of testing (DeAvila, 1990). For example, statistically different percentages of students are identified as non-English-proficient, limited English-proficient, and fully English-proficient by three widely used language proficiency tests—percentage differences that vary depending on grade level of students tested. A student could be classified as fully English proficient on one test yet limited English speaking on another (Ulibarri, Spencer, and Rivas, 1981). Our conclusion need not be to jettison all language tests, but we can appreciate the limitations of the information we are getting.

Cummins' Framework for Bilingual Language Proficiency

One of the most useful frameworks contributing to an understanding of classroom implications of language (or communicative) proficiency has been propounded by James Cummins (1981). Although it is associated with theories of bilingual language proficiency and school performance, much of it is equally applicable to monolingual students or students who speak so-called "non-standard" dialects. The framework moves beyond static lists of components of language proficiency by incorporating a developmental perspective and two major dimensions along which language activities can be scaled. It recognizes the importance of contexts in language learning and language use, taking into account differences between the language demands of the classroom and those of nonacademic settings. And it suggests (on the basis of research) a relationship between proficiency in the first language and proficiency in the second language.

BICS and CALP

Cummins proposes that the language proficiency of many students is misunderstood because of a failure to recognize that fluency in conversational skills does not imply facility with academic uses of languages in the classroom. Cummins has called the former "BICS" (basic interpersonal conversational skill) and the latter "CALP" (cognitive-academic language proficiency). CALP entails skill in using language in *"context-reduced"* situations (some say "decontextualized") to talk about events or ideas that are not clearly tied to current context. It may take up to seven years to develop fully, compared to BICS, which Cummins has said takes about two years. Examples of decontextualized language use might be discussing a science activity completed the day before, or reading a text composed by a distant author on a topic foreign to one's own experience. BICS is by definition "context-embedded," and "is communication [that] derives from interpersonal involvement in a shared reality that reduces the need for explicit linguistic elaboration of the message" (Cummins, 1981, p. 11). In other words, because speakers can draw from shared knowledge and familiarity, they do not have to rely on the language alone to convey meaning.

BICS and CALP are best thought of as two ends of a continuum rather than two completely separate language capacities. Moreover, many school tasks incorporate elements of both BICS and CALP; and conversations among friends may be more or less context-embedded. Furthermore, it would be oversimplifying to assume that BICS develops before CALP in an absolute sense. Although CALP is more associated with school experience, it has its roots in earlier decontextualized experiences (which will be discussed later in the section on "Language Use in the Classroom: Discourse Genres"). And, skill with social language continues to develop beyond the primary school years.

BICS tends to be learned early in the process of acquiring any language, and a student may have well-developed BICS yet have little mastery of CALP. However, this distinction may not be apparent to teachers or others who are in a position to assess the child. What they may see is a child who is quite fluent with English in informal social settings, yet appears to have difficulty learning or expressing him/herself in formal classroom activities. They may wrongly conclude that the student has a learning disability, is not motivated to perform, or is generally slow. In fact, it is difficult to ascertain whether an English learner has a specific learning disability in addition to learning problems attributable to the normal process of acquiring a new language (see Langdon, 1992). For example, the same error patterns one sees in a child who is learning a language may be seen in one who has an actual language disorder; the only observable difference may lie in the *pervasiveness* and *persistence* of such errors (Langdon, 1992).

CALP is developed over a much longer period, generally through classroom experience, although certain activities common to middle-class homes also build CALP. Monolingual English speakers are, of course, developing the CALP register over a period of years; but they have the advantage of doing so in their primary language. Numerous studies (see Collier, 1992, for a summary) have shown that it takes several years for English learners (matched for socio-economic class) to catch up to grade level peers in academic achievement. Paradoxically, those who get greater amounts of instructional support in their first language (L1), balanced with second-language instruction, achieve higher academically (in English) than peers who are taught monolingually in English. "In programs with no L1 support, it may take a *very* long time for language minority students to reach national norms in L2" (Collier, 1992, p. 205). There is a curvilinear relationship, however. In the first two or three years of a program, students instructed monolingually make faster gains in English and do better on tests; but between the third and fifth years, the bilingually instructed students begin to catch up and then surpass those monolingually instructed (Collier 1992, p. 193). This evidence suggests that there are cognitive and academic benefits to continuing to build the first language.

Cognitive Demand

A second developmental aspect of language proficiency has to do with the degree to which a language task is experienced as cognitively demanding. (Figure 4.2 shows these two orthogonal continua and four quadrants defined by them.)

This is an important principle and one that teachers understand well: the difficulty of a task does not reside in the task alone but is relative to the student's developmental level (here, speaking of language development) as well as personal experience. Cognitively undemanding language proficiencies would be those that have been mastered to the point of automaticity. By the early school years, for example, children have usually mastered the pronunciation of most sound combinations of the language, production and comprehension of many types of sentences, and skill in social communication (representing basic competence in elements of the four components outlined by Canale, 1981). These are the skills that one would think of as cognitively undemanding and the first ones to be learned by second-language learners (upper pole of continuum). However, these skills will not move into the cognitively undemanding realm until they have been mastered. Skills that have moved to the upper end of the continuum for native speakers may be near the bottom for second language learners. So, although we can in some general way evaluate the language demands of a classroom/assessment task, we must remember that these demands will be relative to the student's level of language proficiency. (BICS and CALP, representing generic extremes, have been placed in quadrants A and C, respectively.)

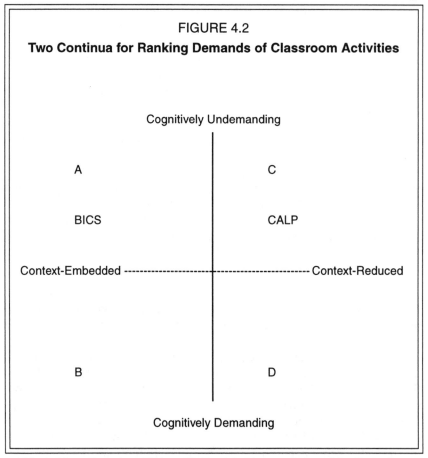

FIGURE 4.2

Two Continua for Ranking Demands of Classroom Activities

Cognitively Undemanding

A   C

BICS   CALP

Context-Embedded -- Context-Reduced

B   D

Cognitively Demanding

Adapted from Cummins, 1981, p. 12. Reprinted by permission of the Evaluation, Dissemination and Assessment Center, CSULA, Los Angeles, California 90032.

Forms of academic discourse in the classroom would be cognitively demanding for all students at the outset—but more so for those who are still in the process of mastering the basic grammatical competence. Tasks can be placed in different quadrants of the scheme, depending on their degree of context-embeddedness or cognitive demands, and relative to a student's development. For example, an assessment that requires a student to write a personal narrative (in any language) about a holiday experience would be more cognitively demanding for a third-grader who is just beginning to learn to write than for one who has been involved in formal schooling since kindergarten. For both students, however, the personalized topic would make the task somewhat more context-embedded—particularly if the students were allowed to talk with each other about the topic beforehand with some teacher support.

The second language learner is at a disadvantage when it comes to producing or comprehending lengthy academic texts (oral or written). As long as she/he has to devote attention to lower-level language skills, there will be less attention capacity available to devote to larger units of meaning and form. This is not to say that children learning a language have to be taught only low-level skills in a hierarchical fashion before getting to big ideas, good books, or rich classroom activities. Rather, it means that they will need instructional supports to participate meaningfully in these activites—increasing context when it is reduced and provision of non-linguistic sources of meaning. Good instruction for students acquiring a second language will use visual information, gesture, and the like to enhance comprehension of the spoken language. However, when the student is left alone to make sense of a text, to take a test without mediation of any sort, the language burden becomes greater. (See Chapter 6 for a thorough treatment of the issues surrounding mediated administration and other measures to improve the fairness and usefulness of assessment with language minority students.)

Relations between First and Second Language Proficiency

The research results cited earlier support another of Cummins' hypotheses: that there is a "common underlying [language] proficiency" (CUP). Thus, content and skills learned in one language transfer to other languages. However, an apparent threshhold must be met. That is, there is a minimum level of language proficiency that must be achieved in order for that language to be a resource. When children are forced to learn a second (usually majority) language before the first is well-developed, and the support for development of the first is not maintained, children may lose real cognitive and linguistic ground. Both languages suffer (Wong-Fillmore, 1991). On the other hand, when the first language is well-developed, a second language is learned more readily; and it is the more academic uses of the second language that tend to benefit. Perhaps this is why 8-to-11-year-old immigrant children have been shown to catch up with English-speaking peers more quickly than immigrant children aged 5 to 7 (Collier, 1987). It is not difficult to imagine why more abstract conceptual knowledge about how print functions, or how to draw on one's own knowledge and experience to elaborate a text would be generalizable across languages. As discussed in Chapter 6, the notion of "scripts" or "schemata" (collections of concepts organized around a recurrent situation, for example, a script for going to the barber or getting ready for school) is useful in thinking about how conceptual knowledge can transfer from one language to another (Saville-Troike, 1991). Immigrant students who have already attended school (like the 8-to-11-year-olds mentioned above) have a script or schema for *"learning in school,"* or *"reading a book,"* unlike many immigrants (both younger and older) who have never had formal schooling; and those who have the script are at an advantage.

Garcia (1992) and Lee (1986), among others, have shown in their research that "bilingual students frequently produce more comprehensive recalls of text written in their second language when they are permitted to use their first language" (Garcia, 1992, p. 5)—as for example, when selected vocabulary is translated for them. Thus, the first language is, in a sense, a resource to the second.

Cummins has pointed out the deficiencies of many definitions of language proficiency as they are operationalized in tests that districts use to evaluate students for placement purposes. He notes that the exact nature of "English proficiency" that would be required to survive in an all-English classroom has been ill-defined and cautions that "a realistic reclassification threshhold of 'English proficiency' is unlikely to be attained by most language minority students until the later grades of elementary school" (Cummins, 1981, p. 41). It is important for teachers to realize, however, that proficiency in the first language is an important index of potential for English language proficiency, particularly in literacy skills. The first language should not be viewed merely as "an interim carrier of content" (Cummins, 1981) until English is mastered. We want to "build on rather than replace entry characteristics of children (Cummins, p. 43)." Mistakes are made when students who have developed a high level of literacy skill in their first language are confined to engagement in low-level tasks in English reading instruction.

Acquiring Literacy: First and Second Language-Learners

"All normal individuals can learn to read and write, provided they have a setting or context in which there is a need to be literate, they are exposed to literacy, and they get some help from those who are already literate" (Heath, 1986, p.23). They will need to learn the conventions of literate language, such as how to use and talk about written texts, how to engage in "culturally valued literate practices" (Greenleaf, 1992, p. 8), as well as code-related conventions such as spelling-to-sound relationships. Here the word "literate" is used to refer not only to reading and writing but ways of talking about text. Some theorists have proposed the term "critical literacy" to encompass the capacity to use language in all of its forms as "a tool for thinking, problem solving and communication" (Calfee and Nelson-Barber, 1991, p. 52). A core component of this definition of literacy is ability to engage in academic uses of language.

It is important to understand that written language skills—at least at the beginning—are dependent on oral language skills. At first, conscious links must be made to the oral language, in terms of mapping of oral units to written units (whether they be sounds, words, or whole texts). Written language is "second-order symbolism," that is, it is a representation of a representation—a secondary symbol system for a primary (oral) symbol system. For students learning to read in a second language, without having done so in their primary language, there is an extra layer of abstraction from their primary symbol system (cf. Oller's concept of the primary language as the basis of all other semiotic systems); that is, they have to make the leap from one primary symbol system to mastery of a different secondary symbol system—one whose primary form they are still learning. It is far easier to learn the principles of literacy in a more familiar language. In fact, English literacy skills are strongly related to first-language literacy skills (Cummins, 1981). Of course, differences and similarities between the first and second languages in their writing systems will matter to some degree as well, for those who have learned to read already. It will be easier to move from one alphabetic writing system to another (as from Spanish to English) rather than from a logographic writing system to an alphabetic one (as from Chinese to English).

Learning to read and write is an example of context-reduced activity that can be made easier by instructional practices. Teachers can, in essence, provide context by preparing students for reading, helping them to see connections to their own experience, using visual images, dramatizations, and the like to ensure that the entire burden of comprehension does not fall on the linguistic code alone. It is easy to see why traditional testing, with its explicit prohibition of contextualizing or individualizing (in order to preserve standardization) would especially penalize second language learners.

Teachers who are not aware of the dimensions to which Cummins refers may tend to assume that students in quadrant A (Figure 4.2), who are able to use language adequately in cognitively undemanding tasks that are context-embedded, have sufficient English language proficiency to participate in an English-only program. Or, as mentioned, they may believe that below-average classroom performance is an indicator of innate learning ability rather than insufficient academic language development. Cummins (1981, p. 17) has suggested that "academic deficits are often created by teachers and psychologists who fail to realize that it takes language minority students considerably longer to attain grade/age appropriate levels in English academic skills than it does in English face-to-face communicative skills."

Needless to say, it would be useful to teachers when they are interpreting student performance to realize that for such (quadrant A) students, academic activities, including assessment, will be experienced as more context-reduced and more cognitively demanding than they will be for fully proficient English speakers. Because second language learners' home sociocultural contexts are less likely to be congruent with that of the school, they will find school activities less context-embedded. The more that links can be made to students' home cultures and languages (providing more meaningful context), the greater are the possibilities for meaningful learning. As Freire and Macedo (1987) state, "the command of reading and writing is achieved beginning with words and themes meaningful to the common experience of those becoming literate and not with words and themes linked only to the experience of the educator" (Freire and Macedo, 1987, cited in Oller, 1992, p. 67).

Particularly with literacy learning, bridges to personal experience (as through the language experience method that has students dictating/writing about their own lives and then reading their own texts) are extremely important. With regard to the assessment context and cultural differences, as discussed in Chapter 2, students from different backgrounds will construe the testing situation differently—contextualizing it based on their own previous experience. American Indian students with traditional backgrounds may not bring a school-congruent notion of testing to their classroom experience, unlike non-Indian students who "know how to be tested school-style" from prior experience (Deyhle, 1987). These are elements of context that go well beyond the issue of whether a student is reading a formal text or participating in a language experience activity.

With a broadened scope of what constitutes literacy, one can see connections among culture, language, literacy, learning, and intelligence. "Literacy viewed from the perspective of communication arising from shared activities with meaningful others cannot be separated from the issues of intelligence, learning, and language . . . literacy becomes entwined with how and what people know—with intelligence" (Miller, 1990, p. 2, cited in Oller, 1992, p. 67).

Assessment of Literacy

While we have focused primarily on oral language assessment, we should at the very least discuss literacy assessment briefly and note some parallels to oral language assessment. For the reader who wants a more detailed analysis of the types of literacy assessments and their appropriateness with language minority students, Garcia (1992) provides an excellent review.

The same shift toward meaning-focused, integrated assessment using authentic tasks is seen in the realm of written language as well as oral. With integrated language arts instruction (in which reading, writing, speaking, and listening are not taught separately) come assessments that combine all four areas. There is a concomitant move away from tests that focus on isolated skills (though for accountability purposes norm-referenced, standardized, multiple-choice tests are often still used), because these are not seen as valid indicators of what we have come to think of as true reading and writing. Tests that basal reader publishers have developed are also in some disfavor because of their tendency to focus too heavily on skills over comprehension (Garcia, 1992).

Informal assessment activities such as story retelling, classroom observations, running records, tape-recordings, reading logs, reading response logs, and think-alouds (Garcia, 1992) may be used by the teacher in conjunction with building a student portfolio throughout the year. But, Garcia cautions:

> . . . informal assessment relies on the teacher's expertise. Teachers who are interested in informal assessment have to be knowledgeable about the literacy process. Informal assessment provides one means for teachers to find out the strengths and weaknesses of their students' ongoing literacy development. However, teachers must know how to interpret this data . . . If they work with second-language children, then they need to make a concerted effort to become knowledgeable about first and second-language acquisition and literacy processes (p. 14).

Language Use

> The meaning of language is not simply in its word meanings and relations but also in non-verbal, stylistic features (intonation, rhythm, volume, emphasis)—and perhaps most of all in its larger intent to convey "respect or disrespect, concern or indifference, intimacy or distance, seriousness or play" . . . (Hymes, 1972, p. xiii) (emphasis added).

Language use incorporates two dimensions. "The first has to do with the goals or functions of language, the reasons why people speak; the second has to do with linguistic and nonlinguistic context that determines how individuals understand and choose among alternative forms of language for reaching the same or different goals" (Bloom and Lahey, 1978). A language cannot be captured by counting and cataloguing linguistic forms, without reference to the circumstances in which it is being used. "What is crucial is not so much a better understanding of how language is structured, but a better understanding of how language is used; not so much what language *is*, as what language is *for*" (Hymes, 1972, p. xii).

Language structures and forms are not used in a vacuum for their own sake; language is used to accomplish something. Language can be used as an instrument to get what one needs, to build relationships (through small talk or expressions of friendship), to express opinions, to gain or share information, to reflect internally on one's knowledge or beliefs, to express emotions, to regulate the behavior of others, to control natural phenomena (religious incantations), to express personal identity, to signal group membership or political solidarity (chanting of slogans or use of "in-group" terminology), to perpetuate cultural values, to imagine or fantasize, to deceive, to amuse, or to analyze itself! The reader will have no trouble expanding this list. Linguist M.A.K. Halliday (1973, 1975) has identified seven functions of language under which all of those listed above can be subsumed (see Table 4.1 for a list and accompanying descriptions).

All of these functions are of importance in the classroom, though the *imaginative, heuristic,* and *representational* seem most closely allied with school learning. Unfortunately, teachers appear to use regulatory language with much greater frequency than any other functional type. Certainly, the most common classroom communication format has teachers regulating most student talk (see "Participant Structures" below).

TABLE 4.1

Functions of Language

Language Function	Defining Characteristics
Instrumental	used as a means of getting things done (the "I want" function)
Regulatory	used to regulate the behavior of others (the "Do as I tell you" function)
Interactional	used to effect interpersonal interactions (the "You and me" function)
Personal	used to express feelings and attitudes, identity of self (the "Here I come" function)
Heuristic	used to investigate reality, learn about things (the "Tell me why" function)
Imaginative	used to create a world of one's own making, including through rhymes, nonsense sound play, riddles, stories (the "Let's pretend" function)
Informative	used to communicate about some thing, express propositions or ideas (the "I've got something to tell you" function)

Adapted from Halliday, 1973, 1975.

The Primacy of the Context of Language Use

Language is always used in a context that influences, if not determines, the form and manner of communication, *how* meaning is negotiated. "Context" can be taken to mean both *immediate* (the situation at hand) and *ongoing* (the larger cultural context in which the speaker has learned to use language). Even with regard to "school language," it is interesting that what counts for proficiency, that is, what is considered appropriate communicative behavior, in one classroom may not pass muster in another (Bennett and Slaughter, 1983). Moreover, as students progress through the grades, they will encounter not only multiple language uses and standards of use but different discourse patterns related to different disciplines and associated with thinking like a mathematician, a historian, or a scientist (Greenleaf, 1992).

Thus students need to become familiar and facile with the ways of using language, presenting ideas, and marshaling evidence that characterize these discourses in order to understand and participate in the academic and public enterprises which are shaped by discourse (Greenleaf, 1992, p. 10).

We could say that there are multiple language proficiencies, drawn on in different contexts. Language is, in fact, a social medium, used in multiple settings for myriad purposes. Therefore, before we go too much further, we may want to ask, "Proficiency for what purposes, in what contexts, and in whose terms? In the classroom? In the community? Judged by the parent, the teacher, the speech and language therapist?"

We cannot make assumptions about people's proficiency with a language by observing it or eliciting it in a single circumstance. Labov's work with Black inner-city students provided a striking example of that fact. Students interviewed by White researchers produced monosyllabic responses, yet in a familiar social setting they were verbally expansive and creative (Labov, 1969). Language use cannot be understood without reference to the power relations of speech communities from which speakers come.

> Classrooms are artificial settings responsive to the particular sociopolitical contexts which affect the use of language. And it is in the classroom where a child's language is first scrutinized and judged by strangers. What the teacher understands or fails to understand, the expressions which are deemed appropriate and those which are not, force the child to confront the social rules governing language (Hymes, in Cazden, John, and Hymes, 1972).

In the case just mentioned, students who appeared low in verbal skill in a formal, impersonal setting became articulate when the power relations changed. Research in numerous cultural settings has shown that when we restrict our concept of language proficiency to how students perform on language tests or in classroom situations, we are illuminating only a small portion of the whole picture. "These findings have cast doubt on traditional assessments of language proficiency based on a limited perception of language as only an abstract formal system of communication" (Casanova and Arias, 1993). Such findings also support the argument for portfolio assessment, because of its ability to capture the context—in fact, shifting contexts over time—of student performance, both for language and academic assessment. (See Chapter 6.)

What constitutes appropriate language proficiency for the school setting is a changing notion. On the one hand, we think of using language in abstract ways to learn (literacy skill with many kinds of texts, classroom discussion and debate, and so on), yet schools are now also embracing the idea of linking the classroom with the real world, developing communication skills for the workplace, embedding abstract concepts in meaningful contexts ("situated cognition") (Lave and Wenger, 1991). Perhaps the lines between academic discourse and the discourse of everyday life will begin to blur somewhat.

Hymes (1972) has argued that to evaluate a person's language proficiency, one must *start* with context. Ideally, one would assess naturally-occurring language in authentic settings. As mentioned earlier, because this is a difficult proposition, intermediate methods have been developed to elicit students' language on a common topic. Contextualized language assessment is a more complex way of determining language proficiency that takes into account the social meanings of texts. A person's discourse is understood in relation to his life situation (culture, experience, power relations with the dominant culture, and so forth) (Fillmore, 1976 in Bennett and Slaughter).

The context in which a teacher or language specialist assesses a student's language proficiency may result in different relations between adult and student (Bennett and Slaughter, 1983). Depending on how the assessment is framed to the student, it may take the form of an *examination, an interview,* or *a conversation*—all of which have different levels of formality and different sorts of expectations of the role of student vis-à-vis adult. Therefore "the importance of the role taken by the adult in eliciting language from students for language proficiency assessment cannot be over-emphasized" (Bennett and Slaughter, 1983, p. 9).

Socially-Based Notions of Appropriate Language

Social values regarding what constitutes appropriate or correct language permeate our ideas of language proficiency. Professor Olga Vasquez (1993) relates a personal experience that illustrates this point. Dr. Vasquez, who identifies herself as Chicana, was traveling in Spain and went to check into her hotel. She addressed the desk clerk with, *Me quiero registrar* ("I would like to check in"), whereupon he informed her with a smirk that there was no such usage of *registrar* in Castilian Spanish and that she should have used the word *inscribir*. Dr. Vasquez says, "The social situation that was created in this brief interaction communicated much about one man's perception of social inequalities. . . . it was clear that his command of standard Spanish positioned him at a higher status—enough to compel him to correct my usage" (Vasquez, 1993, p. 201). One can sense from this episode how denying the validity of someone's language (whether in part or whole) is scarcely a step removed from denying the legitimacy of the person's own identity, both personal and social. In fact, groups often maintain non-standard linguistic forms, dialects, to distinguish themselves from a dominant group. Common language is a source of solidarity. (The expression, "We speak the same language," implies much more than "We both speak Vietnamese.")

Sociolinguistic (pragmatic) conventions are less accessible to consciousness than specific vocabulary or pronunciation; however, when a sociolinguistic rule is broken, we sense that something is very wrong. For example, if a student fails to give any response to a teachers's direct question in front of the entire class, both teacher and student may be suffering from crossed sociolinguistic wires: the teacher taking umbrage at the lack of a demanded response, the student embarrassed at being addressed individually within a group. Although it is accepted European-American instructional practice to examine students individually in the whole group (for comprehension or attention), in some American Indian communities it would be considered rude to address a single person when others are present, thus excluding them (Philips, 1983). In such a circumstance, the teacher may wrongly conclude that the student is uncooperative, incapable of answering, or did not understand the question (a judgment about the student's language proficiency). Other aspects of communication, such as eye movement, gesture, pace and volume of speech are also extremely variable from culture to culture. When teachers are not aware of how such elements can vary, they may believe a student has a learning problem because he/she has failed to learn how to communicate in mainstream ways; or worse, she may believe that the student is expressing hostility when respect is intended or lack of interest when deference is meant.

Dialects

We introduced the topic of "dialects" in Chapter 2, but it merits further attention here. A *dialect* is "a variety of a language that is distinguished from other varieties of the same language by features of phonology, grammar and vocabulary and by its use by a group of speakers who are set off from others geographically or socially" (Webster's Encyclopedic Unabridged Dictionary, 1989, p. 397). All people speak a dialect, though what many people think of as dialects are distinctively regional speech patterns or those associated with low-status groups. So-called *standard English* is simply one dialect among many equally valid and complex dialects of English. What is grammatical to a person depends on what dialect(s) he or she has learned. Problems may arise when "children . . . have difficulty judging what is grammatical in the English of a teacher, and a teacher . . . [has] difficulty recognizing what is grammatical in the normal English of the children" (Hymes, 1972, p. xxxviii).

To understand the language of students, teachers will have to learn about the meanings of language behaviors in students' home communities. Though some forms are accepted by the dominant culture as "standard" and others "non-standard," it will be helpful to understand the social origins of such values. That is to say, there is no inherent superiority in one linguistic convention over another, despite the social value attached to preferred styles and forms. Nor is one language or dialect superior to another. One of the misconceptions about languages is that there are "primitive" languages or dialects that do not allow their speakers to talk about abstract ideas or express logical relationships. "The fact of the matter is that every culture which has been investigated, no matter how 'primitive' it may be in cultural terms, turns out to have a fully developed language, with a complexity comparable to those of the so-called 'civilized' nations" (Crystal, 1987,p.6). (Cf., Hymes, 1972, p. xx: "The vernacular speech of every society or social group, when studied, has been found to be based on complex, profound structures of the same kind.") This would suggest that efforts to expand children's language capabilities should focus more on higher-level language activities than on remediation of dialectal differences. Bilingual research also supports the strategy of focusing on high-level cognitive activities rather than skills-based instruction. In either case, students are more likely to expand language knowledge for meaningful purposes—and to acquire standard forms in the process.

Forms of Discourse

Cazden (1988), Gumperz (1982), Hymes (1972), Heath (1983, 1986), Mitchell-Kernan and Ervin-Tripp (1977), and many others have contributed to our understanding of how language is organized (in terms of styles and genres, for example), depending on its purpose or use. It is not enough to say someone speaks a particular language. Many varieties of language are spoken by any given individual. Communities have multiple registers, or socially determined variants of a language used for particular purposes, such as legal or medical (Crystal, 1987, p. 429), or mathematical, or to recognize social distinctions between classes. Many people speak more than one dialect. Speakers choose the kind of language they will speak according to context or need. Even *silence* is a choice (Hymes, 1972). Some communities speak more than one language; but language is only one of several means of communication available to a community. Each person has a verbal repertoire that includes the means of speaking and the contexts in which he/she may speak, adding up to *ways of speaking* (or in Heath's phrase, "ways with words," Heath, 1983), a set of patterns relating means of speech and contexts of situation.

If we are to understand what children from a community are saying, and how they hear what we say to them, we must come to be able to recognize more than the language of what is being said. We must recognize how the community norms of interpretation are embodied in speech (Hymes, 1972, p. xxx) .

At times, teachers do not recognize as intelligent those language behaviors that are alien to their own cultures. It is "not that a child cannot express himself or that a thought cannot be required of him, but that he expresses it in one style of expression rather than another. Not that a child cannot answer questions, but that questions and answers are defined for him in terms of one set of community norms rather than another, as to what count as questions and answers, and as to what it means to be asked or to answer (Hymes, 1972, p. xxxi) . . . A teacher can do much to shape the environment surrounding language and its use in the classroom (Hymes, 1972, pxxxii) . . . It has become clear that mutual understanding depends not only on common linguistic means, in the narrow sense, but also on common ways of using and interpreting speech (Hymes, p. xxxvii).

Classroom Language

Uses Linked to Discourse Genres

As we have mentioned above, language *use* is an important facet of language proficiency in the classroom. In fact, language use may well be the *most* powerful cultural element in the classroom related to student learning (Heath, 1986; Villegas, 1991). Unfortunately, it is the facet of language about which teachers probably have the *least* awareness.

As mentioned, before coming to school, children learn the language uses of their communities through countless interactions over a period of several years; and different communities value different uses. Most children, however, have opportunities to hear and use language in ways beyond those modeled within their own immediate communities. However, children isolated by distance (social or geographic) from other communities may have little exposure to language uses of people and institutions outside their own communities (Heath, 1986). Some of the more decontextualized (or context-reduced) uses of languages, such as reading texts or talking about experiences remote from the context at hand, may be alien to the language of culturally non-dominant children. Yet, all children will be called on in school to use language in a decontextualized way. For example, even in kindergarten and first grade, classroom routines like "show and tell" require students to talk about past or future events (events not present in the situation). An increased burden is placed on the code (language), as opposed to the shared context. Students need to know how to gauge what listeners know and do not know and express themselves accordingly.

Real-life experiences outside of school, in which children have to explain their needs to people beyond their immediate family, build the ability to use language to supply all the necessary information. Middle-class students from the dominant culture are generally exposed to many more such experiences in which information is given and received in the absence of shared familiar context. Particularly important are interactions in which oral and written communication co-occur, for example when forms have to be filled out or library books signed out (Heath, 1986).

At home, middle-class, "mainstream" parents model for and elicit from their children considerable decontextualized conversation about past and future events, about stories they have read. These practices parallel classroom language events, and they have been shown to be positively associated with later acquisition of literacy. So, there is a continuity for culturally dominant students between home and school that may not obtain for other students.

It is not only second-language learners who may be at a disadvantage in the classroom. Students from non-dominant cultural or ethnic backgrounds or from lower socioeconomic groups whose experience does not match that of the mainstream (as represented by the culture of the classroom) may not be familiar with the discourse genres of the classroom or with the conversational patterns in which they are expected to participate. These *discourse genres* are organizing units of language, or maps for stretches of discourse (Heath, 1986); they are associated with different uses of language, such as obtaining information or telling about one's experiences or what one has learned. There is an accepted (school) "formula" for talking about one's experiences (*account* genre) or talking about how one is going to carry out a task (*eventcast*). (See Table 4.2 for examples of school language uses and the genres to which they are linked.)

	TABLE 4.2	
School Language Uses	**Linked To**	**Discourse Genres**
Label and describe		*Label quests:* Adult names items or ask for their names or attributes ("What?…" What kind of…?")
Recount past events		*Recounts:* Speaker retells experiences or inform- ation known to teller and listener. (Tell about an event, retell a passage read, summarize material, display knowledge in oral and written form)
Follow directions (oral and written) Maintain social interactions of the group		*Eventcasts:* Speaker pro- vides running narrative of events at hand or forecast. (E.g., teacher tells what day's events will be, what steps to take to complete a task; student may be asked to do same.)
Obtain information from non-intimates		*Meaning quests:* Adult seeks student interpretation or explanations. (Interpreting actions or text; test "why" questions)
Account for one's experiences, link to known ideas or events, create new information		*Accounts:* Speaker tells about own experiences to listener or reinterprets known information. (Show and tell, reports) *Stories:* Factual or fictional accounts that follow format of an animate being mov- ing through a series of events with goal-directed behavior.

Constructed from text by Heath (1986), pp. 166-170.

For many children entering school, there is minimal fit between language uses and genres they have learned in their home communities and those that school requires (Heath, 1986), if only in the degree to which these uses prevail in their communities. The accepted formula may vary from one culture to the next, so that even if a child has extensive experience with a genre, that experience may not help the child to use the equivalent genre successfully in school. For example, though storytelling is something apparently practiced in virtually all communities, what counts as a story is quite variable. Some communities of speakers, such as middle-class European-Americans, tell *topic-centered* stories that are characterized by sequentially structured discourse on a single topic. In their version of the story or account genre, it is also considered important to assume little knowledge on the part of listeners and thus be explicit about such things as relationships among characters, which pronouns refer to which nouns, and other information that would be necessary for someone who was not familiar with the context in which the events occurred. Other communities may have a tradition of *topic-associating* stories, that are characterized by multiple-linked topics structured in less linear fashion. They do not have as clear a pattern of beginning, middle, and end. In stories of this kind, which may be told more frequently within a group that shares cultural knowledge and experience, it is not necessary to be so explicit about character identification and tracking of pronouns to their noun referents. A discrepancy in cultural definitions of a genre such as this one needs to be taken into account in assessing a student's grasp of narrative, for example.

Participant Structures

Another aspect of classroom language use that may not parallel the practices of students' home communities has to do with *participant structures*. These are the patterns of discourse that reflect rules about who should speak when. Classroom discourse (conversation, discussion, presentation) is critical to learning and displaying abilities. Unfortunately, the participant structure of most classrooms—what has been called "the recitation script" (Cazden, 1988; Mehan, 1979)—has been shown to adversely affect "minority" students (McCollum, 1991). Figure 4.3 shows the pattern of the recitation script: The teacher initiates virtually all conversation (often by asking a question); a student responds to the teacher (and the teacher usually chooses a student to respond); then the teacher evaluates the student's response. Rarely do students initiate talk or evaluate each other's responses. Calfee and Nelson-Barber characterize the roles of teacher and student in this participant structure as "spectator" and "exhibitionist" (Calfee and Nelson-Barber, 1991).

FIGURE 4.3

Two Possible Participant Structures

Recitation Script

I--------> R--------> E--------> I--------> R--------> E--------> I-------> R

T   S   T   T   S   T   T   S

In the recitation script, all conversation is mediated through and evaluated by the teacher.

Small-Group Discussion Script

The teacher sets the stage by helping the group plan what it will be working on; then participation is semi-independent, scaffolded by occasional teacher monitoring and initiation of questions or comments.

I--------> R--------> R--------> I--------> R--------> E--------> I-------->

S1   S2   S3   S2   S4   S1   S1

R--------> E--------> I--------> R-------->R--------> E--------> I-------->

S2   T   T   S2   S3   T   S1

R--------> R--------> I--------> R-------->E--------> I-------> R-------->

S4   S3   S3   S2   S1   S1   S2

In the small-group discussion, students maintain their own conversation. There may be two or more responses to an initiation, and any member may initiate a subsequent comment or question. At times, the teacher may facilitate student discussion by monitoring it and posing a question of his/her own and perhaps evaluating student responses. Students may evaluate each other's statements.

Note the number of teacher turns versus student turns in each script.

T= Teacher, S= Student, I= Initiate, R= Respond, E= Evaluate

The recitation script is harmonious with a view of the teacher as purveyor of all knowledge and students as recipients, but it is not harmonious with the view of teaching and learning in which the teacher is a facilitator of high-level, self-directed (sometimes cooperative) inquiry on the part of students. Neither is it compatible with the needs of students learning a second language (or developing high-level discourse skills in any language). They need more opportunities to speak and more control over their choices to speak. Finally, there are numerous examples of cultural conflict with this discourse format. In cultures that are said to be more "peer oriented" (such as the Native Hawaiian and the Inuit in Quebec), students are not used to being constantly evaluated by an adult; rather, they rely on feedback from their peers (Eriks-Brophy and Crago, 1993; Jordan, 1985). Ongoing evaluation of every response may serve to "shut them down" in class. Jordan (1985) has talked of "harnessing peer interaction for academic purposes." Figure 4.3 also shows a possible alternative to the recitation script, one that would have students talking with each other (here in small groups), facilitated at times by the teacher.

Domination of talk by a single person is not the norm in some American Indian communities (Philips, 1983). In addition, as mentioned earlier, in such communities, when speaking in a group a person is expected to address the entire group rather than a single individual (as teacher and students do in the recitation script); and in many American Indian communities it is usual for a person to decide when he/she will speak and for how long. A child from a community with these norms of communication would undoubtedly find the recitation script both alien and difficult to participate in.

It is not much of a leap from classroom communication patterns to the arena of assessment. In fact, much of ongoing informal assessment in the classroom takes the form of questioning within the whole group. One wonders how accurate a picture of student learning can be gained when incompatible or discomfiting discourse structures are used. Some of the new assessments would appear to demand new participant structures, such as the "instructional conversation" (Tharp and Gallimore, 1988) or collaborative learning. In the former approach, students take a much more active role in classroom discourse. The teacher facilitates discussion, poses questions, encourages students to respond to each other, and introduces important information at key moments—but is far less regulatory in the traditional sense. Allowing students to participate through a variety of social relations and to have more control over how they will participate makes learning opportunities more equitable. There is no longer only one way to participate that represents a historical, dominant culture norm.

In collaborative learning, students conduct inquiry in small working groups that may draw support from the teacher but are relatively autonomous. This kind of arrangement is beneficial—probably to all students— but especially to students from non-English-speaking backgrounds because

(a) they talk more than in teacher-centered instruction; (b) they use a greater range of linguistic functions (questioning, explaining, clarifying, generalizing, describing, defining, classifying, evaluating); and (c) they put more effort into trying to make their meaning clear to other students without the teacher's help (Garcia, 1988; Swain, 1993).

A form of collaborative learning (small-group projects) has worked better than whole-group and traditional small-group instruction for groups of American Indian students, seemingly in part because of the opportunity for students to control when they speak (Philips, 1983).

If performance assessment were collaborative as well, one would expect to see a greater range of student skills than in an individual assessment, particularly in linguistically diverse classrooms. Research with science performance assessment of English-learners suggests that small-group performance assessment that allows students to use their language of choice to solve problems collaboratively is beneficial for promoting engagement and better performance (Shaw, 1993).

A Comment on Discourse Styles

The issue of cultural differences in discourse styles is too vast to explore in any depth, but it should be addressed, however briefly; because differences in communicative style potentially affect student performances and how they are evaluated by teachers. A couple of examples will suffice to show how this can happen. The typical European-American approach to composing a piece of persuasive writing is to introduce first a thesis (main idea) and then support it with evidence. As suggested earlier, this is in contrast to Chinese or Chinese-American style in which evidence or details are offered first, then a conclusion stated. "Chinese speakers systematically favor steadily unraveling and building up information before arriving at the important message" (Tsang, 1989, p. 243).

As we noted in Chapter 1, research on Black and White communicative styles has revealed some interesting differences. Black style is said to be more spontaneous, improvisational, exaggerated, expressive and personalized, while White style tends toward the methodical, systematic, understated, restrained, and role-oriented (Kochman, 1989). While seeking to avoid assumptions about "all Blacks" or "all Whites," we may gain some insight into possible differences in the ways students communicate in the classroom. One related claim arising from Kochman's research is very suggestive for classroom assessment: that Black style does not exclude emotion and personal belief in argumentation, whereas White style dictates removing both emotion and personal belief and relying on evidence and outside authority alone. Kochman claims that Black speakers he studied find White argumentation to be disingenuous; while White speakers find Black argumentation too emotional.

Suspending the claim that the styles discussed here are used strictly by White, Black, or Chinese speakers (but likely do represent different approaches to argument), we can imagine how they could lead to very different performances on the same assesssment task—equally valid in the eyes of different communities. Even if performance standards are tied to "mainstream" norms of communication, and students are expected to meet them, knowledge of cultural differences in style would suggest that some differences in teaching approach are probably required, not to mention differences in ways of interpreting student performance on classroom tasks.

The Language Demands of Performance Assessments: Some Examples

Educators' concerns about the validity of assessing students in their second language have historically centered around students' degree of mastery of the vocabulary and grammar of that language. Their concerns about the validity of standardized assessments for culturally non-dominant students have focused more on the appropriateness of content. While these concerns continue to be legitimate, as we have mentioned, at least as important as these factors are the *uses of language* that students are called on to understand and engage in themselves. Students whose communities do not use language in ways parallel to the ways of the classroom cannot help but require additional time and support to expand their repertoire of language uses—something they will have to do if they are to succeed. At the same time, teachers need resources to support their own ability to recognize their students' ways of using language, for example, to "hear" a topic-associating narrative as actually having a structure, rather than concluding that a child "has no sense of story structure."

Table 4.3 gives some examples of performance assessment tasks (or items) and identifies the kinds of language demands they appear to make. Of course, these demands can be mitigated or changed by the kinds of interpretation or support teachers offer. The reader will probably be able to discover additional potential language demands for each of these tasks.

Figure 4.4 offers an example of a more complex performance assessment activity. It is a draft of an interdisciplinary fifth-grade task designed at T'saile Public School (in the Chinle Unified Public School District) on the Navajo Reservation in Arizona. This task is designed to be completed over a period of several weeks. It addresses skills related to three content area standards established by the district: environmental and cultural awareness and responsibility, life skills, and communication.

TABLE 4.3

Assessment Activities and Their Language Demands

Sample Assessment Activity	Potential Language Demands
Write a report for a friend who was sick today, explaining to her the various exhibits you saw at the Science Museum in the order you saw them on the class field trip.	Recount a past event, sequencing and reinterpreting information; assume role of teacher to a non-present audience. (Requires considering what recipient already knows, level of detail she needs to comprehend.)
*Tell us anything else about your understanding of this story—what it means to you, what it makes you think about in your own life, or anything that relates to your reading of it. (Segment of an elementary reading assessment.)	Give account of own experience(s), linking to text, elaborating story comprehension.
You are a statistician for a large electronics firm. Design a market survey, construct a graph, and analyze data in various forms regarding consumer preferences and characteristics. Advise your marketing director on an advertising strategy. (Adaptation of an eighth grade mathematics assessment).	Obtain/select necessary information, recount information through multiple representations, interpret and explain; summarize conclusions.
*Imagine that you are a staff writer for a small magazine. One day you are given your "big chance." . . . You are asked to write the final scene of an incomplete story. (Taken from a 12th-grade writing task.)	Complete an account (a story) following prescribed format; comprehend/analyze story so that new segment makes sense. Take on voice of another author, maintaining style.

*Reprinted by permission from *A Sampler of English-language arts assessment* (Elementary) copyright 1994, California Department of Education, P.O. Box 271, Sacramento, CA 95812

FIGURE 4.4

Sample Extended Interdisciplinary Performance Task

Prompt to Student:

In this task you will collect data and information regarding one aspect of deforestation (such as erosion, endangered animals, economics, values, and effect on the bio-system and sacred places) to become an expert in one or more areas. You will conduct an interview about the issues and values of deforestation. You will work in small groups to present your material in a variety of ways, including a debate in which you take a pro or con position.

Re-explanation for student:

You will find out more about deforestation by reading, interviewing, and sharing. You will work in a small group to present your information. To accomplish this task, you will need to:

1. Research one area of deforestation

2. Write interview questions

3. Complete the interview

4. Keep a notebook of your information and data collected, a record of research problems and solutions, and personal reflections.

5. Work with a group to present information about deforestation.

5th grade teachers, T'saile Elementary School, Chinle (AZ) Unified School District in collaboration with Nanette Koelsch, Far West Laboratory.

The T'saile teachers have identified task extensions such as literature studies, role playing, drama, and various other kinds of written and oral presentations and products. The language demands of this rich, extended task are quite evident; many are directly listed. Any one of the activities, such as preparing for and conducting an interview, entails a whole constellation of language skills. Interviews require a real sense of what one wants to know, how a question needs to be posed to get at that information, what sequence of questions makes most sense, and how to phrase questions so that they will be considerate (not too intrusive, for example). The carrying out of the interview requires an equally complex array of language skills. In this case, one assumes that cultural congruence will make at least one set of issues moot. Since the Chinle Public Schools' curriculum is based on the cultural values and knowledge of the Navajo community to which students belong, tasks associated with it are likely to be meaningful and—in some sense—contextualized. However, students will still have to learn how to manage the dual task of keeping an interviewee engaged while taking notes, monitoring whether the desired information is forthcoming, and re-asking or re-phrasing questions if it is not.

Of course, the demands of all of the activities will be relative to students' language proficiency and academic experiences. If one thinks of Halliday's categories of language use, one might judge that the heuristic and informative functions would predominate. At least four of the school language uses outlined by Heath (Table 4.2) would be entailed; and all language arts components would be used (including "performing" if one counts debate as performance).

Figures 4.5 and 4.6 represent two mathematics assessment items published by the California Department of Education as samples for teachers to try out (1991). The first one is for primary grades and is not at all atypical in its language demands. In fact the language demands seem quite minimal at first glance.

FIGURE 4.5

Sample Primary Mathematics Assessment

The Bus Ride

A friend of yours, who just moved to the United States, must ride the bus to and from school each day. The bus ride costs 50 cents. Your friend must have exact change and must use only nickels, dimes and quarters.

Your friend has a problem because she does not yet understand our money, and she does not know how to count our money.

Help your friend find the right coins to give to the bus driver. Draw and write something on a whole sheet of paper that can help her. She needs a sheet of paper that can show which combinations of coins can be used to pay for the 50-cent bus ride.

Be sure to organize your paper so it is clear and helpful for your friend.

Reprinted by permission, from *A Sampler of mathematics assessment,* © 1991 by the California Department of Education.

FIGURE 4.6
Sample Secondary Mathematics Assessment
Survey of Smoking

The journalism class of Exeter High School surveyed 100 of the school's 2,000 students about their smoking habits. The results of the survey follow:

38	Never smoked
11	Current smoker who has smoked less than one year
24	Current smoker who has smoked more than one year
18	Quit smoking less than one year ago
9	Quit smoking more than one year ago
———	
100	Total

Write a short article that could appear in a school newspaper about the results of the survey. Include five statements that show interpretations or conclusions you derive from the survey data.

Reprinted by permission, from *A Sampler of mathematics assessment*, © 1991 by the California Department of Education.

"The Bus Ride" task does not require much written language on the part of the student, but in order to figure out what to do, the student has to read quite a bit of text and understand some specialized vocabulary (*exact change, nickel, dime, quarter, combinations of coins*). Now, consider the secondary mathematics assessment item shown in Figure 4.6. The student, in this case, has to compose a short expository piece that translates quantitative information into language—and something more than a list of conclusions. *A short article that could appear in a school newspaper* will be expected to be appropriately structured and sequenced, expressing the student's interpretations of what is interesting to fellow students about the data presented. This task is far different from answering a set of multiple choice items that get at the student's understanding of the information (for example, "What percentage of the students surveyed used to smoke?": (a) 9%, (b) 24%, (c) 27%, (d) 18%.)

As mentioned in Chapter 1, when language is involved in an assessment, there is always the question of whether one is assessing understanding of the purported independent construct (such as drawing conclusions from statistical data) or actually assessing language proficiency—at least in part. If a student had difficulty with the second example above, a teacher might have trouble divining whether a poor performance was due to lack of comprehension of the statistical data, failure to conceptualize the task, or problems with producing a written piece in a specified time frame. The complexity of the issue is magnified when a student is being assessed through a language other than his/her primary one. Another issue is that with multi-dimensional, integrated tasks (that call on several kinds of language or other skills), breakdown can occur at any point; and the teacher cannot always diagnose where things went wrong by evaluating a student product out of context or without additional information.

Without resorting to extremely technical analyses, teachers can use the frameworks of Cummins, Halliday, and Heath to guide them in evaluating the language demands of classroom tasks relative to the language proficiencies and contexts of their students. Table 4.4 shows a checklist that was adapted for the Georgetown University Evaluation Assistance Center from an earlier one designed by Bernhard and Loera (O'Malley, 1989) based on Cummins' framework.

TABLE 4.4

Interpersonal and Academic Language Skills Checklist

Name: Date:

Directions: Please check skills which have been observed at an appropriate level in either English or the non-English language.

	English	Non-English language
Contextualized/Noncognitively demanding:		
1. Answers basic questions appropriately.		
2. Exchanges common greetings.		
3. Follows general classroom directions.		
4. Participates in routine school activities.		
5. Describes classroom objects or people.		
6. Gives classroom commands to peers.		
7. Participates in sharing time.		
8. Retells a familar story.		
9. Initiates and maintains a conversation.		
10. Follows along during oral reading.		

	English	Non-English language
Decontextualized/Noncognitively demanding: 11. Decodes fluently. 12. Reads noncognitively demanding information, e.g., notes, signs, directions, simple sentences, etc. 13. Writes words and simple sentences. 14. Generates simple sentences. 15. Writes from dictation. Contextualized/Cognitively demanding: 16. Follows specific directions for academic tasks. 17. Uses terms for temporal and spatial concepts, e.g., *first, last; top, bottom; left, right,* etc. 18. Asks/answers questions regarding academic topics. 19. Understands contextualized academic content. 20. Reads stories for literal comprehension. Decontextualized/Cognitively demanding: 21. Distinguishes main ideas from details (oral). 22. Predicts conclusions after listening to story. 23. Understands lectures on academic content. 24. Uses language to reason, analyze, synthesize. 25. Participates in academic discussions. 26. Reads content area information for comprehension. 27. Uses glossary, index, appendices, etc. 28. Writes meaningful short paragraphs. 29. Uses correct language mechanics. 30. Writes coherent stories or reports.		

Adapted from J. Michael O'Malley. (1989). Language proficiency testing with limited English-Proficient Students. In Alatis, James E. (Ed.), *Language teaching, testing, and technology: Lessons from the past with a view toward the future.* Georgetown University Round Table on Languages and Linguistics, 235-244. Washington, D.C.: Georgetwon University Press.

Teachers may also address the following questions as they attempt to evaluate the language demands of classroom instructional and assessment activities:

- What components of language arts are involved in the activity, and how competent is the student with each one?

- How complex are the directions for undertaking the task? (Sentence structures and length, specialized vocabulary, length and complexity of text; dependence on small relational words such as "before," "after," "if . . . then," "because," etc.)

- How flexible is the task in terms of its requirements for language use? Are there alternative ways of expressing understanding or representing information given in language (drawings vs. essays, for example)?

- Even though the task appears to be a non-verbal task, what kinds of hidden language demands does it have (for example, for problem-representation)?

- How can the task be facilitated or mediated? Can additional explanation be offered? Is the student allowed to use a dictionary or other tool?

- How much decontextualized language is being used, or how much will the student have to produce (demands of reading, writing especially)? Does the topic provide any bridges to student experience?

- How many different language functions must the student "pull together" to perform a complex, integrated task (and where might the process break down for a student who is still learning English or who has limited mastery of language functions)?

- How cognitively demanding does the task appear to be, judging from what is known about a student's language proficiency and previous educational experience?

- To what degree does a language use or an associated genre match the student's cultural experience with that use or genre?

Summary and Recommendations

We have introduced several ways of looking at students' language proficiency and emphasized those that focus on meaningful communication within social contexts. We have also emphasized the critical role of language in learning—whether it be in the home community to which the child belongs or in school. At this point, perhaps we ought to remind ourselves that language proficiency does not account for all of the differences in student achievement that one sees between students from dominant and non-dominant cultures. Lack of adequate resources and opportunities to learn, inadequate teacher knowledge about language and culture, and broader social inequities contribute to lower-than-desired performance on the part of some students. Yet, we are optimistic that awareness of the ways linguistic factors influence classroom participation and performance cannot help but improve the way in which language minority students are taught and assessed.

In attempting to appraise the potential language demands of the classroom, we have looked to theorists such as Halliday, Cummins, and Heath for taxonomies or frameworks of language use. We have argued that mastery of language uses and their associated conventions and structures are a more important determinant of student success than mastery of vocabulary and syntax.

We have come to believe that some of the most important understandings teachers can gain from thinking about language in the ways we have proposed have to do with students' need for powerful experiences with extended texts—both spoken and written. A student cannot be expected to succeed in school or in the society at large without the ability to read many kinds of texts (narrative, exposition, poetry, drama, among others) critically, bringing his or her own experience to bear on interpretation of the text. Nor will students succeed without equally strong school-congruent oral discourse skills representing many genres. At the same time, students' home-community forms and uses of language need to be respected and fostered in their own growth. The brain's linguistic capacity is apparently boundless, in the sense that we have yet to identify any limit on the number of languages, dialects, and registers, or uses and variations of genres with which an individual can develop competence.

"Critical literacy," which would encompass the competences mentioned in the previous paragraph, is an essential element in the success of students in a curriculum focused on higher-level thinking. Others, such as Freire, would add that an important element of critical literacy is the ability to evaluate what one reads and hears and thus become empowered to transform the world. If, indeed, there is a nationwide movement toward universally high standards associated with high-level instruction for all students, one could argue that a goal of critical literacy should be the cornerstone of such a movement. To accomplish the goal of critical literacy for all, teachers will have to tailor instruction and assessment to the needs of their own students, considering numerous issues. Table 4.5 is a compendium of suggestions that can serve as a checklist for teachers who seek to promote critical literacy for all students, including those whose first language is not English and those from non-dominant cultures.

TABLE 4.5

Summary Suggestions

1. Add meaningful context to decontextualized activities (such as reading of texts).

2. Draw on the cultural experiences of students.

3. Support continued development of students' primary languages (the conceptual basis for other representational systems).

4. Show respect for a student's first language as the source of his/her personal and cultural identity.

5. Provide maximum opportunity for using one semiotic system to gain entry to meaning in another (using visual or gestural information to enhance verbal, etc.).

6. Give many unthreatening opportunities for students to increase familiarity and comfort with school language uses and genres.

7. Share examples of cultural variations of classroom genres (such as accounts and stories) so that students can see how they differ.

8. Develop awareness of students' competence with various uses of language (by observation, tape-recording, consultation with other professionals).

9. Concentrate on big ideas, the "thinking" part of language rather than discrete skills, while providing context to make input comprehensible.

10. Examine classroom activities in light of their language demands (see above).

11. Ensure an appropriate "mix" of language activities in the classroom (representing all components of language).

12. Provide more opportunities for students to take an active role in classroom discourse (using different participant structures and observing students' responses).

13. Be sure that there is more student talk than teacher talk in the classroom.

14. Decrease regulatory use of language and increase heuristic and representational.

15. Encourage students to learn from each other in group discussions and give evaluative feedback to the group rather than individuals at times (directing attention to informative student responses or encouraging students to respond to each other).

16. Allow students to make choices about how they will participate in classroom discourse.

17. Try different grouping strategies (small-group, student-managed; small-group, teacher-managed; student pairs; short one-to-one instructional sessions; whole-group lessons with and without group responses permitted, etc.), and see who participates and how.

18. Increase collaborative learning opportunities.

19. Increase student choice regarding topics of individual or group inquiry. (Motivation and investment should increase.)

20. Allow students to use whatever language works for them in independent group work.

21. Use the BICS and CALP framework to assess student levels of proficiency and how they intersect with the demands of classroom tasks.

In Chapter 5, we will discuss specific approaches to assessment that are potentially equitable for and informative about all students. With the insights and principles garnered in our exploration of several frameworks of language proficiency we may be able at least to imagine a system or systems that would answer the needs of a multilingual, multicultural student population.

Commentary

Sharon Nelson-Barber
Far West Laboratory

Chapter 4 raises issues of tremendous concern to all educators in our society. With our nation's classrooms populated by more and more students who may speak a first language other than English and who come from cultural traditions beyond those of mainstream America, teachers are now required to know more about world-view differences, language diversity, and ways of interacting effectively with students from a range of cultural groups. This can be quite a challenge given the small percentage of teachers of color in our schools, the fact that teachers are increasingly likely to live outside the communities from which their students come, and the generally inadequate preparation provided to teachers in understanding and handling cultural differences.

As the authors remind us, any lack of shared understanding can be troublesome when teachers are charged with assessing students' intellectual capabilities. Of particular concern is research's suggestion that teachers who know little about their students' backgrounds may be unable to make connections between the content they are trying to teach and the knowledge their students already possess. Also relevant is the notion that teachers may be unable to establish the kinds of relationships with students that motivate them to succeed.

On the other hand, many teachers who *are* successful have learned that the so-called "progressive" strategies and techniques being called for today (for example, active, hands-on exploration and use of resources and structures such as heterogeneous cooperative grouping, etc.) will mean little if teachers are not equipped to fashion a curriculum that is more personal and more directly linked to their students' experiences and shared values, including local language styles. It is this latter category that will be the focus of the commentary, for even though teachers work their hardest to keep responsiveness to students apace with the changing demographics, miscommunication in the classroom remains a serious issue.

Though it makes sense that misunderstandings can occur when the language of the classroom is one that students are just learning, it cannot be stressed enough that teachers and students from different cultural backgrounds can also have difficulty understanding one another despite adequate knowledge of a *mutual* language. In fact classrooms where individuals ostensibly speak the same language can be places where subtle but damaging expressions of difference take place that further increase the distance between teacher and student.

For example, the authors mention numerous communicative strategies that figure significantly in the semantic judgments and cohesiveness of verbal interaction and also convey that these strategies are not the same for all cultural groups. Clearly, dialectal variations in features such as accent and in rules governing grammar or vocabulary can be important sources of misunderstanding between speakers. Still, teachers are likely to make sense of phonological and syntactic differences between dialects, while many of the distinctions that lead to miscommunication between subgroups are more finespun and subliminal. In other words, one might make sense of the grammar and sound system of (Alaskan) Village English; but understanding the conventions of non-verbal communication in these communities is more dependent upon shared knowledge not easily accessible to those from the outside.

For example, if two speakers have a great deal in common with one another, much can be taken for granted in the interaction. When asked to describe and justify work to a teacher from a similar cultural background, a student's task is considerably eased by the background assumptions she shares with the teacher. One the other hand, to speak from the perspective of differences, from an alternate cultural view, is a far more difficult communicative task. In such a situation, common ground cannot be assumed, but instead must be created by the student. To achieve understanding, the student must proceed more slowly, provide more background information, explain assumptions, anticipate objections and misunderstandings, use more specific examples and details. If the student undertakes such a task with the feeling, well founded in experience, that her perspectives are not likely to be taken seriously by the teacher who, in the student's mind, has already determined the "appropriate response," it is likely that the student will view the possibility of achieving real understanding between herself and the teacher as a futile task. Teachers who have little experience outside their own speech communities may be unaware of the complex demands that seemingly simple speech events such as "Show and Tell" place on young children.

In this case even aspects of communicative style that are appropriate—effective and community validated—can reinforce negative conclusions about children's academic potential. If in "Show and Tell" Native children organize their talk according to traditional norms, their "story" may not be presented in a linear fashion with a beginning, middle, and end that leads listeners to an appropriate conclusion. Instead, they may present a series of perspectives on a topic with the expectation that listeners as active participants have the responsibility of making appropriate connections and deciding whether they will be persuaded. Typically, teachers who misunderstand this rhetorical style tend to dismiss such narratives as "rambling" and "ineffectual" and prod their students to "talk only about important things."

Also, as the authors have already mentioned, the notion of speaking before a group or of representing a group perspective can be taboo in Native cultures. Not only might a teacher presume that her students feel comfortable speaking in this fashion, she might also expect them to "show off" new-found knowledge or experience. Many indigenous groups in our society shun this behavior, deeming it boastful and rude. In other words, many Native children are not socialized to exhibit what they know, but instead demonstrate their skills in ways that are less direct—letting excellent work speak for itself, and so forth. As a consequence Native children have been viewed as aloof, withdrawn, or, more tragically, as not having certain skills at all. In these cases the teacher's intuitions about talk and ways of displaying excellence may unwittingly lead to the child's coming away from these experiences frustrated, confused, and misjudged.

Another important communicative issue mentioned in the chapter is that members of some communities of color may be uncomfortable in situations in which they are asked to respond to questions to which it is clear that the questioner already knows (or thinks s/he knows) the answer. The purpose of such questions, typical of teacher-student interaction, is not for the questioner to gain information, but for the respondent to display information, to prove that he or she knows the answer. Sociolinguistic research suggests that children from different cultural communities come to school differentially prepared to participate in conversational exchanges that require them to display informational for its own sake. While numerous language studies reveal that display or test questions are the type most frequently addressed to middle class pre-schoolers (for example, "how many eyes do you have?", "what color is this dolly's dress?", "how many fingers is mommy holding up?"), other researchers found that in some working-class African-American communities children were almost never asked questions to which the adult already knew the answer, because such questions were perceived as having no real communicative purpose. Because classroom instruction relies so heavily on this kind of questioning for both instruction and assessment, it is important for teachers to understand its differential relevance to students.

The fact that adult members of such communities may have learned to handle display questions in order to succeed in school does not mean that they necessarily perceive such questions as serving any real communicative purpose or as an invitation to talk about what they know and believe about a subject. Unfortunately, one of the lessons many students of color have learned as a result of their schooling experience is to draw a sharp distinction between their own knowledge and experience and what it is they perceive the teacher as wanting to hear.

Though we must be careful not to overgeneralize differences, it must also be said that communicative styles are rooted in specific modes of thinking and interacting that are automatic and not necessarily summoned or modified on command. Indeed, a major challenge facing schools of education as they prepare individuals to meet the needs of an increasingly multicultural student population is to define more precisely the common knowledge base and set of experiences that teachers will need to draw upon in adapting to diversity in the classroom. Further broadening the knowledge base to include the perspectives and experiences of teachers and researchers, who themselves come from a diverse range of cultural backgrounds and who possess knowledge about the kinds of teacher behaviors and practices that work most effectively in non-mainstream settings, will be the central challenge of educational reform for the 2000s.

— ⅍ —

Dr. Sharon Nelson-Barber, Senior Research Associate at Far West Laboratory with the Regional Consortium for Science and Mathematics, is a sociolinguist who has taught courses on language, culture and education in the Anthropology Department at Stanford University. Dr. Nelson-Barber's research has centered around communication patterns in indigenous communities in the southwestern United States and Alaska, language issues in education, and linguistic and cultural factors in teacher preparation and evaluation. She is Coordinator of the Native Education Initiative, a national task force whose goal is to improve educational services to American Indian, Alaska Native and Pacific Island students and is a key member of two national committees addressing the development of equitable assessments in mathematics and science. Dr. Nelson-Barber is a frequent speaker at national conferences and the author of numerous articles and book chapters. Most recently her focus has been on culturally-responsive instruction in mathematics and science.

References

Arizona student assessment plan. (1992). Chicago: The Riverside Publishing Company.

Bennett, Adrian and Slaughter, Helen. (1983). A sociolinguistic/discourse approach to the description of the communicative competence of linguistic minority children. In Charlene Rivera (Ed.), *An ethnographic sociolinguistic approach to language proficiency assessment.* Clevedon, Avon, England: Multilingual Matters, 1983, 2-26.

Bloom, Lois and Lahey, Margaret. (1978). *Language development and language disorders.* New York: John Wiley and Sons.

Bonner, John Tyler. (1980). *The evolution of culture in animals.* Princeton, NJ: Princeton University Press.

Calfee, Robert and Nelson-Barber, Sharon. (1991). Diversity and constancy in human thinking: Critical literacy as amplifier of intellect and experience. In Elfrieda H. Hiebert (Ed.), *Literacy for a diverse society: Perspectives, practices and policies.* New York: Teachers College Press, 44-57.

California Department of Education. (1991). *A sampler of mathematics assessments.* Sacramento, CA: California Department of Education.

Canale, Michael. (1981). From communicative competence to communicative language pedagogy. In J. Richard and R. Schmidt (Eds.), *Language and communication.* New York: Longman. (Cited in Cummins, 1981).

Canales, JoAnn. (1989, Spring). Assessment of language proficiency: Informing policy and practice. *Focus.* Southwestern Educational Development Laboratory, Austin, TX.

Casanova, Ursula and Arias, Beatriz, M. (Eds.). (1993). Contextualizing bilingual education. In Beatriz M. Arias and Ursula Casanova, *Bilingual education: Politics, practice, research, Part II. Ninety-second yearbook of the National Society for the Study of Education.* Chicago: University of Chicago Press, 1-35.

Cazden, Courtney. (1988). *Classroom discourse: The language of teaching and learning.* Portsmouth, NH: Heinemann Educational Publishers.

Chinle Public Schools, Chinle, AZ (Fifth grade teachers) (1993).

Cole, Michael and Bruner, Jerome S. (1971, October), Cultural Differences and Inferences about Psychological Processes. *American Psychologist.* Vol. 26, No. 10, 867-876.

Collier, Virginia P. (1987, December). Age and rate of acquisition of second language for academic purposes. *TESOL Quarterly,* 617-641.

Collier, Virginia P. (1992, Winter/Spring). A synthesis of studies examining long-term language minority student data on academic achievement. *Bilingual Research Journal,* 187-212.

Council of Chief State School Officers. (1992). *Recommendations for improving the assessment and monitoring of students with limited English proficiency.* Reston, Virginia: CCSSO.

Crystal, David. (1987). *The Cambridge encyclopedia of language.* Cambridge, England: Cambridge University Press.

Cummins, Jim. (1981). The role of primary language development in promoting educational success for language minority students. In California State Department of Education, Bilingual Education Office. *Schooling and language minority students: A theoretical framework.* Los Angeles: Evaluation, Dissemination and Assessment Center, California State University, Los Angeles, 3-49.

Cummins, Jim. (1982, February). Tests, achievement, and bilingual students, *Focus,* 1-7.

Cummins, Jim. (1989). Empowering language minority students. *Harvard Educational Review, 56,* 18-35.

DeAvila, Edward. (1990, September). Assessment of language minority students: Political, technical, practical and moral imperatives. In *Proceedings of the first research symposium on limited english proficient students' issues.* Washington, D.C.: Office of Bilingual Education and Minority Languages Affairs, 194-245.

Deyhle, Donna. (1987). Learning failure: Tests as gatekeepers and the culturally different child. In Trueba, Henry (Ed.). *Success or failure.* Rowley, MA: Newbury House.

Diaz, Stephen, Moll, Luis C., and Mehan, Hugh. (1986). Sociocultural resources in instruction: A context-specific approach. In *Beyond language: Social and cultural factors in schooling language minority students.* Bilingual Education Office, California State Department of Education. Los Angeles: Evaluation, Dissemination and Assessment Center, California State University, Los Angeles, 187-230.

Duncan, Sharon and DeAvila, Edward. (1985). *Language assessment scales.* Monterey, CA: CTB/McGraw Hill.

Duran, Richard. P. (1985). Influences of language skills on bilinguals' problem solving. In *Thinking and learning skills.* Hillsdale, NJ: Lawrence Erlbaum Associates, 187-207.

Eriks-Brophy, Alice and Crago, Martha B. (1993, April). Transforming classroom discourse: Forms of evaluation in Inuit IR and IRe routines. Paper presented at the Annual Meeting of the American Educational Research Association, Atlanta, GA.

Ervin-Tripp, Susan and Mitchell-Kernan, Claudia. (1977). *Child discourse.* New York: Academic Press.

Estrin, Elise Trumbull and Chaney, Carolyn. (1988, Winter). Developing a concept of the WORD. *Childhood Education,* 78-82.

Fillmore, Charles. J. (1976). The need for a frame semantics in linguistics. In *Statistical methods in linguistics.* Stockholm: Skriptor.

Freire, Paulo and Macedo, Donaldo. (1987). *Literacy: Reading the word and the world.* South Hadley, MA: Bergin and Garvey.

Garcia, Eugene. (1988). Attributes of effective schools for language minority students. *Education and Urban Society,* Vol. 2, No. 4, 387-398.

Garcia, Georgia Earnest. (1992). *The literacy assessment of second-language learners.* University of Illinois at Urbana-Champaign, Center for the Study of Reading, Technical Report No. 559.

Gardner, Howard. (1983). *Frames of mind.* New York: Basic Books.

Gardner, Howard. (1991). *The unschooled mind: How children think and how schools should teach.* New York: Basic Books.

Greenleaf, Cynthia. (1992). The impact of the HERALD Project on student learning. In Cynthia Greenleaf, Rosemary Henze, Genevieve Lau, *HERALD Project evaluation.* San Francisco Unified School District, 1-163.

Gumperz, John J. (1982). *Discourse strategies.* Cambridge, England: Cambridge University Press.

Halliday, M.A.K. (1973). *Explorations in the functions of language.* London: Edward Arnold.

Halliday, M.A.K. (1975). *Learning how to mean: Explorations in the development of language.* London: Edward Arnold.

Heath, Shirley Brice. (1983). *Ways with words: Language, life and work in communities and classrooms.* Cambridge, England: Cambridge University Press.

Heath, Shirley Brice. (1986). Sociocultural Contexts of Language Development. In *Beyond language: Social and Cultural Factors in Schooling Language Minority Students.* Bilingual Education Office, California State Department of Education. Los Angeles: Evaluation, Dissemination and Assessment Center, California State University, Los Angeles, 143-186.

Hymes, Dell. (1971). Competence and performance in linguistic theory. In R. Husley, and E. Ingram, (Eds.) *Language acquisition: Models and methods.* New York: Academic Press. (Cited in Greenleaf without pages)

Hymes, Dell. (1972). Introduction. In B. Courtney Cazden, Vera P. John, and Dell Hymes, (Eds.), *Functions of language in the classroom*. New York: Teachers College Press, xi-lvii.

Jordan, Cathie. (1985, Summer). Translating culture: From ethnographic information to educational program. *Anthropology & Education Quarterly*, 105-123.

Kochman, Thomas. (1989). Black and white cultural styles in pluralistic perspective. In Bernard Gifford, (Ed.). *Test policy and test performance: Education, language, and culture*. Boston: Kluwer Academic Publishers.

Krashen, Stephen D. (1981). Bilingual education and second language acquisition theory. In California State Department of Education, Bilingual Education Office, *Schooling and language minority students: A theoretical framework*. Los Angeles: Evaluation, Dissemination and Assessment Center, California State University, Los Angeles, 51-79.

Labov, William. (1969). The logic of non-standard English. In James E. Alatis, (Ed.), *Linguistics and the teaching of standard English*. Monograph Series on Languages and Linguistics, No. 22. Washington, D.C.: Georgetown University Press.

Langdon, Henriette W. (1992). Speech and language assessment of LEP/ bilingual Hispanic students. In Henriette Langdon, and Li-Rong Lilly Cheng, (Eds), *Hispanic children and adults with communication disorders: Assessment and intervention*. Excellence in Practice Series, Katharine G. Butler (Ed.). Gaithersburg, MD: Aspen Publishers, 201-271.

Lara, Julia. (1992). Response to JoAnn Canales's Presentation, In *Proceedings of the Second National Research Symposium on Limited English Proficient Student Issues: Focus on Evaluation and Measurement, Volume 2*. Washington, D.C.: United States Department of Education Office of Bilingual Education and Minority Language Affairs, 123-126.

Lave, J. and Wenger, E. (1991). *Situated learning: Legitimate peripheral participation*. Cambridge,England: Cambridge University Press.

McCollum, Pamela. (1991). Cross-cultural perspectives on classroom discourse and literacy. In Elfrieda Hiebert, (Ed.), op cit., 108-121.

Mehan, Hugh. (1979). *Learning Lessons*. Cambridge, MA: Harvard University Press.

Miller, L. (1990). The Roles of language and learning in the development of literacy. *Topics in Language Disorders*, Vol. 10, No. 2, 1-24. (Cited in Oller, 1992).

National Council of Teachers of Mathematics. (1989). *Executive summary of curriculum and evaluation standards for school mathematics*. Reston, VA: 1989.

Oller, John W., Jr. (1991). *Language and bilingualism: More tests of tests* (with the assistance of Steve Chesarek and Robert Scott). Lewisburg, PA: Bucknell University Press.

Oller, John. (1992). Language testing research: Lessons applied to LEP students and programs. In *Proceedings of the Second National Research Symposium on Limited English Proficient Student Issues: Focus on Evaluation and Measurement, Volume 2.* Washington, D.C.: United States Department of Education Office of Bilingual Education and Minority Language Affairs, 123-126.

O'Malley, J. Michael. (1989). Language proficiency testing with limited English-proficient Students. In Alatis, James E. (Ed.). *Language teaching, testing, and technology: Lessons from the past with a view toward the future. Georgetown University Round Table on Languages and Linguistics,* Washington,DC: Georgetown University Press, 235-244.

Philips, Susan Urmston. (1983). *The invisible Culture: Communication in classroom and community on the Warm Springs Indian Reservation.* New York: Longman.

Roth, D. (1978). Raven's progressive matrices as cultural artifacts. In W. S. Hall, and Michael Cole (Eds.), *Quarterly Newsletter of the Laboratory of Comparative Human Psychology, Vol. 1,* 1-15. (Cited in Oller, 1991, p. 54)

Saville-Troike, Muriel. (1991, Spring). Teaching and testing for academic achievement: The role of language development. *Focus,* no page numbers.

Shaw, Jerome M. (1994). *Science performance assessment and language minority students: Exploring the interface.* Unpublished Doctoral Dissertation, Stanford University.

Spanos, George, Rhodes, Nancy C., Dale, Theresa Corasaniti, and Crandall, JoAnn. (1988). Linguistic features of mathematical problem solving: Insights and applications. In R.R. Cocking, and J.P. Mestre (Eds.), *Linguistic and cultural influences on learning mathematics.* Hillsdale, NJ: Lawrence Erlbaum Associates, 221-241.

Swain, Merrill. (1993, April). Cognitive academic language needs of culturally and linguistically diverse students. Paper presented at the TESOL Panel at AERA on "Policy and Practice in the Education of Culturally and Linguistically Diverse Students: Views from Language Educators," Annual Meeting of the American Educational Research Association, Atlanta, GA.

Tartter, Virginia C. (1986). *Language processes.* New York: Holt, Rinehart and Winston.

Tharp, Roland and Gallimore, Ronald. (1988). *Rousing minds to life: Teaching, learning, and schooling in social context.* Cambridge, MA: Harvard University Press.

Trumbull, M. Elise. (1984, May). *Metalinguistic skills: Can they be taught?* Unpublished Doctoral Dissertation, Boston University.

Tsang, Chui Lim. (1989). Bilingual minorities and language issues in writing: Toward professionwide responses to a new challenge. *Written Communication*. Vol. 9, No. 1.

Ulibarri, Daniel M., Spencer, Maria L. and Rivas, Guillermo A. (1981, Spring). Language proficiency and academic achievement: A study of language proficiency tests and their relationship to school ratings as predictors of academic achievement. *NABE Journal*, 47-80.

Vasquez, Olga A. (1993). A look at language as a resource: Lessons from La Clase Magica. In M. Beatriz Arias, and Ursula Casanova, op. cit., 199-224.

Villegas, Ana Maria. (1991. September). *Culturally responsive pedagogy for the 1990's and beyond*. Princeton, NJ: Educational Testing Service.

Webster's Encyclopedic Unabridged Dictionary of the English Language. (1989). New York: Portland House.

Wong-Fillmore, Lily. (1991). When learning a second language means losing the first. *Early Childhood Research Quarterly*. Vol. 6, No. 3, 323-347.

Chapter 5

Developing
Equitable
Assessment Systems

If reform is to matter, it must begin with the populations for whom we have drawn these special categories. Curriculum and instruction should first be effective with these students, and then applied to other populations (Secada, 1992).

W e begin this discussion on development of assessment systems with the provocative statement of Walter Secada. Secada decries the failure of educators when developing instructional interventions to focus on the target groups of the interventions as, for example, in the case of Title I/Chapter 1. Most of the interventions have been developed from what was thought to be effective for the general student population. We submit that an approach that focused first on underserved populations would be singularly appropriate for the development of assessments as well. Instead, we have seen a pattern of exempting minority students from assessments or thinking of them after the fact, most notably through the development of a native-language version of an already-developed test for mainstream students. This type of development-by-afterthought will not accomplish the social changes and correction of invalid assumptions that must occur if we are to have a truly equitable educational system—a system that replaces the notions of disadvantage and compensatory education with notions that acknowledge the competence of all students.

Philosophical Framework

In order to build an equitable and effective assessment system, consideration must be given to the philosophical framework for the system and to the principles that are to guide the development. In this section, we proffer a philosophical orientation to the development of new types of assessment systems. This is followed by a section on procedural guidelines for initiating and pursuing such work.

Using a Standards Model

No attempt to develop an assessment system can be deemed in any way successful until and unless the *purposes* of the system are clarified. Tests have been used widely to provide school accountability information, to evaluate school reform, and to communicate to schools about learning targets. As calls for school reform have gained ground and many types of reforms have been implemented, there has been a persistent demand for efficient ways to determine the success of those reforms. This demand points to an underlying tension that is dragging on all efforts to move in new assessment directions—that between two incompatible purposes for testing: (1) gathering information about student achievement or progress toward desired standards and (2) using relative measurements of students, schools, districts, and states. This same tension remained unresolved in the past as, for example, when *norm-referenced tests* were weighed against *criterion-referenced tests*. The increased use of performance-based measures will not eliminate this tension (Taylor, 1994). Assessment systems must be developed that are in harmony with the goals of school reform. As Taylor (1994) points out, for the past 60 years, we have used a *measurement model* as the foundation for norm-referenced test development; the purposes were to assess general knowledge across broad areas, rank students, and compare students, schools, and districts on scales of achievement. The term *standards model* can be used for a conceptual foundation for a system whose function is to "assess how students perform in relation to absolute standards" (Taylor, p. 233). There is considerable risk involved in mixing these models and trying to apply the technology of one paradigm to the other. If educators do not understand this, measurement specialists and policymakers will continue to require the same of performance assessments as for accurate, comparative *measurement*. Although a number of measurement specialists have raised concerns about the potential reliability and validity of performance assessments, to insist on viewing these assessments from the perspective of the measurement model seems misguided. A different set of assumptions underlies the standards model. As defined by Taylor, they are that:

1. We can set public educational standards and strive toward them.

2. Most students can internalize and achieve the standards.

3. Very different student performances and exhibitions can and will reflect the same standards.

4. Educators can be trained to internalize the standards and be fair and consistent judges of diverse student performances (Taylor, p. 243).

The last assumption is, of course, very important to our perspective on developing assessments. It is important to note that efforts to develop criterion-referenced tests in the 1970s were guided by many different methods for setting standards. None of them, however, required the examination of student work to relate it to "standards of quality and performance criteria for defined performances." This focus on student work allows developers to establish performance criteria and levels of performance quality that are considered "excellent" (Wiggins, 1990). The process of reviewing student work and using it to establish performance criteria is one that can provide the opportunity to identify aspects of a performance that may be attributable to cultural and linguistic factors, rather than a presumptive knowledge or skill deficit.

In Alaska, for example, a voluntary writing assessment is used statewide starting in grade 5. It is begun at that grade level because developers felt confident that students who entered school speaking a native language other than English would have gained sufficient proficiency in English by that age to complete the assessment. When the assessments are scored, however, those written wholly in a language other than English are read by raters fluent in that language (if they are available) and are scored in the same way a paper written in English would be. If native language words or grammatical structures are inserted in the writing, as often happens with Yup'ik, the writing is evaluated to determine whether the student has met the criteria for communication (or perhaps enhanced the communication by using native language elements); the paper is scored according to the criteria; the student is not penalized because of a failure to write completely in English. Through the establishment of standards and a review of student work, then, we are able to identify performance criteria that provide a more equitable basis for evaluating student performances.

Special Concerns for Prompt Selection in Alaska*

In Alaska, it is imperative to select prompts for our Statewide Direct Writing Assessment that can inspire students from typical urban schools in a city of 300,000 that locals acknowledge is *"close* to Alaska" to single teacher sites at the tip of the Alaska Peninsula, on Interior rivers, and on islands in the Bering Sea. Our Prompt Selection Committee includes teachers and curriculum and assessment administrators from the North Slope and Kuskokwim River villages as well as Anchorage and Fairbanks, and discussions about the cultural relevance of prospective prompts range from the ridiculous to the sublime. The group has debated whether the traditional Native understanding of "a long time" might put village students at a disadvantage by side tracking them into spending their time trying to interpret a *gussak* question rather than writing. It rejected a prompt about pet dogs because it is meaningless in villages where toddlers are killed and maimed each year when they wander into dogyards filled with sled teams.

Typical discussions took place in 1993 and 1994 as the committee reviewed prompts used in other direct writing assessments. We wanted to be able to do informal comparisons of our students' scores with others. Yet we found five of the nine prospective 1993 prompts for descriptive writing were inappropriate for Alaska. It was obvious to all that asking children who had never left a village of three hundred except to go to fish camp to describe a place like a fair or carnival was absurd. Similarly, rural Native students would have a hard time relating to "vacations." The holistic life view of traditional Natives also made unsuitable a prompt about "a work experience"; these students simply do not see doing what it takes to live divided into that which is work or art or study.

Likewise, in 1994 the committee concluded that a persuasive prompt about losing one's driver's license for failing grades was not one that would elicit a passionate response from rural students who have driven snow machines since they were four and live in villages where the only automobile is the van the school uses to transport materials and people to and from the airstrip. And, in order to make an informative prompt asking for an arts review work, the committee had to add the parenthetical comment that "The program or performance may be live or recorded, *i.e.,* on TV, film, CD."

Clearly, there are special concerns for prompt selection in Alaska directly related to the rural Native culture. Yet every state and school district has populations whose experiences and world views may be equally different from those of the mainstream. Prompts must be selected with a conscious effort toward inclusion.

*Developed and used with permission of Judith Entwife, Alaska Department of Eucation, Juneau, Alaska.

Voices from Another Culture

"Aumyak go get a some water from the lake." said the old woman "But the lake froze over last night grandma." answered Aumyuk. "Don't be lazy and chop a whole in the ice." said the old woman. So Aumyuk a small Eskimo girl about 10 years of age took her seal skin bag a went out of the sud house to get water.

Aumyak lived with her grandparents and mother in a sud hut by a huge lake. The land scape was flate except for a few mountains in the back ground. They lived alone in this vast snow and ice covered land where the air was always cold.

They had come here because the rest of the villagers had died of starvation. The village was about 30 miles to the south. They had moved here because there was some fish in the lake to feed themselves with.

Aumyak's grandma was small like her and her mother. She was about sixty five years old and had gray hair and few wringles. Aumyaks gradpa was just as old and just as fraile. Her mother was pretty for a woman of forty. Aumyak's father was killed while hunting for seals on the lake. His whole crew too drowned with him. There village had about over hundred people before the starvation started. After awhile only half survived. The ones that survived spit up in to small groups and went seperete ways to feed themselves.

When Aumyuk reached the lake she saw a huge fish under the ice. She looked at it for a while and started thinking of a way to kill it. When she had an idea she put a deadly poison into her locked that was around her neck After this was done she went down and started chopping a hole. The great fish heard the noise and went closer to the hole and said "why aren't you afraid of me. Aumyak answered "I am not araid of you, but only wan so wat fomy grandma." The great fish said "go ahead and take some water, but in exchange you must give me something of value to you." "But why!?" she said in a suprised tone! Because you have taken water that I swim in and because this water is very presious too me. So Aumyak took the locket and threw it into the fishe's mouth. As soon has he swolled it the great fish soon died. Aumyak was very happy and excited. She ran home to tell her other and gradmother about the fish. after awhile when the brought the huge fish out Aumyak's grandma asked "why weren't you afraid of this great fihs? The gril said "because if I was afriad then no one would have gotten the great fish.

It took two whole weeks to dry and store the fish. At the end of the two weeks the family had a great feast that lasted for a long time.

Commentary:

This story from the 1990 Alaska Statewide Direct Writing Assessment was written by a tenth grader in response to a prompt to describe an experience of fear, challenge, or discovery. It was scored high in all traits except Conventions. Written in a traditional storytelling mode, it eloquently expresses, as well, the sentence structure, word choice, and voice of Alaska Natives.

The content and style of "Aumyak" stand in high contrast to

that of the next paper, a 1993 piece. Yet both are among the few Alaskan papers that score high in Word Choice. Notice that the eleventh grade author uses the right words, strong and simple, to convey a strong and simple truth about what she has learned outside of school.

What I Have Learned Outside of School

I'm standing outside in snow with my sister and about three other kids my age. Actually with all the kids my age here in False Pass. It's New year eve and we just got done hugging and kissing everyone after the count down. Now we're all standing around looking through the porch railings at the adults drinking and dancing inside. Some are slumped over shaking their butts and hanging their heads. Others smile and look as if they are having a good time. My Aunt and my friends mom are arguing near the door way. It's more or less my friends mom screaming as my Aunt has her mouth open to object but she can't get a word in. Gassy (my friend's mom) pushes my Aunt, she stumbles but regains her balance.

"Get the Hell out of my house!", Gassy screams.

I run around the corner and see my Aunt fall out of the door. her butt's hanging out as her pants hang down around her knees. Windows vibrate as Gassy slams the door. Rolling around on the ground my Aunt mumbles under her breath as she tugs at her pants. Slowly she stands and swaying back and forth pulls her pants up. Still mumbling she stumbles back inside leaving the door wide open. Entertainment's over so I walk back over to laugh at all the drunks trying to dance.

"Time to come in!". Gassy yells.

Looking down at my watch it's about two thirty. "Great now we have to go in and listen to all these fools". I think to myself. Going in we try to dodge all the crying drunks that want to hug and kiss while they tell you how much they love you. Making it to the bedroom with only one hug. I got lucky. Time inches by as we sit telling jokes and mimicking drunks. Every once in a while we hear some woman screaming at their husband. There's a fight or two but we just laugh because that sort of thing happens all the time.

"Party's over!". Gassy announces.

We hear a few thuds as they all get up and try to use the walls as support to make their way to the door way. They're almost gone but of course we can still hear one fool slurring his words while trying to tell his sob story. Finally they push him out and I hear the door lock. I close my eyes but I can't sleep. I think about all the crap that happened here tonight and more that's going to go on. My Aunt will go home and get the shit beat out of her and it will be nothing new because it happens every time she drinks. I see this all the time and if there is one thing I have learned by living in this little town is that I won't end up here drinking my life away or watch anyone else do it.

Commentary:

This fifth grader, writing in response to a 1994 prompt asking for a description of a place close to home you'd like to be and why, gives us a good example of "village English." While his Word Choice and Conventions scores were low and his Sentence Fluency average, his Voice, village English, works for his story and scored very high.

One day me and my friend was walking through the woods looking for a fort. I said where going too far in maybe we should turn back. But he wanted to go on so we went on. I new we was lost because things look different. When Matthew look back he said we were lost. I said see I told you we shouldn't go further in the woods. So we cept on walking we walked for two days with nothing to eat. The third day we finally saw something big and tall like a hotel but it was a beautiful castle. We went up and knock but nobody answer so we went in and looked around. It look like paradise. It had water bed, soda fountain, Honda's snogo's and lots of other good stuffs. The first thing I did was ride honda. When I was riding I saw Caribous and Mooses. So I went home and took a nice hot bubble bath. After I took a bath I ate supper. When I was done eating I went up to my room and read till I fall asleep. The book I was reading is called Tracker. When I woke up I ate breakfast and went out hunting. I caught two Caribous and two Mooses. After I went home we tried to go back home. When we get hungry we wood cook the food and start moving. One day pass we walked really slow no water little bit food. Two days pass no food and Matthew said where probable close to the village. Day three pass we walk on the hill and we saw the village we start running and we reach and lived happily ever after.

Commentary

An eleventh grader writing in 1993 takes us into the future with a paper that scored high in every trait. Notice especially how easy it is to read and how naturally rhythmic the Sentence Structure is.

Our Battle Has Been Won

The year is 2003-March 31. Just three weeks ago seven new members were elected to the board or the Tanana Tribal Council. Those members consist of Cynthia Johnson. Chairman of the Board: Cheryl Roberts, President: Rachel Edwin, Vice Presdent; Sharon Roberts, Secretary; John Folger, Treasurer; Tereasa Dick, Representative #1: and Chris Grant, Representative #2.

On February 9, 2003, the Tanana Tribal Council and all the other state councils received a letter from the federal government saying this:

Throughout the past ten years the State of Alaska has been in a economic slump. The number of available jobs was outstanding. If only there were enough qualified people to take them.

The Federal Government has been giving the Alaska Natives numerous benefits throughout the years. Now we have come to a decision to cut off those much needed benefits, because of the lack of workers in the native villages.

One out of ten Alaska Natives graduate from college each year, the other nine either drop out of school or don't attend college at all. That is something you and your people will have to change. The proxy papers will be sent out in June, so please inform your community of this.

Since then, a plan has been implemented. Our State Representative, Dorothy Jordan, has written numerous letters to the federal government about this issue. Although her actions didn't stop the government from continuing its plan, they helped us figure a way to bring up our economic budget.

In 1993, the State of Alaska had thirtenn regional native corporations ttions. Now there are only three: Doyon, Tozitna, and NANA. The main arguement is over the land that we, the Alaska Natives, own.

Most of the Tozitna shareholders who inherited stock were non-natives. But, in 1999, a new law was passed by the Slate of Alaska, saying that you had to be half or more native to be a shareholder in Tozitna or any other native corporation. Because of this, all the non-natives had to sell their shares back to the corporation. Now the state is saying there aren't enough jobs taken by the Alaska Natives. They say we are living off benefits given to us by them. They argue that we can't run our land because of this.

They are the ones who drove us from our land and forced us into missionaries, where we were told not to speak our language. We fought for what was rightfully ours but all we got out of it was 44 million acres. What is 44 million acres out of 328 million?

Then they hand us benefits, in pay back for the land they took. Of course we took these benefits because they were needed amoung our people and we continue to use these benefits to this day. It was a deal that we couldn't pass up and now they are trying to take them away.

They are asking us to give up our land, but we will not. It seems if they want to take the benefits back then we can take our land back. We will continue to fight until we win.

A new road is being built from Tanana to Rampart, which is half-way done. From the point where there is no land to build on, we will start a bridge joining the North bank of the Yukon with the South bank, right below Rampart. While digging up the land we discovered that we are sitting ontop of a huge oil-well, which has helped us start a new corporation in Tanana. Jobs are being provided to the Alaska Natives who qualify for them. The amount of money is not the problem, the problem is the amount Of educated people in our district. I have have set up eight new scholarship programs for Alaska Natives only. It has been a real challenge for both me, my stafff, and our community to do this, but it seems to be working. Now the percent of Alaska Natives who graduate from college and continue onto jobs is nine out of ten.

Things are running smoothly for us. Our new corporation, The Bidziyhkuh Corporation, which means biggest caribou is bringing in the money. If we continue to prosper our land and continue our schooling we won't have to worry about our land. With our new corporation booming and the oil well our workers have run into up river, pasted the mission grave yard, we ar set for years to come.

Another way to contrast the measurement model with the standards model is in the emphasis placed on reliability; in the former, the primary emphasis is on reliability, while for the latter, the emphasis is on validity. It will be essential to find new ways to establish reliability, because when the function of assessment is to gather information about student learning, the ways to do that expand. We refer, again, to Taylor for differences in the approach to assessment that the standards model will occasion (Figure 5.1).

FIGURE 5.1

1. The standards model allows for the assessment of student work that takes an *extended period of time* to complete, as well as the collection of student *work samples over time*. Growth during the period in which work is gathered is not of concern. The important question is whether the student has achieved the standards.

2. The standards may be achieved early in a student's career for mathematics and late in a student's career for writing. Students may have *many opportunities* to demonstrate their achievements, yet the desired standards remain the same.

3. The standards model allows for performances that *include collaboration as well as cycles of feedback and revision*. Collaboration and revision cycles are typical aspects of adult work, therefore, authentic performances may involve either.

(Italics added; adapted from Taylor, 1994)

"The reliability of the student's assessment, then, is a matter of the degree to which the body of evidence for the student in any given area gives a clear message about whether or not the student has achieved the standards" (Taylor, *Ibid.*).

If a system of assessment is built on a standards model, there are several additional issues to address. Of course, the political, social, and economic conditions that play such a significant role in determining what happens in schools and that affect students must be handled. The organizational structure of schools must also be modified if we want to ensure that all students achieve standards. In the recent report by the Commission on Time and Learning, *Prisoners of Time: Report of the National Education Commission on Time and Learning*, the recommendations address organizational variables related to time. Two of them have relevance to assessment of student learning:

1. Reinvent schools around learning, not time.
2. Fix the design flaw: use time in new and better ways.

Other organizational factors that must be dealt with include student-teacher ratios and the structure of the curriculum. Rather than thinking of a volume of material to cover, teachers should plan to teach central concepts over longer periods of time and focus on helping students learn how to *access* and *use* information to expand their learning. These changes in organizational variables would help to accommodate children who are learning English or whose cultural differences make it necessary for them to "learn" the mainstream culture and that of the school as well.

Attention to Equity Issues

As noted earlier in a statement quoted from Malcom (1991), "Equity concerns must be at the heart of assessment design." Malcom speaks of assessment that would serve equity. Alluding to the agreed-upon need to avoid bias in testing, she states: "What will be tougher than avoiding bias will be building a system from the ground up that supports equity. What considerations would have to be incorporated to construct an equity-supporting assessment?" The conditions that Malcom offers are fairly simple and straightforward. They will serve as a framework for our discussion of issues related to the design and use of equitable assessments.

---

1. Rules about what is to be known must be clear to all.
2. Resources needed to achieve must be available to all.
3. Ways of demonstrating knowledge must be many and varied.
4. Things valued by different groups must be reflected in the original statement of what is to be known.

Rules about what is to be known must be clear to all

In a Ford Foundation report issued in 1990, it was charged that the "American testing system has become a 'hostile gatekeeper' that has limited opportunities for many, particularly women and minorities" (Rothman, 1990, quoted in Freeman and Freeman, 1991). Part of the solution to this dilemma may reside in the consensus-building process in which many educators are now engaged to develop curriculum standards and assessments. As content standards and performance standards (levels of student competence in the content) are established, assessments tied to those standards are developed. It is critical that participation in this process be as broad-based and direct as possible so that varying perspectives are taken into account. What becomes critical when the assessments are used in classrooms is that the students, too, understand clearly the content and performance standards against which their work is being judged. This, in fact, has not generally been the case in the American education system. Study after study for years have demonstrated that teachers grade student work based on radically different criteria, and that idiosyncratic performance resulting from students' linguistic or cultural heritage is rarely understood or correctly interpreted.

Wiggins (1989) asserts that "an authentic test not only reveals student achievement to the examiner, but also reveals to the test-taker the actual challenges and standards of the field." He refers to the information to be gathered through the use of authentic assessments as "evidence of knowing." Acquiring this evidence requires the development and use of assessments that give students opportunities to show good judgment, pose and tackle problems, gather evidence, critique, extend and expand knowledge. Students, teachers, and parents alike must understand and agree that this type of knowledge and skill is what is valued and necessary for survival in an ever more complex world. Similarly, those who serve as advocates for poor students, students of color, or second-language students must subscribe to the standards and performance-based or authentic assessments that are developed. In this way only, will we all begin to feel that rather than being "hostile gatekeepers," tests or assessments are an integral and supportive part of the learning process and that they can serve to enhance the learning opportunity for all students.

The effective use of assessment results to support the teaching and learning process is part of a larger discussion of "consequential validity." Assessments must be evaluated on the basis of their effectiveness in guiding teachers to make defensible choices in instructional planning. The assessment should provide the necessary information to help the teacher plan instruction that will meet students' learning needs. If the results of an assessment show that any student or any group of students is not meeting desirable learning standards, it should lead to serious scrutiny of the instructional program to determine what modifications need to be made so that the program becomes one that is designed to and is successful in challenging all students to learn at high levels, ones that were perhaps not even predetermined. That is, we have a tendency to speak of students' reaching their "potential" or learning at "maximum levels," but if the curriculum and instructional program are open-ended, challenging, and guided by the highest expectations, we may very well be surprised at the levels of learning that children are able to reach. The important point here, however, is that the main purpose of assessment should be to inform and improve instruction for *all* students. This counts most for students who are learning the mainstream language or whose home culture does not match that of the school, because we are most prone to attribute their poor performance to some misperceived barriers to learning, rather than to an instructional program that does not match their learning styles and needs.

Another important concept related to "knowing the rules" of assessments is sometimes referred to as "transparency." The criteria for a performance must be transparent rather than secret so that the criteria themselves can motivate and direct learning. This is another critical factor for students from a non-dominant culture. As many researchers point out, these students face a dual challenge in that they must learn the culture of the school at the same time that they must learn the content of schooling—sometimes in a language other than their native one. These students can benefit immeasurably from information (through explanation, modeling, examples) that helps them understand: (1) what processes and products of learning are valued; (2) how to use language to engage meaningfully with the tools of learning; (3) ways in which to exhibit quality work; (4) how to change, revise, adapt, or modify their strategies to improve their learning; and (5) how to be independent learners.

Resources needed to achieve must be available to all

Under this condition, we would include all aspects of "opportunities to learn." A California Department of Education Task Force developed a report[1] focused on standards for opportunities to learn that includes the following aspects:

Opportunities to learn must reflect:
- enriched, rigorous, and relevant curriculum
- differentiated, high-quality instruction
- extra support for students and teachers
- access to technology
- a safe learning environment
- well-coordinated student and family support services
- fairly distributed resources; and
- coherent policies

California Task Force on School Delivery Standards, 1993

What must also be emphasized is the need to align or draw close linkages between instructional and assessment approaches. In fact, assessment should become largely indistinguishable from instruction. The effectiveness and quality of teaching in American schools is a key factor. Gordon (1993) makes the point that if we are adequately teaching, we don't need to be as concerned about equity of assessment. This doesn't let assessors off the hook; there is much that we can do to assess more equitably at the same time that we effect positive changes in instruction. In the absence of effective instructional intervention in all schools, we will not solve the problem of equity in assessment.

It is clear that the design and implementation of assessments must occur at the local level so that they can be linked to local decisions about curriculum and fit legitimately within the local instructional context. Bilingual educators, for example, have long argued that items on a standardized test do not measure the objectives or content of such programs because they are built on objectives that are unique to the needs of its students. Tests that are imported from the outside with no consideration of the local context are not likely to be sensitive to actual student progress. In essence, then, when we discuss the need to provide adequate opportunities to learn—to achieve proficiency on the standards we establish—we must consider both the need to create challenging learning situations that reflect student needs and the need to design or select assessments that are linked to our instructional design. Malcom poses the challenge to reinvent assessment in a way that reflects how daunting that challenge is: "Curriculum would be based on standards that are rigorous but not rigid; diverse but without compromising the highest standards of excellence; reflective of student and societal needs; derived through interaction of public, discipline, teaching and user communities; world class but distinctly developed to fit America's values and needs" (1991, p. 326).

The issue of access to the best curriculum and teaching situations is discussed in Chapter 3, but it is worth reiterating briefly. Glaser (1988) discusses access to education opportunity and states that "assessments should be designed to survey possibilities for student growth, rather than to designate students as ready or not ready to profit from standard instruction." The approach that Glaser suggests is one that responds to critical questions: Do students who are newcomers to a country have equal access to the best possible education, one that will compensate for the multiple challenges they face? Are the results of tests or other assessments used to ensure that the education they receive will match their needs and optimize their learning or to place them in academic tracks (more accurately, "ruts") that will preclude an equitable education?

Ways of demonstrating knowledge must be many and varied

This particular condition holds tremendous promise for establishing an assessment system that truly can support the learning needs of a very diverse population of students. If this condition, alone, were met, we believe that not just the battle, but a large part of the war would be won.

Adjusting for language differences

First, we must give serious consideration to the issue of assessing the learning of children who began their learning in a language other than English. The problems and concerns surrounding this assessment dilemma are almost legendary, and like many legends, the content gets distorted and is impossible to verify. Many of the efforts to develop English as a Second Language or bilingual programs over the years were based on the premise that linguistic differences or a lack of proficiency in English *caused* the low academic achievement of students from minority language backgrounds. Though the argument is plausible, particularly in cases where students are expected to learn in situations where only English is spoken, we have since come to learn that students' competence in English does not have as much impact on their academic success as do some other factors. Another misconception that has been fairly pervasive is that students are proficient in English when they have acquired fluency in everyday face-to-face communication with their peers, teachers, or families. (In Alaska, they sometimes refer to this as "village English.") This criterion is then used for administering a standardized achievement test in English or placing students in transitional, English-only, or Chapter 1 programs. Placement or non-placement in Chapter 1 programs has actually been one area where this particular assessment dilemma—that of relating English proficiency to academic ability—has been reflected in the most distorted manner. For a long time, Federal regulations held that students who are limited-English proficient (LEP) could be served in Chapter 1 programs only if it was possible to determine that their educational disadvantagement was not due to their lack of proficiency in English. This was, of course, an impossible challenge for Chapter 1 staffs, one that was approached in perverse and diverse ways.

Over the years, educators have also come to realize that looking for evidence of "negative transfer"—indications that the child's native language is interfering with proficiency in English—has prevented us from recognizing and acknowledging "positive transfer." When children learn language, meaning resides in the interactional context. Linguistic forms are ascribed meaning because they are embedded in the context. Over time, the linguistic forms become a more integral part of the meaningful context. Cognitive psychologists have labeled knowledge representations as "schemata" or "scripts." Scripts are organized around recurring situations, processes, or events. Once acquired, scripts or schemata are used to interpret the meaning of similar events whether the language that is used to interact about them is the same or not. Learning does not start all over again when students learn a second language; rather, they interpret meaning in terms of what they already know. Script knowledge, however, is cultural knowledge and learning or adapting scripts is part of the acculturation process that second language students must accomplish. Children also develop specific strategies for processing language—making inferences, identifying main ideas, constructing more complex schemata—and these strategies transfer quite readily to academic tasks in a new language. These are some of the reasons that so-called "sheltered English" strategies are effective with students—they present teaching with contexts clearly identified and use many cues to prompt students to the appropriate scripts (Saville-Troike, 1991).

Language assessment as it has been traditionally practiced has focused on language rather than on language in relation to academic proficiency, and those assessments have evidenced low predictive validity with regard to academic achievement. This suggests that they measure the wrong thing and have limited value. We should be asking the question, "What factors are most significant in predicting academic success for students?" For example, "reading ability in English is the single most important skill determining school achievement beyond the third grade" (Saville-Troike, 1991). Once identified, this constellation of factors should be measured using a variety of approaches.

If the condition identified above—that is, "ways of demonstrating knowledge must be many and varied"—were met and the assessment of language development were multidimensional, we would have come an enormous distance in providing an equitable education for these students. Such a multidimensional approach could be accomplished reasonably using performance tasks, informal measures, structured interviews, writing assessments, and portfolios.

Portfolios as a means of accommodating differences

The use of portfolios is a productive way to meet the condition of multiple measures. Portfolios have the potential of providing a more accurate view of academic achievement because they contain information about students' progress in learning over time and along various dimensions. Portfolios can contain information about language development as students contribute work they do in their native language as well as in English. (See Chapter 6.)

In an assessment development project one of us was involved with in Alaska, one of the participating teachers taught first grade students in what was referred to as a "Yup'ik-first-language school." As the teachers in the project discussed various types of performance and other alternative assessments they wanted to develop for use with their students, this teacher saw few parallels for what would be useful in her program with her young native language-speaking youngsters. When asked about her instructional program, she described the language-rich and story-based activities she provided. As we talked about gathering relevant information about their learning, she began to see how much there would be that could be gathered into portfolios and used to track the progress of these very young learners. We talked about assessing their "sense of story" using Yup'ik and English stories, about comparing their language strategies in Yup'ik and English, about monitoring their writing ability as it developed in the two languages, and the list went on and on. Eventually we both became very excited about all that could be learned about her students and how much it would help her in making instructional decisions.

In Dos Palos Joint Union Elementary School District in California, teachers collected writing samples, conducted interviews, recorded observations of bilingual students, and created and revised Spanish/English writing and observation check sheets. Through the portfolios, these teachers were able to recognize their bilingual students' strengths and growth and to improve their teaching by revealing the activities most effective for their bilingual learners (Freeman and Freeman, 1991).

Portfolios hold considerable promise for all learners and their teachers because they allow both to understand complex processes more fully, to reflect on the learning process, and to explore and examine idiosyncratic approaches to learning. It is an approach that recognizes that assessment can be equitable without yielding the same results for everyone. Wiggins (1989) states this quite well: "We typically learn too much about a student's short-term recall and too little about what is most important: a student's *habits of mind* . . . As the word *habit* implies, if we are serious about having students display thoughtful control over ideas, a single performance is inadequate. We need to observe students' *repertoires*, not rote catechisms coughed up in response to pat questions."

Assessing different habits of mind

The notion of collecting information that allows us to observe students' unique habits of mind is referenced by several researchers and should not be lost sight of. Wiggins (1989) invokes the British and American legal systems to elaborate the concept of "equity": "Blank laws and policies are inherently unable to encompass the inevitable idiosyncratic cases for which we ought always to make exceptions to the rule." As it has been practiced, mass testing treated students' reasons for their answers as irrelevant. Paulson and Paulson (1991) propose an equally provocative concept by discussing portfolio assessment from the perspective of chaos theory—basically that nonlinear patterns show up in very different and unexpected places—and these phenomena are evident in widely separate disciplines. "Chaos refers to deterministic patterns that are so complex that prediction is problematical." In testing, it means that we may react to variation as being random and discard critical information as random error. "Assessing portfolios requires that we seek models that refine and expand our ability to understand human performance as multidimensional phenomena occurring in complex, social contexts." As a final word on this notion, we refer to a statement by Malcom (1991) in her list of descriptors for the reinvention of assessment: "Acceptable 'outlier' responses to assessment questions would be captured and, where appropriate, would be included as training examples for teachers to illustrate the range of appropriate responses" (p. 327).

Self-assessments

In order to become self-sufficient, to operate as independent learners, students need to be able to judge and reflect on their own work. Building on the criterion noted above, that is, that one has to "know the rules," students must cultivate the ability to scrutinize the products of their learning, make accommodations, and develop strategies for learning more, thereby improving their skills and nurturing their talents. Second-language or minority culture students who may exhibit different approaches to learning and communication than is typical of the mainstream culture must be given opportunities to represent their learning approaches in ways that are comfortable for them—to write in their native language until they are able to make the transition to the language they are acquiring, to structure their oral presentation or compositions in ways that are appropriate for them, and to explain or react to their processes of learning through writing, artistic expression, through an interpreter, or in any way that will help them engage in self-reflection. The use of these strategies is important to teachers as well because it will enrich their own awareness of the cultural and linguistic differences in their students' approaches to learning.

Socially-situated assessment

It is perhaps one of the most serious errors we have made in education: assuming that learning is ideally autonomous and should follow this pattern in the classroom. When a teacher uses a recitation mode of teaching, it reflects the assumption that each individual must consume the information presented, absorb it, store it in memory or notes, review it later and reproduce it for an assessment. Typically, then, the individual student is held solely accountable for the result. Unfortunately, the most prevalent assumption in this scenario is that education has done its best to teach the student, and a poor showing on the test is attributed to a student's failure to pay attention, take notes, study, take the test seriously, follow directions, or, to interference from his first language, cultural or family background, to some learning disability, a lack of emotional stability, proper nutrition, or hygiene. Glaser has written extensively on these points and suggests that "assessment situations in which the student participates in group activity should increase. In this context, not only performance, but also the facility with which a student adapts to help and guidance can be assessed."

Extended tasks and contextualized skills

The term, "authentic assessment," was first bandied about because many educators and researchers recognized that assessment should be based on more meaningful tasks that were more closely related to the outcomes that were deemed essential in each subject domain. In the new forms of assessment, many have seen that the assessment opportunities themselves could reflect worthwhile learning experiences that would better capture the relevance and utility of the knowledge and skills students acquire in the domain. The more that assessment is embedded in meaningful contexts, the easier it will be for students, but particularly minority students, to demonstrate what they know and are able to do. When the information to which students must respond in an assessment is abstract and devoid of a context or schema that is explicit and purposeful, their chances for using their knowledge of the world and repertoire of problem-solving strategies to accurately represent what they know are jeopardized. The ability of minority students to respond is confounded because the cues that they typically come to depend on for understanding what is expected of them in school are gone. For example, a minority student may learn to survive in a classroom where spelling lessons are presented from a text that lists the words with meanings and pictures. Perhaps the teacher has the students rehearse spelling the words out loud, the student studies the words with a friend or a family member and manages to pass the test each Friday when she is asked to spell 20 words as the teacher dictates them. If on a more formal test, the student is then asked to complete a spelling subtest where she has to identify the misspelled word from a selection of five, the challenge is quite different and devoid of context.

Scope and comprehensiveness

Using a variety of performance-based assessments means that a greater range of learning can be analyzed, and it is possible to determine what students can do in terms of the particular cognitive demands of the particular task. This, too, is important for minority students because it enhances their chances of demonstrating what they know and are able to do by using multiple pathways to arrive at an understanding of their approach to learning situations and their knowledge of content. The challenge for us as educators will be to determine the most efficient strategies for selecting measures to suit particular purposes and students, for interpreting and integrating information collected, and for using that information to improve instructional programs.

Importance of multiple measures

A primary consideration that must guide the development of an assessment system and will lead to the most valid and reliable information about all students—information that will be essential to designing effective instructional programs—is the use of multiple measures. It is undeniable that the use of one type of test at a single point in time supplies a very narrow slice of information about a student's ability, and that information is subject to vast misinterpretation and misuse, particularly with respect to minority students. As Howard Gardner has observed (in Gifford and O'Connor, 1992), it is too simplistic to say that a student either has or doesn't have certain knowledge. In fact, knowledge that a student cannot tap on demand in the way a test calls for may "show up" miraculously in the context of performing a task that does call for it or in the presence of a supportive adult who asks the right questions. Gardner notes further that few practices are more nefarious in education than drawing broad conclusions from the score of a single test. "Assessment programs that fail to take into account the vast differences among individuals, developmental levels, and varieties of expertise" are increasingly being seen for their serious limitations (Gardner, 1992). If we truly want to get a picture of a child's educational achievement and potential, we *need* multidimensional assessment. This approach is arguably more important with language minority students because of the susceptibility of measures to bias and the potential confusion of a language difference with an educational deficit.

In the context of bilingual-bicultural assessment, multiple measures usually refers to multiple instruments or sources of information. It can also refer, however, to multiple indices of progress over time. In the latter sense, it is a practice that we strongly recommend for all students. Interestingly, we found that this recommendation that multiple measures be used and that individuals be assessed over time is by no means new. Consider this statement from William James in 1915 (as reported in Wolf et al., 1991):

> No elementary measurement, capable of being performed in a laboratory, can throw light on the actual efficiency of the subject; for the vital thing about him, his emotional and moral energy and doggedness, can be measured by no single experiment, and becomes known only by the total results in the long run ... Be patient, then, and sympathetic with the type of mind that cuts a poor figure in examination. It may, in the long examination which life sets us, come out in the end in better shape than the glib and ready reproducer, its passions being deeper, its purposes more worthy, its combining power less commonplace, and its total mental output consequently more important (James, 1915, pp. 135-143).

Using multiple measures (and giving similar weight and value to each of them) will further allow us to accommodate differences in point of view, cultural and linguistic variation, and diversity in cognitive style. Accommodations can be made in content, format, administration procedures, scoring, and interpretation. Such accommodations are much more viable with performance-based tasks and portfolios.

Things valued by different groups must be reflected in the original statement of what is to be known

Test bias can be said to exist whenever a given interpretation of a test score is less valid for a subgroup of test takers (Cole & Moss, 1989). Bias has been distinguished from *unfair test use* by some theorists, with bias being an inherent feature of a test and unfairness having to do with the way a test is used. In actuality, test bias is intimately bound up with use: a test may be biased against certain students when used for one purpose vs. another—for example, reading skill vs. reading skill *in English.*

Content will continue to spark debate related to issues of equity and fairness with new forms of assessments as well, but it is important to note that the *standards and criteria* applied to these assessments as well as the *performance-based formats* used will raise concerns that were not as pronounced in the debate over standardized tests. These concerns have, however, been raised in research or assessment situations where African-American students were asked to reply verbally to typical examination questions or other stimuli presented by an examiner. The students' failure to respond and their use of not much more than monosyllables led the researchers to conclude that they had "no language" or were "non-verbal" (Osser, Wang & Zeid, 1969; Weener, 1969, quoted in Winfield & Woodard, 1994).

Gay and Abrahams (1973) have written extensively about the influence of the "context" on the accuracy of the measure. The testing situation, as they see it, is "defined as being *cold* in the negative sense of that Black term. Black Americans looking at Euro-American interactional style often brand whites as cold and aloof . . . Not only does this environment ignore the means by which significant information is generally passed on among Blacks . . . but it eliminates the possibility of establishing the kind of relationship that makes anything but hostile responses seem appropriate to the testee" (Gay & Abrahams, 1973, p. 333). As they indicate, the testing situation as defined proves only that the student has not learned the appropriate strategies for responding in this particular situation.

Three other culturally-related factors are not taken into account in testing situations that involve African-American students (and students from other cultures who may experience similar discontinuities between the culture of the home and that of the school). Gay and Abrahams point out that the norm for an African-American home is one of a family-based co-operative unit, one in which the mastery of a task is accomplished by observing others, imitating, and asking for help when needed. In a test situation, a child who operates according to these "rules" will be accused of cheating. In addition, it is customary in the Black community for rules to emerge out of a given situation and to apply only for the duration of the event. This notion—that the rules are no longer applicable when the event ends, and that the rules are constantly changing—puts students at a serious disadvantage when they are asked to take a test or perform in certain ways. Finally, the use of direct questioning is one of overriding importance in this discussion, not only with African-American, but other students as well. Direct communication between adults and young children is limited in the Black community, and instances that occur are typically related to the regulation or punishment of behavior. The culture of American schools, however, is based, more or less, on the Euro-American ideal of open lines of communication—questions and answers—between adults and students. The negative effect for Black children who do not operate according to this norm "is compounded, of course, when the questions emerge in the context of a test situation. Here the query technique is combined with the cold medium of the instrument being administered. It is not only that these instruments so often contain vocabulary and concepts foreign to previous experiences of Black youth, but the mode of communication is culturally biased (albeit inadvertently so)" (Gay & Abrahams, 1973).

Similar discontinuities occur and have been reported for Native American students whose typical performance on standardized tests often results in placing them below even African-American students in ability and achievement. Many researchers have examined factors contributing to this performance and have identified a number of significant linguistic and cultural elements that clearly have a bearing on test results. In particular, the Native American's perception of reality or world view often conflicts with the mainstream, Euro-American view. Some English sentences indicate relationships that are not possible in the world view held by Navajos, for example. The dichotomous relationship between fiction and non-fiction that characterizes reality in the mainstream American view is contrasted with the concept of the Navajos (and Hopis as well) who have three types of reality: truth (same as Anglo truth); mythology (encompasses things that used to be true but may not be true anymore); and lies (not fiction—fiction as known in the Anglo culture does not exist). The word "if" does not translate into the Hopi language to indicate a cause and effect relationship (Rhodes, 1988). Thus, if a reading comprehension item is designed to test understanding of causal relationships, Native American students may not answer appropriately for reasons that would not be apparent to most teachers or administrators. It is not difficult to imagine how the poor performance of a linguistic or cultural minority student on a test would not be correctly attributed to differences in the student's native language or cultural background.

Other factors having to do with processing strategies influence performance on tests. Native American performance is influenced by the fact that it is more common for them to make decisions slowly with the intent of being right the first time. Timed tests, therefore, that require quick responses, guessing, and risk taking handicap the Native American student. In addition, the multiple-choice format has presented a problem because many tasks and ceremonial activities in the Native American culture require many people to make decisions; they are made by consensus, thus allowing everyone to feel that they are a part of the solution. This pattern results in a reluctance on the part of a Native American to eliminate choices from consideration; he is more comfortable combining elements from different choices to make a better response.

Thus we recognize from the history of test bias that content bias can negatively affect the performance of minority students, but we also see that process test bias has at least equal potential for inhibiting the performance of these students. "The question of test bias is always valid when dealing with an instrument developed by one culture, primarily for that culture, and yet administered to individuals of another culture" (Rhodes, 1988). In developing standards and assessments that honor diverse ways of knowing and learning, it will be necessary to accommodate differences in processing strategies—communication, decision-making, speededness, and so forth. "The task is to design assessment probes which measure the same criterion from contexts and perspectives which reflect the life space and values of the learner. . . . Thus options and choices become a critical feature in any assessment system created to be responsive to equity, just as processual description and diagnosis become central purposes" (Gordon, no date, in Darling-Hammond, 1994).

Gordon speaks of equity in terms of sufficiency. He asserts that resources must be distributed sufficiently and opportunities for demonstrating competence must be diverse. "You may expose all persons to the same standard, but if the manner in which the standard is presented isn't one that matches the characteristics of each person, one cannot assert that it has been presented equitably" (Rothman, 1994). This point of view will require deep consideration. The content standards that have been or are being developed by national organizations, state departments of education, and, in some cases, by schools, districts, and other groups are now much more commonly characterized by an emphasis on higher-order thinking skills, "habits of mind," and even affective responses to materials read or assessment activities. This shift away from an emphasis on facts and informational fragments demands much more thought about linguistic and cultural influences on a student's ability or proclivity to "inquire," "communicate mathematically," "solve problems," "reflect on a performance," "make inferences about a character's motivations," and so on. As educators who are engaged in pioneering efforts in the land of new assessments are already discovering, this reformation will require support from parents and the general community as well as students, teachers, and administrators. The rationale for the alteration in approach must be explained, conveyed, communicated, and otherwise disclosed as often as possible and necessary. If this "public relations" work is not accomplished, this innovation in assessment procedures deemed essential to school reform by so many well-meaning educators will undermine itself.

Wiggins (1994) uses an interesting term to discuss an alternative climate for testing or assessment. He refers to the need for approaches to be "respectful" and explains that when individuals are not (1) told about the intent or methods; (2) given the opportunity to explain their responses; (3) given timely, accurate, and helpful feedback; (4) provided with adequate resources or time and opportunity to practice, refine, and master a task, then the situation cannot be considered to be one of mutual respect. We think Wiggins' point is well taken and would extend it to include Malcom's notion that "things valued by different groups" must be reflected in the standards and in the assessment. In referring to new forms of assessments as "authentic," Wiggins (1989) conceived of tests that would accommodate the diversity in students' learning styles, aptitudes, and interests. He asked: "Why must all students be tested in the same way and at the same time? Why should speed of recall be so well-rewarded and slow answering be so heavily penalized in conventional testing?" (Wiggins, 1989, p. 712).

What will be very difficult to accomplish in establishing a new philosophy of assessment is the need to develop performance-based tasks that reflect a multicultural perspective. Most tasks that are developed will be heavily influenced by Euro-American culture as has been the typical pattern of instruction within classrooms. As Baker notes, "the schools must find ways to deal with children from cultures, languages, and expectations that mainstream America barely understands, if at all" (Baker, 1994). If the suggested changes do not occur both in the instructional content of the school and in the content of assessments, certain racial/ethnic groups will continue to be favored over others.

Other factors besides test design, test use, and inequality of educational programs contribute to inequities in assessment for children from linguistic and cultural minority groups. Language differences, attitudes toward test-taking, perceived use of tests, attitudes toward competitiveness, achievement motivation, test-wiseness, test anxiety, willingness to guess, and ability to perform within time limits also come into play. This situation is unlikely to change spontaneously with the advent of performance-based assessments. What will, perhaps, remedy the situation is the use of a wider variety of assessments as well as multiple measures to gain a better understanding of a student's achievement.

In an earlier chapter, we referred to Gordon's (1994) comment that the issues we are addressing are "complex beyond measure," and we think it is time to acknowledge again that what needs to be accomplished in establishing a new, equitable philosophy and approach to assessment will, by no means, be an easy course to follow. What *is* abundantly clear to us, however, (and we hope to readers) is that it will be of enormous value— not only to our educational system, but to our society as a whole. The greatest challenge, perhaps, will be for all of us in that society to have enough patience to spend the time necessary to get it right. We offer the procedural suggestions in the next section as rudimentary guidelines in establishing a new system. As more of us experiment and explore new forms of assessment, we will all find ways to enhance this initial set of guidelines and advance along the course toward more equitable and engaging assessments.

Procedural Guidelines for Development

The quest for new forms of assessment that will provide greater support for student learning is still in its beginning stages. A number of writers, organizations, and states have developed documents to serve as guidelines in this venture, but most are still in draft form. From them, from our own experiences, and from suggestions we have culled from early research and the suggestions of others, we have synthesized the following guidelines or procedures to support efforts toward designing assessments that will honor learning, reflect respect for all students, and help to enhance our educational endeavors.

Policy Prerequisites

In educational planning and development, the need to establish policies to guide and protect the implementation of sound practice in assessment is often one that goes unaddressed. Even when they are established, they often are neglected or ignored in the throes of practice. The following sample scenario related to testing decisions illustrates what we mean.

> *Scenario:*
>
> A school principal discusses with his staff the need to test students in a compensatory education program. The decision to test is one that has been imposed by the requirements of the program. The principal asks a selected staff member to choose and buy a test that fits with their existing testing program, can be purchased economically, and has some non-consumable booklets that can be used for several years. At no time does the staff discuss the purposes of testing, how they might use the results to improve their instructional programs, criteria for a test they are willing to administer, what factors would hinder performance for certain students or groups of students and how they would accommodate such problems, or what other measures they might use to flesh out a comprehensive assessment program for their students.

The administrators and staff of a school should establish policies for an assessment program before they begin to choose, design, refine, or develop a set of measures that will constitute their program. They should reflect on and discuss the purposes of assessment and the questions they most want to answer about their students. They must think about the potential of any test or assessment measure to interfere with learning or to harm students; they must discuss how much intrusiveness they want to permit and how to integrate assessment with instruction. They must decide what types of assessment are appropriate for which students and what administration procedures they need to follow or modify to accommodate diverse learners. There are a wide variety of policies that a school (district or state) might decide to establish to frame an assessment program. Readers who are involved in such work may find Malcom's suggestions for "reinventing assessment" a useful starting point for thinking about relevant questions that could be addressed by writing policies to address the needs of the particular situation (Figure 5.2).

FIGURE 5.2

According to Malcom (1991), the following elements would characterize the "reinvention" of assessment:

- Assessment would be aligned with the nationally agreed upon and locally available curriculum
- Curriculum would be based on standards that are rigorous but not rigid, diverse but without compromising the highest standards of excellence; reflective of student and societal needs; derived through interactions of public, discipline, teaching and user communities; world class but distinctly developed to fit America's values and needs.
- Assessment would inform resource allocation rather than simply reflect it. Students would be provided with various modes of assessment, and if a particular mode is found to provide the best instructional information, its use for a particular student could increase.
- Assessment would focus on higher-order skills,use of subject matter, and demonstration of competencies, especially in settings that are contextually meaningful to students.
- Assessment would be continuous and usually indistinguishable from instruction; it would prompt reinstruction and reassessment until the standards are achieved.
- Assessment would change as the curriculum changes toward subject-matter instruction according to the way the discipline is conducted by its practitioners, and as it connects to other fields.
- Assessment would inform student initiative and learning outside of school.
- Teachers would be prominent in the assessment development and scoring process.
- Teachers, developers, and scorers would be reflective of the tested populations and would include males and females and persons from different regions and different racial/ethnic groups.
- Acceptable "outlier" responses to assessment questions would be captured and, where appropriate, would be included as training examples for teachers to illustrate the range of appropriate responses.
- Consistency, inconsistency, and redundancy among assessment results would be captured and used to improve the assessment process.
- Technology would become a more prominent tool of assessment, especially in providing contextually richer questions; assistance to poor readers, non-English speakers, and students with disabilities; and in diagnosing learning problems and misconceptions.
- The use of timed testing would decrease.
- Students would be able to see their own scored assessments (with comments) as well as examples of exceptional and acceptable responses.

- An appeal (or explanation) process would allow students to challenge scoring.
- Assessment results for quality control would be publicly reported, and resources and technical assistance would be provided to assist schools in teaching appropriate levels of performance.
- Standards for school performance would be set at world-class levels, and schools given some period of time, resources, and technical assistance to raise their performance to meet those standards.
- Regular subpopulation sampling and separate reporting would be a part of the assessment process, and appropriate intervention would be put in place where necessary to improve subpopulation scores.
- As in sports performance (in gymnastics and diving, for example), students would be encouraged to demonstrate superior performance in tasks they select, with degrees of difficulty attached. Creativity would be rewarded with additional recognition.
- Single-score reporting would be replaced with scoring that provides more information about competencies, skills, and knowledge attained.
- Scoring would be rich enough to inform teachers of children who move from grade to grade, school to school, or region to region, about what these students have been taught and what level of knowledge they have achieved.

Malcom, Shirley M. (1991). Equity and excellence through authentic science assessment. In G. Kulm & S. Malcom (Eds.), *Science assessment in the service of reform* (pp. 313-330). Washington, DC: American Association for the Advancement of Science.

In addition to Malcom's comprehensive set of guidelines, we suggest three general policy decisions that should be *sine qua non*[2]:

Assessment should support student learning. Information garnered from the assessment should be related to standards and curriculum and used for improvement. The time spent should be seen as valuable because it is tied to educational purposes. The information should include qualitative judgments and examples of student work related to standards and rubrics to illustrate the quality of the work and student progress in learning. The assessments used should be open and transparent to students; they should understand the standards and performance criteria and have the opportunity to reflect on their performances. The assessments should be useful to teachers for planning instruction, provide information about inequities in results by subpopulations, and be used to reflect on and evaluate classroom practice. The information generated by the assessments should be understandable to parents and provide information about their children's learning gathered over time. The assessments should be disaggregated by socioeconomic status (SES), racial-ethnic groups, language, gender, and disability; provide useful school, district, and state data, and be used as a basis for addressing inequities in outcomes.

Assessments should be based on content standards. These agreed-upon standards must have been developed through an open, public process in which all significant parties have fully participated to ensure that the assessments are tailored to various populations. This process should support implementation of the standards by having public discussions; circulating examples, summaries; involving students in reviews; and publication in languages other than English. The assessments should reflect what is deemed most important to learn. "Curriculum, teaching, and assessment must be integrated and mutually supportive elements in the educational process, each serving common goals" (Bass, 1993).

Assessments must be related to opportunity to learn. Standards should also be developed using an open process that addresses the opportunities that students have to learn and develop proficiency in areas included in the content standards. Disaggregated assessment information should be used to address any systemic differences that are revealed by the data. Where inequities in opportunity to learn clearly exist, students should not be penalized. The goal of developing a system that will effectively reach those populations for whom the system has historically been least effective is a "formidable challenge in the design of assessment instruments. They must not operate as a cultural filter, as has previously been the case. Instead, they must be sensitively crafted to accommodate diverse forms of authentic communication and they should assess only what students have had a fair opportunity to learn" (Bass, 1993).

When taken together, the last two recommendations really pose a conundrum with regard to minority students. For too long, children who have been variously labeled minority, LEP, economically disadvantaged, educationally deficient, special needs, and educationally handicapped have been held to standards that were much too low—expectations have been unreasonably low. The fact of the matter is that we really have no idea what children are capable of until we give them the maximum opportunity to learn, to become proficient, to master what lies before them. So we should hold them to the highest standards, teach them to develop higher-order thinking skills. But in doing so, we must acknowledge (as does Denise McKeon [1994] in an excellent treatise, "When Meeting 'Common' Standards is Uncommonly Difficult") that meeting the standards is "a more complex and cognitively demanding task than it is for students who are proficient in English," for example. In the past, the opportunities for such children to learn have been hindered by programmatic deficiencies, teacher preparation deficiencies, and assessment procedures. McKeon suggests five simple steps to ensure that such students as those who are limited-English proficient, will meet the content standards proposed (Figure 5.3).

FIGURE 5.3

1. School and district officials can systematically examine the academic program open to their limited-English-proficient (Ed. comment:substitute any other label here) students. Often, it is helpful to select three of four LEP students with different backgrounds, reviewing the type of course offerings available to fill the special needs of each. Do the courses provide support in learning English as a second language? Do they provide challenging content teaching, either in the student's first language or by "sheltering" the content (that is, teaching academic content along with the language needed to learn it).

2. Using the TESOL[1] Access Standards as a guideline, school personnel can review their approach to educating limited-English-proficient students. The school environment can support LEP students' learning and value their linguistic and cultural diversity (approaches should add to, rather than replace, students' cultural repertoires).

3. State and school district officials can make sure that ESL and bilingual educators are included on teams that develop curriculum frameworks. Often, ESL and bilingual educators use alternative instructional techniques (such as bilingual education or content-based ESL) to teach particular subjects (science, social studies, and so on). If these professionals help to develop curriculum frameworks, they can ensure that the instruction for LEP students is up-to-date, effective, and consistent with local standards.

4. State and district officials can discuss alternative ways to judge the performance of limited-English-proficient students. Some students might show what they know through portfolios. Others, especially those in bilingual programs, might demonstrate achievement in a language other than English.

5. State and district officials can support the development of standards for the discipline of English as a second language. Professional teaching standards for ESL are needed to ensure that its instructors are highly skilled, and content standards are important because many LEP students receive ESL in place of regular language arts.

[1] TESOL (Teachers of English to Speakers of Other Languages) recently formulated a set of opportunity-to-learn standards for LEP students. They are divided into four areas: (1) access to a positive learning environment; (2) access to appropriate curriculum; (3) access to full delivery of services; (4) access to equitable assessment. For a complete explication of the standards, see the Appendix.

As noted, this puzzle is one we can't afford to ignore, that is, developing high standards for all children to meet without thinking deeply about what this will mean for children for whom this will be a formidable challenge. Yet, to some, it seems that it is being ignored. Richard Allington notes, "If 'all' really does mean 'all,' it would seem to me someone would be thinking a little more deeply or commenting a little more precisely on how they expect all students to meet the standards . . . Maybe what they mean is 'almost all' or 'practically all'" (in Viadero, 1993). We hope that is not what they mean, but we agree that this must be given much deeper consideration, and we hope that this book helps to prompt the discussion and policy-setting that must occur.

Establishing Assessment Purposes

One very important aspect of developing an assessment system is to give consideration to the various purposes for testing or assessment. In our experience, we have found that testing is something that has so often been externally imposed or mandated—that school and district staff most often seem to think of it as something that is merely required. They don't expect to use the information in any constructive way because, in many cases, they don't even expect to see the results for a long time—sometimes not at all. If they do review it, they find it of extremely limited usefulness. It has little effect on their instructional programs. Teachers do engage in the development and use of classroom assessments, and in such instances, they are more apt to use the information for instructional purposes; more often, however, they are used for grading. This failure to give consideration to the different purposes for assessment, to the specific questions that need to be answered by use of an assessment, and to the wide variety of tools that are or could be available is justification enough for altering the entire philosophical approach to assessment and to the extant procedures commonly followed.

One way to begin thinking about the purposes for testing with a school or district staff is to use a simple matrix like the one in Figure 5.4 to begin to sort out essential information. We have sometimes found that teachers have difficulty completing the matrix because they have never been given the opportunity (or the responsibility) for thinking about the purposes for an assessment program.

FIGURE 5.4		
What is the purpose of testing?	**What questions do we want to answer?**	**What tools or instruments can be used?**
Assess student accomplishment in language arts	How well do students comprehend what they read?	Written response to story or other non-fiction material
	Are students able to analyze stories for plot, character, setting, and theme?	Story map
	Can students use metacognitive skills to reflect on the writing they do?	Self-reflective response to writing
Report on student achievement by school	How do students do in language arts in this school compared to other schools in the district?	State performance-based assessment Criterion-referenced tests Norm-referenced tests
	How much progress have students made in writing skills?	State performance-based assessment Writing assessment scored with rubric

The use of a matrix or any other planning tool should be couched in a preliminary discussion of priority outcomes for the students in a school or district. The assessment system that is devised should reflect and reinforce the skills and habits of mind you deem most important. Herman et al. (1992) offer some questions to use as starting points:

1. What do you want your students to be able to accomplish in a unit, in a course, in a discipline, or across disciplines?
2. What should students be able to do at the completion of a unit, a course, or a year of study that they were not able to do

before? What critical areas of student development do you want to influence?

3. What important cognitive skills do you want your students to develop?

4. What social and affective skills do you want your students to develop?

5. What metacognitive skills do you want your students to develop?

6. What types of problems do you want them to be able to solve?

7. What concepts and principles do you want your students to be able to apply?

Of course, in all of this, you must also take into account your students who are English learners, who are from a non-mainstream culture, who are learning disabled, or who come from a background of poverty. While the outcomes you value should definitely remain the same, you may have some added considerations:

8. How well do ELLs (English language learners) communicate in English in written and oral formats? How well do they communicate in their native language?

9. Do Native American students demonstrate their skills better when they have been given the opportunity to work with a group first?

10. Do black children express what they know better when the questions reflect a discourse style that is more common for them than a routinized series of basal reader questions? (See Hiebert & Calfee, 1990.)

Do not underestimate or abbreviate this process of discussing purposes of assessment and matching them to outcomes of interest. It will become the infrastructure for the system, and a failure to build this carefully will result in an eventual deterioration of the system. Perhaps, too, we all have to give serious thought to what we consider to be the purposes of school. Taylor (1994) states provocatively that "as a nation we do not all agree on the purposes of schools. Do we believe that schools are supposed to sort students to find the brightest and the best, or do we believe that our democracy will be stronger if we foster the creativity and capacity of every individual? Such questions *should* provoke thinking and broad-based discussion as we all work together to improve education for all children."

Participation in the Process

In contrast to the measurement model by which tests were most often externally mandated and administered as an activity totally separate from the instructional process, the development of alternative assessments is standards-driven and closely tied to the instructional process. By their very nature, alternative assessment measures require that the administrator have a thorough understanding of the content and cognitive skills involved in the subject domain being assessed. This understanding must be shared by all instructional staff to ensure consistency of judgment across the instructional program. The assessment system we are advocating would be designed to improve learning outcomes, and, as such, teachers must be fully cognizant of the purposes and procedures and must be fully committed to the standards on which any assessment is based. Teachers should, therefore, participate in the design, development, administration, scoring, interpretation, and use of many of the assessment tasks and exercises. This is certainly true for any classroom assessments developed by local districts, but it should also be true of assessments developed by states for use in larger-scale assessments. It should become common practice for teachers to review together information in student portfolios, to discuss how the contents reflect content standards, to participate in scoring sessions for performance tasks, and to discuss appropriate interpretation of a body of work as a reflection of student learning.

Professional development for teachers must be a vital part of the movement to new forms of assessment. There is no shortcut to improved assessment of students from non-dominant language and culture groups that does not include increased access for teachers to knowledge about how culture and language affect learning. Pre-service and in-service education opportunities must be made available for teachers to learn more about issues of language and culture. Teachers must have the chance to get beyond mere infusion of multicultural content into existing curricula to strategies that promote inclusion of all students in classroom discourse. With a repertoire of possible ways of grouping students, an awareness of how different styles of communication play out in the classroom, and a framework for evaluating classroom language demands, they can be more responsive. To understand students' classroom performance, teachers need to learn from their local communities. Linking with the community will be crucial—to see communication patterns firsthand, to understand from parents what they value and why, to learn about how children perform at home, and to share with them a "school perspective" (Estrin, 1993).

The close involvement of teachers in the development of effective assessment systems represents a significant change in the role of teachers. Taylor (1994) points out that "teachers will have to become professionals within their disciplines . . . If teachers are to build instruction from essential performances or if teachers are to be able to judge whether students are prepared for performance examinations or to submit their work for formal evaluation, they will have to be good judges of student performances within the assessed disciplines. This requires (a) subject-matter knowledge, (b) an understanding of the processes that are central to different disciplines, and (c) pedagogical strategies that help students approach each discipline in appropriate ways."

In addition to teachers, other important stakeholders, including administrators, counselors, parents, policymakers, and members of the community, should be educated about assessment and involved at appropriate points in the assessment development process. Parents and community members must be involved in reviewing assessment tasks for bias, appropriateness, and meaningfulness, and they should be able to review scoring procedures and understand fully the uses and consequences of assessment. In addition to having parents and members of the community involved in development and implementation, there should be continuous, concerted efforts to enable the community at large to understand the choices that are made with regard to type and format of assessment, the development process, and the contribution that such assessments will make to improved learning for children. If this last task is not attended to consistently, any new assessment system is vulnerable to criticism, and it is likely that efforts to dismantle it will be undertaken.

As we have mentioned elsewhere, it is also important to think about broad-based involvement in formal assessment development processes. Any panel, committee, or task established to develop assessments should include persons knowledgeable about the education of students who are learning English, who are from minority cultures, or who require additional consideration. In a report on federal education programs for limited-English-proficient students prepared by the Stanford Working Group, *Blueprint for the Second Generation* (1994), several recommendations related to participation are included:

1. In LEAs where there are LEP students, school staff and community members that represent LEP students should participate in any discussions about additional local standards for curriculum and instruction. Moreover, the educational needs and contributions of these students must be considered (p. 25).

2. In States with substantial numbers of LEP students in given language groups, the State Plan should include a process for developing content area assessments in the native languages represented by these groups.

Designing Performance Tasks

One component of an assessment system that can provide rich opportunities for students to demonstrate what they know and are able to do is the performance task or exercise (sometimes also called "event"). Many states are including them in statewide assessment systems, and various databases of such tasks are being developed by national organizations and as part of local efforts to develop assessment systems. Performance tasks should be linked very closely to outcome goals (content standards) deemed important by the group developing the tasks. They should be based on an identification of discipline-based content and skills. There are numerous advantages to using performance tasks to assess learning:

- They can provide the opportunity for students to use higher-order thinking skills, use multiple approaches to solve problems, and react to their performance by using self-reflection procedures as part of the exercise.

- Minority or second-language students can demonstrate what they know or are able to do by choosing an approach to the task that is appropriate for them, by writing in their native language, or by reflecting (orally or in writing) about their performance.

- They can represent real-life experiences.

- Both students and teachers can use them as learning experiences and modify their approaches to learning and teaching based on the results of the exercise.

- Various content areas or disciplines can be integrated in one task so that the performance is multi-dimensional.

Despite the complexity involved in developing such tasks and scoring rubrics to use in evaluating student performance, we believe that the benefits far outweigh the challenges involved in developing them. If you are just beginning the development process, we strongly recommend the ASCD publication by Joan Herman et al., *A Practical Guide to Alternative Assessment* (1992). The chapter on "Selecting Tasks" provides very useful information related to the development of tasks. For example, the following set of questions is presented to guide the development of effective assessment tasks:

- Does the task match specific instructional intentions?

- Does the task adequately represent the content and skills you expect students to attain?

- Does the task enable students to demonstrate their progress and capabilities?

- Does the assessment use authentic, real-world tasks?
- Does the task lend itself to an interdisciplinary approach?
- Can the task be structured to provide measures of several goals?

In addition to the general questions identified above, many other questions need to be posed related to eligible content or topics, format of questions included, group or individual work or balance of both, choices of response mode to be given, materials or resources needed, directions to students, administrative constraints, and scoring procedures. Herman et al. also offer a useful set of criteria for evaluating tasks developed:

- Do the tasks **match the important outcome goals** you have set for students? Do they reflect complex thinking skills?
- Do they pose an **enduring** problem type?
- Are the tasks **fair and free of bias**? For example, do they favor either boys or girls, students who have lived in a particular location or region, students with a particular cultural heritage, or those whose parents can afford to buy certain materials?
- Will the tasks be **credible** to important constituencies? Will they be seen as meaningful and challenging by students, parents, and teachers?
- Will the tasks be **meaningful** and engaging to students so that they will be motivated to show their capabilities?
- Do the tasks involve real problems, situations, and audiences? Are the tasks **instructionally related/teachable**? Do they represent skills and knowledge that your students can acquire and that you have the materials and expertise to adequately teach?
- Are the tasks **feasible** for implementation in your classroom or school in terms of space, equipment, time, costs, and so forth?

As noted in the aforementioned document, these criteria are derived from the more general CRESST (Center for Research on Evaluation, Standards, and Student Testing/UCLA) criteria for judging assessment quality (Linn, Baker, and Dunbar, 1991). Using questions and criteria such as the ones given above can ensure that assessments yield valuable information about students and programs.

It is important to include a few words on the structure of problems included in performance tasks. Several researchers who have written about assessment have discussed the difference between *ill-structured* and *well-structured* problems. Problems on standardized tests are typically well-structured: they are clearly stated, provide all the information needed, and a clear procedure exists that guarantees a correct solution. As defined by Simon (1978), an ill-structured problem is "one that is complex, without definite criteria for determining when the problem is solved, without all the information needed to solve the problem, and without a 'legal move generator' for finding all the possibilities at each step in solving the problem." Frederiksen (1984) points out that most of the important problems one faces in real life are ill-structured, as are all of the other social, political, and economic problems we face in the world. An ability to solve ill-structured problems is an example of something that is not taught and not tested in American schools.

In another article we would recommend for guidance on developing performance exercises or tasks, Joan Baron (1991) poses some questions to guide one's thinking in the process of developing tasks, one of which relates to the issue of ill-structured problems:

- Have I included some messy, loosely structured problems in which students have to first structure the problems before beginning to solve them?

The process not only of finding but formulating problems (or generating questions related to a reading passage) are skills that students will find extremely useful when they move into the workplace.

Other questions that Baron submits and that expand on the list provided above include the following:

- Do my tasks have either multiple solutions or solution paths, and do they encourage diverse perspectives?
- Are my tasks structured to encourage students to access their prior knowledge and skills when solving problems?
- Do some tasks require students to work together in small groups to solve complex problems?
- Do some problems require sustained work?
- Do some tasks allow students a degree of choice and control over the course of action needed to solve problems and conduct investigations?
- Do some tasks require students to design and carry out their own investigations?
- Do some of my tasks require self-assessment and reflection on the part of students?
- Are my tasks likely to have personal meaning for the students?

- Do some of my tasks provide problems that are situated in real-world contexts and are appropriate for the age-group solving them?

- Do some tasks allow for transferring the understandings gained and generalizations made in the present task to other related tasks?

Those who begin working on the development of performance tasks will find a striking similarity between good assessment tasks and good curriculum tasks. The differences include the fact that assessment tasks need scoring criteria, are more highly integrative than instructional tasks, and alter the role of the teacher. "The time is ripe to work together to create for our teachers and our students rich assessment opportunities in which students can 'put it all together' and self-monitor their own learning" (Baron, 1991).

The sample performance tasks included in Figure 5.5 will give assessment developers some idea of the kinds of items that are being drafted and tried out with students as part of state and local efforts to develop alternative ways to assess children's learning. It should be useful to review these sample items with regard to the questions listed above in order to gain a greater understanding of what is possible to accomplish with a performance task and how to evaluate the quality. The reader will also find sample tasks and a critique tool in the Appendix that may be used to provide a useful staff development exercise in applying some of the criteria we have been discussing to a review of existing tasks. This kind of review and critique helps to prepare assessment developers for the challenge of the development work.

Ensuring Fairness

Developing assessments for a widely diverse student population must recognize (a) the social, political, and economic realities involved; (b) the relevance of educational opportunities to those realities; and (c) the significance of linguistic and cultural factors to both educational opportunities and socioeconomic realities (O'Connor, 1989). These issues have been debated for years, with critics charging primarily that minority students were not receiving a *comparable education*, so that tests were not fair to them (Sanchez, 1934, in Olmedo, 1981).

FIGURE 5.5
Generic Reading Task

Standards: Communication

Performance Task Domain: Examining, Representing and Evaluating Information

Task Overview: Students will read, interpret and evaluate a literary or non-fiction text. Students will display their understanding of the text through answering questions, reflecting on their own reading, and evaluating their learning. Students will have 3-4 days to complete the task with daily class time provided for discussion and revision. Teachers will discuss the prompt with the entire class prior to individual student work.

Time: 3-4 days

Prompt to Students: You will read a story or selection. After you read the selection, you will show your understanding of the content and the author's writing through the following activities:

1. A short **summary** of significant aspects of the story or selection including its main ideas and important events.

2. A **story diorama** (a three dimensional stage upon which figures can be placed or drawn) about the event in the story that you found to be most important to you. A **quote** from the event or section that you found important and the reasons why you chose the quote.

3. A **graphic or description** of the strategies you used to figure out the meanings of words or ideas in the story, including an example.

4. A **conclusion** about the story that tells about what it means to you, what it makes you think of, or anything that relates to your reading of it.

Instructions for making a diorama using 8½" by 11" paper

Fold point A to point B.

Cut along top edge of folded area (A to B).

Fold triangle in half (from A to B) to form smaller triangle.

Open triangles into diamond.

Cut along any crease from an outer edge (A) to center of diamond (B).

Make a pocket by folding side A over side B.

Secure diorama with a paper clip.

Nanette Koelsch, Far West Laboratory

TASK DEVELOPMENT

I. **Date:** July 30, 1992

Name: F. Kunimoto

Grade Level: 4-6
(for task)

Standards Assessed: 2,6,7

II. **Overview:**

For this task the student will read the selection *The Medieval Feast* by Aliki and participate in class discussions. In small groups, students will compare and contrast a medieval feast to a Hawaiian luau. Students will decide how to share what they have discovered by charting, illustrating, mapping, demonstrating cooking, or writing a summary. Students will then write a reflection about what they learned.

III. **Prompt:**

In this task you will:

A. Read the selection, *The Medieval Feast.*

B. Participate and listen to a class discussion of similarities and differences of a medieval feast with a Hawaiian luau.

C. In a small group you will decide on a presentation that will demonstrate what you learned about medieval feasts and a Hawaiian luau.

D. Write a reflection (for portfolio) about what they learned after comparing the feast to a luau.

Re-explanation:

To accomplish this task you will need to:

A. Read *The Medieval Feast* selection, then participate in a discussion of characteristics of medieval times.

B. Participate in discussion of a Hawaiian luau, then compare and contrast looking for similarities and differences.

C. In a small group students will list on chart paper and share ideas with other students.

D. Each group will be asked to brainstorm possible ways to present to the class what they have learned about the different culture or periods of time.

E.   The members of the group will collaborate and work together to share responsibilities, to produce and present to others, their findings.

F.   Write a reflection about what you learned from the comparisons.

IV. Directions to Teachers:

To administer this task you will need to:

A.   Provide the students with prior knowledge and practice with comparing and contrasting and looking for similarities.

B.   Provide students with prior practice working in a group with assigned roles (i.e., leader, recorder, artist (illustrator), etc.).

C.   Pre-read and get to know the story.

Instructions Prior to Task:

A.   Provide opportunities for group activities to determine group compatibility.

B.   Provide opportunities for charting, mapping, demonstrating cooking, and summary writing.

C.   Provide information/experiences about a luau (i.e., guest speaker, discussion of personal experiences, etc.).

Materials/Resources:

A.   Social Studies textbook on Medieval times.

B.   Reading the selection *The Medieval Feast* by Aliki.

C.   Art supplies (i.e., chart paper, pens, construction paper, scissors, etc.)

V. Time: 1 week

VI. Extensions:

A.   Prepare a medieval feast and invite parents, other students, etc.

B.   Share presentations at the "feast".

C.   Research other culture's feast (i.e., Chinese, African, Greek, etc.).

The Mural Project

Attention sixth grade students! One wall on the exterior of Building A needs a mural. All sixth grade students will have the opportunity to draw a design for the mural. Your design must include a geometric, Southwestern border framing a Navajo scene. The scene should reflect pride and respect for life on the Navajo Nation.

The project will be part of your mathematics, art, culture and language arts classes. Each student will submit a border design and a drawing of a Navajo scene to be painted inside of the border. You will also figure the cost of materials and the estimated time of completion for your mural. All school students and personnel will vote for two winning murals. All sixth grade students will participate in painting the murals this spring.

The finished mural will be 80 inches by 160 inches. Following are the directions for the project.

1. Use the cinderblock paper to design a geometric, repeating border for a mural.

2. Interview at least 10 people about their choice for a Navajo scene that best reflects the local area and culture of the Navajo Nation. Example might be specific landmarks, people, cultural activities, recreation, livestock, plants, legends and more. Graph the results of your interviews on graph paper.

3. Based on the results of your interviews, draw a scene that you feel best represents the local area and culture of the Navajo Nation.

4. Color your scene. (Choose from pastels, paint, markers or other color media).

5. Calculate the cost of material using cost sheets from three local sources. Include cost of paint, primer, brushes and any other needed material. Choose the most cost efficient materials to complete your design.

6. Share your design with classmates. Decide if you should submit your design individually or combine your border or scene with another students' border or scene.

7. Draw your border and scene to proportional scale using tagboard or posterboard that your teacher provides.

8. Write up a proposal for your design. Include estimated cost, time of completion and the cultural value of your project.

Designs will be posted and all students and personnel will vote. Your entire project will be included in your portfolio as a mathematics and language arts project.

Sixth grade teachers, Many Farms Elementary School, Chinle (AZ) Unified School District in collaboration with Nanette Koelsch, Far West Laboratory.

FIGURE 5.6
Standards for Quality Performance Assessments

- **Consequences.** Testing history is full of examples of good intentions gone awry. This criterion requires that we plan from the outset to assess the actual consequences of the assessment. Does it have positive consequences or are there unintended effects such as narrowing of curriculum, adverse effects on disadvantaged students, and so on?

- **Fairness.** Does the assessment consider fairly the cultural background of those students taking the test? Have all students had equal opportunity to learn the complex thinking and problem-solving skills that are being targeted?

- **Transfer and Generalizability.** Will the assessment results support accurate generalizations about student capability? Are the results reliable across raters, and consistent in meaning across locales?

- **Cognitive Complexity.** We cannot tell from simply looking at an assessment whether or not it actually assesses complex thinking skills. Does an assessment in fact *require* students to use complex thinking and problem solving?

- **Content Quality.** The tasks selected to measure a given content domain should themselves be worthy of students' and raters' time and efforts. Is the selected content consistent with the best current understanding of the field and does it reflect important aspects of a discipline that will stand the test of time?

- **Content Coverage.** The content coverage criterion requires that assessment be aligned with the curriculum and, over a set of assessments, represent the full curriculum. Because time constraints will probably limit the number of alternative assessments that can be given, adequate content coverage represents a significant challenge. Are the key elements of the curriculum covered by the set of assessments?

- **Meaningfulness.** One of the rationales for more contextualized assessments is that they ensure that students engage in meaningful problems that result in worthwhile educational experiences and higher levels of motivation. Do students find the assessment tasks realistic and worthwhile?

- **Cost and Efficiency.** To be effective tools, assessments must be cost effective. Labor-intensive performance-based assessments require efficient data collection and scoring procedures. Is the information about students worth the cost and time to obtain it?

(Linn, Baker, and Dunbar, 1991)

The goal in developing and using tests or assessments must be to ensure that specific inferences made from the results are appropriate, meaningful, and useful, a property of test use often referred to as *validity* (Cole and Moss in Linn, 1989). Validity could theoretically be achieved through tests that measure what they were designed to measure and to do so equally well for all groups, but some theorists maintain that there will be no validity in testing until issues of social justice and values are resolved—that inequities in the society will always be reflected in test results, invalidating conclusions about some students. *Some items* on any test will be unfair to *some students.* The difficulty for minority and language minority students is that there is a disproportionate number of such items for them. For example, a common type of item bias in reading comprehension tests that results in lower scores for minority students is found in items that can be answered without reading the passage, by relying on "common (middle-class) knowledge." In such cases, *construct validity* is jeopardized because such test items are testing general knowledge as well as reading comprehension. This same potential risk will be embodied in performance-based assessments that call for students to use their background knowledge and reasoning strategies to make judgments, analyze, or solve problems.

Cultural differences along with language differences affect test performance to the same degree as they do classroom participation. American Indian students may appear to be non-competitive, for example, but not for the reasons often assumed. It is a cultural characteristic of many Indian groups that they do not like to be singled out for recognition and feel ashamed if they are. Assessment that draws undue attention to an Indian student may cause serious stress for the student. The testing situation forces a recognition of the child that goes against social norms. Some alternative assessments that call for or allow students to work cooperatively or discuss a piece of writing may, in fact, ameliorate this situation for some minority students, but it must be examined carefully throughout the development process and when such assessments are administered.

The question of ensuring fairness of performance tasks is a complex one, one that must be given specific attention in developing performance tasks; it is common, however, for it to be overlooked or neglected until well into the development process. Several groups are working on separate sets of criteria for assessments that are responsive to student diversity (for example, FairTest, Stanford Working Group, TESOL). Some of the criteria that have been suggested include the following:

1. Assessment tasks should reflect the diversity of cultures and experiences of students to be assessed.

2. Assessment tasks should allow for different modes of presentation to reflect different learning styles and different cultures.

3. Assessments should be given in students' primary language when it is the student's language of communication.

4. Students should be given a choice of the language in which they will complete an assessment task except when the purpose is to assess the language ability of the student.

5. Assessments should be adapted for students with disabilities so that they can participate in the assessment.

6. Assessments should be validated for significant student populations.

The effects of linguistic and cultural differences on processing strategies will also have to be taken into account when developing and using performance tasks. Teachers who administer the tasks should keep thorough anecdotal records of what they observe the child doing as he or she approaches the task and should ask the child to self-reflect in writing or orally on his or her approach to the task and success or problems. This information should become part of the record on the child's progress in learning. If "rightness" is defined by "a single set of criteria derived from mainstream, Eurocentric cultural values, not by pedagogical appropriateness based on the characteristics of different groups of students" (Gay, 1988), then learning for students is constrained, and judgments about their learning are contaminated. The technical demands of item construction, test design, and psychometrics are discouraging, or even prevent vigorous discussions of what will count as evidence that all students are able to use their minds well (Wolf, Bixby, Glenn, and Gardner, 1991). We need to be at least as concerned with equity and credibility as with reliability and validity.

New modes of assessment also require that children be thoroughly grounded in what is expected of them. They should not be penalized because they are not familiar with a different approach to assessment. For example, many performance assessments allow children to collaborate, encourage revision to arrive at a better final result, and discourage a mere regurgitation of facts as the best response to an item. All students must have access to these presuppositions in order to allow them to challenge old patterns of performance (Wolf et al., 1991). Students must also be allowed a variety of ways of meeting standards and have multiple opportunities to do so.

A few more examples may serve to illustrate further the importance of considering differences in processing strategies if assessments are to be fair. Michael Pavel of UCLA points out that Native American students are ill-served by tests that demand rapid responses and immediate decisions because Native Americans value placidity and patience. Their behavior has sometimes resulted in their being viewed as slow or backward (Rothman, 1993). In addition, William Leap (1988) reported on several characteristics of Ute Indian students that affected classroom performance: differences in question-answering strategies and in styles for processing information from the printed page; resistance to tasks requiring the use of speculation, personal opinion, or judgment; and preference for discussion in terms of concrete rather than hypothetical description.

In discussing the culturally-based behaviors of African-Americans, Gay and Abrahams (1973) related them to test performance:

> . . . testing violated the learned interactional practices of the Black child in a number of ways. First, he is given a written test when he is accustomed to demonstrating his abilities verbally. Second, he is asked to function in-dividually, isolated from his compatriots, when his culture background sanctions cooperative efforts. Third, the environment is rigidly structured and formalized, while, within the Black community, he learns in an infor-mal, social setting. All of these interferences operate on the child before he has opportunity to address himself adequately to the task itself.

Despite the fact that the authors wrote this over 20 years ago, it should be clear that the factors are ones that still operate to affect a student's perfor-mance on an assessment. All of these culturally-based factors must be taken into account when designing assessments.

Most of the alternative assessment measures that are being explored offer genuine potential for student learning and reflection as part of the assessment. Many of the formats being used require a constructed response, ask for students to use their knowledge and learning strategies in the con-text of a meaningful task, or focus on production-type, rather than selec-tion-type responses. Despite all of the potential advantages of alternative assessments, however, we cannot lose sight of the fact that "many forms of bias will remain, as the choice of items, responses deemed appropriate, and content deemed important are the product of culturally and contex-tually determined judgments, as well as the privileging of certain ways of knowing and modes of performance over others" (Darling-Hammond, 1994).

Validity and Reliability

Issues related to the validity and reliability of performance assess-ments are among the most vexatious. Part of the solution lies with our ability to think in new ways about assessment designs and procedures and shift our perspective from a "measurement model" to a "standards model"—as discussed above with reference to Taylor (1994). While we are not psychometricians, statisticians, or measurement specialists, we do think it's important for everyone who will be involved in any way with assessment design to develop an awareness of these psychometric issues and contribute to a new perspective on them. High technical quality is not something that should be sacrificed or neglected when developing performance-based assessments. Researchers at CRESST, for example, have proposed that quality assessments should meet certain standards, regardless of purpose or format. Their proposed standards are presented in Figure 5.6. The features included in this list contribute significantly to an assurance that such assessments can be characterized as valid and reliable.

The need to change perspective when considering validity and reliability is also reflected in assertions made by Grant Wiggins (1994):

> *Tests are intrinsically prone to sacrifice validity to achieve reliability and to sacrifice the student's interests for the test maker's.* All testing involves compromise. Tasks are simplified and decontextualized for the sake of precision in scoring. Limits are placed on the student's access to resources. Standardization establishes a distance between tester and student: the student can neither adapt the question to personal style nor question the questioner (a right, one would think, in a modern society, and something we would encourage in a more personal educational relationship).

Wolf et al. (1991) also suggest that we need to "revise our notions of high-agreement reliability as a cardinal symptom of a useful and viable approach to scoring student performance" and "seek other sorts of evidence that responsible judgment is unfolding." What we must do, it seems, is challenge the traditional definitions and the assumption that reliability as it has been traditionally operationalized is essential to sound practice. Reliability represents the degree to which test scores are subject to errors of measurement. It is typically operationalized by examining the consistency among different observations. Performance assessments make it difficult to generalize across readers and tasks because they are much less standardized; they permit considerable latitude in student response, in interpretation, and in design; they often require an integration of skills and knowledge; and they require expert judgment for evaluation. Developers have had considerable success in establishing reader or rater reliability when scorers receive careful training. They have had considerably more difficulty in establishing acceptable levels of reliability across tasks intended to address the same skills or with portfolios where the tasks vary substantially from one student to the next and where multiple tasks are evaluated simultaneously.

Wiley and Haertel (1992) offer one promising means of addressing reliability without the assumption of homogeneity of tasks. They suggest a careful analysis of tasks to describe the capabilities required, scoring tasks separately for the capabilities, and "examining reliability within capability across tasks to which the capability applies" (Moss, 1994). Validity researchers, on the other hand, working on the development of performance assessments have been building on the work of Messick (1964, 1975, 1980, 1989) and Cronbach (1980, 1988) that includes social consequences in the definition of validity. They stress the "importance of *balancing* concerns about reliability, replicability, or generalizability with additional criteria such as 'authenticity' (Newman, 1990), 'directness' (Frederiksen & Collins, 1989), or 'cognitive complexity' (Linn et al. 1991). This balancing of often competing concerns has resulted in the sanctioning of lower levels of reliability, as long as 'acceptable levels are achieved for particular purposes of assessment' (Linn et al., 1991)" (Moss, 1994).

Moss (1994) suggests that there is a second approach to assuring interpretations of human performances that could be considered an alternative to the one based in psychometrics. She bases this second strategy in hermeneutics.[3] We think that what Moss suggests in terms of a hermeneutic approach to assessment holds considerable promise for all performance assessments, but particularly for the scoring of portfolios and for reviewing the performances of diverse students.

> A hermeneutic approach to assessment would involve holistic, integrative interpretations of collected performances that seek to understand the whole in light of its parts, that privilege readers who are the most knowledgeable about the context in which the assessment occurs, and that ground those interpretations not only in the textual and contextual evidence available, but also in a rational debate among the community of interpreters. Here, the interpretation might be warranted by criteria like a reader's extensive knowledge of the learning context; an ethic of disciplined, collaborative inquiry that encourages challenges and revisions to initial interpretations; and the transparency of the trail of evidence leading to the interpretations, which allows users to evaluate the conclusions for themselves (Moss, 1994, p. 7).

We included Moss's entire comment because we think it describes so precisely the kind of evaluation that we believe will be necessary to ensure equity (to the degree that is possible) in the assessment of diverse students. Assessment must involve the use of multiple measures or "collected performances" viewed as a whole; those who evaluate them must be thoroughly cognizant of what they are looking for in a performance and what the details of that performance tell them about a student's learning and about her linguistic and cultural orientations; and such well-grounded interpretation can most fruitfully take place when interpreters work and discuss together using collaborative inquiry. If such a system truly were in place, we believe that assessment practices would have "scaled the heights." It is hard to imagine that such a process would not go a long way toward improving teaching and learning as well.

Administration, Scoring, Interpretation, and Use

This section includes a number of complex issues that, if treated individually, would require at least a chapter to discuss in depth. It is not our intent to include such discussions in this book, so we are merely providing overviews of potential approaches and things to consider. Performance assessments allow and invite considerably more latitude in administration and response approach than do traditional standardized tests. As a result, considerable work will need to be accomplished to accommodate the shift, not only in goals and intent, but in procedural issues as well. This latitude is extremely important when it comes to English language learners or non-mainstream students. If our goal is to gain a comprehensive understanding of students' progress in learning, it is necessary to use a variety of approaches and truly explore their approach to learning and their ability to convey what they know and are able to do.

At this point, however, it is important to recall our discussion of the identification of purpose or *intent* in the development of assessment systems at the beginning of this chapter. The various approaches we discuss below will vary in their degree and latitude of use depending on the particular purpose. So, for example, if a teacher is using a set of various assessment practices to help plan a more effective program of instruction, given the range of children's strengths and needs in a classroom, then considerably more latitude may be possible than if an assessment is being used for external reporting purposes. While there is clearly a move away from the traditional fully-standardized approach that allowed little variation in administration procedures, it is important to recognize that the latitude that is possible will vary from one assessment situation to another.

To give an example, published performance-based assessments are currently available that allow students to work collaboratively after being presented with a problem in reading or math or that suggest interim drafting and outlining strategies before students actually sit down to produce an individual response to the assessment item. Other assessments permit the use of resources such as calculators and resource documents to complete an assessment task. These examples of changes in the general approach to assessment will require not only extensive examination to determine what type of strategies and how much use of them is appropriate, but also a drastic change in educators' attitudes and perceptions about assessment.

Researchers and developers are suggesting and investigating a variety of approaches to incorporate into performance-based assessment systems. We have gathered some of them into three general categories. While not an exhaustive sample of alternative approaches, we think they represent ones that hold considerable promise for developing more equitable assessment systems—systems that will help to ensure the gathering of more valid information about the learning progress of diverse learners. The approaches we will discuss are included in the following three categories:

1. Flexibility: Choice, Mediation, and Scaffolding
2. Use of Multiple Approaches: Informal, Dynamic and other Forms of Assessment
3. Scoring, Interpretation, and Use of Results

Flexibility: Choice, Mediation, and Scaffolding

A key to meeting the demands of an equitable assessment system is a flexible approach. It should be possible to design assessments that allow for a wide variety of response types and a wide variety of tasks to elicit a single response while maintaining standards (García & Pearson, 1991; Gordon, 1993; Taylor & Lee, 1987). Grant Wiggins, who has written so extensively about "authentic" assessments, emphasizes that such assessments "allow appropriate room to accommodate students' learning styles, aptitudes, and interests. . . . " (Wiggins, 1989). Gordon (1992) also calls for diversity in task content and demands, flexibility in timing entry points and time span of performance, multiplicity in perspectives, and choice involving self-selected and teacher-selected items.

Choice in task or medium for demonstrating competence will be somewhat difficult for educators to accommodate because of our habituated use of a thoroughly standardized approach. Again, purpose plays a role here. If the goal is for the teacher to learn (assess) what students know and are able to do and to ensure that students' linguistic and cultural differences won't invalidate that learning (assessment) process, then giving choice to the student or selecting an approach that better accommodates that student's learning style will lend greater validity. This will probably be one of the most difficult approaches for educators to adopt in the shift from a pervasive use of standardized tests. By giving students a choice of task, the variations that we feel must be built into administration procedures for performance-based assessment to be used in an equitable manner can be fulfilled.

Choice of task can be accomplished by tailoring or modifying an existing performance task that has been designed and tested to a particular cultural or linguistic group. (One example of this was included in Chapter 1.) Assessments should also be constructed in the primary languages that are represented in the student population of a particular school or district to allow English-language-learning students to engage in an assessment task in their native language if it will give a better indication of their academic learning as they continue to develop their competence in English. It is important to point out, though, that simple translations of English assessment tasks are not deemed to be appropriate and constitute a source of many psychometric problems. There are no perfect equivalents across languages; and one is really translating across cultures as well. Some languages, like Spanish, have many dialects. Determining where the overlap of dialects lies so as to produce a translation comprehensible to most speakers of the language presents a considerable challenge (Estrin, 1993). As the American Education Research Association's Standards for Educational and Psychological Testing notes:

> Psychometric properties cannot be assumed to be comparable across languages or dialects. Many words have different frequency rates or difficulty levels in different languages or dialects. Therefore words in two languages that appear to be close in meaning may differ radically in other ways important for the test use intended. Additionally, test content may be inappropriate in a translated version (AERA, 1985, p. 73).

Other aspects of text such as length may be affected by translation. Perhaps most fundamentally, construct validity is jeopardized with translation, that is, it is not clear with a translated test that one is still testing the same presumed underlying abilities or knowledge. Accomplishing choice of task by developing assessments in languages other than English does raise important policy issues that will need to be addressed: Who will be assessed in which language? How many languages can be accommodated? Some of these concerns pertain more to widescale assessments for which comparability between forms is desirable. (When it is the classroom teacher who is accommodating students' needs within the classroom, the problems are somewhat mitigated.) Several states engaged in the development and/ or use of statewide assessments are using or developing Spanish versions. In most cases, they are original—not translated—versions. For the reasons already noted, translation must be regarded as only a partial solution.

Mediation of assessments may be accomplished in a number of ways: by increasing the amount of time given to complete them; by repeating or rephrasing instructions, or giving them in a student's native language; by explaining the meaning of terms; or by allowing the use of adjunct materials or classroom tools (dictionaries, calculators, etc.). As part of the development of the statewide assessment in Arizona (ASAP), a set of guidelines for mediation was developed and is presented in Figure 5.7. In addition, the tables in Figure 5.8 show the counts of students who took the mediated assessment in the March, 1992, pilot of ASAP.

FIGURE 5.7
Guidelines for Mediation*
Arizona Student Assessment Program (ASAP)

The following may be used:

1. Providing flexible scheduling
   -Extending the time allotted to complete the assignment
   -Administering the assessment in several sessions

2. Providing a flexible setting
   -Administering the assessment individually in a separate location
   -Administering the assessment to a small group in a separate location
   -Providing special lighting
   -Providing adaptive or special furniture
   -Providing special acoustics
   -Administering the assessment in a location with minimal distractions

3. Revising assessment directions
   -Reading directions to student
   -Simplifying language in directions
   -Highlighting verbs in instructions by underlining
   -Providing additional examples

4. Providing assistance during the assessment
   -Reading questions and content to the student
   -Signing questions and content to the student
   -Taking dictation

5. Using aids
   -Visual magnification devices
   -Auditory amplification devices
   -Auditory tape questions
   -Masks or markers to maintain place
   -Tape recorder
   -Typewriter or word processor
   -Communication device
   -Calculator
   -Abacus
   -Arithmetic tables

*used with permission, Arizona Department of Education.

FIGURE 5.8
March 1992 Pilot

Counts of Mediated Assessments
(Who Took the Mediated Assessments)

Race/Ethnicity

Race/Ethnicity	All Assessments Count	Percent	Mediated Assessments Mediated	Percent
White	67,004	62.28%	1,230	37.87%
Black	4,290	3.99%	103	3.17%
Hispanic	26,720	24.84%	1,438	44.27%
Asian/PI	2,005	1.86%	76	2.34%
Am. Indian/AN	7,569	7.04%	401	12.35%
Subtotal:	107,588	100.00%	3,248	100.00%
Other*	7,671		242	
Total:	115,259		3,490	

Gender

	All Assessments	Percent	Mediated Assessments	Percent
Male	56,260	49.51%	2,061	61.03%
Female	57,370	50.49%	1,316	38.97%
Subtotal:	113,630	100.00%	3,377	100.00%
Other*	1,629		113	
Total:	115,259		3,490	

Special Program Membership

	All Students	Mediated	Mediated as a % of All Students
Chapter 1	14,474	1,137	7.86%
Bilingual	1,778	329	18.50%
Special Education	3,320	1,600	48.19%
Migrant	1,089	140	12.86%
ESL	4,066	941	23.14%

*(Other): Includes "Other", missing or unusable responses. Mediated figures based on ADE R&D ASAP
Mediated database using SPSS for Windows Report function.
Prepared by: Research and Development, Arizona Department of Education, Phoenix, Arizona

"Authentic tests can be—indeed, should be—attempted by all students, with the tests 'scaffolded up,' not 'dumbed down' as necessary to compensate for poor skill, inexperience, or weak training" (Wiggins, 1989). The notion of **scaffolding** is one that has been introduced in current information about effective instructional practice, but it may be quite a different matter for people to accept it with regard to assessment practice. The general idea is to "talk through" a particular assessment task with a student who seems unable to engage with the task for reasons related to cultural and linguistic diversity. The purpose is for the assessor to:

1. identify the point or points where the student encounters difficulty, for example, with the written directions;

2. give the student support by explaining, paraphrasing, translating into the student's first language, or reminding him or her about similar classroom experiences;

3. modify the task as needed to allow the child to participate;

4. continue until it is apparent that the student is able to engage in the task.

Such a process allows the assessor (who will often be the teacher) to clearly identify the aspects of academic tasks that present problems for students, ways to help them circumvent those problems, and what the student knows or is able to do when the format or content of the assessment does not preclude engagement—that is when the child can appropriately access the information and abilities he has and needs in order to participate in the assessment situation.

Use of Multiple Measures and Approaches: Informal, Dynamic and other Forms of Assessment

As Anastasi (1990) has cautioned, we must beware of using a single assessment score to make decisions about a student. What is needed is a range of assessments administered at different times throughout the school year. Students' performances on different tasks—even within a subject area—can vary considerably, and they change over time. Portfolios offer one possibility of a desirable method of unifying in one place multiple indices of student performance that have been gathered over time (Estrin, 1993). Both performance and portfolio assessments present the opportunity to validate assessments by using data from multiple sources.

Although a standardized test does provide some information about a student's ability, the information reflects a narrow range of ability and is of limited value for planning instruction. A student may complete a multiple-choice test, but it will not provide information about his or her abilities to reflect on learning or to produce learning products. In a discussion of the importance of using multiple indicators, Hiebert and Calfee (1990) point out that performance tests also have limitations. "Many of these programs standardize the topic, the task, and the conditions of administration, which solves some problems but causes others. Some of the more readily identified problems with performance tests are that time may limit test coverage to one or two topics, students who have not been effectively taught to express themselves in writing or speech may be at a disadvantage, and subjective evaluation allows the possibility of bias."

An important concept discussed by Hiebert and Calfee gets at the principal value of using multiple measures, approaches or indicators: *convergent validity*. As noted in Messick (1989), evidence from a number of sources can demonstrate the validity of an assessment in a new view of test standards that represents a significant departure from traditions of psychometric theory and practice. "The third grader who is struggling with writing mechanics but is adept in making oral presentations requires a different assessment approach than one who has the mechanics but lacks imagination. One student may thrive on flowery novels while another enjoys writing reports in science. Both read and write capably under some conditions and less well in other contexts" (Hiebert and Calfee, 1990). Developing a profile of a student that shows consistent achievement "over variations in task, topic, time and other factors" allows one to have confidence in the profile. This approach reflects generalizability theory (Cronbach et al., 1972; Shavelson, Webb & Rowley, 1989) and "provides a method for examining data from many sources for both internal consistency (reliability) and external relevance (validity)" (Hiebert & Calfee, 1990).

One of the primary reasons that the use of multiple indicators and approaches can be so beneficial for assessing students from cultural and linguistic minorities is that the interference of related factors can be numerous and subtle. Heath (1980), for example, found that basal reader discussions were mysterious to Black children in rural areas. Heath identified the fact that they were accustomed to "genuine discourse exchanges," and were, therefore, mystified by exchanges with teachers who asked them questions from the basal reader manual to which they obviously knew the answers. The students' failure to respond was viewed as failure by the teacher. Hispanic and African-American students did even more poorly than white students on a recent NAEP writing assessment when they were given additional time; they did not seem to have the same awareness of ways to use the time to improve their performance (Hiebert & Calfee, 1990).

At least as one alternative approach, consideration should be given to sampling a range of different topics when designing performance tasks such as writing samples. This is difficult, of course, with performance assessments because they are time-consuming by design. Another approach suggested by Miller-Jones (1989) is to use tasks that are specific to the culture and instructional background of students being assessed, but it is "exceedingly difficult to establish task equivalence" (p. 363).

Informal assessment procedures have been gaining much more recognition since the shift to a performance-based assessment paradigm has been felt across the nation. With the widespread call for the use of multiple measures and for assessments that have greater potential for informing instruction for teacher decision-making, informal classroom measures have been receiving greater emphasis. With increasing interest in and development of instructional practice in reading based on a constructivist view of learning, teachers want and need to know how children approach reading; what strategies they utilize in reading; and how factors such as prior knowledge, vocabulary knowledge, interest, and purpose affect reading comprehension. Another way to state this perspective is as King does when she says that "evaluation is expansive, not reductionist. Teachers and students seek to expand and get meaning from their actions, not narrow the focus to one particular item. And when different languages and cultures are involved, the rich information used and gained in making evaluations is a learning asset" (Harp, 1993). The increasing recognition that assessment must be "expansive" has led to the exploration of a variety of approaches to assessment. García (1992) suggests that in planning a classroom assessment system in literacy that includes various informal measures, teachers should ask themselves two questions:

1. What do I need to know about individual children's literacy and language development in order to plan their instruction?

2. What activities and tasks can I use to find out and record this information?

Informal Measures

The sources that we reviewed in order to cull suggestions about informal measures all included very similar lists of options. Examples include: observational records, running records for oral reading (Clay, 1989), story retellings (recounting stories of solution procedures in math, science, etc.), audio and videotapes, written responses to reading (math or other content area activities), student learning records (for example, reading logs), think-alouds, self-evaluations, and student-teacher conferences. A number of them are discussed below.

Observational Records.   Keeping track of students' progress throughout the year can be enhanced through the systematic use of ongoing anecdotal records that provide details of the evidence of students' learning and the context within which it occurred. Teachers' observations are a valuable component of student evaluation, but they often do not take the time to note what they observe. Key observations should be recorded along with interpretations of the events. In addition, it is helpful to organize observations and to follow up on each observation recorded as appropriate. Checklists can also be used to record observations.

García (1992) notes the following examples of key observations: "A teacher might note that Ming-Ling wrote her address in English for the first time, or that Ahmad seemed to have difficulty comprehending the volcano story because he did not appear to know what a volcano was." One important aspect of using this informal measure is that teachers must have the knowledge required to make insightful observations and to note linguistic and cultural factors that influence learning.

Story Retellings. Using this approach, teachers ask students to retell what they have read. The teacher uses some type of story outline or story map (outline of key elements that typically includes setting, problem/goal, initiating event, plot events/episodes, and resolution of the problem). Upon conclusion of the retelling, the teacher may also prompt the student with questions that relate to elements of the retelling or to elements of the story map that have not been sufficiently addressed by the student. This process works very well with English language learners. The teacher should allow the student to retell in the student's native language, to "code-mix," or to provide an example of how well he can complete the task in English.

This procedure can also be adapted for math or other content areas. Students can relate how they went about solving a problem in math, record the procedures used in conducting a science experiment, or relate historical events.

Think-alouds. Subsequent to introduction and modeling by a teacher, students can be asked to read a text and interrupt the reading to "make their thinking public" as they read. A student might, for example, make a comment about a word that she doesn't know and explain her speculation of the word's meaning by making inferences from the text. In a prompted "Think-aloud," the teacher marks the text at key points and asks the student to stop at those points and explain what has been read, to make a prediction, or identify any problems encountered in reading the text. Again, such a process is very appropriate for minority students because it gives the teacher the opportunity to discover the interpretations students are making and the challenges they are encountering. Teachers can gain insights about the learning approaches and learning styles of second-language and culturally-divergent students.

Self-evaluation Forms. Using self-evaluation procedures endows students with the responsibility for their own learning. Students should examine what they know, what difficulties they encountered, and what they want to pursue in their learning. This sort of reflection helps students to develop the metacognitive strategies they need to continue as effective learners.

3rd Grade

Mote and Troll went to the beach. They were having fun at the beach. Suddenly Mote fett a pinched on his toe. He blamd it on Troll. Then started fighting and arguing.

By puting their hands on their heads and their feet in plain sight and nouthi hapend. And they found out the crab was pinching. Ef Molie and Troll didnot find the crab they kodof tatk about it.

Dynamic Assessment

The informal procedures discussed above are sometimes referred to as situated assessment because they are contextualized within the classroom. In a similar fashion, *dynamic assessment* is an alternative form that can be used in both formal and informal contexts. In essence, it is an assessment procedure that provides the opportunity to document the progress children are making with and without support (García, 1992); it is an opportunity for both teaching and learning. This process grows from a Vygotskian vision of education and learning; it assumes the stance that assessment should be directed to finding out what the student is capable of learning (working in the "zone of proximal development") with the assistance of the teacher, rather than to finding out what he already knows. There are different versions of dynamic assessment calling for varying degrees of explicit, mediated learning during assessment (and varying along a dimension from *scripted* to *flexible*), but all emphasize the importance of examining *how* a child learns. Proponents argue that dynamic assessment is an improvement on traditional assessment because it:

- deals with processes as well as products of learning;
- addresses the student's responsiveness to instruction; and
- provides information about potentially effective intervention techniques.

If the main purpose of assessment is to improve instruction and learning (whether as an immediate goal in the classroom or a distal goal of statewide assessment), then we must look beyond *products* of learning and assessment, according to dynamic assessment advocates. Also inherent in this approach is the belief that the search for learning problems should be centered on the instructional environment rather than within the child, because virtually all children can learn if given appropriate instruction—thereby shifting the "locus of failure" (Estrin, 1993). It should be apparent as well that this approach to assessment would work well with diverse learners because it affords the opportunity to gain insights about how children approach learning, which instructional strategies give them the opportunity to learn, and how well they respond to particular techniques.

Curriculum-based Assessment

Curriculum-based assessment (CBA) has arisen as an alternative or complement to standardized testing, particularly with special education students for whom standardized tests often provide inadequate information. But, as with many other innovations that originated with education of the gifted or other special groups, it has potentially broader applications for all students. Curriculum-based assessment represents a procedure for determining the instructional needs of a student based upon the student's ongoing performance vis-à-vis the actual course content taught. For example, unlike standardized tests of reading that do not provide insights into readers' fluency, provide only limited insights into their comprehension, and are a poor match to curricular goals, CBA can directly examine important reading skills through content (for example, vocabulary, text type) that has been taught. Curriculum-based assessment:

- is linked to students' curricula;
- may take the form of a very brief task;
- is inexpensive in terms of time and materials; and
- is sensitive to improvement of students' performance over relatively short periods of time.

The purpose of most norm-referenced tests is to measure individual differences rather than student growth. They may not be sensitive to learning gains when they actually occur, and they may not be given in a timely enough manner to be of any use to instructional planning; they cannot be given too often. In contrast, curriculum-based measures can be given at the end of an instructional unit, at the time appropriate for gaining information about what a student can do.

With CBA, as with portfolios, setting criteria and agreeing on ways of assessing students when CBA is used are two key steps to establishing the validity of the method. The problem with CBA as it is currently characterized in the literature is that it seems to focus on indices of atomistic skills, for example, reading isolated words. In principle, however, CBA need not focus on isolated skills but could center around performances on meaningful tasks. In the special education context, CBA is typically administered individually, not by the classroom teacher but by a testing clinician. Yet, this need not be the case. It seems highly appropriate for teachers to conduct this kind of assessment, whether with individual children, small groups, or whole-class groups. The component of student reflection can be incorporated as well, although it is not clearly identified as a necessary feature of CBA.

Scoring, Interpretation, and Use of Results: Performance-based Assessments

"Some believe that the use of performance assessments may provide a more fair approach to assessing ability than traditional multiple-choice methods" (Hambleton and Murphy, 1992). However, the very nature of a performance assessment introduces the possibility of extraneous error from sources unfamiliar to multiple-choice tests such as those that may arise due to readers, topic selection, and the approach to scoring (Sackett, 1987;

Linn, Baker & Dunn, 1991; quoted in Welch, 1993). The types of error that have been introduced by some researchers raise questions of fairness for performance assessments just as they have been raised with multiple-choice tests.

While many who have developed and trained scorers to use appropriate scoring methods for performance assessments report fairly high inter-rater reliability, we know that *reader effect* does influence results. Though this effect can be controlled to some extent through training, when the gender or ethnicity of an examinee can be determined (especially true of writing assessments), a number of researchers have documented an effect due to reader. Oppler, Campbell, Pulakos, and Borman (1992), for example, found that individuals often receive higher scores from raters of their own race.

In a study conducted on the Arizona state assessment (ASAP), sample texts were developed that represented modifications of the original versions. The text of the versions was identical except for specific elements designed to imply that the student writing the sample was a member of a minority group. One version included a character named Henry, a BMW car, and a trip to the mall; the other featured a character named Hector who drives from a reservation in a truck, spends time with his friends at night, and likes his friends "because they don't call me names like the white kids in town do." The results of the data analysis revealed a significant difference between the scores given to the two different versions. "It appears that the scorers (who were primarily special education teachers), upon identifying the author of a sample as being a minority student, lowered their expectations relative to the ASAP criteria. It is as if the scorers thought 'This is really good for a minority student' and allowed that thought to bias their scoring efforts" (Howell et al., 1992).

Without question, scoring procedures play a significant role in establishing fair and equitable assessments. Stiggins (1987; quoted in Linn, 1991) states that it is critical that such procedures assure that "performance ratings reflect the examinee's true capabilities and are *not* a function of the perceptions and biases of the persons evaluating the performance." There are various sources of error in **interpretation** related to a lack of recognition of the attributes of linguistic and cultural minority students. Fishman, Deutsch, Kogan, North, and Whiteman (1964) referred some time ago to one of them as "deviation error." "By this is meant the tendency to infer maladjustment or personality difficulty from responses which are deviant from the viewpoint of a majority culture, but which may be typical of a minority group. The results of a test might accurately reflect a child's performance or quality of ideation, but still the results should be interpreted in the light of the child's particular circumstance in life and the range of his experiences. . . . There is evidence to indicate that members of a tribe that has experienced periodic famines would be likely to give an inordinate number of food responses on the Rorschach.[4] So too might dieting Palm Beach matrons, but their underlying anxiety patterns would be quite different than those of the tribesmen" (p. 164). While the work just cited emphasizes psychological and intelligence testing, it can be easily seen that such potential errors of interpretation apply to any assessment.

We find the work of Delandshere and Petrosky (1994) to be particularly insightful with regard to interpretation as it is related to newer forms of assessment—ones for which educators are struggling to establish reliability and validity. The article referenced focuses on performance assessment for teachers, but the concepts are certainly relevant to all age levels. As indicated earlier in this chapter in the section on "Philosophical Framework," the development of content standards provides the foundation for an assessment system, and standards become the keystone and define the "broad ideological framework within which . . . performance is captured and interpreted."

As Delandshere and Petrosky define them, "dimensions" are "standpoints or lenses through which the performance can be analyzed and interpreted." Dimensions provide those who are scoring or judging with different perspectives for them to make several different interpretations of the same performance. What is critical in this scheme is that the performance can only be evaluated as a whole; pieces of the performance must be evaluated in the context of the whole, "interpreting from the particular perspectives or dimensions the exercise was designed to capture." Because there is often a collection of evidence that individuals integrate in response to a task, it is vital that scorers make a summative judgment. In this process, judging is seen as a "creation of knowledge"—thus the requirement to make their reasoning visible and criteria-based.

Delandshere and Petrosky liken it to Music's (1989) validation of an interpretive inference "to ascertain the degree to which lines of evidence are consonant with the inference, while establishing that alternative inferences are less well supported." The reader should also notice a similarity to the concept of "convergent validity" discussed above. It also resonates with the general trend toward greater acceptance of qualitative research strategies that has been evident in the research community for a number of years. In fact, the struggle between the use of tests based on a measurement model and assessments based on a standards model also seems quite parallel to the struggle between using/accepting quantitative research methodology versus qualitative research methodology. The important point to make here is that it is extraordinarily difficult to judge or interpret a performance (just as it has been difficult to make judgments based on a single test score from a multiple-choice test), but it is reasonable to judge a performance in relation to established standards. "By rethinking the representation of knowledge as interpretive acts that individuals create in discourse, we have been able to capitalize on the use of ill-structured tasks as opportunities for candidates to produce knowledge" (Delandshere and Petrosky, 1994, p. 17).

The **use** of assessment results is, of course, a critical factor in establishing equity. As stated in draft standards developed by FairTest (1994): Assessments must be "used primarily to facilitate further student learning, not to sort, classify, or track." Decisions should not be made on the basis of one indicator, but on multiple measures collected over time. When assessment data is used to make decisions about placement, those students should not be denied the opportunity to meet content standards that must be established for *all* students. They should not be used for high-stakes purposes unless the assessments can meet development standards. The risks and consequences associated with sorting and tracking students, not only by the fact that it is often done with reference to a single test score but also because the practices themselves are detrimental to student growth and progress, are well documented in the literature. These practices constitute true perils for children, ones we do not want to—and should not—visit upon them. Assessment data should be used, however, to plan excellent programs, ones that give all children fair opportunities to learn.

Inequities associated with testing and assessment are also provoked by the inappropriate use of test results. Unfortunately, bias in assumptions about abilities of language minority students influences the ways test results are used. If low expectations are held for students, low performance on a test will only serve to confirm what is "known" and promote continued low expectations and often relegation to a less demanding program. If, on the contrary, high expectations were held, a student's lower-than-expected test performance would be viewed as an occasion to re-examine and revise the educational program—so as to produce the expected results. In fact, it is a sad truth that standardized tests have often served to compound existing inequities by acting to prevent access to programs (as with tracking practices), or by fostering a diminished sense of self-efficacy in students, completing a destructive cycle that starts with the low expectations held by society.

One final point we would like to make here is with regard to the impact of performance assessment programs on classroom instructional practice. While not much research-based information has accumulated yet, this is certainly the hope and expectation for many who are involved in the development and use of performance assessments. Many practitioners provide anecdotal evidence to support the positive benefits that affect instructional planning and delivery. One study (Almasi, Afflerbach, Guthrie, and Schafer, 1994) that was conducted to examine the impact of a statewide performance-based assessment (the Maryland School Performance Assessment Program) on literacy instruction, administrative support, and student and teacher affect provides some initial indications of this potential impact. While the researchers qualify their findings because they worked in elementary schools "that were purposively selected as exemplars of instructional change," their findings are revealing, if not generalizable.

Through this study, the researchers found that tasks, methods, and materials were altered to "reflect the nature of the assessment itself and the state-mandated outcomes for literacy." They saw evidence of increased writing opportunities, more emphasis on student response to reading, and more student choice in literacy tasks. Instructional methods also included thematic-based instruction, writer's workshop, integrated instruction, and more use of authentic texts. Much more student input and interaction was likewise evident.

Teachers also evidenced a shift toward more reflection and more active engagement in curriculum design. These qualities alone, along with more direct involvement in the design, development, judging, and use of performance assessments could give teachers a much more solid knowledge base and greater awareness of the characteristics and learning approaches of non-mainstream children.

While most educators are heartened by any indication that the development and use of performance assessments will lead to significant improvements in curriculum design and classroom instruction, we must all be careful not to rely too heavily on an accountability system to bring about curricular reform. Shepard (1991) addresses this point directly: "Although I generally concur that more admirable assessments will have a more salutary effect on instruction and learning, I have two reservations about using assessments (however impressive) to leverage educational reform. (a) Under great pressure, the weaknesses of any assessment will be exaggerated. . . . (b) Forcing modes of instruction via external high-stakes assessments detracts from the professional role of teachers" (p. 27). Shepard also suggests that this can be avoided if tasks are sufficiently broad to allow multiple paths to successful performance. This is a strategy that we certainly endorse in the interest of children from non-mainstream groups.

Endnotes

1. *Ensuring Every Student Succeeds: A Report on Opportunity to Learn Standards,* for the National Governors' Association, California Task Force on School Delivery Standards, 1993.

2. Throughout this section, we present some information that has been drawn from a set of standards being developed by Fairtest, the National Center for Fair and Open Testing. While the standards are still in draft form and not

available for distribution, we have participated in invitational forums related to the standards and feel that the information is very useful.

3. Hermeneutics is the science of interpretation.
4. Projective instrument used in psychological testing; commonly referred to as "inkblot test."

Commentary
Linda F. Winfield and Josie Bane

The chapter on "Developing Equitable Assessment Systems" was comprehensive and raises concerns and questions regarding the equity and fairness of alternative assessment currently being developed. Other scholars have noted that tests and fairness are thorny issues not just because of the test "but because of the historical and contemporary use and misuse of standardized tests" (Johnson, 1987, p. 77). Thus, in the past, appeals concerning fairness have been made primarily on sociopolitical or ideological grounds. Some argue that because of the changes in the demographics in the workforce and public schools, the issues of equity and fairness are critical to maintain the viability of America's economy. In brief, America can no longer underutilize human potential of any racial/ethnic group.

Although alternative measures that are direct assessments of a student's performance may be more appropriate indicators of student learning, we feel that any measure must be considered in terms of the function and purpose served. Standardized tests will still be appropriate in certain contexts, as will the use of informal assessment by teachers. No one type of measure in and of itself is a panacea. Whenever critical decisions are made that impact the opportunities and life chances of an individual student (for example, placement in special education or admission to college) multiple sources of information are needed. These sources might include performance-based or more indirect measures of student achievement. We strongly feel that if the purpose and function of the test is not made clear to teachers, the likelihood that the assessment is carried out in a meaningful manner is virtually nil. Moreover, such assessments are unlikely to be used in classroom instruction. On many occasions, teachers do not have a clear idea of the purpose of the test. The need for professional development cannot be emphasized enough, particularly with the newer forms of assessment in which teachers play a significant role. Our understanding of "alternative assessments" is that such measures are performance-based and require an observation or judgment on the part of the teacher. The assumption, however, cannot be made that alternative forms of assessment would prevent unfairness or reduce achievement differences between racial/ethnic groups . There are a number of issues to be considered in terms of: (1) the actual assessment (2) the context, (3) learner characteristics, and (4) antecedent instructional conditions (Winfield & Woodard, 1993).

The Actual Assessment

America's public schools have become increasingly diverse in terms of racial/ethnic groups in attendance. One issue relates to the content of the assessment and the basis for selecting a particular curriculum framework. If one is talking about locally-developed assessments by classroom teachers, this may or may not be as problematic as a state department or a large nation-wide assessment. What measures/steps are taken to ensure that a multicultural emphasis is incorporated throughout? Whose content gets included? If students are required to construct a response in written or oral form, what content is appropriate/acceptable? These issues focus not only on the selection of content but also on the standard being applied. For example, in a study of performance-based literacy tasks taken from the NAEP Young Adult Literacy Assessment (1986), eighth grade inner-city African-American students were administered tasks in a one-to-one situation and asked to "think aloud" about how they would go about solving the tasks (Winfield, 1991). One task was a poem that described a scenario for an individual named Joe which alluded to death, the metal barrel of a gun, and other war paraphernalia. It might be obvious to an adult reader that the passage referred to someone preparing to go to war. When one youngster was asked to explain his interpretation, he replied "He's getting ready to go out in the street." I asked him to elaborate and he replied "he got a gun . . . people get killed in the street where I live." This youngster who was growing up in a drug infested inner-city neighborhood where there had been a rash of violence and innocent children had been hit by stray bullets had read, interpreted, and constructed a response based on his experience and background knowledge. When the youngster and I reexamined the passage together and looked for other clues, he was able to obtain the correct response. The point is that his initial response, according to "the standard" would have been judged unacceptable and considered wrong.

Similarly, if the developer does not include a wide variety of items from different cultural backgrounds, some students may be at a disadvantage. Another eighth grade (Winfield & Weston-Foster, 1991) was asked to solve a quantitative item. He was given a lunch menu and asked to add up two or three items that had been pre-selected and compute the tip. The item required fairly simple addition. The youngster described that he would add the items and gave the correct total but couldn't go any further. When I questioned him, he indicated: "I don't understand what a tip is . . . I know it's money that you leave on the table after you eat but I don't know how much." Another student added the same amount as the lunch total to calculate the tip. When I asked each of the students if they had ever been in a restaurant, one replied "Yea—McDonald's." The other student gave a similar response. Within the background of these youngsters' experiences in fast food restaurants, one does not need to know how to compute tips. **Performance on real life tasks or events will be heavily influenced by background knowledge, exposure, and opportunity to learn specific content—most of which will reflect "mainstream" culture.**

Contextual Conditions

The context of how and under what conditions an assessment is administered will affect the outcomes of racial/ethnic students. Although there is reason to be concerned about the generalizability of performance across specific tasks, there is more reason to worry about the reliability and validity of ratings, scores, and judgments made of the performance of students from various race/ethnic groups. There is a well documented literature on teachers' beliefs (Winfield, 1986) and expectations and their relationship to teachers' classroom behaviors and student outcomes. These expectations are likely to vary for students from various race/ethnic groups and social class. Can we expect teachers' judgments of students' performance to parallel these findings? If performance is assessed through a demonstration or exhibition, to what extent will the students' dialect or accent influence raters' scores? Individuals who speak in certain ways are more likely to be judged as less intelligent and less capable. This phenomenon has been studied extensively—for example, in Canada, negative and pejorative attitudes are expressed toward the French-speaking population because French is the language of less prestige (Lambert, 1967; Seligman, Lambert & Tucker, 1972).

Similarly, if performance is assessed through written tasks, such as essays or portfolios, to what extent do certain syntactic structures or semantically marked features of a particular dialect (for example, double negative in Black English Vernacular) impact the rating a student receives? A consistent use of vernacular may indicate a student's inability to use standard forms, but an occasional phrase may indicate informality (Chaplin, 1988). Additionally, many Latino students may have difficulty in writing because they are not native speakers of English. These and other contextual issues must be addressed to ensure the reliability and validity of performance-based measures for racial/ethnic group students.

Learner Characteristics

For certain groups of learners, the characteristics that they bring to the assessment task may affect their performance. For example, when asked to perform verbal tasks, non-native English speakers might require additional time for processing because of the two languages. Some of the past psycholinguistic research on bilingualism (Kolers, 1968; Lambert, 1972; Mcnamara, 1967) and bidialectical speakers (Baratz, 1969; Winfield, 1978) may inform this issue. Similarly, teachers and assessors need to be concerned with the linguistic complexity when presenting materials for performance-based verbal tasks for this group of learners.

Another category of learners for whom there is concern is that made up of very young racial/ethnic group students whose receptive language skills are more advanced than their productive ones. These children may know more than they can verbalize. The "trickle down" effect in education will eventually result in performance-based kindergarten and preschool assessments. There is a body of research on African-American children conducted by psychologists in laboratory settings in the late 1960s and early 1970s that was based on **performance.** Based on empirical studies, researchers concluded that "poor black kids were non-verbal and had no language." In many of these studies, the context interacted with characteristics of the learner to severely depress children's performance. Children were placed in unfamiliar surroundings with strange white adults. When asked a question, the children would respond in monosyllables. Joan Baratz (1970), Bill Labov (1972), and some other linguists demonstrated the ethnocentric bias in much of this research and the need to address ecological validity—that is, studies in naturalistic settings—which provided a much richer view of the verbal performance and capabilities of these children.

Antecedent Instructional Conditions

Finally, educators and policy makers believe that alternative measures will drive instructional practices. They suggest that assessments that are focused on complex performance and critical thinking rather than "filling in bubbles" on standardized tests will result in changes in teacher behavior and practices focused on more complex knowledge and skills. Empirical work suggests that open-ended response formats provide much better diagnostic information, and tap students' misconceptions. However, this information is seldom used in classrooms for a variety of reasons—the least of which is the actual test used. Factors such as dissemination and translation of research results, the structure of schools and classrooms, the content of teacher education, and the quality of teaching influence the usage of information.

More importantly, would the appropriate content and knowledge get taught to African-American and Latino students? Opportunity to learn is a function of many factors, such as classroom and supplemental instruction; practice, feedback and incentives; academic engaged time; quality of the teacher-student interaction; teacher beliefs; and the nature of the academic tasks. There is sufficient evidence that many racial/ethnic group students are disproportionately placed in lower ability groups or tracks (Braddock, 1989) and as a result opportunity to learn is diminished. Thus, changes must also be made in the social organization of schools to prevent ability grouping, retention, tracking, and other processes that disproportionately impact students from racial/ethnic groups.

Additionally, there are still gross inequities in facilities and resources available to schools that serve large numbers of racial/ethnic group students, particularly in inner cities (Barton, Coley & Goertz, 1991). These schools are more likely to have difficulty recruiting and retaining high-quality staff and faculty. They are more likely to suffer from declining enrollments and budget cuts at the same time that the student population is much needier; that is, the students come from poorer families, have social problems, and have to cope with different languages and cultures. From this perspective, merely changing the form or method of assessment may have some impact on teacher practices and student performance, but the real need is for sufficient resources targeted toward effective staff development and teacher and student support services.

In conclusion, the four areas discussed here—the actual assessment, contextual conditions, learner characteristics, and antecedent instructional conditions—provide some of the issues of concern to those developing assessments. And unless these concerns arc addressed, alternative assessments will be no more fair or equitable or serve as accurate measures of the performance of racial/ethnic students than standardized measures.

— ❧ —

Dr. Julia Lara is the Director of Services to Language Minority Students and Co-Director of the IASA (Improving America's Schools Act) Implementation Project at the Council of Chief State School Officers, Washington, D.C. Her expertise is in advising CCSSO staff and others on appropriate programs for English language learners. She has had a key role in working with various national and state entities to analyze services to language minority students and make recommendations for improvement of policies that affect those students. Dr. Lara has published numerous articles and reports through the CCSSO. Among the best-known are "School Success for Limited English Proficient Students" (1990), "Reflections: Bridging Two Cultures," (1992), and "State Data Collection and Monitoring Procedures Regarding Overrepresentation of Minority Students in Special Education," (1994).

Commentary References

Baratz. J. C. (1969). A bidialectical task for determining language proficiency in economically disadvantaged Negro children. *Child Development*, Vol. 48, 889-901.

Baratz. S. S. & Baratz, J. (1970). Early childhood intervention: The social science base of institutional racism. *Harvard Education Review*, 40, 29-50.

Barton, P. E., Coley, R. J. & Goertz, M. E. (1991). *The state of inequality*. Policy Information Report, Princeton, N. J.: Educational Testing Service, Policy Information Center.

Braddock, J. M. (1989). *Tracking of Black, Hispanic, Asian, Native Americans and White students: National trends*. Baltimore, Md.: The Johns Hopkins University. Center for Research on Effective Schooling for Disadvantaged Students.

Chaplin, M. T. (1988). *A comparative analysis of writing features used by selected black and white students in the National Assessment of Educational Progress and the New Jersey High School Proficiency Test*. Princeton, N.J.: Educational Testing Service, RR-8842.

Johnson, S. (1987). Test fairness and bias: Measuring academic achievement among Black youth. *The Urban League Review*, Vol.11, Nos. 1 & 2.

Kirsch, I. S. & Jungteblut, A. (1986). *Literacy: Profiles of America's young adults* Princeton, NJ: National Assessment of Educational Progress.

Kolers, P. A. (1968). Bilingualism and information processing. *Scientific American*, 78-85.

Labov, W. (1972). *Language in the inner city*. Philadelphia,PA.: University of Pennsylvania Press.

Lambert, W. E. (1967). A social psychology of bilingualism. *Journal of Social Issues*, Vol. 23, 91-109.

Lambert, W. E. (1972). Psychological studies of the interdependencies of the bilingual's two languages, in W. E. T Lambert (Ed.), *Language, psychology and culture*. Stanford, California: Stanford University Press.

Mcnamara, J. (1967). The bilingual's linguistic performance: A psychological overview. *Journal of Social Issues*, Vol. 23, 58-77.

Seligman, C. R., T Lambert, W. E. & Tucker, G. R. (1972). The effects of speech style and other attributes on teachers' attitudes towards pupils. In W. E. Lambert (Ed.), *Language, psychology and culture*. Stanford, California: Stanford University Press.

Venezky, R. L., Kaestle, C. F., and Sum, A. M. (1987). *The Subtle Danger— Reflections on the literacy abilities of America's young adults*. Report No. 16CAEP-01 (Center for the Assessment of Educational Progress, Educational Testing Service, Princeton, N.J.

Winfield, L. F. (1978). Cross-dialect translations as a function of memory load. Paper presented at the 49th Annual Meeting of the Eastern Psychological Association, Inc., Washington, D. C.

Winfield, L. F. (1986). Teacher beliefs toward academically at-risk students in inner urban schools. *The Urban Review,* Vol. 18, No. 4, 253-268.

Winfield, L. F. & Dolph, G. (1988). Context and task performance of high vs. low literacy proficient Black young adults in the NAEP 1986 Literacy: Profiles of America's young adults, in Winfield, L. F., *A study of characteristics of high vs low literacy proficient Black young adults.* Final Report to the Rockefeller Foundation. Philadelphia, PA: Temple University Center for Research on Human Development & Education.

Winfield, L. F. & Weston-Foster, H. (1991, December). Adult and children's literacy proficiency. Paper presented at the National Reading Conference, Palm Springs, CA.

Winfield, L. F. & Woodard, M. D. (1993). Assessment, equity and diversity in reforming American's schools. *Educational Policy,* Vol. 8, No. 1, 3-27.

References

Almasi, J., et al. (1994). The impact of a statewide performance assessment program on classroom instructional practice in literacy. Paper presented at the Annual Meeting of the American Educational Research Association, New Orleans, LA.

American Educational Research Association (with the American Psychological Association and the National Council on Measurement in Education). (1985). *Standards for Educational and Psychological Testing.* Washington, DC: American Psychological Association.

Anastasi, A. (1990). What is test misuse? Perspectives of a measurement expert. In *The Uses of Standardized Tests in American Education: Proceedings of the 1989 ETS Invitational Conference.* Princeton, NJ: Educational Testing Service.

August, D., et al. (1993). *Federal education programs for limited-English-proficient students: A blueprint for the second generation.* Report of the Stanford Working Group, Stanford, CA.

Baker, E. L. (1994). Issues in policy, assessment, and equity. In *Proceedings of the Second National Research Symposium on Limited English Proficient (LEP) Student Issues: Focus on Evaluation and Measurement, Vol. II,* pp. 1-18. Washington, D.C.: U.S. Department of Education, Office of Bilingual Education and Minority Languages Affairs.

Baron, J.B. (1991). Strategies for the development of effective performance exercises. *Applied Measurement in Education, Vol. 4,* No. 4, 305-318.

Bass, H. (1993, October). Let's measure what's worth measuring. *Education Week.*

California Department of Education. (1993). *California Learning Assessment System (CLAS) Equity Guidelines.*

Clay, M. M. (1989). *The early detection of reading difficulties* (3rd ed.). Portsmouth, NH: Heinemann.

Cole, N.S., & Moss, P.A. (1989). Bias in test use. In R.L. Linn (Ed.), *Educational measurement* (3rd ed., pp. 201-219). Washington, DC: The American Council on Education and the National Council on Measurement in Education.

Cronbach, L.J. (1988). Five perspectives on validity argument. In H. Wainer (Ed.), *Test validity.* Hillsdale, NJ: Erlbaum.

Cronbach, L.J. (1989). Construct validation after thirty years. In R.L. Linn (Ed.), *Intelligence: Measurement, theory and public policy.* Urbana: University of Illinois Press.

Darling-Hammond, L. (1994). Performance-based assessment and educational equity. *Harvard Educational Review*, Vol. 64, No. 1.

Delandshere, G., & Petrosky, A. (1994). Capturing teachers' knowledge: Performance assessment. *Educational Researcher. Vol. 23,* No. 5, pp. 11-18.

Educational Researcher (1991, March). Interview on assessment issues with Lorrie Shepard. Vol. 20, No. 2.

Estrin, Elise (1993). Alternative assessment: Issues in language, culture, and equity. San Francisco: Far West Laboratory.

Fishman, J., et al. (1964). Guidelines for testing minority group children. *Journal of Social Issues,* 20, 129-145.

Frederiksen, N. (1984, March). The real test bias: Influences of testing on teaching and learning. *American Psychologist,* Vol. 39, 3, 193-202.

Frederiksen, J.R. & Collins, A. (1989). A systems approach to educational testing. *Educational Researcher, Vol. 18 ,* No. 9, 27-32.

Freeman, Y. & Freeman, D. (1991, January). Portfolio assessment: an exciting view of what bilingual children can do. *Bilingual Education Outreach.*

Garcia, E. Linguistically and culturally diverse children: Effective instructional practices and related policy issues. In Waxman et al. (Eds.). *Students at Risk in at Risk Schools.* Newbury Park, CA: Corwin Press.

Garcia, G. E. & Pearson, P. D. (1990). The role of assessment in a diverse society (draft paper). University of Illinois at Champaign-Urbana.

Gardner, H. (1989). Assessment in context: The alternative to standardized testing. In . B. Gifford (ed.), *Report to the Commission on Testing and Public Policy.* Boston: Kluwer Academic Press.

Gardner, H. (1992). Assessment in context: The alternative to standardized testing. In B. R. Gifford & M.C. O'Conner (Eds.), *Changing assessments: Alternative views of aptitude, achievement and instruction* (pp. 37-76). Boston: Kluwer.

Gay, G. & Abrahams, R.D. (1973). Does the pot melt, boil, or brew? Black children and white assessment procedures. *Journal of School Psychology*, Vol. 11, No. 4.

Glaser, R. (1988). Cognitive and environmental perspectives on assessing achievement, in Eileen Freeman (Ed.), *Assessment in the Service of Learning: Proceedings of the 1987 ETS Invitational Conference.* Princeton, NJ: Educational Testing Service.

Gordon, E. W. (1994). In Rothman, R. (Winter, 1994). Assessment questions: Equity answers, Proceedings of the 1993 CRESST Conference. In *Evaluation Comment*, UCLA: Los Angeles.

Gordon, E. W. (1992). Implications of diversity in human characteristics for authentic assessment. CSE Technical Report 341. Los Angeles: National Center for Research on Evaluation, Standards, and Student Testing.

Hambleton, R.K. & Murphy, E. (1992). A psychometric perspective on authentic measurement. *Applied Measurement in Education, Vol. 5*, No. 1, 1-16.

Harp, B. (Ed.). (1993). *Assessment and Evaluation in Whole Language Programs.* Norwood, MA: Christopher-Gordon Publishers.

Heath, S. B. (1986). Sociocultural contexts of language development. Selections from *Beyond language: Social and cultural factors in schooling language minority students.*

Herman, J. L., Aschbacher, P. & Winters, L. (1992). *A practical guide to alternative assessment.* Alexandria, VA: ASCD.

Hiebert, E. & Calfee, R. (1990). Assessment of literacy: From standardized tests to performances and portfolios. In Samuels, S.J. & Farstrup, A. (Eds.), *What research says about reading instruction* (2nd ed). Newark, DE: International Reading Association.

Howell, K., Bigelow, S. & Evoy, A. (1992). A qualitative examination of an authentic assessment.

Kirst, Michael W. (March 1991). Interview on assessment with Lorrie Shepard. *Educational Researcher*, Vol. 20, No. 2, 21-24.

Leap, W. (1988). Assumptions and strategies guiding mathematics problem solving by Ute Indian students. In Cocking, R.R. & Mestre, R.P. (Eds). *Linguistic and cultural influences on mathematics.*

Linn, R.L. (Ed.). (1989). *Educational measurement* (3rd ed.). New York: American Council on Education, Macmillan Publishing Company.

Linn, R.L., Baker, E.L. & Dunbar, S.B. (1991). Complex, performance-based assessment: Expectations and validation criteria. *Educational Researcher, Vol. 20*, No. 8, 15-21.

Malcom, Shirley (1991). Equity and excellence through authentic science assessment. In G. Kulm & S. Malcolm (Eds.), *Science assessment in the service of reform* (pp. 313-330). Washington, D.C.: American Association for the Advancement of Science.

McKeon, D. (1994). When meeting "common" standards is uncommonly difficult. ASCD: *Educational Week*, Vol. 51, No. 8.

Messick, S. (1989). Validity. In R.L. Linn (Ed.), *Educational measurement (3rd ed.*, pp. 13-103). Washington, DC: American Council on Education and National Council on Measurement in Education.

Moss, P. A. (1994). Can there be validity without reliability? *Educational Researcher*, Vol. 23, No. 2.

Newman, F. M. (1990). Higher order thinking in teaching social studies: A rationale for the assessment of classroom thoughtfulness. *Journal of Curriculum Studies Vol. 22*, No. 1, 41-56.

O'Connor, M. C. (1989). Aspects of differential performance by minorities on standardized tests: Linguistic and cultural factors. In *Test Policy and Test Performance: Education, Language and Culture*, Bernard Gifford (Ed.). Boston, MA: Kluwer Academic Publishers.

Olmedo, E. L. (1981). Testing linguistic minorities. *American Psychologist*, *36*, 10, 1078-1085.

Oppler, S. H. et al. (1992). Three approaches to the investigation of subgroup bias in performance measurement: Review, results, and conclusions. *Journal of Applied Psychology, Vol. 77*, 201-217.

Paulson, F. L. & Paulson, P. R. (1991). The ins and outs of using portfolios to assess performance. NCME, Chicago.

Rhodes, R. W. (1988, November). Standardized testing of minority students: Navajo and Hopi examples. Paper presented at the Annual Meeting of the National Council of Teachers of English, St. Louis, MO.

Rothman, R. (1993). A.C.T. unveils new assessment, planning system. *Education Week, XII*, 24, 1,17.

Rothman, R. (1994, Winter). Assessment questions: Equity answers, Proceedings of the 1993 CREST Conference. In *Evaluation Comment*, UCLA: Los Angeles.

Saville-Troike, M. (1991, Spring). Teaching and testing for academic achievement: The role of language development. *NCBE*, No. 4.

Secada, W. G. (1992). Race, ethnicity, social class, language, and achievement in mathematics. In Grouws, Douglas A. (Ed.), *Handbook of Research on Mathematics Teaching and Learning*. New York: Macmillan.

Shavelson, R.J. , Webb, N., & Rowley, G.L. (1989). Generalizability theory. *American Psychologist, Vol. 44*, 922-932.

Shepard, L.A. (1982). Definitions of bias. In *Handbook of methods for detecting test bias*, R.A. Berk (Ed.), pp. 9-30.

Simon, H.A. (1978). Information-processing theory of human problem solving. In W.K. Estes (Ed.), *Handbook of learning and cognitive processes: Vol. 5. Human information processing* (pp. 271-295). Hillsdale, NJ: Erlbaum.

Taylor, C. (1994, Summer). Assessment for measurement or standards: The peril and promise of large-scale assessment reform. *American Educational Research Journal*, Vol. 31, No. 2, pp. 231-262.

Taylor, O. & Lee, D. L. (1987). Standardized tests and African-Americans: Communications and language issues. *The Negro Educational Review*, Vol. 38, No. 2-3.

Viadero, D. (June 2, 1993). The rhetoric and reality of high academic standards. *Education Week*.

Welch, C. J. (1993). Issues in developing and scoring performance assessments. Atlanta: American Educational Research Association.

Wiggins, G. P. (1989). A true test: Toward more authentic and equitable assessment. Bloomington, IN: *Phi Delta Kappan*.

Wiggins, G. P. (1990). Secure tests, insecure test takers. In J.L. Schwartz and K.A. Viator (eds.), *The prices of secrecy: The social, intellectual and psychological costs of testing in America*. A Report of the Ford Foundation. Cambridge, MA: Educational Technology Center, Harvard Graduate School of Education.

Wiggins, G. P. (1993). *Assessing student performance*. San Francisco: Jossey-Bass.

Wiley, D. E. & Haertel, E.H. (1992). Extended assessment tasks: Purposes, definitions, scoring, and accuracy. In R. Mitchell & M. Kane (Eds.), *Implementing performance assessment: Promises, problems, and challenges*. Washington, DC: Pelavin Associates.

Winfield, L. F. & Woodard, M. (1994). Assessment, equity, and diversity in reforming America's schools. *CSE Technical Report 372*. Los Angeles: National Center for Research on Evaluation, Standards, and Student Testing.

Wolf, D., Bixby, J., Glenn, J. III, Gardner, H. (1991). To use their minds well: Investigating new forms of student assessment. In Grant, G. (Ed.) *Review of Research in Education*, Vol. 17, Washington, D.C., American Educational Research Association, 31-74.

Chapter 6

Portfolio Assessment: Potential for Equity

... the keys to meeting the assessment needs of a diverse student population are a flexible approach to assessment and a dramatically improved teacher knowledge base.

Georgia Earnest Garcia and P. David Pearson, 1991, p. 2

A student's performance is best understood in context; this implies that when interpreting results, the examiner will consider various contextual factors.

Nancy Cloud, 1991, p. 220

Why Focus on Portfolios?

Portfolio assessment holds out the possibility of both flexibility in design and use and contextualization of student performance—two features that have been repeatedly identified as keys to equitable assessment. Because of these attributes and others related to portfolios' emphasis on empowerment of students as learners, we have decided to devote a full chapter to examining the potential of portfolios as an unbiased and equitable form of assessment for ethnolinguistically diverse students. We must stress, however, that teachers' knowledge about assessment, domains of learning, cognitive psychology, and cultural and linguistic factors in the classroom is at least as important as any assessment process or tool.

Another strong reason to investigate portfolio assessment in depth is that, if used well, it both reflects and promotes instructional practices that have been identified as effective for English language learners. However, although a few of these practices are specific to the needs of students learning via a second language, most are not. By and large, they represent an approach to instruction that recognizes students as active, social constructors of knowledge who are capable of and benefit from developing autonomy over their own learning. Table 6.1 shows how many of these instructional practices or features intersect with features of portfolio assessment. We will be framing our vision of portfolio assessment shortly, but we want our readers to understand from the start some of the reasons we are enthusiastic about the possibilities of portfolio assessment.

What Is Meant by "Equity in Assessment?"

As we have noted earlier, *equity* does not mean *equality*. What is fair and just, or what contributes to a fair and just outcome for students may differ from one environment to another. *Equity* has been interpreted by educational reformers to mean the right [for students] to achieve at levels sufficient to participate productively, and in a rewarding way, economically and civically (Resnick, 1994). More narrowly, with regard to assessment itself, equity has been conceived of as the provision of opportunities to students to demonstrate what they actually know in a given subject area (Romberg, 1993).

Public advocates of assessment reform tend to agree on the importance of making assessments more informative to the instructional process, with the ultimate goal of improved student learning. Arising from an increased awareness that learning potential can be developed—not just measured—is an emphasis on using assessment to identify "instructional methods that actually change children's ability to learn" (Shepard, 1992, p. 308).

Although linking of assessments to classroom instruction is usually called for, not all who are involved in this public conversation recognize the implication that if such linking is to take place, contexts of learning must be taken into account in the design, administration, interpretation, and use of any assessments. Variations in culture, ethnic and language background, economic and social status, and learning opportunities all contribute to the larger context in which students are assessed. If responsibility for assessment and the power to exercise such responsibility are actually shifted to teachers (and to students), then genuine adaptation of assessments to the needs of particular communities can take place.

TABLE 6.1

Complementarity between Features of
ELL-Appropriate Classrooms and Portfolios

Elements of good ELL instruction	Features of Portfolios
Opportunities to deal with big ideas, whole texts	Authentic activities are used as source of assessment information.
Thematic and/or project-based learning	Complex performances, or sample components of them can be captured.
Use of drama, visual represent- ations, art, multi-intelligence activities	A range of performances in different modalities is permitted and desirable.
More student talk, less teacher talk	Student reflection on own performances/learning is promoted.
Opportunities to use language for variety of meaningful purposes	All forms of language are permitted; focus is on meaningful classroom activity.
Collaborative learning opportunities	Portfolios do not require strictly individual performance.
Multiple ways to participate (grouping patterns, discussion formats)	Portfolios have flexibility to capture range of participation.
Links to personal experience, latitude for choice in projects, reading materials, etc.	Student choice, interest, affect can be annotated; portfolios are individualized and represent personal goals, investment.
Links to home and community, sense of belonging	Student choice is encouraged; annotation by student, parent included.
Trusting climate in which to take risks	Sense of individuals' values is communicated; respect for student work and thinking are conveyed.
Use of first language permitted, not punished	Any language can be tape-recorded, written. Student and parent can dictate, record, etc.
Supports for friendships between ELL and ELP* students	Portfolios can be used as vehicle for students to get to know each other.

*English-language proficient

In a sense, assessment of student progress may become more a matter of negotiating meaning, of interpretation, than of psychometrics (Belanoff, 1994). The tension between validity and reliability that arises when standardization is reduced may resolve itself in the direction of validity, particularly if an integrated view of students' performances and learnings takes the place of a focus on individual samples of performance out of context. If multiple performances of different kinds are evaluated through different perspectives (teacher, student, parent), what may emerge is a deeper sense of a student's capabilities. In that instance—in the case of portfolios—there is less of a rationale for standardizing an assessment to the point that one removes all of the context that makes it meaningful. Certainly, if we subscribe to the notion that knowledge and meaning are socially constructed, then we must maintain reference to the social context of the student in assessment to understand the student's meanings.

The tension between standardization and contextualization of assessment is highlighted in the arena of equity for diverse students, as it is in the realm of portfolio assessment. If we adopt a social constructivist theory of learning, we are led to a vision of portfolio use that situates concerns for reliability lower on the scale than concerns for authenticity and fairness in assessment. Such a stance would be compatible not only with the needs of diverse communities of learners, but with goals of assessment reforms that focus on active learning and student autonomy in a "thinking curriculum." As Moss (1994) observes:

> There are certain intellectual activities that standardized assessments can neither document nor promote; these include encouraging students to find their own purposes for reading and writing, encouraging teachers to make informed instructional decisions consistent with the needs of individual students, and encouraging teachers and students to collaborate in developing criteria and standards to evaluate their work (p. 6).

As has often been said, this alternative approach to assessment in practice not only aligns assessment with instruction but blurs the line that separates instruction and assessment. Some educators such as Reuven Feuerstein (1980) have consciously incorporated instruction or "mediation" in assessment in order to get at a child's learning potential—that is, the child's maximum possible performance with teacher assistance. They would suggest that the only fair way to assess a child's learning potential—given inequities in opportunities to learn—is by "staging real instructional experiments" (Shepard, 1992, p. 309) in which one observes how the child performs with teacher guidance. Guided assessments have been shown to reveal learning potential of some children that traditional measures have dramatically underestimated (Shepard, 1992, p. 309). And it could be argued that it is more equitable to assess learning potential than achievement when opportunities to learn have not been equitable. Portfolio assessment offers opportunities for the kind of guided or "dynamic" assessment espoused by Feuerstein and others.

It is not surprising that those who are concerned about equity for students of ethnic and linguistic minority backgrounds are both hopeful and fearful vis-à-vis alternative assessments. If, as Hilliard (1990) has said, the reforms do not result in improved instruction (and, by extension, learning) for all students, nothing will have been gained. In fact, improved instruction has been openly stated as the primary goal of assessment reform in several states (for example, California and Arizona). At the classroom level, an assessment innovation like portfolios can stimulate the kind of climate that promotes student independence and engagement in learning (Camp, 1990, p. 10), if there are real opportunities to do meaningful intellectual work. For teachers, there is the promise of higher-quality information on which to base understanding of student learning and thus instructional planning.

As mentioned, portfolios offer opportunities not only for more informative but for fairer depictions of student learning and understanding because of their potential for flexibility and for linkage to the contexts of learning. Here the term "contexts" refers to prior experiences in school and out ("antecedent conditions"), the state of a student's English/other language development, the student's demonstrated interest and engagement, and the immediate conditions under which the task was accomplished—including setting, teacher support, materials, time taken, and other factors. Understanding of the context may be the greatest boon to improved interpretation of student performances. In fact, it has been strongly argued that to use test or assessment data without reference to context is invalid (Anastasi, 1990).

Moving toward an Assessment Culture

As suggested in Chapter 1, portfolios and other forms of performance assessment *per se* will not be powerful or useful unless those who use them have a fundamental understanding of and belief in the views of learning and instruction to which they are linked—and are able to act in accordance with those views. It has been argued that what is important is not the surface features of portfolios but rather their deep conceptual structure (Calfee, 1994). Those taking the most sanguine perspective believe we are moving from a "testing culture" toward an "assessment culture," one of "defining and documenting what it is to use a mind well" (Wolf et al., 1991)— *interpreting and informing* versus *measuring*. Along with this shift, we will undoubtedly find ourselves struggling to develop or embrace a set of values and practices that are harmonious with a portfolio culture—re-evaluating the utility of the psychometric maxims that have guided our understanding of testing and assessing.

Perhaps portfolios are the best hope for a tool that can support the ideals of an assessment culture. In fact, some (Duschl and Gitomer, 1993, among others) have used the more specific term "portfolio culture" to signify a classroom environment in which the emphasis is shifted from "management of actions, materials and behaviors to management of reasoning, ideas, and communication" (Duschl and Gitomer, 1993, p. 3), from an activity focus to a thematic inquiry focus. In keeping with their stance, these authors have worked with middle school science teachers to develop portfolios that demonstrate how students understand, communicate, reason with and construct scientific knowledge (p. 5). Underlying the shift identified by Duschl and Gitomer is a fundamentally different set of relations between teacher and students—one in which students have increased autonomy over their own learning and the evaluation of it, and teachers are expert guides rather than dispensers of knowledge. As Chancer (1994) says, "This type of assessment belongs to the student, yet the teacher has never had a more important, active role in setting in motion the structures that support a portfolio classroom" (p. 15).

Portfolios: A Process Tool

Our working definition of portfolio here is:

a process tool to link instruction and assessment that entails both teacher and student selection and evaluation of student work against criteria known to both and results in a structured collection of such work, gathered over time.

In reality, portfolios are not purely assessment, but rather a combination of instruction and assessment; in a sense they exist at the intersection of instruction and assessment (Paulson and Paulson, 1990). Lucas (1992) calls them a form of "reflective evaluation, a kind of formative feedback the learners give themselves" (p. 2). Some see their value primarily as a vehicle of instructional change, for transforming the curriculum (for example, Purves, 1994) and not as assessments in the traditional sense. From these points of view, outcome data useful for accountability purposes would be seen as only a by-product (Lucas, 1992, p. 9). Herman et al. (1992) state that portfolios qualify as assessment only when "(1) an assessment purpose is defined; (2) criteria or methods for determining what is put into the portfolio, by whom, and when, are explicated; and (3) criteria for assessing either the collection or individual pieces of work are identified" (Herman et al., 1992, p. 72). But standardizing portfolios risks obliterating their principal advantages, and if they cannot be adapted to local contexts and reflect genuine student choice and ownership, they may become compromised beyond usefulness.

In our minds, the process, particularly the collaboration between teacher and student around the issues of assessing student learning and setting learning goals is at the core of portfolio assessment. Collections of student work have always been kept by teachers, but the process we are discussing has not been commonly used. Although decisions about what to put in a portfolio and how to score it tend to dominate conversations about comparability and aggregation for purposes beyond the classroom, in the classroom the focus should be on the processes and learnings that are revealed by selecting and evaluating a variety of products and processes against a set of known criteria.

Paulson & Paulson (1990) present a "cognitive" portfolio model reflecting a constructivist approach that is focused on the *processes that students must be able to engage in* to produce work that meets agreed-upon criteria. Their version of portfolio assessment has three mandatory components: criteria for selection of pieces to go in the portfolio, criteria for merit, and evidence of student self-reflection (p. 60). One criterion that sometimes goes unmentioned is that portfolio pieces should reflect important instructional goals (Herman et al., 1992). Bringing the student back into the picture, we would stress also the importance of the student's learning goals.

Types of Portfolios

Distinctions have been made between "working portfolios" and "show" portfolios (Farr and Tone, 1994) or "process" and "presentational" portfolios (Yancey, 1992 c.f., Wolf et al, 1991—"process-folios"). The working or process portfolio is a dynamic tool—with products in various states of completion or perfection, whereas the show portfolio is typically a collection of a student's best works, much like an artist's portfolio. An example is the end-of-program portfolio used by high school seniors to qualify for a certificate of proficiency in a vocational domain or to use with prospective employers.

Figure 6.1 shows one possible way of thinking about the relationship between a working portfolio and a presentation portfolio. In effect, there may be three layers to the process: a working folder from which student and teacher select pieces to go in a more formal working portfolio from which only a few pieces are kept at the end of the year for a presentation portfolio that is a summative document sent on to the next year's teacher. For any portfolio that is shared with an audience, students should have say-so over which of their performances or products they want to make public (Hackett, 1993). Of course, portfolios may represent any instructional content. Perhaps the most common are writing portfolios—often expanded to represent other language arts. Interdisciplinary portfolios, such as the Chinle, Arizona school district has developed (See the section at the end of this chapter), are not altogether uncommon at the elementary school level. Portfolios will take shape in different ways depending on their purposes and the populations with whom they are used; and any given system can be expected to evolve over some time, as teachers and students experiment with portfolios.

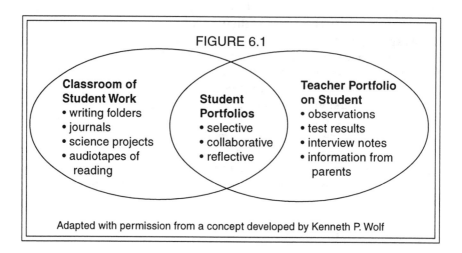

FIGURE 6.1

Classroom of Student Work
- writing folders
- journals
- science projects
- audiotapes of reading

Student Portfolios
- selective
- collaborative
- reflective

Teacher Portfolio on Student
- observations
- test results
- interview notes
- information from parents

Adapted with permission from a concept developed by Kenneth P. Wolf

Multiple Uses of Portfolios

There is no single best use for portfolios. In fact, Ruth Mitchell (1992) once documented some thirty-five legitimate portfolio uses. (Table 6.2 lists some of the most common purposes for classroom and school-level portfolios.) However, it is probably unwise to use a portfolio for too many purposes, particularly ones that may conflict in their demands. The broad distinctions in use relate to "widescale" versus classroom or "school-scale" portfolios and to process versus presentational modes.

TABLE 6.2
Common Uses of Portfolios at the Classroom and School Level

- Student self-evaluation of progress
- Student goal-setting
- Teacher evaluation of student progress
- Instructional planning
- Teacher monitoring of instructional success
- Reporting to parents and family
- Reporting to administration (school level accountability)
- Coordinating student programs among several specialists
- Program monitoring

Widescale Use

Widescale portfolio use is typically associated with statewide accountability efforts, such as the states of Vermont, Rhode Island, and Michigan have mounted. The purpose of such portfolios is to determine to what degree districts and states are meeting their instructional obligations or—when results are disaggregated—how well certain groups of students (by sex, grade, ethnicity, socioeconomic status, or program) are faring. Student performance outcomes on such portfolio assessments may not be accessible or useful to classroom teachers and to students.

Because of the perceived need to standardize tasks, the links to student interest and experience and to classroom instruction tend to be lost when portfolios move beyond the school level. Flexibility in administration and interpretation may also be reduced. When portfolio contents are scored by outside groups, as they usually are, the results may be available only in the form of a score—which may not be very informative to the teacher and student. Nor do scorers have context information to enhance understanding of performances. In addition, the whole sense of a portfolio as a collection of student work over time (the developmental perspective) is lost in the widescale context, at least as such portfolios are currently constituted and examined. A serious equity concern is that standardized portfolio tasks may not exist in a student's first language; and despite policies of inclusion, English language learners may be excluded from tasks or simply not be able to complete them without greater accommodations than the usual mediation procedures can provide.

Classroom Use

The second major arena of portfolio assessment is the classroom, and here it usually has several related purposes: to give the teacher valuable information about what kind of instruction and curriculum planning need to be done (through the monitoring of student progress), to engage students in the evaluation of their own learning and in setting additional learning goals, to let students and teachers in on each other's thinking about what is being learned, and to show parents and others a portrait of student progress. The classroom portfolio almost seems like a different form of assessment from the widescale portfolio, with its links to context, the freedom to assess when appropriate (rather than on demand), student ownership, and procedural flexibility. If we insist, as some do, that student ownership and reflection are defining features of portfolio assessment, we may question the legitimacy of using the term "portfolio" for widescale assessments—at least as they are currently designed.

Teachers can use the portfolio process with each other to help establish consensus about what constitutes a "good enough" or "superior" student performance on various kinds of tasks. In the case of schools where teachers from the dominant culture are in the position of evaluating students from non-dominant groups, moderating student performances in concert with teachers from non-dominant groups can potentially reduce bias and increase cross-cultural understanding.

Portfolios represent both the *inquiry* and *reflection* components of learning (Yancey, 1992)—documenting intellectual activity, thinking about what has been learned, and setting new learning goals. In a sense, inquiry and reflection/evaluation/goal-setting really constitute one cyclical process. We have suggested that portfolios' greatest value lies in their ability to promote student self-evaluation of or reflection on learning in collaboration with expert models of evaluation (teachers) (D'Aoust, 1992; Farr and Tone, 1993; and others). The process may be even more important for non-mainstream students whose construal of *what* is going on in the classroom and *why* may be less congruent with the teacher's notions of the purposes of instructional events than that of mainstream students. It presents another chance to get clarifications in a one-to-one or small-group situation.

Another implied purpose of classroom portfolios is to help teachers to assess their instruction and its effectiveness with all students and to guide planning of subsequent instruction. The same instructional strategies may not be equally beneficial to all students (Gomez, Blaue, and Bloch, 1991). But there is no direct route from reflection on student performance to modification of instruction; and early reports of teachers' efforts to use portfolios to inform instruction suggest that teachers need support to translate portfolio data into instructional planning (Calfee, 1994; Au, 1994)—

one more reason to insist upon opportunities for collaborative reflection among teachers.

Conferencing and close observation of individual students and groups of students are necessary complements to portfolios (Gomez, Blaue, and Bloch, 1991; Hackett, 1993). Because of the complexity of factors affecting the learning of cultural and linguistic minority students, strategies to enhance understanding of the context and conditions of student learning are doubly important.

We want to focus on the portfolio not as a pristine archive or summary of exemplary student work but as a somewhat more messy, interactive, developing and developmental classroom tool that can be shaped by the needs of students and teachers. Yet all of the major issues we raise and steps to equity that we offer apply as well to widescale applications of portfolio assessment for linguistically and culturally non-dominant students. The question of how well widescale assessment can actually respond to the needs of all students remains unanswered, as does the question of how useful and meaningful data gathered through such assessment can be.

Criteria for Valid and Equitable Performance Assessments

It is important that portfolios and other forms of assessment have "systemic validity," that is, that they promote the kinds of instructional changes in educational systems that will support high-level learning for all students. To be valid and equitable, they need to have fair consequences for each individual student as well. Table 6.3 specifies a set of criteria for valid alternative classroom assessments.

These criteria, many of which have been proposed by research and assessment development groups such as the National Center for Research on Evaluation, Standards and Student Testing (CRESST) at UCLA (Linn et al., 1991) and FairTest (1994), get at the core notions of meaningful assessment. They address the purposes of assessments, the nature of the assessments themselves and their relationship to learning and instruction, conditions of administration, and uses.

"Authenticity" has been a byword of the assessment reform movement. At the heart of authenticity is the idea that assessment takes place in the context of work that students have been thinking long and hard about (Frederiksen, 1994) and calls upon lower-level skills in the service of higher-order mental activity. Newmann (1991) has used the term "authentic instruction" to refer to instruction that assists students to pursue complex questions, topics, and interests deeply. Such instruction would indeed demand some individualization or tailoring of assessment, because students within a classroom would not all be investigating the same topics. Use of the term "authentic assessment" to refer only to performance tasks, portfolios, and exhibitions raises hackles on occasion, because it suggests that all other forms of assessment are "inauthentic." Most proponents of the reform would likely continue to argue that assessments that examine skills in a decontextualized format are inauthentic. However, others cite research to show that alternative assessments do not necessarily yield information about students' facility with particular skills and argue for the use of both norm-referenced standardized tests and alternatives (Lindholm, 1994).

TABLE 6.3
Criteria for Valid Alternative Classroom Assessments

1. Are curriculum-linked and tied to known standards

2. Promote high-level learning for all students (systemic validity)

3. Are scored according to performance criteria known to teachers, students, and parents

4. Are flexible (form, administration, interpretation)

5. Provide for multiple ways and multiple opportunities to meet the same standards

6. Reflect opportunities to learn

7. Are cognitively complex

8. Call on multiple intelligences

9. Are used primarily to facilitate student learning and not to sort, classify, or track (FairTest)

10. Are authentic, meaningful opportunities for learning in themselves and are transparent to students

11. Entail opportunities for self-assessment

12. Are culturally reponsive/allow for variation in language, in cognitive and communicative style, and in beliefs and values

13. Integrate skills

14. Are used appropriately and are useful for the purpose for which they are designed

15. Inform student and teacher about how to organize future efforts

To be equitable and valid, portfolio systems must stack up against these criteria. Teachers need to examine their practices against these criteria, and through collaborative effort they will have to set in place mechanisms to ensure that the criteria are consistently met. Critical concerns for students from non-dominant groups have to do with the following criteria in Table 6.3: (5) provision of multiple ways and multiple opportunities to meet standards; (12) provisions for variations in language, and cognitive and communicative style; (14) provisions for appropriate use. These criteria need to be operationalized, to get beyond egalitarian rhetoric to specific strategies for ensuring that they are met. Discussion of student work, student classroom participation patterns, and community values and practices needs to take place among teachers that will lead to decisions about how cultural variation can be acknowledged and reflected in portfolios and their use. When teachers from more than one classroom are designing tasks that will be completed by all students at a grade level, they need to discuss how the task can be accessible to all students—allowing for different ways of engaging in it. As discussed in Chapter 4, tasks need to be evaluated for their language demands and consideration given to modifications that allow all students to participate in them.

To put criteria for equity in assessment in perspective, we need once again to refer to the larger context in which portfolios and other assessments operate. If portfolios are to be empowering to students, partly through responsiveness to contexts (including cultural), they must be linked to teaching and learning that is equally empowering and responsive. "Portfolio discourse" (Koelsch, 1994) can be the vehicle for linking school with the community outside the classroom only if communication is two-way at every step—in the formulation of standards, the design of curriculum and instruction, and the design and use of assessments. Figure 6.2 highlights the role of portfolios, situating them within the context of other important elements of an equitable instructional system. Community-school relations are depicted as mutually informing and influencing.

Standards

To be fair, assessments should be linked to agreed-upon content standards: What is it we want students to know and be able to do? And performance standards (the criteria for what counts as good performance) should be known to teachers, students, and parents. A student has a right to know why he/she is being assessed, how he/she will be judged, and how the assessment outcomes will be used. Equity advocates are pressing home the point that to be fair to students with different backgrounds and school experiences, assessments must take multiple forms and be administered in ways that make sense to the student and setting.

FIGURE 6.2

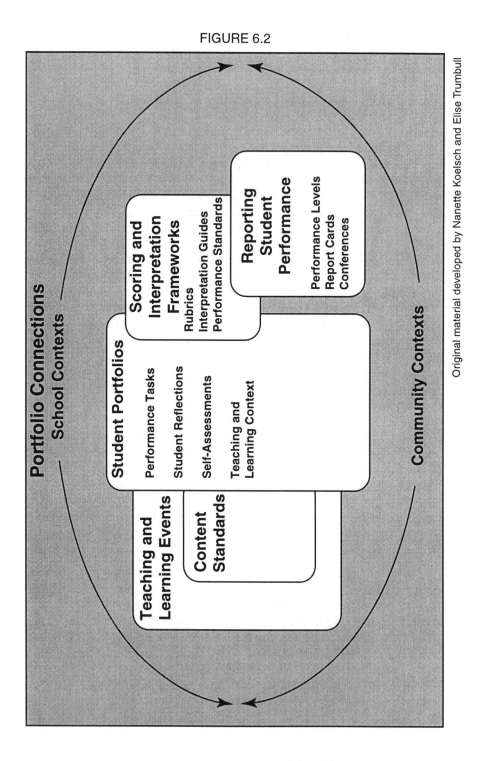

Original material developed by Nanette Koelsch and Elise Trumbull

A troubling question is, "Who sets standards?" It is easy enough to say that they should arise from a consensus of the community from which students come, but how does that take place? What constitutes the community, and how can all components of the community as defined be represented in the standards-setting process? In reality, standards are neither neutral nor representative but tend to reflect the values of the dominant culture—only one segment of the community. Furthermore, there is a danger in thinking of standards as permanently fixed. Things change, and even the best community-based standards may need to evolve or be interpreted in a different light at a later date.

The problem of representation is compounded when such a process is extended to the national level. However, the broader reforms with which portfolio assessment is associated entail profound changes in the roles and relationships of teachers, parents, students, and community vis-à-vis each other—essentially changes in the direction of more equal distribution of rights and responsibilities in the educational process. So, for the next several years we will be learning how to make that process and the resulting standards more inclusive and more representative. To the degree that we are able to do so, equity will be increased for our students.

In like fashion, performance standards must be flexible enough to incorporate cultural variation. For example, as we discussed in Chapter 4, oral and written discourse strategies (for telling a story, explaining, or developing an argument, e.g.) are different across communities of speakers. As Ball (1993) has shown through her research, African-American students may use rhetorical devices in their written discourse that are traditionally associated with oral forms. For example, they may use *narrative interspersion* in an expository piece, that is, they may interject narrative to illustrate a point. Teachers who do not understand this to be an accepted strategy in African-American discourse might be inclined to rate it as a deviation or deficiency—as something not learned rather than as a strategy mastered. In addition, students' "reading" of the expectations of assessment, of what it is they are supposed to display or show off, varies by ethnic group and by sex; so uniform assessments potentially underestimate the knowledge and understanding of some students.

A process for linking standards to student work to obtain evidence that standards have been met is essential. Figure 6.3 shows one group's visual conceptualization of the relationship between standards and the sources of evidence that would go into students' portfolios. In this case, six reading standards are represented (in shorthand). A summary graphic like this one can be used to organize thinking and planning about portfolios.

FIGURE 6.3

Portfolio Plan: Hawaii

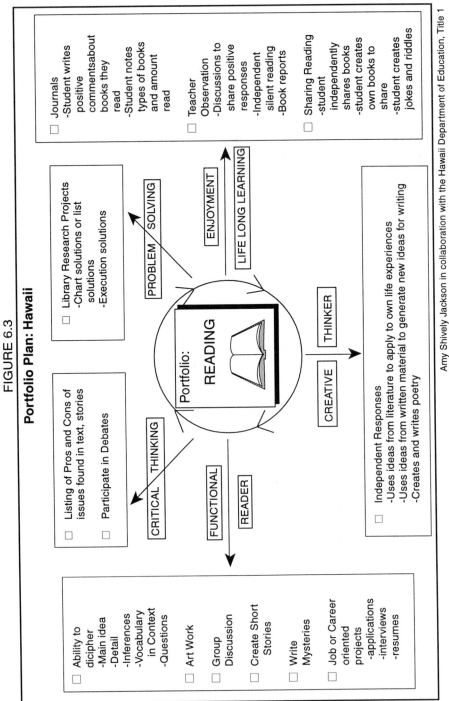

□ Journals
-Student writes positive commentsabout books they read
-Student notes types of books and amount read

□ Teacher Observation
-Discussions to share positive responses
-Independent silent reading
-Book reports

□ Sharing Reading
-student independently shares books
-student creates own books to share
-student creates jokes and riddles

□ Library Research Projects
-Chart solutions or list solutions
-Execution solutions

PROBLEM SOLVING

ENJOYMENT

LIFE LONG LEARNING

Portfolio:
READING

CRITICAL THINKING

FUNCTIONAL

READER

CREATIVE

THINKER

□ Listing of Pros and Cons of issues found in text, stories
□ Participate in Debates

□ Independent Responses
-Uses ideas from literature to apply to own life experiences
-Uses ideas from written material to generate new ideas for writing
-Creates and writes poetry

□ Ability to dicipher
-Main idea
-Detail
-Inferences
-Vocabulary in Context
-Questions

□ Art Work

□ Group Discussion

□ Create Short Stories

□ Write Mysteries

□ Job or Career oriented projects
-applications
-interviews
-resumes

Amy Shively Jackson in collaboration with the Hawaii Department of Education, Title 1

While it is easy to generate lists of principles for valid and equitable assessment, it is challenging for teachers and administrators to translate such principles into action—particularly when inequities continue to exist in the larger society. In the last segment of the chapter we will take a look at the experiences of some school districts around the country—putting some practical "meat" on the theoretical "bones" and showing how these districts have met some of the challenges.

Positive Features of Portfolios for Diverse Classrooms

Table 6.4 summarizes the features of portfolios that make them a potentially valid, equitable, and valuable form of assessment for students from non-dominant linguistic and cultural groups. In the next few pages, we will examine these features more closely, present some guidelines for ensuring that they are capitalized on, and review some examples of worthy efforts.

Flexibility

Portfolios have the flexibility to include products in any language or in any form (student writing, student dictations to teachers, tape recordings, drawings, photographs, even videotapes). Activities that are culturally appropriate for a student can be jointly chosen by teacher and student; or they can be modified to accommodate student interests or learning style and still draw on common proficiencies or understandings.

In fact, unlike other assessments or testing instruments, the portfolio process has the potential for the flexibility necessary to accommodate culture-based curriculum and instruction in any language. Part of this potential is currently being tested by fifth-grade teachers in the Chinle Public Schools on the Navajo Nation in northeastern Arizona. These teachers, in collaboration with a consultant, Nanette Koelsch, are designing a portfolio process that will link their Navajo curriculum and integrated, cross-disciplinary standards to the state's *Essential Skills Frameworks*. Their plan is to use the portfolio process for both classroom instructional and student self-evaluation purposes as well as for accountability to the State for students' mastery of Essential Skills. The Chinle portfolio system is discussed in greater detail in the final segment of the chapter.

Another element of flexibility has to do with the use of time. Traditional standardized assessment has usually required that time of administration be held constant, something that is not the case with the kind of work that goes into portfolio assessment or with the process of selecting and evaluating such work.

TABLE 6.4

Positive Attributes of Portfolio Assessment
for Diverse Classrooms

Are Flexible
- whole process can be mediated as needed
- may include products of any type
- may include products in any language (oral, written)

Convey Context
- can be annotated by teacher, student, parent
- can include information about culture, language
- can explain conditions of learning

Show Development
- have no ceiling, no floor (start where child is and go where child can go)
- include entries from extended time period

Incorporate Multiple and Complex Measures
- do not rely on single scores or scores alone
- include many types of performances
- can include indices from extended projects

Communicate
- are more transparent in meaning to all audiences
- make the classroom more "visible" to parents

Promote Self-Assessment, Reflection, Metacognition
- serve as process tool through which teacher and student communicate, learn about each other's thinking

Support Inquiry and Development of Skill in Argumentation
- engage students in setting goals, making choices about learning
- promote use of evidence to make judgments, frame argument

Finally, any classroom activities that may serve as assessments or yield products that can be assessed can be mediated by teachers in ways that traditional assessment cannot be. Teachers may translate, rephrase, or elaborate instructions. They may provide other forms of assistance such as explanations, reframing of the task, or suggestions for sources of additional information. There need not be the artificial dichotomy between instruction and assessment that means, "I have stopped helping you learn. Now you're on your own to sink or swim." What is important, however, is that some form of annotation be included to show the degree and type of teacher assistance the student needed to engage in and complete an activity successfully. (See "Annotation" below.) It is helpful to the depiction of a student's learning profile to include in the portfolio similar performances that are both assisted and unassisted.

Ability to Reflect Contexts

Because portfolios can reflect the contexts of student learning and classroom instruction, they have the potential to be a more meaningful and valid form of assessment. Products and processes associated with instructional activities that are part of the classroom curriculum, rather than on-demand tasks alone, can be assessed through the portfolio process. In conjunction with specified standards (content and performance) and criteria for judging to what degree they have been met, students can engage in authentic learning tasks that are tailored to their developmental level and instructional experiences. As Edmund Gordon (1993) and others have said, it should be possible to design multiple tasks or activities that assess the same standards—meaning that teachers do not all have to use the same activity to assess a student's progress toward a standard but can use tasks that make sense in the context of their own classrooms.

At times, teachers at a given grade level within a district may choose to give the same performance task to different groups of students and jointly score them. These scored tasks may be entered into student portfolios. The tasks should have congruence with the curriculum, and teachers can have students complete them when it makes sense in the context of ongoing instruction. On-demand assessments—those that are administered on a predetermined schedule rather than at natural junctures in instruction—introduce an artificiality and discontinuity to the process. Not surprisingly, there is some evidence that they also introduce much more performance anxiety than assessments that are indistinguishable from instruction (Estrin, 1995).

Annotation

Context is not communicated by a product alone. Teacher and student annotation—explanatory notes—are often necessary to convey the circumstances of the performance. Although the meaning or importance of a particular piece of student work may be evident to teacher and student, it may not be evident to a parent or other portfolio audiences. It is helpful to have an explanation of why a product was selected and how it was selected, that is, the criteria and the process of determining that they were met. The criteria may have to do with processes that the performance can reveal or with standards relating to outcome (what the product itself looks like). Pieces can be labeled "work in progress" or "best example so far of X." Because it can be time-consuming to annotate portfolio entries, teachers have devised numerous tools to simplify the task. They may use stick-on notes for temporary commentary, either placed directly on student work or collected on a clipboard to be retrieved and put in portfolios later. Some teachers communicate with students via such stick-ons (assigning a grade or giving critique) and remove them in favor of later student commentary.

Others use small spiral notebooks of 3 x 5 cards to write observations about individual students; the cards can be detached later and put in a portfolio or working folder as desired. Of course, observational checklists can be used as well. Another method of ensuring that observations about the work of all students have been recorded routinely is to use a calendar with blocks for each day. The teacher jots down comments and reviews them periodically to see that each student has been observed at desired intervals.

Products of classroom instruction, along with teacher and student commentary about the meaning and circumstances of classroom activity, can reveal much about classroom opportunities to learn—the nature of curriculum and instruction. Teacher annotation is *very* important in contextualizing student performance, particularly for students who are using a language other than their first.

Annotation can be done by either student or teacher and can describe:

- strategies that worked (or did not) for the student
- the student's affective response to an activity or task
- the length of time the activity took
- the degree to which the student persisted with a difficult element of the task
- a description of the setting/situation
- explanation of the kind and degree of teacher or peer assistance (mediation) offered (including translation)
- any other information that the teacher or student believes is important to understanding the performance at hand.

Annotation should also address, when appropriate,

- the nature of language use—which language, in which forms (oral, written), for what purposes, with what assistance.

Developmental Perspective

Most assessments, including performance tasks, are designed with students of a certain age, norm group, and level of development in mind. This means that they will always be too difficult for some students, too easy for others, and inappropriate because of a lack of match to instruction or cultural/linguistic orientation for still others. The portfolio process need not exclude any child, because it can document a student's development over time, beginning with whatever his/her level of development in various domains might be, using appropriate tasks and indices. Progress can be followed and assessed against standards, for teacher, student, and child to see. If expected progress is not being made, teacher and student have a set of authentic performances to look to as a source of explanation rather than test scores based on sampling of bits and pieces. In addition, a cumulative body of work to which students can refer in assessing their own progress provides understandable reference points of growth.

Multiple Measures

If there is a single most important caution to be observed in assessing all students—but particularly English language learners or students from non-dominant groups—it is that one should never rely on a single score to make an educational judgment about such students. Multiple types of assessments completed at different times are necessary to developing any sort of full picture of student ability or achievement. Simply by virtue of gathering in one place over time several kinds of performance, one is conveying the message that many indicators must be considered to understand a student's level of development. Portfolios can also be of great use in cases where students are receiving services from several specialists. Student work from more than one setting can be included in a portfolio, if different service providers collaborate (and with the student) to establish a process and criteria for inclusion and judgment of work.

Because portfolios can include non-written products such as audio and video tapes, drawings, and other visual representations, they can be used with students who are still learning the language of the classroom. The significance of these artifacts will need to be explained through annotation; in some cases, existing rubrics may capture important aspects of such products. Understanding of student learning will be enhanced by evaluating a variety of products and processes in multiple contexts (for example, different social groupings, using a range of materials and modalities), but great caution must be exercised in interpreting the performances of English language learners. It can hardly be said too often that because language mediates nearly all instruction in some way, the performances of students being taught and/or assessed via a second language must always be suspected of misrepresenting their learning. Nevertheless, in combination with more formal measures, the portfolio can contribute invaluable information to understanding a student's language development and learning and can be used to assist decision-making about program placement and need for special services.

Student Choice, Autonomy, Orientation as "Learner"

Historically, student choice has been exercised in relatively few domains: selecting a library book (probably with teacher or librarian guidance), volunteering for classroom jobs, choosing a free-time activity, or perhaps picking a piece of artwork or writing to display on the bulletin board. It has rarely extended to defining a long-term project on a topic of interest or setting one's own learning goals with the help of a teacher—the kinds of self-determined actions that would support development of autonomy.

The classroom portfolio process is clearly associated more with the latter kinds of choice than the former. If the student's participation in the portfolio process is to be most authentic and educationally beneficial, it must extend beyond selecting what goes into the portfolio—though that is an important step. A constructivist approach to learning would suggest that students need to be able to choose—with teacher guidance—how they will work, what language they will use, with whom they will work, what topics of interest they want to learn more about, how much time they need to complete their work. They also need the opportunity to make assisted judgments about how well they have learned something and when they are ready to move on to more difficult work. Allowing students choices is one natural way to encourage, accommodate, and incorporate culturally-diverse interests, experiences, and ways of learning in the classroom. Beyond that, portfolios can help nurture students' identities as learners—as writers, as mathematicians, as scientists (Yancey, 1992) when they use the discourse of those disciplines to examine and reflect on their work.

Students who are learning English need to feel that they have real choices about how and when they use their first language in particular—for both affective and cognitive reasons. We know that prohibitions of first-language use engender shame and fear and that freedom to use a first language to get more information about a task or to frame it for oneself helps students succeed with difficult work. Allowing students to choose topics they will investigate can provide a natural conduit to students' experiences, promoting a sense of ownership and inclusion in the classroom.

Encouraging students to choose when they are ready to display knowledge or present items for portfolio inclusion shifts responsibility onto their shoulders and communicates high expectations for student autonomy along with a respect for culturally variable styles.

If we want students to value inquiry and to be autonomous learners, we need to support them in discovering the gratification of exploring big ideas and solving challenging problems. Only through such a stance will we help students become thoughtful, engaged learners who can make decisions, set their own goals, and sustain interest in difficult cognitive work. Ideally, we will engender a love for and deep satisfaction in hard work well done, whether it be in the context of solving a tough mathematics problem, expressing a strong emotion successfully in poetry or painting, or using a computer program to design a futuristic car.

Intrinsic Versus Extrinsic Motivation

As Marshall (1992, 1993) has shown, students' perceptions of the purpose of classroom tasks and of themselves as learners are shaped to some degree by the ways in which teachers frame tasks. Some teachers tend to present tasks as work to be completed rather than as opportunities for learning. Of course they intend for students to learn in the process, but the only goal apparent to students may be to finish the work. Other teachers frame their instruction to students in terms of what can be learned, emphasizing "the importance of thinking and understanding over 'right answers' and completed worksheets" (Marshall, 1993, p. 1). Students in classrooms with learning goals are more likely to come to see themselves as learners.

The most powerful uses of portfolios entail students' perceiving themselves as learners who can make decisions and choices about their own inquiry, and that is something that will develop only with the guidance of teachers who do not see the learning activities of the classroom as "work" or—even worse—as "drudgery." Portfolios are compatible with learning goals and intrinsic rather than extrinsic rewards, such as remote (both in the sense of distance from the curriculum and from immediate usefulness) test scores or end-of-course grades. Extrinsic rewards are not likely to support the kind of sustained motivation and effort required for authentic learning. In the words of Catharine Lucas,

> Although summative assessment, whether it generates external test scores or classroom grades, has typically had enormous impact on the way students and teachers work and learn, it nonetheless remains, in a sense, peripheral to the learning process itself . . . Caring about grades, those external stamps of approval or disapproval that teachers rely on to motivate achievement, can go only so far to guarantee meaningful effort (1992, p. 3-4).

Choices about how to accomplish classroom work and use language are critical to fostering any student's sense of belonging in the classroom. In cognitive/learning terms, choices allow students to participate in ways that are culturally-appropriate for them. For example, as mentioned in Chapter 4, students from a variety of cultural backgrounds have been shown to have greater classroom success when they have the opportunity to work somewhat independently with peers rather than in small groups in which the teacher controls the communication—an example of autonomy teachers may not initially be comfortable with or anticipate as feasible.

If the portfolio process is to have full impact, it needs to be tied to culturally responsive instructional patterns; otherwise, we will never see the full learning potential of students. A classroom set of portfolios in which each one is nearly identical to the next, in which there is no hint of a student's home language or personal experience, is testimony to missed opportunities in instruction and assessment. (And we have seen such classroom sets for groups in which 75 percent or more of the children are English language learners.)

As mentioned, in an effort to ensure that all students have been assessed on the same standards, teachers often give students the same task to complete. However, choice can be built into such tasks. In their "Deforestation" task (Table 6.14, p. 307), the Chinle teachers have made sure that students have choices about (a) aspects of the larger topic which they will research, (b) whom they will interview to gather background information, (c) the ways in which they will keep their data and report on it, and (d) the kinds of products they will create and share with the class. At the same time, particular scientific and mathematical concepts, language arts skills (including ways of using language), and social skills will be demanded of all students.

Reflection/Self-Evaluation, Development of Metacognitive Skills

We have said that portfolios embody both inquiry and self-evaluation. Self-evaluation is involved in the selection of what goes in the portfolio, in reflecting on one's performances and learnings, and in deciding on learning goals. To be aware of what one knows and select strategies for improving upon that is to be *metacognitive*. Brown et al. (1992, cited in Shepard, 1992, p. 314) define metacognition as "the ability to allocate one's mental efforts efficiently, to plan, monitor, oversee, orchestrate and control one's own learning." Many elements of metacognition are entailed in successful portfolio use.

Students do not automatically develop metacognitive, reflective, self-evaluative skills or dispositions; and they may have had little experience in evaluating their work before being exposed to the portfolio process. In addition, although what we think of as the essential mental processes that make up intelligence are likely the same across cultures, different cultures will call on them to be used or manifested in different ways (Cole and Scribner, 1974; Sternberg, 1986). Moreover, the kind of verbal self-regulation that seems to characterize higher-functioning students (Biemiller and Meichenbaum, 1992; Vygotsky, 1978) may not be "available" to students who are struggling with a second language or whose experience does not match school expectations.

It appears that students for whom classroom tasks are not overly demanding have "surplus capacity" to reflect out loud on what they are doing "while consolidating skills during independent work periods." (Biemiller and Meichenbaum, 1992, p. 76). And it may be that if students have no opportunity (or do not learn) to verbalize about their performance, they may not be able to tap that knowledge about their performance later (Biemiller and Meichenbaum, 1992). We know that explaining and justifying one's position lead to better understandings in the explainer. (Recall the discussion about dependency on language for task or problem representation in Chapter 4).

Others have identified "mastery-oriented children" who "spontaneously instruct themselves to slow down, try new tactics, evaluate the task more systematically," and so forth. (Brown, 1988, p. 313, referring to Dweck & Bempechat, 1983). In contrast, "failure-oriented children" seek to avoid situations in which they may fail, thus foreclosing opportunities to learn. Portfolios would seem to be the perfect vehicle for helping students to become mastery-oriented critics of their own learning, to "regard errors as information that can be useful" (Brown, 1988, p. 313).

Students may not have facility with the language of self-evaluation or peer-evaluation and will need help from teachers at the outset. The portfolio process asks students to engage in some rather high-level, metacognitive reflection; and this process is predictably dependent on language. (All the more reason to select tasks carefully, to provide additional teacher or peer scaffolding, and to allow language choice.) Perhaps, in Piagetian fashion, we should strongly consider modeling and eliciting a new or developing skill (self-reflection) in the familiar context of well-learned tasks. Cross-age tutoring, which allows one student (even an academically lower-functioning student) to give academic assistance to another, has been suggested as another way to encourage verbalization about one's understanding or skill. This experience could complement the portfolio process. Certainly, students who are routinely able to take on leadership roles in the classroom (for example, in cooperative groups) get more opportunities to develop and reinforce the ability to reformulate their own knowledge—a sort of "rich get richer" effect.

It is possible that a student still learning English may very well be able to verbally self-regulate or reflect in his/her first language, something that may not be apparent to a teacher and may need to be explicitly encouraged. Teachers may have to model the reflection process first (Camp, 1992, p. 65), posing questions that direct students to look beyond surface features of their work (such as mechanics in writing) toward important aspects, for example, "What did you most want your reader to get from this piece?" (in regard to a written composition). Even older students are not readily able to reflect on their own work without assistance from teachers (D'Aoust, 1992; Hackett, 1993).

Table 6.5 gives some examples of reflection questions teachers have used. We should be wary, however, of relying on rote reflection questions or formats. We want to "be careful not to let written self-evaluations become the worksheets of the '90s" (Juneau's *Language Arts Portfolio Handbook*, 1993). Reflection, if genuine, may depend on creating an environment in which students can feel free and trusting—even silly and playful (Yancey, 1994). And a single, well-polished summative reflection at the end of a portfolio should not be the only indicator of reflection.

Student-Teacher Portfolio Conferences

As we have said, portfolios should be an opportunity to learn about learning—to become metacognitive (c.f., Paulson, Paulson and Meyer, 1991). Portfolio conferences are also an opportunity for teachers to learn about how students think, what they are interested in, their disposition toward various topics and forms of learning, and what helps them persevere with a difficult task. They also present the opportunity for student and teacher to collaborate to develop a common framework and language about learning (Gomez et al., 1991).

Teachers' inferences about student learning can be markedly enhanced by portfolio conferences with students (Hackett, 1993), either individually or in groups. Through conferencing, students can continue to develop understanding of the purposes of portfolios and understanding of teachers' expectations, values, and philosophy of teaching. They can also develop knowledge about specific learning strategies and content area concepts the teacher may want to highlight. Equally important, they can talk about personal concerns and how they feel about the work. If assessment is viewed as a collaboration to construct evaluative information and to help the student learn to participate in the classroom community (Hackett, 1993), the need to understand "where students are coming from" both cognitively and personally becomes clear. Perhaps more than we acknowledge, the personal and the academic are intertwined (Gold, 1992).

TABLE 6.5

Sample Reflection Prompts and Questions

I have chosen this piece because . . .

What I think this piece shows about me is . . .

What I liked most/least about [the story, the activity, etc.] was . . .*

What I learned/what I would like to know about [the topic] . . .

What was most interesting to me was . . .

If I had the chance to do this activity again, the next time I would . . . because . . .*

What did you do if you had a problem or didn't understand something?

What problems did you have with the activty? What would you tell another student about how to succeed with the activity?

Did you have any problems with the language of [the instructions, the story, the text, the resource materials, the group discussion, your small group working together . . .]?

What kind of problems?

What did you do to help yourself understand or communicate?

What do you think could help you next time with the langauge?

How can other students or I help you with the language?

(Some "meta" questions about the portfolio itself)

What was the best thing about keeping a portfolio?**

What were the drawbacks?**

Did your writing (or other process) or thinking change over the marking period/year because of keeping a portfolio?**

Did your attitude toward your writing [other complex skill] change?**

*Adapted from California Assessment Collaborative, 1993, p. 59
**Adapted from Gold, 1992, p. 25

Conferences between teacher and student, whether individual or group, can reveal things not apparent from a student's performance. As Mercado and Romero (1993) observe, bilingual students, particularly at the secondary level, can be excellent informants about their own learning needs.

Enabling bilingual students to explain or clarify what they mean and to tell us what their specific needs are, in whatever language they choose, is especially important for intermediate and high school students who are able to articulate these needs. Moreover, by reflecting on the strategies they use to learn language and to learn instructional content, bilingual students may be able to assume a more active role in their own development (p. 157).

All students need "sustained opportunities to internalize standards and ways of questioning and improving the quality of their work" (Wolf et al, 1991, p. 59), and conferencing can offer one such opportunity. However, a single method of conferencing with students from various cultural backgrounds may not fit all needs. Some students may be uncomfortable with demands to display knowledge directly or to do so when the teacher is ready—especially if they are not ready. The portfolio process may rely a great deal on one-to-one conversations between teacher and student, particularly in the context of reflection and goal-setting conferences. Some students may not be comfortable with such conversations. As mentioned in Chapter 4, some American Indian, Alaska Native and Hawaii Native students may find such a communication setting awkward or alien. If talking between adults and children has been discouraged in the student's community (Chamberlain and Medinos-Landurand, 1991), things may not neatly fall into place during a portfolio conference. Likewise, in some communities, children are taught to respond to adults' questions in limited fashion (Chamberlain and Medinos-Landurand, 1991); so free-flowing interchange, with elaborate reflections on the part of the student, will not materialize easily. Sometimes students are more comfortable expressing themselves in writing than orally.

Teacher Feedback

Students can be overwhelmed with too much in the way of questions or feedback. However, feedback is necessary to evaluating accomplishment of goals and to setting new goals (Marzano, 1994). Students who have not had the experience of evaluating their own learning may be able to offer only a global assessment of their abilities or performance. Noted cognitive psychologist, Ann Brown, has talked about her first attempts to work with a ten-year-old boy, Daniel. Faced with what he took to be a memory game, Daniel queried Brown, "Didn't they tell you I don't got no memory?" Brown says of her work with Daniel:

It would take many sessions of systematically mapping out the specific nature of his memory problem, providing feedback about just where the problem was acute but also where there were no problems at all, before

Daniel could derive a more realistic evaluation of his learning problems and, as a consequence, would be willing to attempt active learning strategies to overcome a recognized specific problem (Brown, 1988, p. 313).

Although Daniel was diagnosed as learning disabled, his tendency to global self-assessment is probably not uncommon, especially among younger and/or less successful students. We cannot expect students to analyze their strengths and weaknesses in learning without coaching in how to do so. English language learners may wrongly attribute their difficulties in accomplishing academic work to general learning deficits. Teachers can help them, through the portfolio process, to understand how to characterize their own patterns of performance in more fine-grained ways and thus to target specific goals. The benefits of more realistic self-evaluation could conceivably extend to a greater commitment to learning. As Brown has observed (1988), the reverse has been shown to be true: children who perceive themselves as learning disabled avoid work and fail to commit themselves to learning.

One suggestion is to limit feedback at the outset of the portfolio process to one statement about something done well and something that needs future focus—a strength and a goal (Camp, 1992). Eventually students can learn to ask and respond to such questions themselves, alone or with a peer. However, students who are learning English or who have not mastered standard forms of English may need very explicit feedback about their performance in order to set realistic goals for themselves.

Robin Scarcella (1994), a professor who teaches university-level ESL (English as a Second Language) classes and who has conducted research on sources of Korean-Americans' written language problems, reports that evaluation practices that focus solely on meaning or how well a student conveys ideas may not be enough for English learners. Is it really acceptable for a student to write, "I remember when U.S. involved in war at the Iraq. It remind me war my country"? Although the meaning is clear here, the student might have serious difficulty expressing less obvious relationships without accurate use of the "little words" (function words such as "of, by, for, with," or relational words such as "therefore, because, if . . . then") which frequently signal important relations when more complex ideas are involved.

The example offered (a fictional version of a similar example given by Scarcella) may be evaluated as acceptable at a certain developmental level. But, Scarcella would argue, to be considered *proficient* a student must do better than that and deserves explicit feedback on what is missing. Many of her students are angry or frustrated that they have not received corrective instruction earlier. In a frequently cited article, Lisa Delpit (1986) has reported similar concerns with regard to instruction of African-American students. She suggests that a strictly meaning-focused curriculum that does not ensure that minority students perfect certain skills is inequitable and ineffective.

Personal Conative and Affective Insights

Anastasi (1990) neatly articulated how motivation, interest, and effort (conative variables) contribute to ongoing development of aptitudes. As one chooses certain activities over others, particular skills get enhanced (to the exclusion of others), leading to the seeking of further experiences that draw on the developing skills. It is easy to see how a child might develop certain (valued) aptitudes within one community (home) only to enter another community (school) where such aptitudes are invisible or not called upon. It becomes the school's job to discover those aptitudes, build on them, and engender interest in developing new ones.

Some have suggested that portfolios (in this case literacy portfolios) are "places for students to show who they are" (Hansen, 1994, p. 33). Students' outside-of-school activities and selves are relevant to who students are in school, the knowledge they bring to the classroom, how they learn. We recognize this truth when we talk about constructing meaning in interaction or transaction with text, when we ask students to write personal-experience narratives, and when we ask students to compare a historical event with an event in their own lives. Perhaps we should allow students to bring written products or other kinds of artifacts from beyond the school walls to put in their portfolios—with the requirement that they explain the importance of these items to themselves as learners. As Hansen (1994) says, students' literacy is not "school property" (p. 30). Nor is their mathematical problem-solving or social science theorizing. "They need not leave their real selves on the doorstep when they enter school" (Hansen, 1994, p. 33). This last statement has a poignancy in the context of the school experiences of students from non-dominant groups.

For English language-learners or students whose home culture is different from that of the school, portfolios can offer an opportunity to reflect on personal experience and potentially give insights to a receptive teacher about cultural differences and their effects on classroom participation. Conferencing with the teacher can be the occasion for building vocabulary about learning, culture, and language. Portfolios may also, as mentioned, provide an important outlet for expression of personal feelings (Gold, 1992, p. 28). We know that the *conative* and *affective* aspects of learning are often overlooked, but they are extremely critical, especially for students who may not feel at home in the classroom. It is not simply a matter of expressing feelings, but of having the opportunity to evaluate what is meaningful for them in their learning experience and to set meaningful goals for themselves. ". . . if one believes the current research and theory on motivation, assessment that is truly 'authentic' can be conducted only within the context of students' passionately seeking meaningful goals, because it is only within such a context that students' true strengths and weaknesses are displayed" (Marzano, 1994, p. 42). Moreover, individual motivation to perform in school is not uniform across cultures (Deyhle, 1987; Philips, 1983; Ogbu, 1992).

Brown (1988) talks about the "pleasure of understanding" (p. 316). She suggests that deep understanding brings intrinsic rewards; when students intentionally work to expand their understanding, to take ownership of expertise, they are engaging in really effective learning. At such times, students monitor their comprehension better than they do when they are engaged in work outside their domains of interest. When they are not motivated to learn about something, they do not "recruit the same deliberate strategies to help them understand better" (Brown, 1988, p. 316). (Compare these observations with Marshall's, p. 275, this chapter.)

The validity of assessments is intimately yoked to student motivation and interest: if a student finds a task or topic uninteresting, there is no way we will see his or her highest possible performance. Once again, we argue for the need to match student experience and interest and classroom instructional and assessment activities (keeping a sensitive eye on sociocultural and linguistic influences). The greater the distance between students' experience and the culture of school, perhaps the greater the importance of explicit links between the two, such as through personal portfolio entries.

Bilingual researcher Stephen Krashen (1983) coined the term "affective filter" to highlight the emotional component of second language learning, particularly in the social context of the classroom. In addition to the cognitive constructive processes that go on in learning, there is an emotional layer that may serve to block or admit new experiences and ways of knowing. Of course, it is not only language-learning that has an emotional connection. In fact, "the emotional cannot be divorced from the cognitive, nor the individual from the social" in any learning situation (Brown, 1988, p. 311, citing Brown et al., 1983). When students feel valued and understood, they are more inclined to take risks in learning and have access to their full intellectual potential. When they do not feel valued, they are prevented from taking risks to explore their full potential. It is an unfortunate truth that racial and ethnic prejudice continue to blind our society to the capabilities and worth of many of its citizens and that our educational institutions reproduce that state of affairs, despite the desires of many— perhaps most—teachers not to do so (McCarthy, 1988; Pang, 1988; Scheurich, 1993; West, 1993).

Effective Communication Tool

Portfolios have been used in numerous ways to communicate with parents and others concerned with a student's progress. At parent conferences it has sometimes been students who take the lead by talking about their own work—in English and/or another language. Parents' responses may be recorded by the teacher or student, in writing or in other forms. In the New Hampshire literacy portfolio project (Hansen, 1994), students had a sheet titled "What do you think of my portfolio?" for each reviewer (fellow students, parents, other family members) to fill out.

Unlike norm-referenced test results that may seem arcane to most parents, actual student work is understandable to parents. If work is annotated, parents can get a sense of the "interactions around the work, making the classroom more visible to them" (Murphy, 1994). If rubrics, standards, or developmental scales are included in the discussion, parents can begin to understand the evaluative rationale. Again, the communication can be two-way, with parent commentary incorporated formally in the portfolio itself. One format used by some teachers is to have a brief conference between teacher and parent and then have a student review portfolio contents, perhaps in combination with moving through various stations in the classroom that display student work or activities in progress. Like students, however, parents may need time and support to develop a common "portfolio language."

Parents delight in seeing artifacts from both home and school, and their understanding of their children's learning can be increased by seeing what their children choose to put in a portfolio and hearing why those things were chosen (Hansen, 1994). Portfolios also communicate, in a sense, to students. There hardly seems any question that full-fledged performance products offer a more fertile ground for discussion of progress than do standardized test scores. Particularly in the case of English language learners who have to reach some criterion score on a norm-referenced language assessment to be moved from program to program, portfolios offer very important complementary information. Cooper (1994) has described how his ELL high school students more readily understood how to formulate learning goals and study to meet them through the portfolio process than on the basis of standardized test results.

Inquiry and Argument

Threaded throughout the previous section are multiple references to the "inquiry" function of portfolios, and we want to elaborate briefly on this aspect because inquiry is so much at the heart of new visions of schooling. Used well in an "inquiring classroom," where all members are learners, including the teacher, portfolios help not only in goal-setting for meeting curriculum requirements but also in expanding students' notions of what they can investigate and explore. "Inquiry" has an open-endedness to it that "meeting standards" does not necessarily entail. It is this sense of expanding and exploring that one associates both with intellectual development and mastery as well as with realization of personal empowerment as a thinking and participating citizen—a goal of pluralistic education. It is not difficult to see how a portfolio culture is harmonious with such social goals.

We want to mention the role of the portfolio process in relation to the ability to use evidence in argument here, because it is an important cognitive ability and because portfolios, by requiring students to evaluate their progress against criteria, using evidence from their work, should support its development. As has been shown in research with intermediate school students, even when they have gathered evidence to examine a hypothesis, students may have real problems using the evidence systematically to draw conclusions (Duschl and Gitomer, 1993). They may not be able to analyze or explain which piece of information made them draw a conclusion or how they used it to draw a conclusion. Given the variability in ways of arguing and using evidence (and in using other information besides evidence, such as personal beliefs) in different cultural communities, teachers might find the argumentation used in connection with portfolios illuminating vis-à-vis their students' approaches. They could then help students to see alternatives, without negating the value of the student's orientation to argument. For example, it may be acceptable to use feelings as evidence for some kinds of argument (response to a piece of literature or something a class member has written) and not for others (judging an explanation of mathematics problem-solving).

Grading or Scoring Portfolios

Conflicts with Traditional Grading Practices

Portfolios and other alternative assessments raise questions about the relations between their scoring and traditional grading schemes. How are teachers to translate portfolio scores (if, in fact, portfolios are scored) or evaluative information arising from them into grades? How do rubric-based scores, for example, map onto letter grade systems? How do they relate to "percentage correct" on traditional tests? As Seeley (1994) notes, "researchers and professional organizations encourage teachers to use multiple assessment measures but give little indication of how to incorporate them into a grade for report cards" (p. 4). Nevertheless, a district must come to some agreement about what grades mean and how they are arrived at. Administrators and teachers may not anticipate the collision between traditional reporting systems and ways of reporting outcomes of new forms of assessment. Sperling (1994) argues that ". . . a performance assessment program and meaningful parent report form, like twins, must be conceived together . . ." (p. 10).

One thing is clear: if teachers and schools have moved to standards-based assessment, grading students relative to each other (norm-based grading) will not make sense. Grading, particularly at secondary and post-secondary levels, has often been a norm-referenced process, with teachers either loosely or assiduously adhering to a bell-curve distribution that dictates a few top grades, a few low grades, and a lot of grades in the mid-range. The bell curve distribution appropriately describes randomly variable human traits such as height and weight, but it is not appropriately applied to complex human performances that depend heavily on particular experience such as intelligence or academic success (contrary to the assumption of Herrnstein and Murray, 1994).

Wiggins (1994) has called the grading curve a "harmful self-fulfilling prophecy" (p. 152). It ensures that only so many students will succeed and causes students to "underestimate their potential to achieve and to overestimate the differences between themselves and other students" (Wiggins, 1994, p. 154). As with "intelligence," school success is _not_ dependent on fixed biological traits of individuals but _is_ highly dependent on the kinds of experiences students have. "In addition, modern research has shown that the seemingly direct relationship between aptitude or intelligence and school achievement depends upon instructional conditions, not a probability curve" (Guskey, 1994, p. 16).

What many people forget is that _tests have been constructed to produce the bell curve performance result_. It is not a natural result of mass testing (Wiggins, 1994, p. 154). To attain the desired statistical result, student performance differences are exaggerated, causing students to have an unrealistic view of their performance differences. "By design, at least half of the student population is made to feel inept and discouraged about their work" (Wiggins, 1994, p. 154). And low scorers are expected to continue to be low scorers. Dramatic improvements in scores are considered anomalies and would be cause for suspicion of cheating or lack of reliability of the test. English language learners, racial and ethnic minority students, and students who live in poverty are once again disproportionately among those who are affected in such negative ways by testing practices.

A Range of Alternatives

So, what are the choices? Some suggest that the portfolio itself not be graded but that it be used to "displace some dependence on grades . . . to shift attention from grades to work that reflects the student's development and thinking" (Mumme, 1991, p. 13). Some educators believe that scoring or grading portfolios is incompatible with the purpose of portfolios. Others suggest that if grades are important, the portfolio can provide summative evidence for a grade (Mumme, 1991, p. 13). Some question the value of grading at all, noting that considerable research supports the contention that grading deters students from becoming deeply interested in and taking pleasure in learning tasks—or in choosing challenging tasks over easy ones (Kohn, 1994). While high grades may serve as a reward, low grades have a negative effect on students, causing them to "withdraw from learning" (Guskey, 1994, p. 16)—hardly an outcome any teacher would seek.

One criticism of existing grading practices has been that they are not fair, because they are idiosyncratic. Teachers do not all grade on the basis of the same criteria, and some grade "easier" than others. Whether to factor in a student's effort in the process of making a judgment about a grade is a highly disputed issue. Moreover, it has been shown that teachers do not uniformly apply the effort criterion to their students. Teachers may reward lower-achieving students for effort by inflating their grades, while they grade higher-achieving students or those perceived as having higher ability more strictly on actual achievement (Seeley, 1993). Perhaps this tendency reflects the inherent contradiction teachers sense in their roles as both advocates for and judges of students—roles that may be very difficult to reconcile (Bishop, 1992). And there are questions of purposes, uses, and consequences of grading. Are grades intended simply to give information about student achievement? Are they also intended as reward or punishment (affecting self-esteem) or as sources of decisions about students' eligibility for programs (cf., Brookhart, 1993)? Once again moving to a new assessment paradigm suggests an opportunity to re-examine practices we as educators have taken for granted.

A Hermeneutic Approach

With or without supporting grading, some educators look to an interpretative (or, more specifically, *hermeneutic*) process of negotiating understanding of a student's performance by student, teacher, and parent as a source of the most valid information (Belanoff, 1994). In this version of portfolio assessment, students' roles in evaluating their own work carry over beyond the formative phase into the summative. A hermeneutic approach seems to be highly compatible with the purposes and philosophy often associated with classroom portfolios because of its recognition of the interrelationships among text (the curriculum or what is taught), context, and individual and because of its emphasis on understanding the parts (for example, pieces in a portfolio) in relation to the whole. Scoring schemes often fail to account for how one evaluates the portfolio as an integrated whole.

The hermeneutic approach to interpretation of complex human phenomena is holistic and integrative, seeking "to understand the whole in light of its parts, repeatedly testing interpretations against the available evidence until each of the parts can be accounted for in a coherent interpretation of the whole" (Moss, 1994, p. 7). Entailed in the hermeneutic approach is a belief in the importance of context and the superiority of judgment of those who are closest to the context—i.e., students, teachers, and perhaps parents, in the case of portfolios—"honor[ing] the purposes and lived experiences of students and the professional, collaborative judgments of teachers" (Moss, 1994, p. 10). Outside, more objective judges who rely on decontextualized criteria would not be interpreters of choice.

Even this brief foray into hermeneutics is enough to both tantalize us with possibility and disturb us with questions about psychometric reliability and fairness. The tension is really the same one we have had to tolerate all along: that of posing equitable assessments that recognize context and student variation against standardization to achieve comparability across students or classrooms. As Moss (1994) notes,

> From a psychometric perspective, the call for "detached and impartial" high-stakes assessment reflects a profound concern for fairness to individual students and protection of stakeholders' interests by providing accurate information. From a hermeneutic perspective, however, it can be criticized as arbitrarily authoritarian and counterproductive, because it silences the voices of those who are most knowledgeable about the context and most directly affected by the results (pp. 9-10).

Rubrics and Developmental Scales (Continua)

Grading systems *can* be aligned with systems of scoring performance tasks or other forms of alternative assessment. For example, the Tucson (Arizona) Unified School District is piloting a method of reporting student progress that supplants the old report card with a rubric-based reporting system parallel to that used by the statewide assessments (Clarridge and Whitaker, 1994). Students receive not letter grades but rubric-based scores, along with the performance-level descriptions accompanying the rubrics. But moving to such new systems may be more of a communication problem than a technical one. Clarridge and Whitaker emphasize the importance of both parents' and teachers' having a thorough understanding of the curriculum and the underpinnings of the progress report. They believe communication is "the major key to acceptance" (p. 9).

Portfolios, themselves, can be scored, using one or more rubrics, in the same way as individual performance assessments are scored. However, arriving at a method for determining an overall score for a body of work can be difficult; and in some cases it may be desirable to give multiple scores, representing performance along various dimensions (achievement, growth, effort, skill in particular subject domains, for example).

As suggested, it is possible to focus on growth rather than absolute performance, to focus on gains rather than rank. Some assessment systems, such as the Juneau, Alaska <u>Language Arts Portfolio,</u> use developmental continua for purposes of showing student growth and explaining to parents their child's development. Table 6.6 shows Juneau's developmental continuum for reading (K-2).

While developmental scales tend to focus on positive development, rubrics may use positive language at upper score points but define lesser performances only in terms of superior ones. In the worst case, a less-developed student performance is defined only in negative terms. Consider the following example from the Oregon Department of Education's Scoring Guide to "Communication."

> Level 5—Clear and complete communication: The student gives a complete response with clear, coherent, unambiguous, and elegant explanations.

> Level 3—Partial or incomplete communication: The student's explanation is unclear, inconsistent or not complete.

> Level 1—Limited or lack of communication: The student's explanation is not understandable or not present.

The Oregon rubric has additional details clarifying the meaning of each score point, but these continue in the same vein. Performances below the optimum level are seemingly viewed as negative, inadequate attempts rather than as representing some level of positive development. An apt parody of a rubric of this sort is found in Table 6.7. Our commentary here is not intended to be a smug critique of Oregon educators or of others who are struggling to explore new ways of assessing student learning. The shift in ways of thinking about these myriad interrelated instructional and assessment issues presents us all with serious challenges, and it is virtually impossible for any single group of innovators to anticipate all of the pitfalls or missteps along the way.

TABLE 6.6

Name _____

Juneau Primary Reading Continuum

	Emergent	Beginning	Developing	Expanding	Independent
Comprehension	• Relies on memory for reading • Responds to stories • May label pictures • May tell a story from pictures using oral language • May pretend to read • May invent text with book language • Focuses on pictures for meaning rather than print	• Reads simple books in which text is repeated; (illustrations provide a lot of support) and demonstrates understanding in the following ways: -Recalls random details -Recognizes when the reading isn't making sense -Shows understanding that print carries meaning	• Reads books with varied sentence patterns; (illustrations provide a moderate amount of support) and demonstrates understanding in a few of the following ways: -Recounts sequence of events -Summarizes story -Predicts what will happen next -Backs up statements with proof from reading -Connects experiences with reading	• Reads books with long descriptions, challenging vocabulary; (illustrations provide low support) and demonstrates understanding in several of the following ways: -Remembers sequence of events -Summarizes story -Predicts what will happen next -Backs up statements with proof from reading -Connects and builds to draw conclusions -Uses prior knowledge with relevant information from the story to form an opinion -Connects experiences with reading	• Reads books with long descriptions, challenging vocabulary; (illustrations provide very little or no support) and demonstrates understanding in most of the following ways: -Remembers sequence of events -Summarizes story -Predicts what will happen next -Backs up statements with proof from reading -Connects and builds to draw conclusions -Uses prior knowledge to form an opinion -Evaluates/Judges character, authors, books • Verbally responds to literature in depth and is beginning to shift this ability to writing

TABLE 6.6 (con't)

	Emergent	Beginning	Developing	Expanding	Independent
Skills/ Strategies	• Identifies own name on print • Understands "how" books work, e.g. top and bottom and front to back	• Recognizes that letters carry sounds • Begins to use context, grammatical, and/or phonics cues and cross checks with pictures * Matches words spoken to words in print • Locates a known word • Understands concepts about print, e.g. direction-ality, sentence, word, letter, space, beginning, end	* Increases and refines use of context, language, and/or phonics cues, and begins to use cross checking to self correct • Begins to pause at appropriate places when reading orally • Knows the meaning of a period, question mark, and exclamation mark • Follows single step written instructions	• Uses a variety of ways to cross check and self correct • Begins to read orally with expression and with appropriate pauses • Knows the meaning of quotation marks and commas • Follows two step written directions	• Self corrects automatically • Confidently reads a story with appropriate expression • Follows written multi-step directions • Begins to ask questions about the structure of language
Attitudes/ Behavior	• Shows curiosity about print in environment • Participates in the oral reading of familiar stories	• Is willing to read • Focuses on print, supported by pictures • Reading is vocal	• Selects books independently • Shows familiarity with titles and authors • Is beginning to read silently	• Chooses appropriate books to read for pleasure • May choose books by author, topic, or a specific information • Usually reads silently for an extended period of time, sometimes vocalizing when text is difficult • Reads lengthier material	• Chooses to read a variety of materials for a variety of purposes • Often chooses reading over other activities • Reads silently for extended periods of time • Recommends books to others

Select the column(s) that best describe how a child habitually and naturally reads from a variety of materials at his/her instructional reading level. (Instructional Level Material that is challenging but not frustrating with normal classroom instruction and support.)

Juneau, Alaska School District, Language Arts Portfolio 1994. Used with permission

TABLE 6.7

Superman Rubric

Performance Factors	Outstanding	Very Effective	Effective	Marginally Effective	Ineffective
Producing Quality Work	Leaps tall buildings in a single bound	Must take a running start to leap over tall buildings	Can only leap over short buildings or medium buildings (no spires)	Crashes into buildings when attempting to jump over them	Cannot recognize buildings at all, let alone jump them
Using Work Time Effectively	Is faster than a speeding bullet	Is as fast as a speeding bullet	Not quite as fast as a speeding bullet	Would you believe a slow bullet?	Wounds self with bullets when attempting to shoot gun
Accepting Responsibility	Is stronger than a locomotive	Is stronger than a tornado	Is stronger than a hurricane	Shoots the breeze	Full of hot air
Job Knowledge	Walks on water consistently	Walks on water in emergencies	Washes with water	Drinks water	Eyes water
Communicating Effectively	Talks with God	Talks with employees	Talks to himself/herself	Argues with himself/herself	Loses arguments with himself/herself

A language arts assessment tool that has been developed specifically with a multicultural and multilingual population in mind is the California Learning Record (CLR) (1993-94), which is based on the Primary Language Record, a British assessment tool. The CLR can be used in conjunction with a portfolio system; it renders a developmental portrait of a student. The CLR illustrates the value of documentation over time for students learning English. Teachers use an eight-page form to document student background information, student performance throughout the school year, conferences with parents and parent comments, student self-assessment, and summative information for the next year's teacher. A key assumption underlying the CLR is that school learning builds on home learning and that schools need to use information about students' home experiences to make appropriate instructional changes within schools. As Mary Barr, Director of the California Learning Record Project observes, "It [the CLR] encourages the view that the home or primary language and culture are bases for academic learning" (*California Learning Record Handbook*, 1993-94, p. v).

The CLR requires extended observation and description of student performances, along with student and parent input. This information is used to interpret students' development along developmental scales. Tables 6.8 and 6.9 show two reading scales (devised for the Primary Learning Record) that assess students according to two different continua: dependence-independence and inexperience-experience. The scales associated with the CLR can be used by teachers to derive both numerical scores and narrative descriptions.

Table 6.10 is a sample narrative relating a second-grade student's report on her own reading progress and preferences recorded by the teacher at a teacher-student conference.

The value of this kind of assessment for students from a range of backgrounds is the degree of context that can be captured. One can see reflected in the developmental scales the positive assumptions about what students *can do* rather than a focus on goals they may not have met.

In norm-referenced scoring and grading, the need for standardization is great. Fairness depends on all students' being given the same assessments so that comparisons can be made; students are graded relative to each other. As we know, this demand for fairness through sameness can bias results for students who have not had certain educational opportunities. In portfolio assessment, fairness would derive from matching of assessment activities to students' instruction and to their linguistic needs, among other considerations. It would also seem important to factor student motivation, disposition to learn (in various subject areas), and information about social, cultural, and language variables into the interpretation of performances. In recognition of the importance of motivation and self-perception with regard to literacy, the Juneau Language Arts Portfo-

TABLE 6.8

California Learning Record Developmental Continuum

Becoming A Reader: Reading Scale 1

Dependence				Independence
1 **Beginner Reader**	**2** **Non-Fluent Reader**	**3** **Moderately Fluent Reader**	**4** **Fluent Reader**	**5** **Exceptionally Fluent Reader**
• Does not have enough successful strategies for tackling print independently.	• Tackling known and and predictable texts with growing confidence but still needing support with new and unfamiliar ones.	• Well-launched on reading but still needing to return to a familiar range of texts.	• A capable reader who now approaches familiar text with confidence but still needs support with unfamiliar materials.	• An avid and independent reader, who is making choices of materials.
• Relies on having another person read the text aloud.	• Growing ability to predict meanings and developing strategies to check predictions against other cues such as the illustrations and the print itself.	• Beginning to explore new kinds of texts independently. • Beginning to read silently.	• Beginning to draw inferences from books and read independently. • Chooses to read silently.	• Able to appreciate nuances and subtleties in text.

California Learning Record: Handbook for Teachers, K-6 and K-12, Preview Editions, © 1993-94 California Department of Education.

TABLE 6.9

Experience As A Reader Across The Curriculum:

Reading Scale 2

Inexperienced ———			——→ Experienced
Experience as a reader has been limited. Generally chooses to read a very easy and familiar text where illustrations play an important part. Has difficulty with any unfamiliar materials and yet may be able to read own dictated texts confidently. Needs a great deal of support with the reading demands of the classroom. Over dependent on one strategy when reading aloud, often reads word by word. Rarely chooses to read for pleasure.	Developing fluency as a reader and reading certain kinds of material with confidence. Usually chooses short books with simple narrative shapes and with illustrations. May read these silently; often re-reads favorite books. Reading for pleasure often includes comics and magazines. Needs help with the reading demands of the classroom and especially with using reference and information books.	A confident reader who feels at home with books. Generally reads silently and is developing stamina as a reader. Is able to read for longer periods and cope with more demanding texts, including novels. Willing to reflect on reading and often uses reading in own learning. Selects books independently and can use information books and materials for straightforward reference purposes, but still needs help with unfamiliar material, particularly non-narrative prose.	An enthusiastic and reflective reader who has strong established tastes in fiction and non-fiction. Enjoys pursuing own reading interests independently. Can handle a wide range and variety of texts, including some adult material. Recognizes that different kinds of text require different styles of reading. Able to evaluate evidence drawn from a variety of information sources. Is developing critical awareness as a reader
Inexperienced reader	Less experienced reader	Moderately experienced reader	Experienced reader
			Exceptionally experienced reader
Language 1 ———		↗	
Language 2 ———		↗	

Both scales are adapted with permission from those which accompany the *Primary Language Record Handbook*, developed and copyrighted by the Center for Language Primary Education, Webber Row Teachers' Centre, Webber Row, London SEI 8QW, in 1988 and distributed in the US by Heinemann Education Books, Inc. ISBN 0-435-0856-6

California Learning Record: Handbook for Teachers, K-6 and K-12, Preview Editions, © 1993-94 California Department of Education.

TABLE 6.10

Excerpt from California Learning Record Handbook

Grade Two, girl
Language: Spanish - English

Jeannear, whose recorded conference with the teacher is shown opposite, is in a primary language class. She is obviously confident about her literacy skills, which she is beginning to transfer to her reading and writing in English. She checks books out of the library in both English and Spanish, prefers to read in her primary language as yet in order to read faster (and more, her teacher can conclude) and enjoys support from her parents who not only get her to a library but read what she writes.

Hilary Hester's "Stages of English Learning, included in this Handbook as Appendix E, are useful in understanding how Jeannear's teacher can build on her prior experience and her confidence as a reader and writer in the classroom.

"More and more I find myself thinking about how useful this record will be especially with my children. So many of them come to school with problems that are too big for them to handle and we are not aware so we make judgments, like 'He never pays attention.'"

Original

"Yo me siento feliz con libros. Me gusta leer mucho, estudiar mucho escribir cuentos, canciones y poesia hacer reportes de los libros que leo". Jeannear trajo 9 libros de la bibloteca escuela, en inglés y español: Me gusta todo lo que pasa en los libos, tambien a mi papa y mama. Ella dice que ella lee a sus padres y que ellos tambien le leen libros a ella: Expreso que aprende mucho leyendo y escribiendo, siente que debe de estudiar mucho porque do grande desca ser maestra pero que para serio te qye saber todas las cosas del mundo, para cuando mis alumnos me pregunten alog e gusta leer en español e inglés, prefiere hacerlo en español porque entiende mas lo que lee y por lo tanto "acabo el libro más rapido". Le gustan los de inglés porque ma y mas libros de ingles en las bibliotecas. Cuanto leo en inglés y no entiendo algo miro las figuras, pienso un rato y ya entiendo. Le gusta escribir y escribir muy bien, pero solo quiere escribir si alguien (compañeros, maestros, padres) va a leer lo que escribe.

Translation

I feel happy with books. I like to read a lot, to study a lot, to write tales, songs and poetry, and to write reports about the books I read. Jeannear bought 9 books from the school library, both in Spanish and English. "I like everything that goes on the books, and so do my parents. She said that she reads to her parents and her parents read to her. She expressed that she learns a lot by reading and writing, she feels that she has to study a lot because when she grows older she wants to become a teacher, but in order to do so "I have to study a lot to know everything in the world, to be ready when my students ask me something". She likes to read in Spanish and English although she prefers to read in Spanish because she understands better when she read and therefore "I finish to read the book faster". She said she like to read in English too because she can figure and more books written in English than in Spanish, in the library. "When I read in English and I don't understand something I look at the pictures. I think for a while and I understand. She likes to write and she writes very well but she only want to write if somebody (peers, teachers, parents) is going to read what she writes.

California Learning Record: Handbook for Teachers, K-6 and K-12, Preview Editions, © 1993-94, California Department of Eudcation.

lio system has included a Reading Attitude Interview and Continuum. (The Continuum is shown in Table 6.11.) While attitudes toward books and reading are important, caution is necessary in inferring attitudes from behavior, particularly in culturally-mixed groups of children. The attributes listed at the positive pole of the Juneau Reading Attitude Continuum may not define a good attitude across all cultural communities or all personalities within the same community. Absence of qualities such as "Likes to read to others," "Enjoys reading aloud," "Thinks friends like to hear him/her read aloud" may not indicate a negative attitude toward reading but rather a different way of relating to others or a cultural variation related to public performance.

There *is* a normative element to standards and scoring systems in that they reflect expectations that students of certain grade levels will be able to grasp certain concepts and apply skills within a range of levels. The reality is that because of ongoing inequities in access to excellent learning experiences and individual differences in motivation and interests, there will continue to be some gaps in student performance independent of ability. Two related points are germane, however: one important purpose of reforms should be to narrow the gaps, so that there are not vast differences in student achievement (particularly such systematic ones based on socio-economic status, race, and ethnic group membership); and individual patterns of achievement should reflect not inequities in the educational system but individual choices and proclivities. The right to achieve mastery, that is, the right to educational experiences that support authentic and high-level learning for all students must be the goal.

Incentives, not Disincentives

We might ask ourselves how grading and scoring practices can best be used to support students' understanding of their own progress in learning and assist them in setting goals for themselves. How can we make scoring and grading serve as incentives rather than disincentives to persevere in school? It seems clear that one important step would be to focus on accomplishments and growth rather than perceived deficiency. A portfolio represents a body of work, over time that should be evaluated that is, in terms of progress. One solution proposed by Wiggins with regard to the grading dilemma is to "give all students the 'same' demanding work but differently scaffolded assessments, based on equitable expectations" (Wiggins, 1994, p. 173). For less able students, or students using English as a second language, teachers would not reduce the complexity of curriculum, instruction, and assessment but would give more assistance to students so that they could participate.

TABLE 6.11
For Use in Discussions, as Appropriate
Juneau First Grade Portfolio
1993-94
Reading Attitude Continuum

NEGATIVE ATTITUDE

- Not always sure how s/he feels about reading to others (scared, embarrassed)
- Not sure how well s/he can read
- Resistant and often does not like to read aloud; feels or acts confused
- Avoids the task of reading independently
- Often needs assistance by another reader or has others read aloud to him/her
- Views reading as work or something someone tells you to do
- May articulate that s/he is "not" a good reader
- Would rather stick to familiar books
- Little confidence in abilities as a reader

NEUTRAL

- Reading to others is okay but would rather not
- Feels s/he is not a good reader
- Does not always like to read aloud—says it's hard
- Will take part in independent reading, but not on a consistent basis
- Rather be read to than to read independently
- May say s/he is not a good reader
- Often needs assistance to move to a more challenging book

POSITIVE

- Views reading as a chance to learn
- Likes to read to others
- Feels good about how well s/he can read
- Enjoys reading aloud
- Thinks friends like to hear him/her read aloud
- Enjoys reading independently
- Able to choose appropriate level books
- Often chooses to read to self rather than have others read to him/her
- Views reading as fun and a way of learning more
- Self-initiates the reading task
- Likes the challenge of a new book
- Perceives self as a good reader

Juneau, Alaska School District, Language Arts Portfolio, 1994. Used with permission.

Scoring/Grading Decisions

If portfolios are to be scored, it has to be determined whether they will be scored as a whole or whether individual entries will be scored separately with no aggregate score. Teachers and students will have to decide on criteria for selecting pieces to go into the portfolio and for judging the quality of the pieces (Herman et al.). Then, teachers will need to decide whether scores reflect progress and improvement in combination with performance (against a set of standards) or simply performance. Herman et al. (1992) pose the following questions:

- Will progress or improvement be assessed?

- How or will progress be evaluated?

- How will different tasks—videos, art work, essays, journal entries, and the like—be compared or weighted in the assessment?

- What is the role of student reflection in the assessment?

- What is the role of parental input? (p. 72)

Teachers (and students) will have to determine the dimensions along which portfolios or their entries will be scored. For example, it is typical in scoring written performances to score them along three or more dimensions (strength of ideas, text cohesion, and mechanics, for example). With English language learners in particular, these dimensions might be weighted quite differently. A dimension such as willingness to take risks in writing, or to persevere with difficult texts in reading could be valued. The process of defining exemplary performances and gathering samples for students to see may be even more important for students who have come from very different kinds of school systems in other countries. If rubrics are used, they will need to be tested and reviewed to determine whether they capture or point to key aspects of performance and development. Scores should be truly descriptive of what students have learned, and if they are not, then they are not useful.

As with all of the innovations in assessment we have been addressing, new approaches to scoring and grading offer the chance to make educational practices more equitable. But once again, we must be cautious not to penalize students on the basis of language or culture and not to develop remedial or second-tier systems that belie an assumption of inferiority in "different" students. Students need to benefit from grading, not suffer from it. Somehow, as Peter Elbow (1992) has invited us to do, we must "embrace contraries": on the one hand, we must hold students to high standards and help them develop visions of what that means in their own terms; and, on the other, we must not overwhelm them with criticism so that they see no way to succeed in our eyes.

Portfolio Examples in Diverse Communities

The following examples of portfolio use in communities that are ethnolinguistically diverse demonstrate some of the power and value of portfolios as well as the difficulties of realizing their maximum potential.

The KEEP (Kamehameha Elementary Education Program) System

Started in 1971, KEEP is a rather well-known program designed to incorporate elements of Native Hawaiian culture in classroom instruction. The program is renowned for its use of conversation, story-telling, and collaborative learning congruent with Native Hawaiian cultural practices.

Learning in Hawaii Native communities tends to be more peer-oriented; that is, children learn from older siblings and learn with their siblings as a group rather than as individuals or in a one-to-one child/adult arrangement. In contrast to what is common in European-American conversational practices, several people may speak at once; or one person may begin a narrative that is picked up by another. KEEP consultants work with public schools (beyond KEEP schools) through the Hawaii State Department of Education to provide in-service education for K-6 teachers. Most recently, KEEP consultants have been working with teachers to establish a literacy portfolio assessment system that is harmonious with a "whole literacy" approach to language arts instruction (Au, 1994). The term "whole literacy" is used rather than "whole language," because the greatest focus is on written language and because the program deviates from whole language philosophy by using grade-level benchmarks of achievement and teacher-directed lessons with students grouped by ability.

The emerging KEEP portfolio system is designed for both instructional decision-making and program accountability. In keeping with goals of fostering student ownership of literacy and willingness to use reading and writing, the portfolio documents affective as well as cognitive behaviors and outcomes. The portfolio also focuses on higher-level thinking and comprehension (areas that were not well-assessed through existing standardized tests). What goes into these portfolios is a direct index of what is happening in the classroom in language arts instruction, representing six broad aspects of literacy. Table 6.12 shows these aspects and the sources of information teachers use to assess their development. For example, a student's response to a story she has read, showing both understanding of the meaning of the story and her own feelings about it might be included. Some of the measures were developed by teachers and consultants in KEEP; others were adapted from published examples. It is important to note that each aspect of literacy is defined in operational terms and that it is pegged to an expected grade-level performance.

TABLE 6.12

Project KEEP Portfolio Assessment Measures

Aspect of Literacy	Sources of Data
ownership	teacher observations and student surveys
writing process	teacher observations and samples of writing produced during writers' workshop
reading comprehension	samples of written responses to literature
language and vocabulary knowledge	samples of written responses to literature
word-reading strategies	running records
voluntary reading	teacher observations and voluntary reading logs

Table from Portfolio Assessment: Experiences at the Kamemeha Elementary Education Program. In *Authentic Reading Assessment: Practices and Possibilities.* Sheila Valencia, Elfrieda H. Hiebert, and Peter P. Afflerbach (Eds.), 1994. Reprinted with permission of Kathryn Au and The International Reading Association.

Appropriate performance levels were established with reference to the curriculum framework of the Hawaii State Department of Education; the reading objectives of the National Assessment of Educational Progress (NAEP); a widely-used standardized test series; and recently published basal reading, language arts, and literature programs. Teachers were to ensure that products or indices of student performance in each aspect of literacy were collected on an ongoing basis; students would be formally evaluated via portfolio in the fall and spring. Summary data sheets would be used to tally student performances (as above, at, or below grade level). Data could be aggregated for each classroom on each aspect of literacy in terms of numbers of students performing at, above, or below grade level.

Many of the challenges teachers may expect to face as they begin to use portfolios surfaced in the KEEP portfolio project. First, it was by no means a simple matter for teachers to make the leap from traditional assessment (standardized norm-referenced tests and criterion-referenced tests of skills) to portfolio assessment. Portfolio outcomes did not translate neatly into implications for instructional practice. Second, teachers did not recognize the potential for using daily activities (such as responses to literature) as an opportunity for multiple assessments. Rather they tended to assign special uniform texts as one-time assessments to all students. These outcomes are not surprising, considering the kinds of assessment teachers were accustomed to using and the usual separation of formal assessment from instruction.

The KEEP example is interesting from another standpoint. Despite the program's culture-based instruction, the portfolio approach used by the schools does not seem to capitalize on or accommodate cultural elements. One would expect to hear about steps taken to use the talk-story format to assess students' ability to connect literature themes to their own lives or to use peer-oriented communication events to get at comprehension. Perhaps teacher observations were applied to such settings, but the expected approaches are not highlighted in the reporting. In fact, teachers do not seem to have recognized portfolio assessment as an opportunity to make assessment more congruent with instruction; they appear to have been content with traditional evaluation. From the description of the portfolio process, one would not know that it took place in Hawaii as opposed to a more culturally homogeneous, European-American community. Finally, student choice and reflection on learning are apparently absent from this system. So, a key opportunity to make assessment meaningful to students is overlooked.

It should be noted that although the portfolio assessment system did not readily inform teachers of what to do about instruction, aggregated data were useful for program evaluation in pointing out areas of strength and weakness across classrooms in the six aspects of literacy. As a result, KEEP staff were able to identify in-service education needs.

Rather than be judgmental about the gaps in the KEEP portfolio approach, we may want to focus on understanding the complexities of integrating multiple elements to arrive at a successful portfolio system. In this case, demands for comparability and record-keeping may well have obviated other possibilities (such as for tailoring to classroom contexts). In addition, the project was orchestrated not by classroom teachers but by outside consultants from KEEP. The experience chronicled by Au is a reminder of the number of elements that must come together if portfolios are to realize their potential for reflecting cultural context and supporting culturally-responsive instruction and assessment.

Chinle, Arizona Public Schools' Portfolios

Sixteen fifth-grade teachers in the Chinle Public Schools have been engaged in developing portfolio assessment that aligns Chinle's Navajo culture-based curriculum with the state's Essential Skills (curriculum)

Frameworks (Estrin and Koelsch, 1994). The same portfolios will be used to assess student learning for both classroom instructional purposes and as one form of statewide accountability. The teachers have drafted a set of integrated (and to some degree cross-disciplinary) standards in four areas: Life Skills, Communication, Environmental and Cultural Awareness and Responsibility, and Mathematical Understanding and Power. They are developing tasks and rubrics that address learning in language arts, social studies, science and mathematics. Their goal is an assessment system that is manageable for educators, students, and parents and that supports exemplary teaching, learning, and assessment.

Table 6.13 shows the most recent draft of three of the Chinle standards. Navajo cultural values are woven throughout all of the standards and are reflected in the rubrics. For example, the Life Skills standard and rubric call for students to demonstrate cultural awareness in terms of their own values and those of the community and to understand the cultural narratives of their community. The expectations for students to display knowledge of healthful ways of living is also harmonious with the Navajo philosophy, which views health as a result of the synthesis of well-being of mind, body, and spirit. Rather than identifying life skills such as knowledge of how to use the telephone, take public transportation, or get assistance in an emergency, the focus is on more complex and global capacities and orientations (healthful living, communication, cultural knowledge, sense of independence and self-direction).

Both the Life Skills and Environmental and Cultural Awareness and Responsibility standards include reference to the importance of history on current life—something that the Navajo community is keenly aware of in daily life, as adults and children grapple with the complexities of maintaining traditions and re-creating their culture in tension with the dominant culture.

The Chinle teachers have begun to develop some performance tasks for the portfolios, which they believe will integrate multiple, high-level skills in the context of meaningful issues. The "Deforestation Task" (Table 6.14) not only requires students to expand their understanding of a topic of deep economic and social import to the Navajo Nation but it incorporates skills from all four standards. The task also gives considerable latitude to students for choices, particularly with regard to the kinds of linguistic products they will be developing.

Standard   Rubric

TABLE 6.13
Portfolio Assessment

Life Skills: Shá Bik'eh Hózhóón
Students will be able to analyze, synthesize, apply, evaluate and produce knowledge for basic life skills.

I	II	III	IV	V
Student is able to state an opinion.	Student is able to express personal opinions.	Student is able to identify and relate with others of the same opinion.	Student is able to present and defend personal beliefs and values.	Student is able to reflect on past experience and apply knowledge to the future.
Student is able to identify components of a community.	Student is able to identify the role of services available within the community.	Student is able to communicate understanding of his/her role in a family to the community.	Student is able to portray personal and community relationships through communication.	Student is able to relate personal perspective and the perspective of others in the community.
Student is able to list facts but does not make strong connections.	Student is able to relate a process of sequencing.	Student can demonstrate role of cultural narratives and their cultural meanings.	Student is able to use past events to reflect on current issues.	Student is able to analyze a social and economic organization in a community.
Student is able to illustrate meaning by creating a story.	Student has conceptual knowledge of cultural narratives and their cultural meanings.	Student shows a sense leadership.	Student is able to integrate cultural meanings with works of imagination through projects.	Student is able to demonstrate a complex understanding of cultural narratives and cultural meanings in past and future.
Student is able to identify personal goals with guidance.	Student is able to identify personal goals and is aware of personal needs.		Student is able to forecast knowledge of personal goals.	Student is able to express personal vision goal beyond self and community.
				Student is able to show independence and self-direction.

Standard   Rubric

TABLE 6.13 (con't)
Portfolio Assessment

Communication

Students will communicate their academic, social and affective knowledge and understanding to a variety of audiences for a variety of purposes.

I	II	III	IV	V
Audience Student is able to demonstrate some sense of audience.	*Audience* Student is able to demonstrate some sense of audience needs and interests.	*Audience* Student is able to maintain a sense of audience throughout the piece.	*Audience* Student is able to respond to needs of audience and keep audience interested.	*Audience* Student is able to transcend the requirements of the audience to inspire.
Process Student is able to create a form of communication that may or may not be relevant to the task.	*Process* Student is able to follow some parts of the process of a particular type of communication presentation.	*Process* Student is able to follow a process for effective communication.	*Process* Student is able to apply given process independently for effective communication.	*Process* Student is able to select and apply an appropriate process for any given type of communication.
Relevance to task Student is able to create a form of communication that may or may not be relevant to the task.	*Relevance to task* Student attempts to stay within the dimensions of the task.	*Relevance to task* Student is able to stay within the dimensions of an assigned task.	*Relevance to task* Student is able to extend the dimensions of an assigned task.	*Relevance to task* Student is able to extend the task to create larger implications of understanding.
Sources of information Student is able to locate specific information from a given source.	*Sources of information* Student is able to select or locate one or more sources for information.	*Sources of information* Student is able to use a variety of sources for information.	*Sources of information* Student is able to compare and apply a variety of sources for information.	*Sources of information* Student is able to evaluate, compare and formulate a variety of sources for information.
	Voice, insight, personhood Student is able to communicate some sense of personal understanding of a given source of information.	*Voice, insight, personhood* Student is able to communicate personal understanding or interpretation of information.	*Voice, insight, personhood* Student is able to apply, in a new way, personal understanding of information.	*Voices, insight, personhood* Student is able to make judgments and assign personal values about prior knowledge and new information.
		Purpose Student is able to identify a particular sense of purpose in communication.	*Purpose* Student is able to demonstrate a particular sense of purpose in communication.	*Purpose* Student is able to analyze the purpose of the communication.

Standard   Rubric

TABLE 6.13 (con't.)
Portfolio Assessment

Environmental and Cultural Awareness and Responsibility
Students will develop an awareness of their local and global environment through exploration of the cultures and ecosystems within them. They will be able to identify systems of organization and cause and effect relationships which exist in the world now and historically in order to effect change.

I	II	III	IV	V
Student is able to identify factual knowledge of past and/or present.	Student is able to describe factual knowledge of past and/or present.	Student is able to apply and/or analyze factual information learned.	Student is able to compose a project that shows synthesis of factual info.	Student is able to evaluate facts and express a position.
Student is able to identify cause and effect within an environment or culture.	Student is able to describe a cause and effect relationship within an environment or culture.	Student is able to indicate the relevance or importance of a cause and effect relationship by clearly describing why a specific cause and effect relationship is important.	Student is able to analyze the interrelationships between components of cause and effect relationships.	Student is able to critique cause and effect relationships with the support of factual knowledge.
Student is able to identify the elements which compose a system.	Student is able to describe elements within a system.	Student researches to find evidence of the interrelationships between the elements of a system.	Student is able to synthesize the inter-relationships within and between systems.	Student is able to evaluate the importance of different systems as elements of our world.

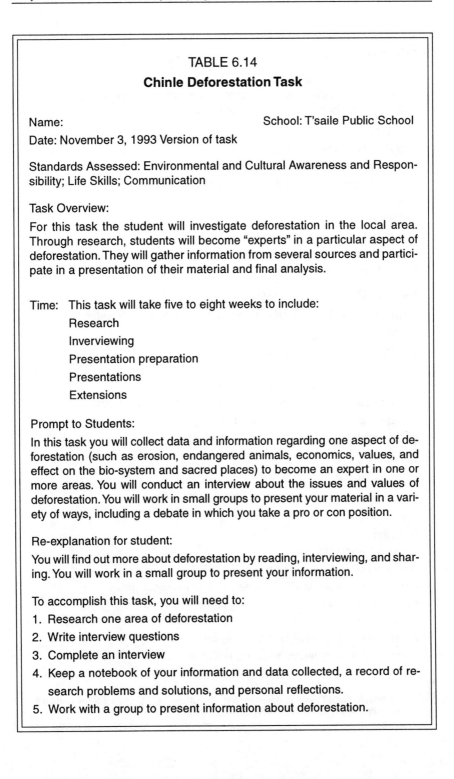

TABLE 6.14
Chinle Deforestation Task

Name: School: T'saile Public School

Date: November 3, 1993 Version of task

Standards Assessed: Environmental and Cultural Awareness and Responsibility; Life Skills; Communication

Task Overview:

For this task the student will investigate deforestation in the local area. Through research, students will become "experts" in a particular aspect of deforestation. They will gather information from several sources and participate in a presentation of their material and final analysis.

Time: This task will take five to eight weeks to include:

      Research

      Inverviewing

      Presentation preparation

      Presentations

      Extensions

Prompt to Students:

In this task you will collect data and information regarding one aspect of deforestation (such as erosion, endangered animals, economics, values, and effect on the bio-system and sacred places) to become an expert in one or more areas. You will conduct an interview about the issues and values of deforestation. You will work in small groups to present your material in a variety of ways, including a debate in which you take a pro or con position.

Re-explanation for student:

You will find out more about deforestation by reading, interviewing, and sharing. You will work in a small group to present your information.

To accomplish this task, you will need to:

1. Research one area of deforestation
2. Write interview questions
3. Complete an interview
4. Keep a notebook of your information and data collected, a record of research problems and solutions, and personal reflections.
5. Work with a group to present information about deforestation.

Directions to the Teacher (Task Administration):

Instruction Prior to Task:
Prior to using this task for assessment, the following concepts, processes and skills should be familiar to the students:

Ecosystem
Classification of trees and species
Interviewing techniques
Research, data collection and analysis techniques
Presentation formats
Graphics
Communication Skills
Presentation techniques
Presentation technologies

Materials/Resources/Technology:

Libraries (School library, NCC library, Forestry Dept., W.R. Educ. Ctr.)
Videos
Computers
Forestry Dept.
Material to prepare presentations
        art material, camcorders, T.V., Video tapes, tape recorders
Transportation to interview as needed
Written material: books, magazines, pamphlets

Task Extensions:

Literature Studies
Role Playing
Drama, Plays
Mapping
Visits to Chapter House
Presentation to Council meetings
Creation of 1 hour "news" video as whole class presentation
Field trips: Logging co., libraries, logging areas
Creative Writing
Informative writing: essays, written reports
Persuasive writing: letters to editor, editorials
Art

5th grade teachers, T'saile Elementary School, Chinle (AZ) Unified School District in collaboration with Nanette Koelsch, Far West Laboratory.

It remains to be seen whether the Chinle portfolio system can serve two masters: classroom instructional and assessment needs and accountability to the state. It is clear that the project will be invaluable to the educational community because of the extent and depth of the effort; the considerable resources available to the district in terms of culture-based curriculum development, skilled staff, and outside support; and the emphasis on linking cultural context to local and widescale assessment. For more detail on the Chinle portfolio experience, see Shirley Fields' personal account in Chapter 7.

Summary

Portfolios as a vehicle to unite instruction and assessment hold special promise for ethnolinguistically diverse classrooms because of their ability to reflect context, be used in flexible ways, and engage students and parents in the learning process. It is an understatement to say that many complex and interacting components have to come together for portfolios to fulfill this promise. If portfolios are to reflect the social, cultural, and linguistic contexts of students, teachers must have requisite knowledge about how these factors operate in the classroom. In addition, teachers will have to make explicit their philosophies and theories about learning, teaching, grading, collaborating with parents, and relating to students as they go about making decisions regarding portfolio use. However, despite these demands, the word from the field is that teachers and students like portfolios and value them when they are used in the powerful ways we have described. We look forward to more examples of portfolio use in diverse communities and encourage all of our colleagues in schools and universities around the country to write about their own experiences.

Commentary

Kathryn H. Au
Institute for Native Pacific Education and Culture

In a cogent and thoughtful manner, the authors argue that the use of portfolio assessment has the potential to improve the educational opportunities of students of diverse cultural and linguistic backgrounds. They cite the flexibility of portfolios as a key advantage, particularly for students of diverse backgrounds whose language and background knowledge are not reflected in standardized tests. Portfolios offer teachers a better chance of recognizing students' strengths. Students' progress can be charted on their own terms, rather than in comparison to other students or to external standards. Portfolios have motivational value as well, in developing students who are autonomous, self-directed learners.

I agree wholeheartedly with the authors' overall conclusions about the potential of portfolio assessment. Rather than reiterating their arguments, I would like to raise several questions to be addressed if this potential is to be realized.

If we were to achieve equity, how would it look? Previously, equity was a concept applied to students' opportunities. As a result, teachers tried to be scrupulously fair, for example, meeting with each reading group for exactly the same amount of time every day. Then we discovered that some students required more time than others in order to master the same material. We also learned that what occurred during lessons differed from one reading group to the next: instruction for better readers tended to focus on constructing meaning from text, while instruction for struggling readers tended to focus on accurate word calling. Furthermore, we discovered that the rich got richer and the poor got poorer. The gap between the better readers (those who entered school at a higher level of proficiency in reading) and struggling readers grew as time went on.

In present, more sophisticated formulations, equity is usually seen in terms of outcomes as well as opportunities. This does not imply that every student must achieve at the same level. Rather, it implies that we should seek to attain similar levels of achievement across groups. Through such efforts we would expect to see, for example, a closing of the gap in literacy achievement, with African-American and Hispanic-American students as groups achieving at the same level as European-American students as a group.

Exactly how can portfolios help with concerns for equity of outcome? As the authors imply, we must work toward improving classroom instruction and assessment at the same time, recognizing that the two are virtually inseparable in situations where a high value is placed on the situatedness and authenticity of tasks. We have a good idea of what successful instruction is like. For example, we know that the struggling readers of diverse backgrounds require lessons that focus on meaning and that build on the language and interactional patterns they bring from the home. If such high-quality instruction is unavailable, portfolios will largely serve the purpose of documenting continued failure, as standardized tests have done. We need more documentation of the successful use of portfolios to guide instruction, leading to higher levels of achievement by students of diverse backgrounds.

Can portfolios be designed both to meet the needs of individual students and to document improvement in the achievement of groups of students? If so, how? An example is seen in work at the Kamehameha Elementary Education Program (KEEP), where we attempted to develop such a system of portfolio assessment, in the context of implementing a whole literacy curriculum. We wanted our students, the majority of whom were of Native Hawaiian ancestry, to engage in setting goals for their own growth as readers and writers and to develop ownership of literacy. We also wanted them to be able to read and write as well as other groups of students at their grade levels throughout the United States.

In our first two years of experimenting with portfolios, we were successful in improving students' ownership of literacy, but two-thirds of the students performed below grade level in reading comprehension and the writing process. In our third and fourth years of work with portfolios, we succeeded in bringing two-thirds of the students to average or above-average levels of achievement. We believe that one of the key factors in this turnabout was the use of grade level benchmarks or standards. Teachers became thoroughly familiar with the benchmarks and focused instruction on them. They made the benchmarks visible to students. Students identified and then labeled items in their portfolios to serve as evidence that they had met various benchmarks.

The KEEP portfolio assessment system had the effect of improving the quality of the literacy instruction provided to students. From the start, teachers agreed that the benchmarks represented what they thought the average first grader, second grader, third grader, and so on should be able to do by the end of the year. However, they doubted that their students could achieve at these levels. In the third and fourth years, we worked with expert teachers, giving them the support they needed to focus on providing instruction that would enable students to meet the benchmarks. The teachers were amazed at the students' progress. A third grade teacher declared, "I will never again set limits on what my students can do."

Benchmarks or standards can help to raise expectations for the achievement of students of diverse backgrounds. But the raising of expectations is not enough. Teachers require considerable time and staff development support, in the form of workshops and network meetings, to develop the expertise to provide students with high-quality instruction and to implement portfolio assessment. It is not difficult for teachers to introduce portfolios to students, particularly if portfolios are simply collections of work. But it is difficult for teachers to put in place a process of interacting with students around portfolios. It is still more difficult for teachers to strike a balance, creating an approach to portfolios that will meet the needs of individual students as well as the standards of evidence required for a reliable reporting of group results.

Does the use of portfolios in combination with grade level benchmarks violate the philosophy underlying the use of portfolios? Some say yes. In my opinion, the answer depends first on the goal one has in mind for using portfolios, and second on the distinction between means and ends. For example, the goal of the KEEP portfolio assessment system was to improve students' literacy achievement. Literacy achievement was operationally defined in terms that related to success in the larger American society. Teachers, parents, school administrators, and policy makers endorsed this view of literacy achievement. The ends, then, were the same as for most other American students. However, the means were somewhat different. KEEP teachers used culturally responsive forms of instruction, such as the talk story style of discussion and peer teaching-learning interactions, means effective with Hawaiian students although perhaps not with students of other cultural backgrounds.

At KEEP we wrestled long and hard with issues of accountability. The term has come to have negative connotations for educators. However, we felt it was vitally important to know how well our students were performing under the new whole literacy curriculum. We had several choices about how accountability could be achieved. The easiest approach was to continue to rely exclusively on standardized tests. We rejected that approach because the tests did not measure the kinds of literacy we believed important. Another approach was to introduce some new tests—performance assessments that would better reflect the kinds of literacy going on in the classroom. We rejected that approach because we believed specially designed and administered performance assessments would impose still another layer of testing onto an already busy school schedule. A final approach was to design a portfolio assessment system that could do double duty: serve the needs of students and teachers in the classroom while at the same time meeting the needs for program evaluation.

Our nation faces no greater educational challenge than achieving equity for students of diverse backgrounds. Fortunately, whole language, the process approach to writing, literature-based instruction, and other promising movements have come to the fore, setting the stage for portfolios and other alternative forms of assessment. Following a wave of initial enthusiasm for portfolios, many conceptual and practical issues have surfaced, as discussed above. If portfolio assessment is to prove of real use in meeting the challenge of educating all children, the time to tackle these difficult issues is now.

— ঽ —

Dr. Kathryn H. Au is an educational psychologist and professor at the University of Hawaii in Honolulu. She teaches courses focused on issues of language, literacy and culture. For a number of years Dr. Au was head of a team responsible for development of a K-6 grade whole literacy curriculum used by about 150 public school teachers affiliated with the Kamehameha Elementary Education Program (KEEP) throughout the state of Hawaii. Her major research interest is in the literacy development of students from cultural minority backgrounds. Dr. Au has published over fifty journal articles and book chapters, is co-author of Literacy Instruction for Today and is President-Elect of the National Reading Conference.

References

Anastasi, Anne. (1990). What is test misuse? Perspectives of a measurement expert. In *The Uses of Standardized Tests in American Education, Proceedings of the 1989 ETS Invitational Conference*, Princeton, NJ: Educational Testing Service, 15-25.

Assessment alternatives in mathematics, an overview of assessment techniques that promote learning. (1989). Prepared by the EQUALS Staff and the Assessment Committee of the California Mathematics Council Campaign for Mathematics. Regents, University of California.

Au, Kathryn H. (1994). Portfolio assessment: Experiences at the Kamehameha Elementary Education Program. In Valencia, Sheila W., Hiebert, Elfrieda H., and Afflerbach, Peter P. (Eds.). *Authentic Reading Assessment: Practices and Possibilities*. Newark, DE: International Reading Association, 103-126.

Ball, Arnetha F. (1993, Summer). Incorporating ethnographic-based techniques to enhance assessments of culturally-diverse students' written exposition. *Educational Assessment*, Vol. 1, No. 3, 255-281.

Belanoff, Pat. (1994, April). Concluding remarks at Conference on Evaluating Writing through Portfolios: The State of the Art, Sponsored by the National Center for the Study of Writing, held at Stanford University.

Biemiller, Andrew and Meichenbaum, Donald. (1992, October). The nature and nurture of the self-directed learner. *Educational Leadership*, Vol. 50, No. 2, 75-80.

Biemiller, Andrew. (1993). Lake Wobegon revisited. *Educational Researcher*, Vol. 22, No. 9, 7-12.

Brown, Ann L. (1988). Motivation to learn and understand: On taking charge of one's own learning. *Cognition and Instruction*, Vol. 5, No. 4, 311-321.

Brown, Ann L., Campione, Joseph C., Webber, Lynne S., and McGilly, Kate. (1992). Interactive learning environments: A new look at assessment and instruction. In Gifford, Bernard R. and O'Connor, Mary Catherine. *Changing Assessments: Alternative Views of Aptitude, Achievement and Instruction*. Boston, MA: Kluwer Academic Publishers, 121-211.

Calfee, Robert. (1994, April). Discussion at Conference on Evaluating Writing through Portfolios: The State of the Art, Sponsored by the National Center for the Study of Writing, held at Stanford University.

California Assessment Collaborative. (1993). Charting the Course Toward Instructionally Sound Assessment. A Report of the Alternative Assessment Pilot Project. San Francisco; Far West Laboratory.

Camp, Roberta. (1992). Portfolio reflections in middle and secondary school classrooms. In Kathleen Blake (Ed.). *Portfolios in the Writing Classroom:*

An Introduction. Urbana, Illinois: National Council of Teachers of English, 61-79.

Camp, Roberta. (1990, Spring). Thinking together about portfolios. *The Quarterly,* Vol. 12, No. 2.

Chamberlain, Pat and Medinos-Landurand, Patricia. (1991). Practical considerations for the assessment of LEP students with special needs. In Hamayan, Else V. and Damico, Jack S. *Limiting bias in the assessment of bilingual students.* Austin, TX: Pro-Ed., 112-156.

Chancer, Joni. (1994, Winter). The teacher's role in portfolio assessment. *Portfolio News,* Vol. 5, Issue 2.

Clarridge, Pamela Brown and Whitaker, Elizabeth M. (1994, October). Implementing a New Elementary Progress Report. *Educational Leadership.* Vol. 52, No. 2, 7-9.

Cloud, Nancy. (1991). Educational assessment. In Hamayan, Else V. and Damico, Jack S. *Limiting bias in the assessment of bilingual students.* Austin, TX: Pro-Ed., 219-245.

Cole, Michael and Scribner, Sylvia. (1994). *Culture and thought: A psychological introduction.* New York: John Wiley and Sons, Inc., 1974.

Cooper, Winfield. Personal Communication, April 22, 1994.

D'Aoust, Catherine. (1992). Portfolios: Process for students and teachers. In Yancey, Kathleen Blake (Ed.). *Portfolios in the writing classroom: An introduction.* Urbana, Illinois: National Council of Teachers of English, 39-48.

Delpit, Lisa D. (1986, November). Skills and other dilemmas of a progressive black educator. *Harvard Educational Review.* Vol. 56, No. 4, 379-385.

Deyhle, Donna. (1987). Learning failure: Tests as gatekeepers and the culturally different child. In Trueba, Henry (Ed.), *Success or failure.* Rowley, MA: Newbury House.

Duschl, Richard A. and Gitomer, Drew H. (1993, April). Emergent conversations about portfolio assessment. Paper presented at the Annual Meeting of the American Educational Research Association, Atlanta, GA.

Dweck, Carol S. and Bempechat, J. (1983). Children's theories of intelligence: Consequences for learning. In Paris, S.G., Olson, G.M., and Stevenson, H.W. (Eds.), *Learning and motivation in the classroom.* Hillsdale, NJ: Lawrence Erlbaum Associates, Inc., 239-256.

Enoki, Donald Y. (1992, April). Student portfolio and profiles: A holistic approach to multiple assessment in whole language classrooms. Paper presented at the Annual Meeting of the American Educational Research Association, San Francisco CA.

Estrin, Elise Trumbull. (1995). *A Case Study of Assessment Reform in Arizona, Part II.* San Francisco, CA: Far West Laboratory.

Estrin, Elise Trumbull and Koelsch, Nanette. (1994, April). Capitalizing on portfolio features to ensure equity for ethnolinguistically diverse students. Paper presented at the Conference on Evaluating Writing through Portfolios: The State of the Art, Sponsored by the National Center for the Study of Writing, held at Stanford University.

Fairtest, Center for Fair and Open Testing. (1994). National Forum on Assessment Meeting on "Indicators," Far West Laboratory, San Francisco, CA, March 16, 1994. [Draft indicators drawn from "Criteria for the Evaluation of Student Assessment Systems."]

Farr, Roger and Tone, Bruce (1994). *Portfolio and performance assessment: Helping students evaluate their progress as readers and writers.* Fortworth, Tx: Harcourt Brace College Publishers.

Feuerstein, Reuven. (1980). *Instrumental enrichment: An intervention program for cognitive modifiability.* Baltimore: University Park Press.

Frederiksen, John. (1994). Personal Communication at Fairtest National Forum on Assessment Meeting on "Indicators," held at Far West Laboratory, San Francisco, CA, March 16, 1994.

Garcia, Georgia Earnest and Pearson, P. David. (1991). The role of assessment in a diverse society. In Hiebert, Elfrieda H. (Ed.). *Literacy for a diverse society. Perspectives, practices and policies.* New York: Teachers College Press.

Gearheart, Maryl, Wolf, Shelby A., Herman, Joan L., Whittaker, Andrea K., and Baker, Eva L. (1992). Writing portfolios at the elementary level: Designing and implementing methods of assessment. Paper presented at the CSW Portfolio Conference, March 20-21, 1992.

Gold, Sue Ellen. (1992). Increasing student autonomy through portfolios. In Yancey, Kathleen Blake (Ed.). *Portfolios in the writing classroom: An introduction.* Urbana, Illinois: National Council of Teachers of English, 20-30.

Gomez, Mary Louise, Graue, M. Elizabeth, and Bloch, Marianne N. (1991, December). Reassessing portfolio assessment: Rhetoric and reality. *Language Arts,* Vol. 68, 620-628.

Gordon, Edmund. (1993, November). Human diversity, equity and educational assessment, Paper presented at the Annual CRESST Assessment Conference, Los Angeles, CA.

Guskey, Thomas R. (1994, October). Making the grade: What benefits students? *Educational Leadership.* Vol. 52, No. 2, October, 1994, 14-20.

Hackett, Rachelle Kisst. (1993, April). The functions of teacher-student portfolio conferences within an assessment system. Paper presented at the Annual Meeting of the American Educational Research Association, Atlanta, GA.

Hansen, Jane. (1994). Literacy portfolios: Windows on potential. In Valencia, Sheila W., Hiebert, Elfrieda H., and Afflerbach, Peter P. (Eds.), *Authentic reading assessment: Practices and possibilities.* Newark, DE: International Reading Association, 26-40.

Herman, Joan L., Aschbacher, Pamela R., and Winters, Lynn. (1992). *A practical guide to alternative assessment.* Alexandria, VA: Association for Curriculum and Supervision.

Hilliard, Asa G. III. (1990). Discussion (of "What is test misuse? Perspectives of a measurement expert," Anne Anastasi). In *The uses of standardized tests in American education: Proceedings of the 1989 ETS Invitational Conference,* Educational Testing Service, 27-33.

Kohn, Alfie. (1994). Grading: The issue is not how but why. *Educational Leadership.* Volume 52, No. 2, October, 1994, 38-41.

Krashen, Stephen D. and Terrell, Tracy D. (1983). *The natural approach.* Hayward, CA: Alemany Press.

Language Arts Portfolio Handbook, (1994). Juneau, AL: Juneau School District.

Lindholm, Kathryn J. (1994, April). Standardized achievement tests vs alternative assessment in bilingual education: Are results complementary or contradictory? Paper presented at the American Educational Research Association annual meeting, New Orleans, LA.

Linn, Robert L. (1990, Spring). Essentials of student assessment: From accountability to instructional aid. *Teachers College Record,* Vol. 91, No. 3, 423-426.

Linn, Robert L. and Hambleton, Ronald K. (1991). Customized tests and customized norms. *Applied Measurement in Education,* Vol. 4, No. 3, 185-207.

Lucas, Catharine. (1992). Introduction: Writing portfolios—Changes and challenges. In Yancey, Kathleen Blake (Ed.). *Portfolios in the writing classroom: An introduction.* Urbana, Illinois: National Council of Teachers of English, 1-11.

Marshall, Hermine H. (1992). Seeing, redefining, and supporting student learning. In Marshall, Hermine H. (Ed.). *Redefining student learning: Roots of educational change.* Norwood, NJ: Ablex, 1-32.

Marshall, Hermine H. (1993, April). Children's understanding of academic tasks: Work, play, or learning. Paper presented at the Annual Meeting of the American Educational Research Association, Atlanta, GA.

Marzano, Robert J. (1994). Commentary on "Literacy portfolios: Windows on potential." In Valencia, Sheila W., Hiebert, Elfrieda H., and Afflerbach, Peter P. (Eds.), *Authentic reading assessment: Practices and possibilities.* Newark, DE: International Reading Association, 41-45.

McCarthy, Cameron. (1988, August). Rethinking liberal and radical perspectives on racial inequality in schooling: Making the case for nonsynchrony. *Harvard Educational Review,* Vol. 58, No. 3, 265-279.

Mercado, Carmen and Romero, Migdalia. (1993). Assessment of students in bilingual education. In Arias, M. Beatriz and Casanova, Ursula (Eds.), *Bilingual education: Politics, practice, research, Part II.* Ninety-second Yearbook of the National Society for the Study of Education. Chicago, IL: University of Chicago Press, 144-170.

Messick, Samuel. (1992, July). *The interplay of evidence and consequences in the validation of performance assessments.* Research Report. Princeton, NJ: Educational Testing Service.

Milliken, Mark. (1991). Portfolios across the curriculum. In *Workshop 3: The politics of process.* Atwell, Nancy (Ed.). Portsmouth, NH: Heinemann Educational Publishers, 46-57.

Mitchell, Ruth. (1992). *Testing for learning.* New York: The Free Press.

Moss, Pamela A. (1994, March). Can there be validity without reliability? *Educational Researcher,* Vol. 23, No.2, 5-12.

Mumme, Judy. (1990). *Portfolio assessment in mathematics.* Regents, University of California.

Murphy, Sandra. (1994, April). Perspectives on portfolio assessment: Implications for teachers and students. Paper presented at the Conference on Evaluating Writing through Portfolios: The State of the Art, Sponsored by the National Center for the Study of Writing, held at Stanford University.

Newmann, Fred M. (1991, February). Linking restructuring to authentic student achievement, *Phi Delta Kappan,* 458-463.

Ogbu, John. (1992). Understanding cultural diversity and learning. *Educational Researcher,* Vol. 21, No.8.

Pang, Valerie Ooka. (1988, August). Ethnic prejudice: Still alive and hurtful. *Harvard Educational Review.* Vol. 58, No. 3, 375-379.

Paulson, F. Leon, Paulson, Pearl R. and Meyer, Carol A. (1991, February). What makes a portfolio a portfolio? *Educational Leadership,* 60-63.

Paulson, F. Leon and Paulson, Pearl R. (1990). How do portfolios measure up? A cognitive model for assessing portfolios. Paper presented at a conference, Aggregating Portfolio Data, August 2-4, 1990.

Philips, Susan Urmston. (1983) *The invisible culture: Communication in classroom and community on the Warm Springs Indian Reservation.* New York: Longman.

Purves, Alan. (1994, April). Portfolios as metaphor and the metaphors in portfolios. Paper presented at the Conference on Evaluating Writing through Portfolios: The State of the Art, Sponsored by the National Center for the Study of Writing, held at Stanford University.

Resnick, L. (1994, Winter). Cited in Rothman, R., Assessment questions: Equity answers, Proceedings of the 1993 CRESST Conference. *Evaluation Comment*, Los Angeles: UCLA. p. 2.

Romberg, T. is cited in National Council of Teachers of Mathematics (1993). *Assessment standards for school mathematics*. Reston, VA: NCTM.

Scarcella, Robin. (1994, February). Assessing the Writing of ESL Students. Paper presented at the Annual Meeting of the National Association for Bilingual Education, Los Angeles.

Scheurich, James Joseph. (1993, November). Toward a white discourse on white racism. *Educational Researcher*. Vol. 22, No. 8, 5-10.

Shavelson, Richard J., Webb, Noreen M., and Lehman, Penny. (1986). The role of symbol systems in problem solving: A literature review. CSE Report No. 269, Center for the Study of Evaluation, Graduate School of Education, University of California, Los Angeles.

Shepard, Lorrie A. (1982). Definitions of bias. In Berk, Ronald A. (Ed.), *Handbook of methods for detecting test bias*. Baltimore, MD: The Johns Hopkins Universiy Press, 9-30.

Shepard, Lorrie A. (1991). Negative policies for dealing with diversity: When does assessment and diagnosis turn into sorting and segregation? In Hiebert, Elfrieda. H. (Ed.), *Literacy for a diverse society, Perspectives, practices and policies*. New York: Teachers College Press.

Shepard, Lorrie A. (1990). Discussion (of "What is test misuse? Perspectives of a measurement expert," Anne Anastasi). In *The uses of standardized tests in american education: Proceedings of the 1989 ETS Invitational Conference*, Educational Testing Service, 37-44.

Shepard, Lorrie A. (1992). Commentary: What policy makers who mandate tests should know about the new psychology of intellectual ability and learning. In Gifford, Bernard R. and O'Connor, Mary Catherine, *Changing assessments: Alternative views of aptitude, achievement and instruction*. Boston, MA: Kluwer Academic Publishers.

Sperling, Doris H. (1994, October). Assessment and Reporting: A Natural Pair. *Educational Leadership*. Volume 52, No. 2, 10-13.

Sternberg, Robert J. (1986). Teaching intelligence: The application of cognitive psychology to the improvement of intellectual skills. In Baron, J.B. and Sternberg, R.J (Eds.), *Teaching thinking skills: Theory and practice*. New York: Freeman, 182-218.

Vygotsky, Lev S. (1978). *Mind in society: The developement of higher psychological processes*. Edited by M. Cole, V. John-Steiner, S. Scribner and E. Souberman. Cambridge, MA: Harvard University Press.

Welch, Catherine J. (1993, April). Issues in developing and scoring performance assessments. Paper presented at the Annual Meeting of the American Educational Research Association, Atlanta, GA.

West, Cornel. (1993). *Race matters*. Boston, MA: Beacon Press.

Wiggins, Grant P. (1993). *Assessing student performance: Exploring the purpose and limits of testing*. San Francisco, CA: Jossey-Bass Publishers.

Wiley, David E. and Haertel, Edward H. (1992, March). Extended assessment tasks: Purposes, definitions, scoring and accuracy. Paper prepared for the California Assessment Program.

Wolf, Dennie Palmer and Baron, Joan Boykoff. (1992). Thinking about strong performance assessment tasks and from tasks to portfolios. Presentation at a workshop co-sponsored by the Office of Testing, Evaluation and Research, San Francisco Unified School District; Performance Assessment Collaboratives for Education, Harvard Graduate School of Education; California Assessment Collaborative, February 27, 1992.

Wolf, Dennie, Bixby, Janet, Glenn, John III, Gardner, Howard. (1991). To use their minds well: Investigating new forms of student assessment. In Grant, G. (Ed.), *Review of Research in Education* Vol. 17, Washington, DC: American Educational Research Association, 31-74.

Yancey, Kathleen Blake. (1992). Portfolios in the writing classroom: A final reflection. In Yancey, Kathleen Blake (Ed.), *Portfolios in the writing classroom: An introduction*. Urbana, Illinois: National Council of Teachers of English.

Yancey, Kathleen Blake. (1994, April). Dialogue, interplay, and discovery: A rhetoric of reflection. Paper presented at Conference on Evaluating Writing through Portfolios: The State of the Art, Sponsored by the National Center for the Study of Writing, held at Stanford University.

Chapter 7

Voices
from the
Field

The endeavor to develop new forms of assessment that we have documented in various ways in this book has repeatedly been characterized as one that is building from the "grass roots." It is described by virtually every developer as an evolving process—a process that becomes defined fully only in the doing. This multifaceted and multiform endeavor is also one that demonstrates clearly the value of collective and collaborative thinking and will likely succeed only if educators at all levels and with various kinds of expertise continue to share, argue, and experiment. It is from this perspective that we have sought to include in the book both the commentaries at the end of chapters and the reports from colleagues in the field represented in this chapter. We imagined that readers would be tantalized (and occasionally sobered) by discussions of assessment system development and implementation—both the benefits and the challenges. Although many examples have been sprinkled throughout the book, there is nothing like a first-hand report from someone who is engaged in bringing about reform in the light of public scrutiny and in real time. It is one thing to propose new or reformed educational practices from the somewhat safe and often unchallenged position of theorizer, researcher, academician, or commentator. It is quite another to take the very public and risky step of reforming traditional educational practices without full confidence of the outcomes. It's not much of a mental stretch to liken it to the voyages of many explorers who sailed off across vast oceans or took off from launch pads with considerable uncertainty as to what challenges awaited them.

The accounts that follow represent a range of projects, experiences, points of view, geographic locations, and student cultural and ethnic backgrounds. The writers are teachers, district administrators, state-level administrators, clinicians, and researchers—with some falling in more than one category. We are very appreciative of these contributions, not least because they come from busy people who need all the time they can muster to do the jobs they have taken on. Moreover, we recognize that all of the efforts described are in progress and that, in some sense, all of these explorers are logging their journeys long before they are able to see their destinations on the horizon and with full knowledge that more turbulent waters await them. It is worth noting also that it was not easy for us to find examples of assessment explorations where those involved were truly paying attention early in the journey to issues of student diversity and ways to accommodate the needs presented by that diversity. We commend all of the contributors because they have responded to the challenge in exemplary ways: they have not addressed these issues only as an afterthought. We hope that other developers will borrow their good ideas.

Common threads across all of these accounts have to do with how assessment practices have been designed to meet the needs of all students, including those from culturally and linguistically non-dominant communities. Some of them relate to development processes and others to implementation. They represent a wide range of alternative assessment practices—development of performance-based tasks, student conferencing, administration and scoring, and use of portfolios.

These accounts are loosely organized according to whether they focus principally on issues related to the development of performance-based assessments or on issues related to implementation, including the relationship between assessment and instruction. For easy reference, the topics of these commentaries are listed below.

Development of Performance-based Assessments

Unschooled Immigrant Children: Developing an Assessment System that Makes Sense (Revising teacher belief systems to develop an assessment system for immigrant students in middle grades—Liz Wolfe, Redwood City School District, California)

Getting Beyond Simple Translation (Issues in translation and other assessment development practices that continue to marginalize members of non-mainstream linguistic and cultural communities—Verma Pastor, Arizona Department of Education).

The Evolution of the Alaska Direct Writing Assessment (Selection of prompts and scoring considerations in the development of a statewide writing assessment to be used with many different language groups—Judith Entwife, Alaska Department of Education)

Rosie's Walk and Other Stories: Teacher Development of Performance Tasks (Development of literature-based writing tasks by teachers in an urban setting for a diverse population of students—Robert Shorb, Alvord School District, Riverside, California)

Implementation and Connections to Instruction

"The test was explein with secretly words": Reflections on Performance Assessment of English Language Learners (Students' reactions to the experience of performance-based assessments in science—Dr. Jerome Shaw, Far West Laboratory, San Francisco, California)

Helping Diverse Students Take Charge of their Learning (Development of "frameworks" and strategies for students in a clinical setting—Dr. Susan Glazer, Rider University, New Jersey)

"I can tell why things happen": Student Self-reflection (Use of student-led conferences with classroom portfolios—Karen Mitchell and Bernie Sorenson, Juneau, Alaska, School District)

Student Projects on the Navajo Reservation (Changes in instruction as a result of a statewide performance-based assessment—Shirley Fields, Chinle School District, Arizona)

DEVELOPMENT OF PERFORMANCE-BASED ASSESSMENTS

Unschooled Immigrant Children: Developing an Assessment System that Makes Sense

Liz Wolfe is has been Director of Bilingual Education for the Redwood City School District in the San Francisco Bay Area since 1991. Redwood City is a district that has become increasingly diverse in recent years, and it has taken pride in its efforts to provide high-quality programs for immigrant students and others who are in the process of learning English. The district has sought alternatives in assessment that are informative and appropriate for its English language learners. Here, Ms. Wolfe talks about one program she has had a key role in developing.

For close to ten years, the Redwood City School District, located in the San Francisco Bay Area, has been faced with the challenge of a growing number of unschooled immigrant children enrolling in its elementary schools. Different educational programs, with varying degrees of success, designed to best meet the needs of these children, have been started, stopped, continued, and enhanced. Over the years, we have received anecdotal information from teachers suggesting that certain aspects of the programs seemed to be meeting the educational needs of the children, but, in 1993, we decided that more objective and quantifiable assessment information was needed.

Our project focused on the unschooled immigrant child enrolling in our middle schools (grades 6-8). This group of children seemed to be made up of those who faced the most challenges in "fitting in" to a traditional middle school structure. (In our district, there are approximately twenty children who enroll in our middle schools each year who have had less than a second grade education in their home countries). Our first step was to bring the teachers who worked with these students in the two middle schools together to discuss their programs, their experiences, their concerns and their beliefs about what the best educational program should be for what we began to call the "literacy" students. We spent a lot of time in these discussions, because even though all of the teachers believed very strongly in appropriate programs and high-quality instruction and curriculum, there was a variety of beliefs as to what this all should look like.

Through these discussions, we brought belief systems into focus—and into conflict. Debates continued over the issues of providing students with grade-level instruction (and the support necessary to be successful) in order that the program and its enrolled students might be seen to be of equitable status with the rest of the school and the need to start with the knowledge the students bring to the program and build from there.

Our project went on to develop standards and aligned authentic assessments in language arts and math to be used in our literacy program. This was a two-year process, with the end result being that we feel like we know now some of what we need to know to truly begin this project!

Through the powerfully enabling process of developing and scoring assessments, we were able to address our belief systems on how students learn. We now share the belief that the background from which the students come is a determining factor in what kind of instruction the children will succeed; in other words, we need to start with what the students know and build experiences for them that are relevant and meaningful.

We believe that every single day in school is essential to our literacy students. Every moment in a class in which a student is exposed to new material, has the opportunity to manipulate, read and discuss and work with other students, and is able to pursue special interests on his/her own brings him or her closer to the goal of being a successful, contributing participant in a rapidly changing world.

We believe that our English learning students learn best in the language in which they are most proficient. We are committed to educating students in their primary language so that they receive equal access to instruction and educational opportunities.

A by-product of this process that I feel to be outstanding is the type of questioning and discussing that takes place among the teachers involved in this project. All of the teachers agree that involvement in this project has helped them better "see the horizon"—where they are heading, and what they need to do to get there.

A program has now been defined for our literacy students; we call it the "Language and Literacy Academy." This program has standards for language arts and math and authentic assessment measures that will give us program information ("Did we teach this?") and student information (Did they learn it?"). A writing portfolio design will be implemented this year. Students at both middle schools who are new to the country and have less than 2nd grade skills in their primary language will be enrolled in this self-contained class that will be limited to no more than 15 students.

The remaining newcomer students will be incorporated into the existing bilingual programs at the two sites and taught with grade level materials and expectations. They will also be assessed in their primary language, as well as in English (to measure their progress in oral English fluency).

For the eighth year in a row, our middle school program looks different for our newly enrolling immigrant students. However, for the first time, we will be able to get more than anecdotal information about the effectiveness of the program. Students in the Language and Literacy Academy will be given an authentic assessment that will measure their growth in language arts and math after one year in the program. No standardized assessment exists that gives us this kind of information for this age population. Students enrolled in the grade level bilingual program will be given both standardized assessments (*Aprenda*) and our district developed performance based assessments (7th grade) in language arts and math in Spanish that measure their progress toward existing standards.

Are we finished revising our middle school program for unschooled immigrant students? Probably not. Are we finished examining our belief systems about what unschooled immigrant students need and are capable of? Definitely not. Finally, however, we are able to take real objective information about students from our assessments to help us in our program revisions and examinations. We can only get better.

Getting Beyond Simple Translation

Verma Pastor has been Director of Bilingual Education in the Arizona Department of Education since 1990. Pastor and her staff have worked both with Riverside Publishing Company, original developers of the Arizona Student Assessment Program (ASAP) assessments, and with colleagues in the Arizona Department of Education's ASAP unit to ensure that the assessments will be appropriate for English language learners and bilingual students. For speakers of Spanish, assessments in Spanish have been developed. For speakers of other languages, techniques for mediation of assessments have been recommended.

I think these new kinds of assessments are pointing out that *all* teachers, not just bilingual staff, need to understand language issues in relation to assessment. In Arizona, at least 35 percent of our students K-12 speak a language other than English in their homes. The state has formally recognized the value of bilingualism by mandating foreign language in elementary schools, but that doesn't mean children develop fluency. As a border state, we (Arizona) may benefit from NAFTA, because it may push some awareness of the advantages of bilingualism, at least for economic purposes; and it may push us beyond "Cómo estás?"

This is the larger context in which we are developing parallel ASAP assessments in Spanish, the language other than English spoken by the largest number of students. We have not yet resolved the issue of whether or how to develop ASAP assessments in some or all of the American Indian languages spoken in Arizona. Speakers of Navajo constitute the largest language group after Spanish-speakers, and we, along with our colleagues in Indian Education here at the Department, are in the process of determining how to address the needs of Navajo students. However, the issues we have faced in developing appropriate assessments in Spanish are undoubtedly basically the same ones that will have to be faced by test developers dealing with English language learners from any language community.

Our first big hurdle was working with the publisher to get beyond simple translation of the English assessments into Spanish. Our idea was to develop "parallel" assessments in Spanish, but it was not immediately evident to the publisher why you couldn't simply do a direct translation. So many words appear to translate easily. But there is a real difference between direct translation and wording something in another language in a way that speakers of that language would word it. The most obvious examples are idioms and figurative language (for example, "kick the bucket" or "the world was his oyster"—neither of which can be translated word-for-word into Spanish), but it is true with ordinary language as well.

Humor, in particular, is very difficult to translate. As an example, one of the twelfth-grade reading assessments used an excerpt from Russell Baker's autobiography, *Growing Up*. In English, the piece is quite funny, and the language, itself, contributes to the humor. At one point, Baker speaks of his mother's fear that he wouldn't make anything of himself. She said to her son, "You've got no more gumption than a bump on a log." At first, the publisher translated "bump on a log" as "un bordo en el tronco," a word-for-word translation that doesn't convey an equivalent meaning. "Gumption" was translated as "iniciativa," an accurate translation, as far as it goes. In a later translation, the whole reference to "bump on a log" was omitted. A sentence in which Baker noted that his mother had detected "distressing evidence of a bump budding on a log" was translated as "angustiosa evidencia de mi falta de ambición"—"distressing evidence of my lack of ambition." Again, the general idea comes across, but you can see how the sound of the original language added to the humor; and in Spanish the reader has to work very hard to discover that this is a humorous piece of writing. You can get the story in translation, but it loses the "juice." What kind of information about the reader's comprehension can we really be getting in such a case?

People often simply do not understand the issues in going from one language to another. Consistency in word choice is another matter. For example, different dialects of Spanish use different words for the same concept: bananas or plátanos, sombria or paraguas (umbrella). These are not interchangeable for speakers of a single dialect, so a choice has to be made, depending on whether most Spanish-speaking students are Mexican-American, Cuban-American, Nicaraguan-American, or from another background.

Another equally important issue came up in designing Spanish assessments in reading and writing. Do you simply use English-language authors? There is literature in Spanish; there are children's stories. We need to recognize that reading of good literature occurs in other languages, that there are other authors besides American and British. We think that to do a literacy assessment, we should go in search of authors writing in Spanish. We want to expose children to Mexican-American writers from our region, and others who are developing assessments in Spanish need to take their own locale into consideration. In New York, I am sure that it would make sense to look to Puerto Rican authors and, in Florida, to Cuban authors. There is no point in simply translating to Spanish from English.

Ensuring that the concepts being assessed in a second language match the concepts being assessed in English is a difficult problem. You don't need to duplicate exactly, but you do need to ensure that you are assessing essentially the same thing. I would say that choosing literature is the most difficult area. With ASAP, as we have tried to link reading, writing, and mathematics thematically, we have tended to start with the piece of literature and work from it to writing and mathematics; so that choice is critical. It is also very time-consuming.

I want to stress that bilingual staff often do not get to be involved in assessment development until there is a finished product in English. Typically there is no simultaneous development. This is a real problem. There should be bilingual staff on the assessment development team, because most educators do not have the kind of background in language acquisition or bilingualism to realize what the issues are. Staff from students' cultures need to participate from the beginning; and with large groups, you can't simply have one Spanish-speaking person, one Navajo-speaking person, and so on. Because of the power relations and money issues, those people will be marginalized—not through anyone's intentions; that's just how it tends to work. I do think that the experiences that publishers are having with states in developing assessments are making them realize the need for materials in other languages. Speakers of Spanish are the largest group, so materials are coming out in Spanish, such as Houghton Mifflin's Spanish literature series. (It is so important for self-concept to see your own language in print in the classroom. You understand what's going on; you feel good. I would like to see all children have this experience.)

There is one other issue that those in other states who are developing assessments in more than one language need to be aware of: If you are going to pilot the English language assessments, you should also pilot the second-language assessments. In Arizona, perhaps because we were a year behind in developing the assessments (in Spanish compared to English), we failed to pilot the Spanish assessments. In a way, this penalizes the Spanish speakers. It perpetuates a sense that they are behind, that they are something less. Of course, they *aren't* less; but they *become* less because they don't know English. Somehow intelligence gets confused with English proficiency, and teachers unconsciously assume children are less intelligent if they don't speak English well. When we allocate funding for assessment—or whatever—for "normal kids" and then find that there's no money left for "special populations," we communicate that these students are of less value or potential. I am hoping that Goals 2000 will push "special students" into the forefront, that we will think about them at the same time as we do "mainstream" students.

My advice to anybody is that if they are going to create new assessments, get a team going early with all languages represented as well as different grade levels. We need to be aware of language, and we need to be culturally sensitive. Even when content is chosen because it seems to be appropriate for children from a certain culture, it may not be sensitively used. For example, there was an assessment that included a story about a Navajo weaver. The name of the child in the story had been changed from a Navajo name to an English-sounding name because "the Navajo name was hard to pronounce." If there is anything people from non-mainstream cultures have been sensitive about, it is having their names changed or being forced to change them because people cannot pronounce them. If we all sat down together at the beginning rather than adapting or translating from what has already been developed, we would be far better off. It is one thing when you are invited to be a participating member from the beginning, and it's another to be asked just to review something after it has been done. You run into time crunches; people resent your criticisms or questions. People feel they don't have time to take your suggestions into consideration. There are always things they haven't thought of, and it is frustrating to them to have to redo what they thought was nearly complete. I think it is clear what needs to be done, and I hope that we have learned from the process we have gone through in Arizona. Perhaps others can learn from us as well.

The Evolution of the Alaska Direct Writing Assessment

Judith Entwife is the Language Arts Specialist for the Alaska Department of Education. Besides working with the Statewide Direct Writing Assessment, she has spearheaded the collaborative development of state English/Language Arts Standards and a framework for their implementation. This includes a document addressing current issues and a resource kit of materials supporting and expanding upon the content, instruction, assessment, and professional development sections of the document.

The Alaska Direct Writing Assessment is an evolving system. It began with discontent with the standardized test that was then the only way many students and programs were being evaluated in our state; developed through a phase of holistic scoring of student samples; and has become institutionalized as an analytic assessment. Similarly, the grade levels tested, the prompts, and the design for production of student samples have changed as we gain experience in identifying and meeting the needs of our state.

Like many states, Alaska responded to calls for educational accountability in the 1980s by mandating a nationally normed, standardized test. Because of concerns that these tests did not examine what Alaska educators valued in writing or the cultural diversity of our state, teachers began to look for something more authentic. In response to emerging research and practice as taught in Alaska State Writing Consortium institutes, educators moved away from teaching the discrete skills typically measured by standardized, multiple choice tests and began investigating ways to find out not students' relative knowledge *about* writing, but how well students actually *write*.

Teachers initially involved in ASWC institutes discussed and practiced holistic scoring. As more teachers received training, earned experience in the method, and returned to share what they had learned, there was growing dissatisfaction. "So if a paper gets a 3, what does that mean, really?" "How can I give a student . . . a score that reflects the fact that he has great ideas, but needs a lot of work on spelling?" "I need more clear, specific diagnostic information." After three years, ASWC leadership began to investigate other ways to assess writing.

In 1989, the Alaska Department of Education collaborated with the ASWC, the University of Alaska, and other school districts to conduct its first inter-district direct assessment of writing, using an analytic model of scoring. Student writing was evaluated by trained teacher/raters using a five-point scale to measure six traits: ideas and content, organization, voice, word choice, sentence structure, and conventions. The model so accurately reflected what Alaska educators believe is important in writing that more than half of the state's school districts have volunteered to participate each year, paying their teachers to travel to Anchorage to receive training and to rate papers from across Alaska. Further, parents, business people, and the community at large concurred; they supported a state standard that requires students to write well in six traits (slightly altered in nomenclature to be more clear to the general public). The State Board of Education adopted that standard as a regulation in 1994, along with a regulation encouraging performance assessments like the Direct Writing Assessment, institutionalizing the scoring method.

Evolution occurred, too, in grade levels assessed. When the assessment began as a pilot in 1989, students at the tenth grade level were asked to produce writing samples. In 1991, the Writing Assessment Advisory Group met to consider whether to continue at that grade level. The group, representing both urban and rural, largely Alaska Native districts, suggested that the assessment expand. Grade eleven was chosen over grade ten for the top end of the assessment, largely because it was near enough to graduation to give a sense of "exit abilities," yet still allowed students, teachers, and districts a chance to focus on revealed needs before graduation. Policy makers chose fifth grade for the low end. A high percentage of students in this state enter kindergarten or first grade speaking an Alaska Native language, and many rural schools and whole districts emphasize teaching writing in that first language. Waiting until fifth grade to assess writing statewide would allow those students to become proficient enough in English to participate fully. (Even then, Native words and phrases appear in student samples. As long as communication is not adversely affected by it, this does not lower any trait score. In fact, it has been known to enhance ratings of such traits as voice and word choice.) Interestingly, while the response to the fifth grade floor has been anticipated, popular demand has moved the high end assessment back to grade ten. We speculate that that was done because of the testing burden already experienced at eleventh grade.

Yet another area of the Alaska Direct Assessment that continues to evolve is prompts. Depending on what questions we hoped to answer in a given year, the number of prompts, genre, and choice among prompts have varied. Early assessments offered only one narrative prompt to which all students wrote in an effort to establish baseline information. One of those same narrative prompts was offered four years later to allow comparisons not only with the levels of student performance, but also the reliability of raters over time. Both proved positive. For four years, we randomly distributed prompts in three different genre to see if a common assumption among Alaska educators was true. Results showed no obvious differences in scores among those assigned "easy" genre (narrative/

imaginative) and those with "hard" ones (expository or persuasive). At the urging of teachers who expressed the need for students to have more control over the topic to do their best work, the Prompt Selection Committee provided a choice between two prompts within the assigned genre in 1993 and 1994. For 1995, the districts, rather than students, will be allowed to choose. New research indicating that prompts are seldom of equal difficulty and that students often choose to their own disadvantage led us to rethink student choice among prompts. District desire to focus on local goals influenced the state to give the choice of genre to the districts. The genre, themselves, however, seem to have stabilized with the passage of state standards in writing. As students are expected to write well "to inform, to describe, to entertain, to persuade," prompts will be constructed to elicit those genre.

The one thing that has remained the same through all these changes in prompts is the selection process. Again, in recognition of the diverse cultures in our state, Alaska looks to a representative committee to construct or choose prompts. Even something as seemingly universal as writing an article for the school newspaper, a letter to the editor of the local newspaper, or a letter to the mayor is meaningless to large numbers of Alaska students who populate villages across vast expanses of the State. There can be no understanding of implied audience or engagement on the part of students who have never experienced a newspaper of any kind and for whom elders, not elected officials, are the group to persuade to your view. Prompts are written or revised accordingly by teachers, curriculum specialists, and university representatives from Juneau to Kuspuk and Fairbanks to Bethel.

Certainly, equal care has been taken to make sure the directions for students to produce their samples reflect what we know about the writing process. While we originally thought two fifty-minute periods of writing on two different days was generous (and, indeed, teachers early on reported that that was more time than students needed), we quickly moved to three periods over three days to accommodate the pre-writing, drafting, revising, and editing that good instruction and the students themselves demanded. Now an advisory group has formed to collect research for review concerning time for peer response in the process. It is possible that the directions will evolve to include this aspect of writing as early as 1996. This kind of evolution will ensure that teachers of writing will continue to believe, as teachers who participated in the 1994 assessment say, the assessment "identifies well the critical parts of good writing," and "the rubric covers the areas I stress in writing workshop . . . " Likewise, novice teachers of the process will continue to find that, "going through the writing assessment helped me clarify my goals for teaching students to write."

We expect the Alaska Direct Writing Assessment to continue to evolve as our knowledge of instruction, assessment, and the needs of our local districts and their diverse student population grows.

Rosie's Walk *and Other Stories: Teacher Development of Performance Tasks*

Robert Shorb is the Coordinator of Special Projects in the Alvord Unified School District. He is responsible for categorical programs, testing and assessment, vocational education, and technology throughout the district. Because of these responsibilities, he is very interested in curriculum reform and the effects on student learning. It was the need to develop additional criteria for measuring student outcomes, besides the results of standardized tests, that initially motivated the move toward portfolio assessment in his district. As the work progressed, it became more apparent over time that the portfolio was a good tool for teachers to assess their own curriculum and success with students and how their learning is developing over time.

In 1985, the Alvord Unified School District had an enrollment of 9,000 students; the population had grown to 16,000 in 1995. During this same span of time, the Limited English Proficient (LEP) population grew from 700 students to 3,000. One of the resultant challenges has been to find ways to maintain and improve the learning climate for this rapidly expanding and diverse population of students.

In the district's search to find a solution to some of the learning dilemmas, the development and use of authentic assessments came to be seen as a vehicle that policymakers in the district felt would address many of the concerns about student learning. The district selected a nationally-known consultant to provide teachers and administrators the background necessary to implement a reading and writing program based on performance assessment. The consultant began by providing elementary teachers a full day of inservice on how to develop reading and writing activities with accompanying rubrics to score them. He also gave teachers the basics for starting to implement the practice of using student portfolios. He has followed up the initial workshop by providing additional workshops for teachers at all grade levels during the past three years.

Following the initial inservice, grade-level teams of teachers were brought together to write activities similar to those being used in the language arts portion of the California Learning Assessment System (CLAS) tests for students. These activities are based on the grade level literature series, using such stories as *Rosie's Walk* and *Brown Bear, Brown Bear*. These reading and writing activities were designed to fit into the student's regular instructional program during a defined time of the year, and they incorporate both group and individual work. The activities conclude by having the student write to a prompt, which gives them a reason to write and an audience to address. Student responses are then scored utilizing a rubric that the teachers have developed for that particular prompt. Anchor papers selected from actual student responses are used to assist with the scoring. These scores are then collected and compiled by the district for each student. This information provides additional evidence of the student's learning progress that supplements the student's standardized test scores. This year the writing activities were duplicated in Spanish for Spanish-speaking LEP students.

The district is now in its fourth year of having students do the writing activities and keeping portfolios. The writing activities have been revised, and some have been rewritten as teachers' knowledge and understanding of the process and student outcomes of performance assessments have evolved.

The purpose of having teachers participate in these authentic assessment tasks has been as much for them to re-think their instructional strategies and techniques as it has been an attempt to gain additional information about students. The process of portfolio assessment has been relatively successful in that teachers are now making decisions based on student work, rather than just using a textbook for a learning guide. The practices of doing the writing activities and keeping student work in portfolios are in place in the district, and many teachers have become quite proficient in the process. Other teachers are very resistant and see it as just something else the district is requiring them to do—rather than viewing it as an integral part of their instructional program.

Preliminary indications are that it has resulted in most teachers having a better understanding of how their students think and learn. It has also broadened teachers' perceptions of their students' capabilities. Most teachers see the benefits of having students maintain portfolios, a process that incorporates cooperative work, performance-based tasks, and student self-reflection on their learning over time. Teachers also find the portfolios a very powerful tool when conferencing with parents about how their children are doing because the actual evidence of what the student is doing is right there.

The district has given all elementary and intermediate schools a $1,500 stipend that is shared by two or three teachers for the purpose of supporting and advancing authentic assessment practices at their sites. The teachers who receive this stipend have responsibility for insuring that information about the writing activities and portfolios get to all teachers in a timely manner. The Learning Facilitators also serve as a resource for new teachers and/or those experiencing difficulties with performance-based assessment and/or the portfolio process.

The district is finding that the established practice of utilizing the writing activities and portfolios are very beneficial for a variety of purposes such as Program Quality Reviews and Coordinated Compliance Reviews (statewide monitoring and evaluation processes used in California). A wealth of information about student work collected in the portfolios is available to individual teachers, the school, and the district. One of the emerging challenges has been how to effectively manage all the additional information.

The keeping of portfolios containing the teacher-designed writing activities are important in a multicultural setting because they require teachers to communicate with each other about what the students are doing. Many of the activities also require the students to work with each other in groups. The resultant student products in the portfolios provide evidence that all students have talents and skills that probably would not be recognized if only traditional instructional and assessment practices were being utilized. The use of portfolios allows each student to include things they like and are proud of in their learning experience.

The portfolios provide the student with evidence of their learning which clearly demonstrates to them, their parents, and the teacher the progress they are making. This capacity to demonstrate student learning provided by the portfolios has a very powerful impact on all students and their parents regardless of their background.

IMPLEMENTATION AND CONNECTIONS TO INSTRUCTION

"The test was explein with secretly words": Reflections on Performance Assessment of English Language Learners[1]

A former elementary and secondary science teacher, Jerome M. Shaw is a science specialist with Far West Laboratory. He recently completed his Ph.D. at Stanford University, where his dissertation focused on using performance assessment with high school science students whose native language is other than English. For this work he received the Outstanding Dissertation Award from the National Association for Research in Science Teaching.

Performance assessment holds the promise of providing a more equitable measure of student performance. This is particularly true when hands-on assessment is aligned with similarly oriented curriculum and instruction. Such congruence can readily be found in inquiry-based science classrooms utilizing performance-based assessments. Nevertheless, serious concerns arise when such techniques are used to assess the academic achievement of ELLs.

I am an educator concerned with the reform of science education and the education of linguistically diverse students. After more than a decade of classroom teaching, I turned to research with just such students. Although recently graduated as an educational researcher, my heart is in teaching. More specifically, I maintain an avid interest in the learning experiences of students, especially those from diverse ethnic and linguistic backgrounds.

Performance assessment has promise and peril. As a former science teacher, I can appreciate the elegance and alignment of performance assessment and hands-on instruction. It is in some ways a new and others an old feature in science education reform. Hands-on evaluations such as lab practicals are a long-standing staple of laboratory science classes. However, only a select group of students were privy to such courses. Current reform efforts call for an inclusive approach in which all students are the beneficiaries of a rigorous science education. Widespread use of performance assessment is often an integral part of this vision. For my doctorate, I investigated the implementation of a performance assessment in high school science classes composed of and designed for ELLs. The results of this research form the basis of my comments.

The students in my study represented seven non-English language backgrounds, primarily Spanish and Vietnamese, and possessed an intermediate level of proficiency in English. The teachers were veteran science instructors with training in and experience with instructing ELLs. The performance assessment was designed to measure science content knowledge and process skills over a span of four 50-minute class periods, alternate days of which were spent in group and individual work. Everyday instruction and the sample assessment were provided in English only. Nonetheless, linguistic support was available to students from their peers, bilingual and English language dictionaries, and occasional teacher translation (Spanish only).

In this as in any ELL assessment context, a central issue is to what extent the assessment functions as a measure of ELLs' proficiency in English or the domain in question, scientific literacy in this case. Feedback from both students and teachers involved in the study shed light on this dilemma.

Through words and action, it was evident that, as with mainstream populations, ELLs responded favorably to the active, hands-on nature of performance assessment. Many students described the assessment as enjoyable and educational. Take, for example, this comment from a Vietnamese junior on a post-assessment questionnaire:

The [performance assessment] was really fun and exciting because I can learn a lot of things that I really don't know.

During the actual assessment, several students expressed the desire to continue working on the day's task. Such interest was motivated by a positive engagement with the activity as well as frustration with the time allotment. As a Filipina sophomore explained: *I don't like the test because I don't finish the experiment, then the bell will ring!*

There were several sources for this "time tension" that are germane to ELLs. First, teachers spent considerable time and effort "scaffolding" the assessment—for example, reading instructions aloud, and providing numerous verbal and visual clues for key terms and concepts. While promoting student comprehension, time spent in these activities thus diminished the amount of time students had to engage directly with the task.

Second, students themselves often struggled with understanding what the assessment was asking them to do. As the title for this commentary implies (words written by a Latino sophomore), comprehension of English vocabulary was an issue. A Vietnamese sophomore commented: *Sometimes I don't understand what did the test want to talk?*

Specifically, difficulty with English comprehension was cited as being related to two factors: vocabulary level and sentence length. In addition, ELLs expressed anxiety over having to respond in written English. One Vietnamese senior commented: *I don't like take the test have much writting because it very diffcult for me when I writting.*

These difficulties have several implications for the use of performance assessment with ELLs. One observation would be to seriously consider time requirements placed on ELLs when being assessed. Possible solutions include augmenting the time allotted for mainstream students to removing a time restriction altogether. Such decisions should be made with respect to the measurement intent of the assessment—for example, is speediness of response an ability under scrutiny?

Design-wise, assessments intended for use with ELLs should be carefully reviewed for clarity of communication. In acknowledgment of the fact that some concepts or language neither can nor should be "dummied down," emphasis should be placed on "contextualizing" language. This includes accompanying text with informative illustrations along with the above-described "scaffolding" techniques. The requested form of student response is another design feature deserving serious consideration. For ELLs, the decision needs to be made whether or not responding in a language other than English is permissible. Such a choice can only be granted given the availability of raters who can score such responses. The involvement of a native Spanish speaker and my own bilingual ability made such an option available to Spanish-speaking students in the study. However, the responses of those students who chose to reply in Spanish displayed a lack of proficiency in the native language (that is, spelling and grammatical errors necessitated the "translation" of these responses into comprehensible Spanish).

Beyond choice of language, performance assessments can also provide flexibility in type of written representation—text, charts, drawings, and so on. ELLs in the study made ample use of opportunities provided to "use illustrations as part of your answer." Such enhancements often assisted raters in fully understanding a student's response and thus assigning an accurate score.

Teacher guidance surfaced as a significant factor for improving the delivery of performance assessment to ELLs. Teachers welcomed the opportunity to provide such help (for example, the above-mentioned "scaffolding") while students cited such assistance as highly beneficial. Explained a Latina freshman: *The questions was easy so when we don't know English we can asked the teacher what you don't know and the teacher can explain your question.*

Such guidance needs to be provided with care. Teachers may take liberty to clarify instructions or questions for students to the extent that the assessment is still able to perform its measurement function. What needs to be avoided is explaining a concept or procedure whose possession, comprehension, or use is intended to be measured by the assessment. This is akin to the difference between helping a student understand a question versus giving away the answer.

As implied in a previous comment, scoring responses of ELLs on performance assessments is another area deserving serious attention. The focus of my comments here is on the scoring of responses written in English by ELLs. As a practical matter, it was found that reading "difficult" responses aloud aided raters' understanding and subsequent reliable scoring. The "difficulty" of these responses is related to English spelling, semantics, and syntax expressed by ELLs. Many of these constructions are "typical" for transitional users of English and bear resemblance to the ELLs' native language. For example, it is common for a native Spanish speaker to substitute the letters "th" for "d" as in writing "thoes" for "does." Knowledge of such constructions, preferably born from first-hand experience with ELLs, is an important prerequisite for raters of ELL responses, especially in high-stakes circumstances.

In summary, my experience with the use of performance assessment with ELLs leads to several practical recommendations. These can be framed around the categories of assessment design, delivery, and the decisions one makes based on the results. (See Tables 7.1 through 7.4.)

Performance assessments should be designed to maximize student comprehension of what the task is asking them to do. Relevant strategies include accompanying text with illustrations and providing examples of important concepts.

Teachers should be allowed to deliver performance assessments to ELLs in a manner that again emphasizes student comprehension of the assessment's demands. Additionally, ELLs should be provided sufficient time to respond completely to an assessment. Each of these actions needs to be undertaken in a manner that does not compromise the measurement intent of the assessment.

Finally, decisions made regarding the accuracy or adequacy of an ELL's response should be made after applying concerted efforts to ensure rater comprehension of a response. Effective strategies include reading challenging responses aloud and assuring that the rater is knowledgeable of typical English constructions made by ELLs. Taken together, these actions can do much to realize equitable measurement promised by performance assessment.

Endnote

1. "English Language Learners" (ELLs) refers to students whose first language is not English, and encompasses both students who are just beginning to learn English (often referred to as "limited English proficient" or "LEP") and those who have already developed considerable proficiency. The term underscores the fact that, in addition to meeting all academic challenges that face their monolingual peers, these students are mastering another language... The term follows conventional educational usage in that it focuses on what students are accomplishing, rather than on any temporary "limitation" they face prior to having done so. (LaCelle-Peterson, M. & Rivera, C. (1994). Is it real for all kids? A framework for equitable assessment policies for English language learners. Harvard Educational Review, 64(1), 55-75. p. 55)

TABLE 7.1

**Summary of Design Attributes of the
Science Performance Assessment**

Favorable	**Unfavorable**
• Clear Procedures With Illustrated Instructions	• Unclear Questions with Difficult Vocabulary and Long Sentences
• Groupwork	• Individual Work
• Intellectual Challenge	• Simple Problem
• Practical Applications	• Lack of Practical Applications
• Hands-on Activities	• Excessive Time for Completion (Day One)
	• Too Open-Ended (Day One)
	• Insufficient Time for Completion (Days Three and Four)
	• Lengthy Text Responses (Days Two and Four)

TABLE 7.2

**Student Recommendations Specific to
Performance Assessments**

Orientation	Recommendations
Student-Centered	• Don't Be Nervous
	• Follow the Steps One-by-One
	• Be Really Careful, Pay a lot of Attention, and Work Together as a Group
	• Apply What You Know and Try to do the Best You Can
Teacher-Centered	• Explain the Meaning of Words with Simpler Words and Examples
	• Give Us More Time
	• Guide the Students so They Know What to Do
Test-Centered	• Don't Give Us so Many Questions or Something We Can Hardly Understand
	• Write the Sentences More Easy to Understand
	• Be Specific
	• Graphing Question Need to be Change
	• We Need More Times to Finish and Complete the Test

TABLE 7.3

Teacher Recommendations for Improving Performance Assessments

Orientation	Recommendation
Student-Centered	• Do a Team-Building Activity for Student Groups
Teacher-Centered	• Make Instructions and Directions Comprehensible for Students by Using Visuals Such as Pictures, Diagrams, and Drawings
	• Provide Information to Students in a Prescribed Format
Test-Centered	• Use Simple Language on Student Written Materials (e.g., Shorter Sentences, Simpler Concepts)
	• Allow Two Hours for Each Day of the Assessment, With up to 20 Minutes of that Time Each Day for Teacher Orientation - Instruction
	• Have Students Work in Pairs for Groupwork Sessions

Table 7.4

Recommendations Resulting from the Scoring Session

Orientation	Recommendations
Student-Centered	• Provide Instruction on the Content Being Assessed
	• Discuss Performance Standards Prior to the Assessment
Teacher-Centered	• Be Familiar with Either Students' Native Languages or Transitional Expressions of English Literacy or Both
	• Participate in the Development of Tasks and Rubrics
Rubric-Centered	• Reduce the Number of Criteria
	• Accompany Rubrics with "Decision Trees"
Task-Centered	• Calibrate the Soup Cans (EP)
	• Tell Students to Draw a Line Graph
	• Direct Students to Cite the Source of Their Specific Evidence

Helping Diverse Students Take Charge of their Learning

Dr. Susan Mandel Glazer is Director of the Center for Reading and Writing at Rider University in Lawrenceville, New Jersey, and past president of the International Reading Association. She is also the author of Portfolios and Beyond.

The Center for Reading and Writing serves a diverse population of students, ages six to sixteen. Gifted, average, and learners with special academic needs are referred for development with oral and written language skills. During the school year, they come primarily from ten to twelve districts in a metropolitan area of New Jersey and Pennsylvania. The summer program is attended by students from all over the East Coast, including Florida, New York, and Connecticut. The students come from many ethnic and socioeconomic backgrounds. We have Asian-American students, Spanish-speaking students, quite a number of inner-city Trenton students, high-socioeconomic status immigrant students from Europe for whom English is a second language, along with middle-class White students from both ethnically isolated and integrated settings. In this past school year, we enrolled twelve homeless children, one who had been shifted from family to family.

Some students come to the Center for enrichment and others because they are experiencing reading, writing, and language difficulties in school. Our program works on all aspects of language. Some students may use a variety of dialects of English to communicate; others lack control over certain aspects of language, such as awareness of story structure or the ability to use an elaborate vocabulary—despite adequate oral interactive skills. We have found, for example, that some of our Asian-American students have adequate language skills but are overly cautious about making errors. It seems that they are concerned with using "correct English," and rather than making an oral error, many choose to say nothing. Other students have a sense of story structure but do not have a sufficient command of English to compose in their second language. Some students, often those who speak Spanish and others who are language-delayed, have particular difficulty with pronouns. Generally, however, there are a lot of similarities in needs. We challenge all of our students to high-quality performance. We do this by guiding students to be in charge of their own learning. This is achieved by using a series of frameworks that guide children to read and respond to text. The same frameworks are used by all children, ages five through sixteen. This provides consistency and, therefore, security which facilitates growth over time. Our teachers get away from empty praise, such as "very good" or "terrific." They will say, instead, "It is important that you wrote the story in English. You will learn to use the language that way!" This provides feedback that helps them confirm behaviors and gives them the impetus to repeat desired behaviors. During the school year, students are seen once a week for two hours (3:30 to 6:00 p.m.).

During the summer, we have an intensive program of three and one-half hours per day, three days a week for the month of July. We use self-monitoring portfolios successfully to accommodate the needs of all kinds of learners. Our structured system permits self-assessment that guides and informs students of their strengths and needs. Children, in turn, inform parents of their progress in a parent/child/teacher conference. Of course, we use what we learn from portfolio (alternative) assessment to plan instruction.

Our alternative assessment process begins by identifying strengths and needs and then aligning those to a plan of instruction. We observe students' oral and written comprehension in response to listening and reading, written and oral composition, independence, and vocabulary development. These categories also provide the format of students' portfolios. We use a combination of standardized and authentic assessment tools that we have developed to guide instruction. The alternative assessment tools are often used as instructional frameworks. For example, a child's retelling of a story is recorded on audiotape and analyzed using one of our frameworks. The child will learn to use the framework, which teaches them the language used to describe story structure. Children will realize that the story elements that they recalled after reading are those that they need to use to compose their own stories. It is important to listen to students' oral language because that often informs us about their writing. All assessment and instruction involves students. Students are engaged in ongoing reflection; they create their own ongoing assessment guide showing "What I know (have studied)," "What I need to learn." We guide children to self-monitor ("I included an introduction . . .", and so on). Our focus is always on guiding students to see their own growth.

Dialogue is a major tool used for all activities. Everybody dialogues with their teacher in a journal. Another form of interchange is using "mailboxes." Kids post letters to each other and to faculty and staff in envelopes on the wall; teachers, custodians, and observers who visit write back to children. Students are given additional opportunities to interact orally because we work with the students in groups of six to ten; we believe that interaction is very important for growth. In initial sessions, we assess in groups of two to four students. We use collaboration even in more formal testing because we believe we learn more about what students can do when we see them interacting with their peers.

Over time we have worked hard to develop strategies for making our assessment and instruction unbiased and as culture-fair as possible. For example, our materials are free of pictures that "decorate." We have found it very risky to use visuals from commercial materials as they are often theatrical. A seemingly innocuous drawing, for example, of a teacher standing over a child may not match a child's expectations and could be offensive. Most instructional strategies, if culture-fair, can be used across content and ability levels. Choral reading, using multiple copies of a text (drawing on multicultural literature) are appropriate for most students. Our goal is to focus on strategies that students of many cultures, abilities, religious groups, both sexes—groups that value different kinds of information and texts—can use. We want children to take these strategies with them as they study through varied contexts in school. In some ways, teachers need to stay out of the way and use consistent frameworks that permit children to take charge of their learning. Perhaps the most important tool we use to assess student strengths and needs is observation. But good observation (and interpreting what one sees as it relates to instruction) depends on knowledge of human and academic development and how to interpret behaviors in light of developmental characteristics. Teachers need to know a lot about developmental stages, especially about language, language use, and cultural factors in learning.

Finally, I want to stress the importance of the conferencing process in using portfolios. We do a lot of conferencing. Parents are informed by their children about what they are doing. We use a checklist matched to our instructional practices to guide these child/parent/teacher conferences. These facilitate children's discussions about their learning and progress. The conference guide checksheets are continuously revised for clarity of language and ideas. We want to share with parents, learn from them, and develop a common language for talking together about their child's learning. When classroom and community discourse come together, students stand a better chance of success with literacy and with learning in general.

"I can tell why things happen":
Student Self-reflection

Karen Mitchell is an elementary Language Arts Specialist (Chapter 1 and Migrant Education) in the Juneau, Alaska School District. For the last eight years, she has taught 3rd grade. She also has spent ten years teaching 5th, 2nd, a 1st-2nd combined, and a pre-first grade class.

Over the last four years, including prior to the implementation of the Juneau School District's formal portfolio program in the third grade, I have been using student-led conferences in my third grade classroom. Student-kept working portfolios used as a means of collecting work for these conferences helped to solve the problem of how to compile work and where to keep it. Our portfolios have mainly consisted of language arts and math sections, accompanied by projects from other curricular areas to be presented at the conference. The scored writing assessment entries coordinated by the district have also been included as an integral part, as well as student self-reflections, teacher narratives, and letters from parents. In reviewing these portfolios, students and parents had sample work from each previous quarter to compare with the present one. Except for the writing assessment samples and the student-corrected record of spelling lists taken from the Sitton list[1] along with weekly paragraphs and dictation exercises, none of the language arts material in our portfolios was scored numerically.

Artifacts from these working classroom portfolios have been used in the Juneau School District's formal language arts portfolios, which are compiled throughout the elementary school years. These more "formal" and cumulative portfolios contain student- and teacher-selected writing and reading samples, marked developmental continuums (similar to the *California Learning Record* scales), assessments, student self-reflections, and teacher narratives. Each year since its inception in 1991, an additional grade level has been added to the district portfolio process, so that, at a district level, the portfolios now contain cumulative information from first through fourth grades, with fifth grade entries being planned for this year. For purposes of clarity, the formal district portfolio and the working, classroom portfolio will be distinguished as such in the text of this narrative.

I began working with student-led conferencing as a result of being associated with Terri Austin, an elementary teacher from Fairbanks, Alaska. Through the years I've taught, I have had the reading and special education teachers in our school, along with parents and practicum students from the University of Alaska, Southeast, help with the children's evaluations. The Harborview Elementary School faculty has been wonderfully supportive in meeting with their former students to reflect on the work of previous years. On a number of occasions, they helped my students practice giving their conferences, as did students in district fifth grade and middle school classes.

Along with another colleague, as a result of my practice with and "fine-tuning" of student-led conference procedures, I have now done extensive training throughout the Juneau school district in the use of student-led conferences and the development of working, classroom portfolios. The Juneau School District administration, especially Annie Calkins, Director of Curriculum and Evaluation, has been exceptionally supportive and instrumental in providing training opportunities for me.

Last year, among my 26 students, I had several from Mexico who were Spanish speakers, at different stages of linguistic development, depending on the number of years they had been in the United States. I had two

Filipino boys who spoke their dialect at home, as well as a Thai student who was adopted into an English-speaking family two years ago. There were also Alaska Native students who had second language influence, although they came from English-speaking homes. One student was multilingual in Spanish, Farsi, and English. Over the years, I have also had a number of Tlingit children who, although they speak English as a first language, have been greatly influenced by their ancestral language. This rich mix of cultures and languages is entirely representative of the population of Harborview School as a whole, as we have had a great growth of immigrant families in the last few years.

As I have worked with student-led conferencing during these years, I have refined the students' working portfolio to become an accumulation of the whole year's work in our classroom in all subject areas. Each student, in collaboration with me or another teacher with whom s/he works closely, compiles and arranges the portfolio at each conference period. Each portfolio reflects that individual student, and I can't say that in the overall process I have done things much differently for culturally or linguistically diverse children. The reason for this feeling may come from the fact that this process is a relatively new experience for all students, and each step must be carefully explained and discussed with each of them for successful implementation. Each child and family contributes to the classroom portfolio; each one is unique.

In the implementation of this process, I have noticed a difference in the ability of English as a Second Language children to evaluate themselves and explain to their parents how they are doing in school. This was especially true last year when, for the first time, I had a number of students (rather than an isolated *one* I had usually had in previous years) who were not native speakers of English. Because of this, I had to do a lot of confidence building and explaining in the first quarter as I introduced the concept of student-led conferences. Before starting on the classroom portfolios, I held a session in which the children worked in groups to define what it meant to be a learner, a risk-taker, and a team member. Each group, which had been assigned one topic, had an adult monitor, and brought back their list of traits to the class, who added more. These notions were reinforced by self-evaluations in each subject where the children had to write about themselves in terms of those subjects. Any student who needed it got individual help and was able to dictate. Students who needed translation or language-based assistance were helped by the bilingual teacher. She also contacted parents to talk to them, in their home language if possible, about the importance of the conferences, explaining how to allow their child to take the lead. In some respects, I feel these bilingual conferences were some of the most successful. The children shared their portfolios with parents in their own language; the parents, in turn, asked questions and shared concerns with them. The message of what a student had learned was conveyed directly instead of through me; children had to confer with parents and teachers, read and understand different types of narratives and letters written by themselves, parents, and teachers; and they had to make a working plan with their parents to improve and set goals for the next quarter.

In one of the conferences I observed (my role is as an overall observer and sometimes participant with the three to four conferences that are occurring simultaneously), Selena was showing her father her graph for spelling tests. I understand Spanish well enough that I was able to follow their conversation. It was evident that she hadn't been studying, and the father shared that concern with her. Together Selena and her father talked about a plan to study the words. By the next quarter's conference, her scores improved considerably, along with the spelling in her written work.

Each classroom portfolio had all the "standard" entries of the district portfolio, but the work contained within Selena's was reflective of her progress each quarter, and there was a wider array of subject matter. The affective section of the classroom portfolios contains a behavior checklist with a comparative side to show progress over two quarters; a short narrative from another teacher in the building with whom each child had to arrange an interview in the first quarter, describing how that teacher saw the child as a learner, as a team member, and as a risk-taker; and a letter from the parent to the child, telling how that parent saw his or her child as a person in the world as well as a student, and some goals they had for the child during his or her third grade year.

I would say that I got the smallest number of parent letters from bilingual parents, perhaps because I didn't really take enough time to explain the letter to them, or have the bilingual teacher contact them early enough in the year to tell them they could write them in Spanish or another home language. I would be more cognizant of this fact in the future, so that all of the children would have letters to read over with their parents on the day of their conference.

The adaptations I tried with the ESL children were not apart from the rest of the class, because *all* of the children were figuring out what self-evaluation was, and they all needed to discuss and explore this issue for themselves. When I introduced the behavior checklist, I read each statement aloud and circulated around the room to be sure everyone understood and gave their best evaluation of themselves at the time. Students who wished could go ahead and complete it on their own. Sometimes I would explain a short sentence in Spanish, or have the bilingual teacher help later if I didn't know. For the Thai student, I did as much as I could with the class, and then later he worked with the resource teacher one-on-one to gain more understanding. Because the checklist was simple and understandable to begin with, most students gained understanding and internalized it as they used it during the year. Debriefing sessions after lessons and frequent self-evaluation also helped when doing this evaluation for the portfolio.

The language arts section of the classroom portfolio was the most extensive. The resource teacher and I adapted the Harborview Reading Skills Profile for everyone. This profile contains things commonly found on checklists, such as frequently used word attack strategies, ability to sustain silent reading, and comprehension strategies. Instead of the adult-oriented language on the original profile, such as "cause and effect," we substituted statements like "I can tell why things happen." This adaptation helped all students understand what was involved in the reading process. This profile was done individually with each child each quarter. It brought about conversations about how evaluations were done. It helped show the child examples of how s/he demonstrated that skill, and I shared my own anecdotal notes with her/him. Since three of us shared responsibilities during the reading block in my classroom (myself, the resource teacher, and the bilingual teacher), we shared the responsibility of these reading evaluations with the children, and all helped the children prepare that section of their portfolios. There is very little we kept secret: except for the most sensitive issues, children were involved in or aware of issues involved in every parent conference or home contact.

Before we began doing the reading and writing self-evaluations, I led a cooperative group lesson in which the children had to read examples of third grade self-evaluations written by other third grade children. Using an overhead, the samples were read aloud by the class and then were re-read in groups. They were then to discuss the examples, and rate them weak, average, or strong. After they were finished, we came together to review the results and the reasons for their ratings. Almost every group rated the same one the weakest, because it was merely a short statement saying "I've improved."

On a large piece of chart paper, I listed their criteria for an effective narrative: it is specific, and addresses not only spelling and mechanics, but also story characteristics such as order, voice, and other traits (my words used to paraphrase theirs). After this exercise, the children wrote their own evaluations while looking at the pieces in their writing folders. They also chose one or two to represent the quarter in their classroom portfolio. Any child who wished could dictate their evaluation, and they were free to write their narrative in their home language, although none chose to do so. A few of the stories they had chosen as samples were in Spanish, however, and the two students who were proficient in written Spanish before coming to the United States continued to write some pieces throughout the year.

In the third quarter, the Thai student chose a piece he had written about his trip from Thailand with his new family and his feelings at the time. He chose this piece of writing over another I had recommended to him as more polished, explaining that because it was more personal (my wording) and meant more to him it should be the one to go into the portfolio. This showed a huge improvement, both in his language skills and his ability to self-reflect in English. In the beginning of the year, we had merely asked him, "Which one do you like?", and he had picked one with no understanding of why he had picked it, other than to share it with his parents.

I don't think there is anything magic about working with second language children. I believe that treating them as everyone else is a large part of the "answer" to effective instruction. We must support their needs as a matter-of-fact part of the normal day, just as we would help any child. If we make sure that all the children have frequent opportunities to be part of small group and individual work, then no one feels outside of the normal happenings of the class. Because children are looking at their own strengths and celebrating what they can do well directly with their parents at conference time and discussing weaknesses in a problem-solving atmosphere, children receive affirmation and are able to set realistic learning goals.

In the portfolio and student-led conferencing in my class, it has been imperative, whenever possible, to affirm the children's and the parent's use of their first language in school as well as in the home. This affirmation has led to several excellent, whole-class discussions about other languages, and how children who do not speak English feel when immersed in an English-speaking environment for the first time. Most of the time, all of us want to feel the same, and then, at times, we want to feel special. Celebrating differences comes with the individual choices contained in each portfolio: in the child's choice of reading to be represented, in the chosen piece of writing each quarter. Most of all, inviting parents into the classroom to celebrate and discuss the portfolio at conference time with their child, as well as giving them a voice in the portfolio process, brings it all together.

Endnote:

1. Sitton, R. (1993) *Rebecca Sitton's Spelling Sourcebook.* Spokane, WA: Rebecca Sitton.

Response to Karen Mitchell

Bernie Sorenson is Supervisor, ESL and Title VII/Multicultural Education Programs, Juneau School District. Before his three years as Title VII Coordinator, he was the Reading Specialist at Harborview School for four years, and a Chapter 1 and first grade teacher in Montana.

As the supervisor for the ESL and Title VII multicultural programs in the Juneau School District (JSD), I have spent many hours reading and researching appropriate forms of assessment for the linguistically and culturally diverse students in our district. My research has led me to believe that portfolio assessment and student-led conferences are two very promising practices. Both forms of assessment support current research (Cummins, 1986; Hornlar-Fradd & McGee, 1994; Navarrette, 1993) in the field of language development for diverse populations, which leads one to the conclusion that our assessments should better be able to tell us when our LEP students have reached full English language proficiency. Currently, most assessments of English language proficiency are not sufficient and often perpetuate the myth that if a students *sounds* proficient, then he must be proficient in all areas of language performance. Cummins (1981) believes that the perpetuation of this myth also tends to diminish educators' awareness of the difficulties students have in developing broad academic skills.

Portfolio assessment and student-led conferences such as the ones used in Juneau have the potential to eliminate this myth about our LEP students. With these types of assessments, students are required to demonstrate their knowledge and use of the English language in a variety of contexts. For example, an LEP student in Karen Mitchell's classroom would be expected to collect evidence that he is progressing over a period of time. This student would be asked to articulate and set learning goals and finally be able to sit down with his parent and discuss his learning goals, achievements, and needs. In order for a student to be able to do this successfully, he must develop the ability to apply ideas and information in a variety of contexts, synthesize what he knows, draw conclusions and inferences, analyze information, and determine its relevance and applicability to his life. The student must finally be able to evaluate his performance in relation to goals and make judgments. All of these skills demand a deeper understanding of the English language.

The portfolio process used by the JSD also demands this kind of English language knowledge from their LEP student population. In the district portfolio process, students are not required to conference with their parents; however, they *are* asked to set goals and write self-reflections as early as grade one, and more and more teachers like Karen Mitchell are figuring out ways to have students demonstrate a deeper understanding of themselves as learner, risk takers, and team members.

In summary, when teachers are asked to involve their LEP students in assessment processes such as portfolios and student-led conferences, we are, in a sense, setting higher expectations for the English language development of all of our LEP students.

Student Projects on the Navajo Reservation

Shirley Fields is a fifth-grade teacher at Many Farms Elementary School in Chinle Unified School District, Chinle, Arizona. She has taught in the district for 12 years. Ms. Fields is part of a group of fifth-grade teachers in the district who have been working with an outside consultant to develop a portfolio assessment system that can be used for both classroom assessment and statewide accountability purposes. (The project is discussed briefly in Chapter 7.) Teachers have designed complex performance tasks that assess multiple "Essential Skills" (skills that the state of Arizona requires students to master and be assessed on) as well as student learning in terms of locally-developed, culturally-congruent standards. Here, Ms. Fields talks about her own experiences with moving toward a new kind of assessment system and takes us through an activity she designed to help her students develop the capacity to engage in more complex, open-ended tasks. The reader can see the numerous ways in which Ms. Fields scaffolds the students' participation, as well as the kinds of specific performance criteria she believes her students will need to be aware of in order to make a final presentation successfully.

I believe it is essential to briefly describe Many Farms Elementary School, the district in which it functions, and its communities. This description will substantiate much of what I want my audience to become aware of. Many Farms Elementary School is part of one of the biggest school districts on the Navajo Reservation, Chinle Unified School District, a district that emerged in the 1960s. It serves children from a wide geographical area. There are about four hundred kindergarten through sixth grade students attending Many Farms. About 99 percent of the student body is Navajo. Out of the 99 percent, about 90 percent are bilingual Navajo and English speakers. Many of these students commute from very traditional homes located at some distance from the school, so they spend nearly half of each 24-hour day away from home.

The communities that Chinle Unified School District serves are located in the central part of the Navajo Indian Reservation; therefore access to frequent socializations with the dominant culture is rather scarce. Thus, the language and culture remain strong, and they always have been.

In terms of our assessment program, in the past, the district made confident use of standardized tests to measure students' progress from year to year. In the late 1970s and into the mid-1980s, the district supplemented these tests with a local district-wide criterion-referenced test.

Now, in the 1990s, the Arizona Student Assessment Program (ASAP, a statewide, mandated program) has been implemented, and, as part of that program, we have begun development of a portfolio system for upper elementary students. My first year of involvement with portfolios was in the 1993-94 school year.

In some ways, I see that the process of the ASAP portfolio system reflects the culture of my students because of the standards and assessment tasks that we, ourselves, have drafted; but it has also led to struggles and frustrations for the students. This also applied to me as well. For a while it was like we were all blindfolded and felt our way to our destination. Many of the frustrations and struggles stemmed from just the utilization of the resources. Reading and comprehending the materials we used for instruction and assessment took great effort for these children. The ultimate endeavor in terms of an assessment task was for children to reproduce and interpret the learned concepts in a written paper and to discuss them. Personalities, attitudes, behaviors, languages abilities (both in English and Navajo), the degree of acculturation, and mental capabilities of the students all played a tremendous role in their success with complex assessment tasks.

During all the years I've taught, much of my teaching methodology depended on textbooks. When I got involved with the portfolio system, I altered many of my teaching methods. The following is a description of an extended activity I did with my whole class, including the procedural steps I took them through.

1. First, knowing that the students had some exposure to reading about early explorers and the settlements that followed, we brainstormed about these ideas.

2. I then put the students into small groups of three to four (of mixed low, medium, and high abilities). Each group decided which explorer and their settlements to write about.

3. I put a chart on the board. On this chart were about five or six questions: Who were the explorers? When did the exploration take place? Where did it take place? What part of the country was the exploration made for? Was the exploration a success? Who were their Indian neighbors?

4. I made an arrangement with the librarian for the use of the library ahead of time.

5. Our next step was to find information in the library using the card catalog and using reference books.

6. Right before we took our excursion to the library, I reminded the students about using their best behavior. I also gave each child five blank papers for note-taking.

7. The students checked out the books. This was about when the frustration level ascended.

8. I encouraged the students to read at least two to three times—and maybe even more—before starting to take notes. Many times during this period I sat with one group at a time to read and discuss. I simplified the information, using words they were more familiar with or that were more frequent in their vocabulary.

I collected the students' work nearly every day to check their progress. This was to ensure them that I was keeping up with their work. On their folders which had all their work I posted comments such as, "You need to reword this line." "Watch your spelling." "What do you mean by this?" "Who is doing the drawing?" "These are not in order."

Our ultimate goal was to create a booklet with hand-drawn pictures, a table of contents, map, timeline, bibliography, and the story. Presenting it to classmates was the final product. This last activity presented another obstacle for the students. For this reason, I outlined six criteria on the board:

1. fluency/clarity, loud voices   0   1   2   3   4   5

2. understanding own project   0   1   2   3   4   5

3. communicating project to class   0   1   2   3   4   5

4. staying within time   0   1   2   3   4   5

5. looking up at audience   0   1   2   3   4   5

For each criterion, I rated the child's presentation: 0 = no attempt, to 5 = excellent work. Each child kept up with his score. On their first presentations, some made no attempt. But on their second time around many of them tried. The third time (and videotaping time), one or two students out of each class made no attempt.

Many times I used the student's own language to "cross" the message to them. This is how I came to see that the English language is so elaborated and the Navajo language so general.

My advice to instructors of children whose language is other than English is to be very open-minded about who your children are—their language abilities (both in English and their native languages) their personalities, attitudes, mental abilities, and their degrees of acculturation.

Concluding Thoughts

Edmund W. Gordon

Assessment Alternatives for Diverse Classrooms helps to fill a serious gap in the educational assessment literature. Despite years of debate concerning the appropriateness of the use of standardized tests of educational achievement and intelligence in the assessment of learners whose backgrounds differ from the English-speaking, middle-class, European-American population, we have very little specialized information available to guide practice. The available literature reminds us that there are problems in this area. There is an abundant treatment of the cases for and against the claims that traditional tests are biased. No one can claim a lack of information concerning the fact that people differ in a variety of characteristics and life conditions. What these differences mean for educational intervention and educational assessment is the insufficiently treated question. It is into this gap in available knowledge and technique that Estrin and Farr have stepped with a very useful collection of information and commentary.

This book places the problems of educational assessment for diverse populations in the context of changing notions concerning both education and assessment. These changes in the ways that we think about teaching, learning, and assessment are used to inform their chapters on "Language in Instruction and Assessment" and "Developing Equitable Assessment Systems," both of which chapters provide guidance for assessment policy and practice. The authors use a constructivist perspective concerning learning, teaching and, ultimately, assessment to frame wise observations referable to educational reform. They see special promise in the current trend toward performance assessment, and devote a full chapter to a discussion of the potential of the use of portfolios in education for redressing some of the problems of instruction and assessment, especially as these problems are associated with learners whose pedagogically relevant characteristics differ.

I find a high degree of affinity between the thinking and work of these authors and the current direction of some of my own work. In my monograph *Human Diversity and Assessment*, I assert that the most fundamental issues concerning human diversity, equity, and educational assessment have to do with the effectiveness and sufficiency of teaching and learning practices. I argue that when teaching and learning are sufficient and truly effective, most of the problems posed for equitable assessment, as a function of diverse human characteristics, become manageable. It is when teaching and learning are insufficiently effective with the wide range of students served by schooling that problems arise in the pursuit of equity in the educational assessment of diverse human populations. Thus it can be argued that the problems of equity in educational assessment are largely secondary to our failure to achieve equitable outcomes through educational treatments. However, the fact that these problems of equitable educational assessment are only secondarily problems for assessment, does not mean that they should not be engaged by the assessment community, even if they cannot be solved through assessment alone.

It is not by accident that existing approaches to the standardized assessment of educational achievement are insufficiently sensitive to diversity in the populations of students served and pluralism in societal demands upon them. Prevailing standards by which academic competence is judged are calibrated in large measure against either: (a) what most persons at a specific level of development can do; or (b) what we agree is necessary in order for students to engage the demands of the next level of work. The fact that some persons have greater difficulty than others or seem unable to achieve those standards is generally thought to be a problem of individual and group differences in abilities or productivity, and is not thought to be a problem of the appropriateness of the assessment instruments or practices. In our efforts at being responsive to diverse learner characteristics and plural (that is, multiple-concurrent) social standards, prevailing wisdom suggests that there may be limits to what can be done in the design and development of assessment technology and procedures. We may be able to make the assessment process more instructive and supportive of diverse learning experiences. We may find varied contexts in and vehicles through which students can demonstrate their competencies. Our items could be made more process-sensitive and could give less emphasis to narrowly defined products. But in the final analysis, the assessment procedure is most likely to reveal the effectiveness of the teaching and learning to which students have been exposed. Thus, the facts of diversity and pluralism may have more serious implications for teaching and learning practices than for the design of equitable assessment technology and practices.

Human beings are thought to differ in their pedagogically relevant characteristics, and increasingly, we live in a world that places multiple-concurrent demand upon our competences. All of us, more and more, are called upon to function in multiple contents, cultures, and languages. The most effective among us are multi-lingual and multi-cultural. Thus pedagogical intervention must be responsive to this diversity and pluralism in order to meet criteria for educational sufficiency and effectiveness. Equitable assessment must be influenced by these developments, even if it may be less responsive to both than is educational intervention. However, this differential in potential effectiveness which favors teaching and learning does not eliminate the assessment community's responsibility to be responsive to the complex facts, problems, and challenges of population diversity and contextual-cultural-linguistic pluralism. Here it is useful to distinguish between the status and functional characteristics of learners. There is little in the differential **statuses** of learners (class, ethnicity, or gender) that should require changes in the design and management of educational assessments, but there may be several ways in which teaching, learning, and assessment can be made more appropriate to the **functional** characteristics (learning styles, interests, sources of motivation) of students. These functional characteristics may adhere to status groups that share life conditions and experiences in common, but it is their manifestations in the attitudes and behaviors of learners that are determinant. This is the primary source of challenge to equitable teaching, learning, and assessment. However, it is essential that we understand and agree that this concern with diversity, pluralism, and equity rests upon a commitment to universal standards of competence, that is, the same standards for all populations, even though we may be able to agree upon differential indicators of change or progress toward those standards. Standards or criteria for competence or mastery cannot be based upon different entry or exit characteristics of learners. Population-specific norms may be useful in planning pedagogical intervention, but they are irrelevant to the certification of educational achievement. Yet, if we are to measure progress, our instruments must be sensitive to changes within specific populations. The task then is to find assessment probes (test items) that measure the same criterion from differential contexts and perspectives that reflect the life spaces and values of the learners. Our indicators must be valid with respect to the criteria used and must be capable of eliciting culturally indigenous behaviors that may reflect appropriate and incremental movement toward the chosen criteria. To do this will require that we find ways to provide students with learning and testing opportunities that are appropriate to the standard, equivalent to the standard, and yet adequate to evoke relevant and sufficient responses. These may be approached through:

1. attention to the engagement potential and interest power of our probes;

2. attention to the relevance of diverse referents and points of reference; and

3. attention to the capacity of items and tasks to be mapped on the learner's existing schemata, styles, and response repertoires.

This kind of fluidity or flexibility in our probes will require that we come to some agreement concerning the core knowledges, competencies, and understandings that are fundamental to developed intellect and re-sponsible citizenship. Then we must permit some choice with respect to how and in which knowledge, competence, and understanding sub-do-mains the student will learn or the examinee will demonstrate her or his competence. Thus, options and choices become a critical feature in any teaching, learning, and assessment system created to be responsive to eq-uity, just as processual description, diagnosis, and learner enablement must become central purposes behind these systems. In this book, Estrin and Farr help to point the way to the achievement of these ends.

Leadership Statement
of Nine Principles
on Equity and Educational
Testing and Assessment

March 12, 1993

Equity has been the dominant theme in national education policy for the past three decades. The focus has been upon providing early preparation for disadvantaged pre-schoolers, compensatory education for disadvantaged elementary and high school youngsters, and financial assistance to help the neediest students gain access to college. At the 1989 Education Summit in Charlottesville, the President of the United States and the fifty state governors began shifting the spotlight away from providing minimum skills and opportunity for the disadvantaged toward higher standards for all American students. They produced six national goals aimed at making every American student internationally competitive by the year 2000 regardless of current achievement levels or economic status.

The National Education Goals Panel, established in 1990 to monitor progress toward achieving the goals, has been severely hampered by the absence of national standards that specify what students must know and be able to do, and national tests and assessments that measure the progress of students toward achieving the standards. To address the feasibility of setting national standards and developing and using appropriate tests, Congress appointed the National Council on Standards and Testing (NCEST) which recommended that Congress enact legislation to establish a system of national standards and examinations. Following the lead of the National Council of Teachers of Mathematics, which in 1989 published "world class" mathematics standards, the U.S. Department of Education awarded grants in 1992 to six professional organizations to develop new "world class" standards in the following six subject areas: science, history, civics, geography, English, and the arts. The standards from these six organizations are scheduled to be published next year.

As policy makers move forward to develop new standards and assessments, they should consider including the following principles, which will help to insure that both equity and quality are dominant themes:

1. New assessments should be field tested with the nation's diverse population in order to demonstrate that they are fair and valid and that they are suitable for policymakers to use as levers to improve outcomes before they are promoted for widespread use by American society;

2. New standards and tests should accurately reflect and represent the skills and knowledge that are needed for the purposes for which they will be used;

3. New content standards and assessments in different fields should involve a development process in which America's cultural and racial minorities are participants;

4. New policies for standards and assessments should reflect the understanding that standards and assessments represent only two of many interventions required to achieve excellence and equity in American education. Equity and excellence can only be achieved if all educators dedicate themselves to their tasks and are given the resources they need;

5. New standards and assessments should offer a variety of options in the way students are asked to demonstrate their knowledge and skills, providing a best possible opportunity for each student to perform;

6. New standards and assessments should include guidelines for intended and appropriate use of the results and a review mechanism to ensure that the guidelines are respected;

7. New policies should list the existing standards and assessments that the new standards and assessments should replace (e.g., Chapter 1 standards and tests, state-mandated student standards and tests) in order to avoid unnecessary and costly duplication and to avoid overburdening schools, teachers and students who already feel saturated by externally-mandated tests;

8. New policies need to reflect the understanding by policy makers of the tradeoff between the types of standards and assessments needed for monitoring the progress of school systems and the nation versus the types of standards and assessments needed by

teachers to improve teaching and learning. The attention and resources devoted to the former may compete for the limited resources available for research and development for the latter;

9.   New policies to establish standards and assessments should feature teachers prominently in the development process.

20 signatories

Guidelines for Equitable Assessment

Diversity and Equity in Assessment Network

FairTest, Cambridge, MA

The administration of over 100 million multiple-choice, norm-referenced, standardized tests in U.S. classrooms each year for accountability
and other purposes has led to educational practices that are harmful to
many students. Whether they be readiness, achievement, I.Q., aptitude or
college admissions exams, these tests often fail to accurately measure the
depth and range of students' knowledge, problem-solving abilities, critical thinking and other skills. The use of these exams by schools, districts,
states, and the federal government has served to narrow and limit classroom curricula.

The widespread use of multiple-choice standardized tests has been
especially harmful to those who have not been served well by our nation's
schools—students of color and language minority, low-income, and female students. Generations of children have been and continue to be denied access to educational resources and excluded from appropriate instruction as a result of flawed tests. The tracking and labeling, limiting of
access, and narrowing of curricula which have resulted from using these
tests have disproportionately hurt students who already face barriers due
to their family income, race, gender, ethnicity, language, and physical differences.

Since testing influences so many aspects of schooling, profound
changes in assessment must be a fundamental part of educational reform.
High quality assessments from which all children will benefit must be
designed and implemented along with other comprehensive restructuring efforts which dismantle the barriers to effective schooling. Failure to
address issues of equity, access and due process, as well as the linguistic,
class, and cultural diversity of students relative to assessment, will only
accelerate the downward spiral of our schools' effectiveness.

We the undersigned believe that the main purpose of educational assessment must be to advance learning for **all** students, and that particular attention must be paid to the needs of those who have been historically excluded.

Traditional concerns of reliability and validity must be addressed, but alone they will not ensure fair and beneficial assessment practices. And while new forms of assessment are needed, they will only be helpful to the extent that they are unbiased, measure what they purport to measure, are appropriately used and are connected with high quality curricula. We therefore call on policymakers to use the following guidelines for testing and assessment programs and practices:

• **Appropriate Assessment.** Strive to ensure that assessments are appropriate to the purposes for which they are being used and are sensitive to a diverse student population.

• **Inclusion.** Ensure that those involved in decision-making about educational goals, assessments, usage of assessment measures, and setting of standards reflect and are responsive to the diversity of our nation's students by involving people of color, parents, and advocates for historically-excluded groups.

• **Authentic Assessment.** Support the design and implementation at the school and district levels of authentic performance assessments (integrated with curriculum and instruction, based on students' actual work, and resembling real-life situations) that foster teaching and learning. Such assessments should encourage student self-reflection and decision-making, emphasize students' strengths, and be adaptable to diverse student populations.

• **Instruction and Resources.** Ensure that students are provided the instruction and resources that enable them to perform well. It is unfair to hold students accountable for their performances on tests while there is no requirement for the systems that administer the tests to provide students with the means and educational resources to perform well.

• **Staff Training.** Ensure adequate staff training so that curriculum developers and teachers are able to prepare and use culturally- and developmentally-appropriate classroom-based assessment. Such training should be done both before and during the implementation of new assessments. Parents and other representatives of the local community should be used as resources in designing and implementing this training. By involving such representatives, (particularly when there are great differences in background between the teaching staff and the student population), issues which significantly affect the educational process, including language, ethnicity, class, race, gender, and culture, can begin to be addressed.

• **Students with Disabilities.** Include students with disabilities in the performance assessment process so that they are given the opportunities to be evaluated with assessments that enable them to accurately demonstrate their achievement.

• **Language-Minority Students.** Incorporate into the design and implementation of performance assessments those elements and characteristics that enable language-minority students to benefit from instructional practices and assessment outcomes. This includes providing opportunities for students to be assessed in their primary language.

• **External Tests.** Limit the use of external, "on-demand" tests or assessments that are not part of daily classroom practice. When such assessments are used, they should model good curriculum and instruction and serve to enhance rather than impede learning. The need for district or state accountability information must be balanced with the need to prevent excessive testing of students and to limit potential narrowing of curricula and instruction.

• **Use of Tests.** Ensure that no single test/assessment or limited set of assessments is ever used as the sole basis for important educational decisions. This includes eliminating the use of cut-off scores (test scores at or above which one passes, below which one fails). Important educational decisions include screening, school entry, placement, tracking or reclassification, retention, promotion, graduation, teacher evaluation, awarding of scholarships, and college admissions. The limited scope and accuracy of information obtained by relying on a single test score often results in the misassessment of students' skills and abilities. Relying solely on test scores also creates situations in which qualified students are unfairly denied access to educational opportunities, resulting in harmful, lifelong consequences. Instead, schools, districts, and states should utilize information gathered over time in a variety of contexts from different kinds of indicators, such as teacher observations, performance-based exams, portfolios, or projects. Students should be allowed to pursue multiple paths to demonstrate comparable levels and degrees of achievement.

• **Test-Takers' Rights.** Establish a Test-Takers' Bill of Rights which provides "due process" protections for students and their parents/guardians. It must assure, for example:

- the right to appeal important educational decisions made on the basis of assessment results;

- the right to multiple indicators of achievement/knowledge when important decisions are made;

- equal opportunity for language minority students;

-   assessment findings and due process information in the first language of the parent/guardian;
-   access to assessment instruments and procedures so that students understand what is expected of them and the standards by which they will be evaluated;

• **Assessment System Criteria.** Utilize the eight *"Criteria for Evaluation of Student Assessment Systems"* developed by the National Forum on Assessment. The National Forum *"Criteria,"* which has been endorsed by over 100 organizations nationally, provides guidelines for developing assessment system practices which will help to ensure that all students benefit from assessment policies.

• **Assessment Accountability.** Investigate and establish ways to independently monitor and hold assessment systems accountable. One example is the Educational Impact Statement for Assessments developed by FairTest.

• **Chapter 1.** Amend the testing requirement of the federal Chapter 1 program to allow for use of authentic performance-based assessment approaches which benefit all students for whom the program is intended. The current law, which requires only annual norm-referenced standardized testing, has been a major factor in the perpetuation of unsound assessment practices.*

• **National Exams.** Congress should not legislate the creation of a national exam/examination system. National exams, even if voluntary, will likely compound the already existing problems associated with testing. Moreover, simply administering new tests and expecting them to address other historic problems is not the answer. Students of color, language-minority students, young women, and students from low-income families will yet again be disproportionately represented among those who fail due to inequitable treatment.

In conclusion, policymakers, educators, parents, community organizations, and businesses must make it an educational priority to help correct current harmful educational testing practices and to support new, educationally-beneficial assessments which meet the guidelines listed above. Assessment must be equitable for all if education is to be excellent for all.

---

*This policy was changed in the reauthorized legislation, the Improving America's Schools Act of 1994. The new legislation allows for the use of performance-based assessments.

Appendix B

Guide to National Efforts to Set Subject-Matter Standards

Subject Area	Lead Organization(s)	Completion Date	Contact for Information or for Copies
Arts	Music Educators National Conference; American Alliance for Theater & Education; National Art Education Assoc.; National Dance Association	March, 1994	MENC Publication Dept., 1806 Robert Fulton Dr., Reston, VA 22091-4348; (703) 860-4000.
Civics and Government	Center for Civic Education	November, 1994	Center for Civic Education, 5146 Douglas Fir Rd., Calabasas, CA 91302-1467; (800) 350-4223
Economics	National Council on Economic Education	Uncertain	Dr. Robert Highsmith, Economics America, 1140 Avenue of the Americas, New York, NY 10036; (212) 730-7007
English/Language Arts	International Reading Association; National Council of Teachers of English	Draft available January, 1996	Liz Spalding, (217) 328-3870, ext. 226 or Maria Drees, ext. 290 at NCTE
Foreign	American Council on the Teaching of Foreign Languages; American Association of Teachers of French; American Association of Teachers of German; American Association of Teachers of Spanish & Portuguese	Spring, 1996	For a draft copy: American Council on the Teaching of Foreign Languages, 6 Executive Plaza, Yonkers, NY 10801-6801; (914) 963-8830

Subject Area	Lead Organization(s)	Completion Date	Contact for Information or for Copies
Geography	National Geographic Society; National Council for Geographic Education; Association of American Geographers; American Geographical Society	Spring, 1995	National Geographic Society, P.O. Box 1640, Washington, DC 20013-1640, (800) 368-2728
History	National Center for History (available both in United States and world history)	Spring, 1995	National Center for History in the Schools, University of California at Los Angeles, 10880 Wilshire Blvd., Ste. 761, Los Angeles, CA 90024-4108
Mathematics	National Council of Teachers of Mathematics	March, 1989	Virginia Williams, National Council of Teachers of Mathematics, 1906 Association Dr., Reston, VA 22091-1593, (800) 235-7566
Science	National Academy of Sciences; American Association for the Advancement of Science; American Association of Physics Teachers; American Chemical Society; Council of State Science Supervisors; Earth Science Coalition; National Association of Biology Teachers	Winter, 1995	Standards Project at National Science Education Standards, 2101 Constitution Ave., NW, HA 486, Washington, DC 20418, (202) 334-1399
Social Studies	National Council for the Social Studies	Winter, 1994	National Task Force for Social Studies Standards, National Council for the Social Studies, 3501 Newark St. NW, Washington, DC 20016-3167

Sample Performance Tasks
and
Critique Tool

Mimi Task

You are on a short Mimi expedition. Your job is to measure and weigh as many different whales as you can for the Mimi's scientific records. You have only 3 days to travel to the whales, to make your observations and to travel home.

1) How many total hours do you have to get your job done? (Figure the number of hours in 3 days.) _____ total hours
   You will have to sleep and eat about 10 hours of each day, so subtract 30 hours from the total hours. _____ work hours

2) Look at the map below. You will choose the pod or pods that you will travel to, and the route that you think will help you do the best job. Remember, your job is to weigh and measure as many different whales as you can.
   A. Which route did you choose?   ❐ Route #1   ❐ Route #2
   B. Why did you choose that route?
   _____
   _____
   _____

   C. It takes the boat 1 hour to travel 20 miles. Figure out how many hours you will need to travel to the whales and back home (round trip). _____ travel hours

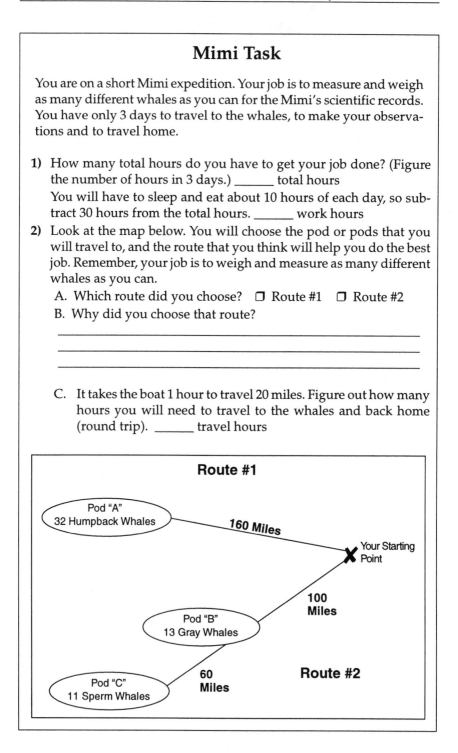

D. How many hours will you have to observe and measure the whales? (Subtract travel hours from your *work* hours.)
_____ observation hours

3) You have only 3 days to make your observations because a storm is coming. As the storm gets closer, the temperature is changing. Use the information below and graph each day's high temperature.

	Day 1	Day 2	Day 3
High temperatures	84°	70°	56°

Graph each day's high temperature on the graph below.

Temperature Graph	Day 1	Day 2	Day 3
100°			
95°			
90°			
85°			
80°			
75°			
70°			
65°			
60°			
55°			
50°			
45°			
40°			
35°			
30°			

The temperature changed _____ degrees from Day 1 to Day 2.
The temperature changed _____ degrees from Day 2 to Day 3.
The temperature changed _____ degrees from Day 1 to Day 3.

• You are keeping a trip log for the three days of your trip. Think about what you would do and see each day and describe it in the log form below. A sample log entry will get you started. (Complete sentences are NOT necessary in a log like this.)

Sample Log Entry: *Day 1. 3:00 p.m., temperature 73°, seas calm, partly cloudy. Sighted 1 female fin whale with her calf off the port bow. She was 71 feet long and weighed almost 52 tons. Kept them in sight for 30 minutes before they swam off to the southwest. It is amazing how big a 70 foot animal really is! I hope we see a killer whale soon.*

Day 1 _____

_____

_____

_____

Day 2 _____

_____

_____

_____

Day 3 _____

_____

_____

_____

4) You have returned home from your Mimi trip. You are trying to explain to other students about the whales. You will use things that we see often to show what size and weight whales are.

Average adult whale measurements:

Whale	Length	Weight
fin whale	70 feet	50 tons
sperm whale	60 feet	65 tons
gray whale	45 feet	45 tons
killer whale	30 feet	8 tons
humpback whale	50 feet	45 tons

Please show your work as you solve these problems.

A. How heavy is a whale? Think about a full-grown sheep. It weighs about 100 pounds. How many sheep would it take to equal one ton? (Note: 1 ton equals 2,000 pounds) There are ____ sheep in one ton.

B. How many sheep would it take to equal the weight of each whale listed below?

     sperm whale = _____ sheep

     humpback whale = _____ sheep

     fin whale = _____ sheep

C. How long is an adult whale? Think about a school bus. A bus is about 30 feet long. About how many buses would it take to equal the length of each whale listed below?

     sperm whale = _____ bus(es)

     humpback whale = _____ bus(es)

     fin whale = _____ bus(es)

5) What can you find in this school building that is equal to a baby whale's length? Find something in this building that is about equal to the length of one of the baby whales listed below. You may put together objects to equal the whale's length. (Example: *"Sarah (4' 10") plus Shannie (4' 2") plus a desk (3') plus one math book (1") equals a 13' baby sperm whale."*) Or, you may find one item that is the same length as a baby whale. (Example: *1 library bookcase equals a baby humpback whale (15').*

baby sperm whale	13 feet
baby humpback whale	15 feet
baby gray whale	14 feet

A. What did you find here at school that is about equal to the length of one of the baby whales listed above? Look at the two examples above and tell about your measurement below.

_____

_____

_____

B. What have you learned about the length and weight of whales by comparing their length and weight to familiar animals and object?

_____

_____

_____

5th Grade Teachers, Chinle Elementary School, Chinle (AZ) Unified School District in collaboration with Nanette Koelsch, Far West Laboratory.

Name: Dennis M. Rose   School: John C. Freemont
Date: February 25, 1994
                    Science Task Assessment
Grade Level: Fifth

I.   Standards Assessed: Science (Scientific Inquiry), Language Arts (Writing, Reference Skills, and Reading)

II.   Task Overview
        For this task the student will demonstrate their understanding in writing of how a Scientific Method could be used in individualized science experiments.

III.   Time: This task will take 18 forty minute science periods of instruction and 10 forty minute periods of individualized science experiments. Time may vary according to amount of instruction.

IV.   Prompt to Students:
        In this task you will:
        A. Choose and do three individualized experiments.
        B. Complete these questions on three five by eight cards:
            1. **What do you think will happen?** (This is the hypothesis part of the assessment. Practically any reasonable answer is accepted.)
            2. **What did you do?** (This is a procedure question.)
            3. **What happened?** (This is an observation and results question.)
            4. **Why?** (This question will determine their understanding of what they have learned and show their reasoning.)
            5. **What did you learn?** (Here is the student's stated conclusion, based upon the hypothesis, procedure, and results parts of the assessment).
        C. Your experiment does not have to be a success in order to receive a good evaluation.
        D. Choose one card for teacher evaluation.

V.   To accomplish this task you will need to:
        A. Pay attention to the instruction given during six mini-science units (Light, Energy, Electricity, Magnetism, Geology, and Matter) for background information.
        B. Construct an ongoing vocabulary list of words and terms from the mini-units to be used in your science experiments.
        C. Complete each activity or assignment that may be associated with the mini-units.
        D. Complete three individualized science experiments.

VI.   Directions to the Teacher (task administration):
        To administer this task you will need to:
        A. Read and discuss the various science lessons to be used as background information for the science experiments.
        B. Demonstrate all related experiments that pertain to each lesson.
        C. Explain each related activity sheet and what is required to work them.

      D. Explain what each question on the five by eight card means (Each card is to have the five questions written on it with ample space for answers.

      E. Keep an ongoing vocabulary list on the chalk board for student use.

      F. Emphasize the non use of the word "it" to refer to something.

VII. Instruction Prior to Task:

      Prior to using this task for assessment the following concepts, processes and skills should be familiar to the students:

      A. Knowledge of correct spelling and ability to write complete and logical sentences.

      B. Ability to organize and place information with correct questions.

      C. Ability to read and choose information wisely.

VIII. Materials/Resources/Technology:

      A. Several individualized science experiments in kit form (Kits may include experiments in electricity, geology, light, magnetism, biology, chemistry, illusions, physics, weather, color, mirrors, and home based experiments ranging from simple to complex).

      B. Enough five by eight lined cards for students to do three experiments.

      C. Copies of the following books by Milliken Publishing Company: *Basic Science Concepts: Light, Universe, Plants, Energy; Basic Science Concepts: Electricity, Geological Processes, Animals, Matter; Basic Science Concepts: Basic Science Experiences For Grades 4, 5, 6.*

      D. Use of various related filmstrips and/or videos.

      E. Teacher prepared handouts and activity pages from Milliken Books.

      F. Science equipment for teacher to perform related experiments in each of the six mini-units, such as:

        1. Flash light.

        2. Translucent material (enough for each student).

        3. A prism

        4. A glass of water and a straw.

        5. A small electric light bulb, a switch, some insulated wire, and a dry cell.

        6. A bar magnet and a compass.

        7. Examples of some rocks and a streak plate.

        8. A yard stick, two balloons, and some string.

        9. A Radiometer to demonstrate solar energy.

        10. A watch with a luminous dial to demonstrate radioactivity.

        11. A lemon, baking soda, and some soap.

        12. Pictures of molecules and other related items.

IX. Task Extensions:

      A. An understanding of how a scientific method can be used in solving a problem.

      B. An understanding of when to use a scientific approach to a problem.

      C. An understanding of how scientists do their experiments and write up their findings.

Dennis Rose, Fifth grade teacher, Carson City (NV) School District in collaboration with Nanette Koelsch, Far West Laboratory

Applied Linear Measurement _____

Standard: Science, Measurement, Length

Shell: Investigating the World

Time: 3-4 days

Task Overview: Students create a desk cover for their desk decorated to go with any area you are currently studying. They will create their own standard for measuring and practice with their standard (but not their desk). They will estimate the length and width of their desk top then find the exact measurement using their standard. They will measure and cut their cover to fit their desk top. Last, they will explain how they created their cover. This task is an assessment of the measurement unit in FOES. It extends what they've learned about standards, estimation and measurement.

Prompt: Create a desk cover for _____ . You will need to find a standard from your desk to measure your desk top with (but not a ruler). After practicing measuring other items in the room with your standard, you will estimate the length and width of your desk. Then measure with your standard. Use that measurement to cut an exact cover for your desk top. Explain your steps in creating your desk cover.

Criteria:
1. Find a standard
2. Practice measuring and estimate length and width of desk top
3. Measure your desk top with your standard
4. Use your measurement to create a cover
5. Explain your steps in creating the cover

Name: _____

1. What is your standard? Describe and draw.

Using your standard:

2. Estimate your desk width _____

    Estimate your desk length _____

3. Give the actual measurement for your desk top using your standard

    Width _____

    Length _____

4. Explain steps to making desk cover

Student Evaluation:

Was your estimation close?   Yes   No

Did your cover fit your desk?   Yes   No

Third grade teachers, Carson City (NV) School District in collaboration with Nanette Koelsch, Far West Laboratory

More Stories Julian Tells

Why Frogs Wear Shoes

Standard: Reading/Literature

Performance Shell: Task Shell 3: Examining, Representing and Evaluating Information

Task Overview: Students will read, interpret and evaluate a literary text. Students will display their understanding of the text through answering questions, reflecting on their own reading, and evaluating their learning. Students will have 5-6 days to complete the task with daily class time provided for discussions and revision. Teachers will discuss the prompt with the entire class prior to individual student work.

Time: 5-6 days

Prompt to Students: You will read a story. After you read the selection, you will show your understanding of the content and the author's writing through the following activities:

1. Construct and illustrate a four-part fold-out which is to include:
   a) The title and author
   b) Beginning
   c) Middle
   d) End of the story

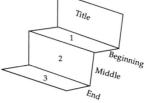

2. Write a brief description of the beginning, middle and end, in complete sentences. Attach written work to four-part fold-out.
3. A story diorama featuring the beginning, middle or end of the story.
4. Conclusion: Write a brief report about the story that tells about what it makes you think of, or anything that relates to your reading.

*Revision: Task Overview - Students will read, interpret and evaluate a literary text, concentrating on identifying the beginning, middle and end of the story.

Standard: Social Studies/Communities

Shell: Examining Representing, and Evaluating Information

Time: 4-5 days

Task Overview: Students will review the elements required for a community: primary and secondary needs. Students will illustrate the important features of their community through constructing a model and writing about how their community meets the needs of its inhabitants. Students will have 4-5 days to complete the task with daily analysis. Teachers will discuss the prompt with the entire class prior to individual students work. (Can be done individually, partnered or in cooperative learning groups).

Prompt: You will build a model of an imaginary community that must include the following information based on the needs discussed in following:

1. Natural surrounding, buildings and other man-made features which help meet the needs of the people in your community.

2. A written description of your community which includes a name and how the community meets the needs of its inhabitants.

3. You will present model and read report to class.

Third grade teachers, Carson City (NV) School District in collaboration with Nanette Koelsch, Far West Laboratory

Mathematical Reasoning,
Jewelry Making and Selling

Standards: Mathematical Understanding and Power, Life
                      Skills

ASAP Cluster: Mathematical Reasoning 8M9

Overview: Students plan a jewelry making business to earn
                      money. They calculate costs of supplies and tools,
                      determine costs of specific jewelry, and determine
                      profit. They choose the most profitable jewelry to
                      make given their end goal of making $130.00 in
                      profit.

Jewelry Making and Selling

Name_____ Date_____

You need $130 dollar to buy a Game Boy. You will make and sell jewelry to earn the money. You will figure out the costs of making the jewelry, and then figure the profit that you can make from selling it.

Look at the tables that show the costs of materials needed for making each piece of jewelry. On the next pages, you will figure out how many and what kinds of pieces you will make to earn the money you need. Use these charts to help you.

Table 1   Cost of Silver

	Item	Cost
Silver:	6" x 12" sheet	$36.00

Use the above chart to answer this question. Show your work in the space below.

1. How much does the silver cost per square inch? $_____

Table 2   Amount of Silver Needed for Jewelry

Ring	2 square inches of silver 2 in.²
Bolo Tie	4 square inches of silver 4 in.²
Bracelet	6 square inches of silver 6 in.²

2. How much will the silver for each piece of jewelry cost?

   Ring $_____   Bolo Tie $_____   Bracelet $_____

Table 3   Jewelry Sale Price and Profit

Item	Sale Price	Profit
Ring	$8.00	
Bolo Tie	$16.00	
Bracelet	$8.00	

3. Figure out the profit for each piece of jewelry and write it in the chart above. Show your work.

4. Use the patterns below to make 2 different combinations of jewelry on 6" x 12" pieces of paper. Use ALL of the silver with each combination.

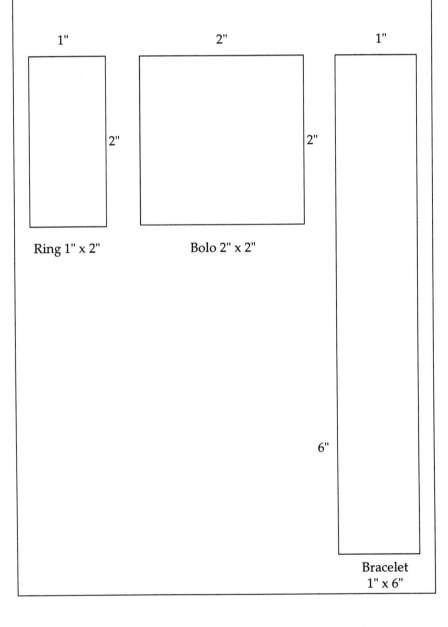

Ring 1" x 2"   Bolo 2" x 2"

Bracelet
1" x 6"

Combination #1			
	How Many?	**Profit Each**	**Total Profit**
Rings			
Bolo Ties			
Bracelets			

Comination #2			
	How Many?	**Profit Each**	**Total Profit**
Rings			
Bolo Ties			
Bracelets			

5. Use Table 3 to figure the total profit from making and selling the jewelry in each combination. Write the amount of total profit in the tables above. Show your work.

6. Use the tables to decide which combination makes the most money for you. Which combination did you choose? _____ Tell how it made more money for you than the other one. ____

    _____

    _____

    _____

    _____

    _____

    Show your work below.

7. Your goal was to make at least $130.00 profit from the sale of the jewelry that you made and sold. Did you make your goal?

    _____

    How much money did you make? _____

    What advice would you give someone who was doing this problem about how to solve it to make enough profit?

    _____

    _____

    _____

    _____

    _____

8. In the space below, draw the design of one of the pieces of jewelry that you made.

Sixth grade teachers at Chinle (AZ) Unified School District in collaboration with Nanette Koelsch, Far West Laboratory

Measurement Task
Building a Model

Standards:	Mathematical Understanding and Power, Life Skills, Environmental or Cultural Understanding and Responsibility
ASAP Cluster:	Measurement 8M4
Time:	2 weeks
Overview:	Fifth grade students will plan, design, and build a scale model of a building from an historical time period.
Prompt:	You are going to plan, design and build a scale model of a _____ (Examples: Colonial shop, architectural building, home). This project includes several parts. You will keep a building journal explaining your math, design a scale drawing, and build your scale model. You will also write a paragraph or more about your building and how it was used by people who lived in the time period.

Scale for buildings: 1 inch equals 1 foot; 1 square inch equals one square foot.

To accomplish this task you need to:

1. Plan your scale design. Because you cannot build a life size building you have to build to scale (a smaller size that keeps the same proportions). This means you have to calculate the area of the building; height of walls, perimeter around building, area of doors and windows using your scale.

2. Keep a building journal of your planning. As you calculate the size of all the parts of your building, you will write down your math and your thinking in a journal. The journal also lists any questions you have, vocabulary you learn, and anything else about your building you wish.

3. You must submit a scale drawing of your building before you build it. The drawing includes the scale, area, height of walls, area of door and windows. Your building journal is turned in with this drawing.

4. Along with your drawing, write a paragraph or more about your building. Explain how it was used by the people who lived then. Write about the size of the actual building and what tells about the time, the people and how they used the building.

5. Build your model, using a larger scale if necessary.

6. Optional: make artifacts for your building.

Fifth grade teachers, Chinle Unified School District in collaboration with Nanette Koelsch, Far West Laboratory

Standards: Communications, Life Skills

Performance Task Domain: Investigating the World

Task Overview: For this task, the student will research his/her family lineage and create a family map, a poem, and an autobiography.

Time: 2-3 weeks.

Prompt to Students: In this task you will research your family's lineage and create your own family and/or clan map. You will write an autobiography of your life and a poem about family.

Re-explanation for Students: To accomplish this task you will need to:

1. Interview relatives about your family.
2. Investigate other documents or sources for information about your family (such as, family records, Navajo tribe, family trees, role numbers, baby books, land use permits).
3. Create your immediate family's map.
4. Design a symbol for your paternal and maternal lineages or nationalities.
5. Extend your research to include larger family.
6. Create extended family map.
7. Create a legend below your map to explain symbols.
8. Write an autobiography of your life from your earliest memory to now. Include information on school and family.
9. Write an original poem about your heritage. Your poem may be bilingual or in the language of your choice.

Verna Clinton, Fifth grade teacher, Tsaile Elementary School, Chinle (AZ) Unified School District in collaboration with Nanette Koelsch, Far West Laboratory

Heritage Task

Sample Format for Family Map

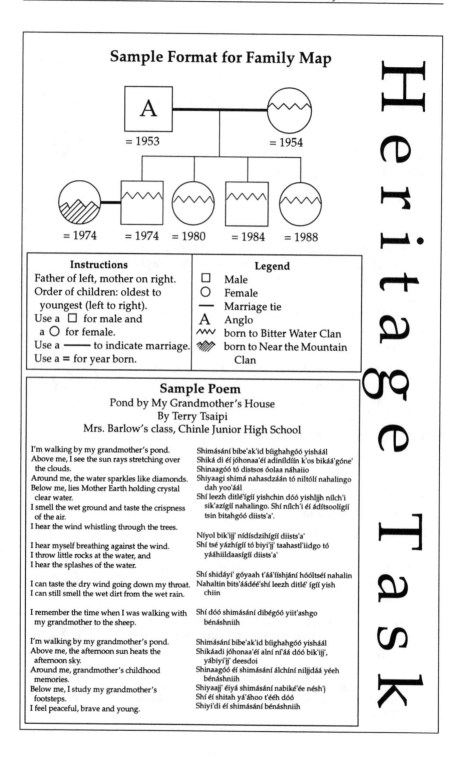

Instructions
Father of left, mother on right.
Order of children: oldest to
youngest (left to right).
Use a □ for male and
a ○ for female.
Use a —— to indicate marriage.
Use a = for year born.

Legend
□   Male
○   Female
——   Marriage tie
A   Anglo
〰   born to Bitter Water Clan
▨   born to Near the Mountain
      Clan

Sample Poem
Pond by My Grandmother's House
By Terry Tsaipi
Mrs. Barlow's class, Chinle Junior High School

I'm walking by my grandmother's pond.
Above me, I see the sun rays stretching over
  the clouds.
Around me, the water sparkles like diamonds.
Below me, lies Mother Earth holding crystal
  clear water.
I smell the wet ground and taste the crispness
  of the air.
I hear the wind whistling through the trees.

I hear myself breathing against the wind.
I throw little rocks at the water, and
I hear the splashes of the water.

I can taste the dry wind going down my throat.
I can still smell the wet dirt from the wet rain.

I remember the time when I was walking with
  my grandmother to the sheep.

I'm walking by my grandmother's pond.
Above me, the afternoon sun heats the
  afternoon sky.
Around me, grandmother's childhood
  memories.
Below me, I study my grandmother's
  footsteps.
I feel peaceful, brave and young.

Shimásání bibe'ak'id bíighahgóó yisháál
Shiká di éí jóhonaa'éí adiníldíín k'os bikáá'góne'
Shinaagóó tó distsos óolaa náhaiio
Shiyaagi shimá nahasdzáán tó niltólí nahalingo
  dah yoo'áál
Shí leezh ditlé'ígíí yishchin dóó yishljjh nílch'i
  sik'azígíí nahalingo. Shí nílch'i éí ádítsoolígíí
  tsin bitahgóó diists'a'.

Níyol bik'ijj' nídísdzihígíí diists'a'
Shí tsé yázhígíí tó biyi'jj' taahastl'iidgo tó
  yááhiildaasígíí diists'a'

Shí shidáyi' góyaah t'áá'ííshjání hóóltséí nahalin
Nahaltin bits'áádéé'shí leezh ditlé'ígíí yish
  chiin

Shí dóó shimásání dibégóó yiit'ashgo
  bénáshniih

Shimásání bibe'ak'id bíighahgóó yisháál
Shikáadi jóhonaa'éí alní ní'áá dóó bik'ijj',
  yábiyi'jj' deesdoi
Shinaagóó éí shimásání álchíní niljjdáá yéeh
  bénáshniih
Shiyaajj' éiyá shimásání nabiké'ée nésh'j
Shí éí shitah yá'áhoo t'ééh dóó
Shiyi'di éí shimásání bénáshniih

Heritage Task

Mathematics Measurement Assessment
Designing a Dream House for Grandmother

Use the following formulas to solve the problems in this task:

Area = L x W (length times width)

Perimeter = 2L + 2W or sum of all sides

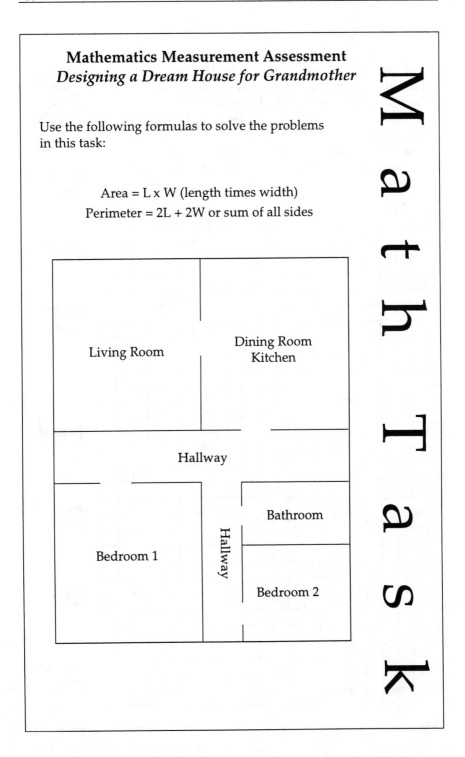

Living Room

Dining Room
Kitchen

Hallway

Bathroom

Bedroom 1

Hallway

Bedroom 2

M a t h T a s k

1. You are going to design a house for Grandmother. The total area of the house will be 1120 square feet. (Use the box below: each square = 1 square foot.) Grandmother wants her bedroom to be 15' x 14' and she wants the family room to be 12' x 23'. She also wants one more bedroom, a kitchen and a bathroom. You are to design a floor plan for Grandmother's house that includes all of the above. Color each room a different color.

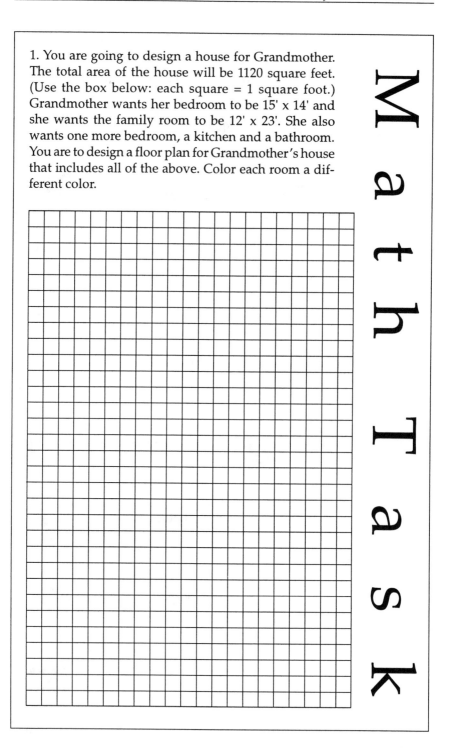

Math Task

2. Measure the spaces and complete the chart below.

Room	Size	Area
Grandmother's Room	15' x 14'	210 sq. feet
Family Room	12' x 23'	276 sq. feet
Bedroom 2		
Kitchen		
Bathroom		
Other:		
		1120 sq. feet

M a t h   T a s k

3. Find the perimeter around Grandmother's house. Show your work below. Explain how you found the perimeter.

4. Evaluate your design. Do you think your grandmother would like to live in her dream house? Explain your reasoning by giving examples.

Fifth grade teachers, Chinle (AZ) Unified School District in collaboration with Nanette Koelsch

Performance Task Review Form*

Directions:

Task review questions are divided into five sections: Cognitive Aspects, Attitude Aspects, Performance Aspects, Instructional Aspects, and Administration Aspects. Respond to each question by circling "N" (no) or "Y" (yes). A section for comments or observations is provided at the end of each section. **Please note that many of these questions can best be answered after having students try out the task.**

Cognitive Aspects

1. Does this task assess a meaningful part of the content standards?   N   Y

2. Does the task ask students to combine several abilities, strategies, or viewpoints to complete the task?   N   Y

3. Does the task provoke different correct answers or problem solutions from students?   N   Y

4. Does the task require students to self assess?   N   Y

5. Will this task motivate students to learn?   N   Y

6. Is it an integrated or thematic task that combines several subject areas?   N   Y

7. Does the task require students to construct an answer or solution?   N   Y

8. Does the task enable teachers to identify student strengths?   N   Y

9. Will students enjoy doing this task?   N   Y

10. Will students be able to successfully complete this task?   N   Y

Affective Aspects

1. Were students able to complete the task   N   Y

2. In administering the task, were you able to observe different levels of student work?   N   Y

3. Did the task allow you to observe persistent student behaviors?   N   Y

4. Did the task allow you to observe students being creative?   N   Y

5. Did the task allow you to observe students' appreciation for learning?   N   Y

Additional Comments or Observations:

_____

_____

_____

_____

Performance Aspects

1. Does the task promote student investigation?   N   Y

2. Does the task incorporate student use of technology?   N   Y

3. Does the task allow students to show their understanding in different ways, e.g. verbally, visually, or in writing?   N   Y

4. Does the task specify an audience to which the solution is to be addressed?   N   Y

5. Can students practice or rehearse for this task?   N   Y

6. Does the task have application to real life experience?   N   Y

7. Does the task allow you to observe a student's process for completing the task, a student's final product, or a student's performance?   N   Y

Additional Comments or Observations:

_____

_____

_____

_____

Performance Aspects

1. Were the assessment criteria made clear to the students prior to the assessment?　　N　Y

2. Was the task integrated as part of class-room instruction?　　N　Y

3. Does the task allow students to be active learners?　　N　Y

4. Does the task ask students to identify or record their "prior knowledge"　　N　Y

5. Does the task have a group work component?　　N　Y

6. Does the task allow students to work independently of the teacher's assistance?　　N　Y

Additional Comments or Observations:

Administrative Aspects

1. Does the task seem to assess too many concepts?   N   Y

2. Did students understand the task directions?   N   Y

3. Are the rating/scoring criteria clear?   N   Y

4. Do you think students feel successful with this task?   N   Y

5. Do you think the format or approach of the task reflects a bias against any student or group of students?   N   Y

Additional Comments or Observations:

_____

_____

_____

_____

_____

_____

The TESOL Standards: Ensuring Access to Quality Educational Experiences for Language Minority Students

Teachers of English to Speakers of Other Languages (TESOL) offers the following standards of access to help schools judge the degree to which programs of special assistance are helping language minority students to meet the National Education Goals. The standards have been developed by the TESOL Task Force on the Education of Language Minority Students, K-12, in the US. They are based on the most current research on language learning in academic settings.

Access to a Positive Learning Environment

1. Are the schools attended by language minority students safe, attractive, and free of prejudice?

2. Is there evidence of a positive whole-school environment whose administrative and instructional policies and practices create a climate that is characterized by high expectations as well as linguistically and culturally appropriate learning experiences for language minority students?

3. Are teachers, administrators, and other staff specifically prepared to tailor instructional and other services to the needs of language minority students?

4. Does the school environment welcome and encourage parents of language minority students as at-home primary teachers of their children and as partners in the life of the school? Does the school inform and educate parents and others concerned with the education of language minority students? Does the school systematically and regularly seek input from parents on information and decisions that affect all critical aspects of the education of language minority students, their schools and school districts?

Access to Appropriate Curriculum

5. Do language minority students have access to special instructional programs that support the second language development necessary to participate in the full range of instructional services offered to majority students?

6. Does the core curriculum designed for all students include those aspects that promote (a) the sharing, valuing, and development of both first and second languages and cultures among all students and (b) the higher order thinking skills required for learning across the curriculum?

7. Do language minority students have access to the instructional programs and related services that identify, conduct and support programs for special populations in a district? Such programs include, but are not limited to, early childhood programs, special education programs, and gifted and talented programs, as well as programs for students with handicapping conditions or disabilities, migrant education programs, programs for recent immigrants, and programs designed for students with low levels of literacy or mathematical skills, such as Chapter 1.

Access to Full Delivery of Services

8. Are the teaching strategies and instructional practices used with language minority students developmentally appropriate, attuned to students' language proficiencies and cognitive levels, and culturally supportive and relevant?

9. Do students have opportunities to develop and use their first language to promote academic and social development?

10. Are non-classroom services and support services (such as counseling, career guidance, and transportation) available to language minority students?

11. Do language minority students have equal access to computers, computer classes and other technologically advanced instructional assistance?

12. Does the school have institutional policies and procedures that are linguistically and culturally sensitive to the particular needs of language minority students and their communities?

13. Does the school offer regular, non-stereotypical opportunities for native English-speaking students and language minority students to share and value one another's languages and cultures?

Access to Equitable Assessment

14. Do language minority students have access to broadly based methods of assessing language and academic achievement in the content areas that are appropriate to students' developmental level, age, and level of oral and written language proficiency in the first and second languages? Are these measures non-biased and relevant? Are the results of such assessments explained to the community from which the student comes in the language which that community uses?

15. Do language minority students have access to broadly based methods of assessing special needs? Again, access is further defined by using measures that are non-biased and relevant, the results of which are explained to the community from which the student domes and in the language which that community uses.

The Authors

Beverly P. Farr is a Senior Research Associate and Title I Technical Assistance Center Director at Far West Laboratory for Educational Research and Development, San Francisco, California. She received her Ph.D. in Reading Education from Indiana University. Areas of special interest include psycholinguistic and sociolinguistic processes involved in learning to use language; effective teaching strategies in reading and language arts; and the use of appropriate assessments for creating optimal opportunities for all students to learn.

Elise Trumbull is a Senior Research Associate at Far West Laboratory for Educational Research and Development, San Francisco, California. She received her Ed.D. from Boston University in Applied Psycholinguistics. Areas of special interest include sociocultural influences on learning and schooling; cross-cultural literacy issues; relationships between language and cognition; assessment; the role of language in assessment; first and second language acquisition; and the social and political aspects of bilingualism.

Author Index

Subject Index

Ability-centered approach
for English language learners, 22
Academic success for students
factors in predicting, 191
Acceleration,
as a factor in assessment tasks, 355-356
and assimilation, 81
Access to learning in educational reform, 60
Accountability, in portfolio assessment, 315
Accretion model of learning,
associated with existing measurement culture, 24
Achievement differences in assessments,
issues in consideration of, 240-244
Active learning, 256
Activity focus in assessments, 258
Additive bilingualism, 111
Affective aspects of learning, 282
Affective filter, in second language learning, 283
Alaska, 49, 179-183, 190-191, 278, 289, 298, 331-334, 347-354
Alaskan Village English, 168
Alignment
in curriculum and assessment, 25
of curriculum and instructional practices, 100
Alphabetic writing system, 141
Alternative assessments
criteria for, 263-264
defined, 240
used as an instructional framework, 346
Alternative measures, as driving instructional practices, 243-244

American Sign Language, 122, 125
Analytic model of scoring, 331-332
Annotation in portfolios, 271-273
Antecedent instructional conditions in assessments, 243-244
Argument
as influencing assessment and evaluation, 16
style, 15
Arizona, 27, 67, 157, 159, 222, 227-228, 236, 257, 259, 269, 288, 302, 327-330, 354-360
Army Mental Tests, 39
Assessment activities
language demands, 158, 164
Assessment creation
cultural sensitivity in, 330
Assessment culture, 257
defined, 26
Assessment data
use of in instructional design, 101
Assessment design
equity concerns in, 186
psychometric issues in, 221
Assessment development, 66
fairness criteria, 216, 219
involvement of teachers in, 211
procedural guidelines for, 202
processing strategies, 219-220
review by parents and community, 212
Assessment evaluation
learner characteristics in, 242-243
Assessment probes, 359
Assessment procedure
informal, 231
as revealing effectiveness of teaching and learning, 358